Ultimate Festival & Travel Guide Rome & Beyond

Unique Experiences, Unmissable Events, Unparalleled
Itineraries Featuring the Art, History, and Architecture of
Rome and Charming Towns Nearby

Katerina Ferrara

IMMERSION TRAVEL PUBLISHING

ISBN (Paperback): 979-8-9915871-6-7

ISBN (Hard Cover): 979-8-9915871-7-4

ISBN (eBook): 979-8-9915871-8-1

DISCLAIMER

The author is not a travel agent. All opinions, experiences, and views expressed are those of the author based on my personal travel experiences. Businesses and websites recommended in this book may change ownership, rebrand, or close.

The author has received no compensation or sponsorship from any recommended businesses.

Contents

Explore More and Stay Connected!

Thank you for joining me on this journey through the wonders of Italy.

Unlock the Secrets of Italy with Insider Expertise!

Allow me to be your personal guide, sharing exclusive insider tips, handpicked experiences, and essential travel insights to help you uncover Italy's hidden gems, iconic landmarks, and cultural treasures like never before.

Whether you're dreaming of strolling through ancient ruins, indulging in authentic cuisine, or immersing yourself in Italy's vibrant festivals, I've got you covered! https://katerinaferrara.com/

KaterinaFerrara.
com

Sign up for my free monthly newsletter today and receive your FREE downloadable guides, packed with:

- Curated itineraries for unforgettable journeys

- Expert travel advice to maximize your time and budget

- Practical tips for stress-free planning

- Hidden gems and must-visit spots beyond the tourist trail

Join a community of passionate travelers and start planning your next Italian adventure with confidence! Sign up now and get instant access to your exclusive guides:

https://katerinaferrara.com/

Let's make your trip to Italy extraordinary! Sign Up Today!

Travel Italy Book Series

Available now:
Book 1: *Ultimate Festival and Travel Guide Sicily (Available in English, Italian, and Sicily in Celebration Dual-Language)*
Book 2: *Rome 2025 Jubilee Year Travel Guide*
Book 3: *Ultimate Festival and Travel Guide Rome and Beyond*
Book 4: *Ultimate Festival and Travel Guide Puglia*
Book 5: *Ultimate Festival and Travel Guide Venice and the Veneto*
Arriving in 2026
Book 6: *Milan and Lombardy Ultimate Festival and Travel Guide*
Book 7: *The Italian Lakes Ultimate Festival and Travel Guide*
Arriving in 2027
Book 8: *Florence and Tuscany Ultimate Festival and Travel Guide*
Book 9: *Naples, Amalfi Coast and Campagna Ultimate Festival and Travel Guide*

CHAPTER ONE

Introduction to Festival Travel

Discover the Joy of Including Celebrations in Your Journey

Picture yourself stepping into a medieval piazza as night falls, where flickering torches cast dancing shadows on ancient stones. The rhythmic thunder of drums draws closer, and suddenly you're swept into a procession that has wound through these same narrow streets for centuries. The air is rich with the aroma of feast-day delicacies: simmering sauces, roasting meats, fresh-baked sweets. Around you, locals share wine and laughter, welcoming you not as a tourist but as part of their living tradition. As the evening ends, fireworks burst against the sky, illuminating Roman monuments that have witnessed these same celebrations for a thousand years. This is Festival Travel, where you don't just visit a destination, you become part of its story.

Welcome to a side of Italy that many travelers overlook, one of ancient traditions and an unforgettable cultural heritage. As someone who has traveled to Italy for over 25 years and immersed myself in its vibrant culture, I've discovered that Italy's heart beats the strongest during its festivals.

This is more than travel. This is becoming part of a story that began millennia ago and continues to unfold with each festival, each feast, each celebration.

These magical moments define festival travel in Italy: experiences that pierce the veil between past and present, between visitor and local, between watching and belonging. Here, in the festivals and sagre of Lazio, every celebration is a gateway to understanding the soul of a place through its most joyous expressions.

In this guide, we'll journey together through Rome and the hidden corners of Lazio, where each festival tells a unique story. From the Eternal City's magnificent celebrations that draw pilgrims and culture seekers from across the globe to intimate village sagre nestled in medieval hill towns where grandmothers still make pasta by hand, you'll discover celebrations that transform ordinary moments into extraordinary memories. Each festival offers more than just a spectacle: it invites you to experience the living essence of Italy and its timeless traditions.

Your Key to Rome and Lazio

This book is born from my experiences attending these extraordinary events. It is more than a travel guide; it is a companion to help you uncover the living spirit of Italy. Yes, it includes the essentials such as top sights, walking tours, restaurant and hotel recommendations, but more importantly, it highlights the celebrations that transform everyday towns into unforgettable destinations.

Rome's rich tapestry of culture is woven through every corner of Lazio. From the Colosseum, which still evokes the power of the Roman Empire, to the frescoed cathedrals of Viterbo, from Tivoli's Villa d'Este gardens to Tarquinia's Etruscan tombs, this region is steeped in living history. Festivals animate this legacy. They fill city squares and medieval villages with music, food, faith, and celebration.

But Rome is more than monuments. It is a city that lives its traditions out loud. In neighborhoods and hill towns alike, ancient stones are transformed into stages. History comes alive not only in museums but in festivals that fill the calendar, in recipes passed from generation to generation, and in the timeless rhythms of Italian life.

What This Guide Offers

City Highlights: Discover what makes each town unique, from Rome's grandeur to the charm of Ciociaria.

Living History: See how Etruscan, Roman, and medieval traditions shape life today.

Natural Wonders: Journey from Lazio's vineyards and lakes to the cliffs of Sperlonga and beaches of Gaeta.

Local Life: Find the small moments that make travel meaningful, from morning markets to quiet piazzas.

Food Finds: Based on countless meals and recommendations from Roman friends, this book highlights authentic places to eat that celebrate local ingredients.

Festival Focus: While this guide covers all aspects of travel, it shines a spotlight on the celebrations that turn everyday places into unforgettable experiences.

Discovering Festival Culture

I didn't always know about this incredible world of Italian festivals. My husband and I started our international travels on our honeymoon in 1997, and we have made it a priority to return to Italy each year. Our journey began like that of many travelers, exploring Italy's famous landmarks and savoring its cuisine. But it was during a visit to a small town in Sicily that everything changed.

Surrounded by the festival's sights, sounds, and smells in the town square, I felt a change, something delightful. The locals welcomed me with such warmth and pride in their traditions that I couldn't help but be drawn in. That moment sparked my love for Festival Travel: a way of engaging with Italy that goes beyond sightseeing to truly becoming part of its living traditions.

Each festival since has only deepened this connection. I'll never forget following the scent of roasting chestnuts to a tiny village square on a crisp fall day, or watching in awe as a solemn religious procession illuminated a medieval street.

These experiences aren't just memories; they're windows into the heart and soul of Venice and the Veneto, revealing the genuine spirit of its people. They've inspired me to create the **Travel Italy Book Series**, which will eventually grow to include 22 Festival and Travel Guides covering all of Italy's diverse regions.

Understanding Feste and Sagre

What Sets a Festa Apart from a Sagra?

As you explore this guide, you'll naturally pick up some Italian along the way, starting with two essential festival terms: 'festa' and 'sagra.'

A festa (plural: feste) often grows from Roman Catholic traditions, like Ferentino's Festival of Saint Ambrose or Viterbo's Santa Rosa. Yet not all feste are religious: they encompass everything from Rome's Cinema Festival to Grottaferrata's historic fair (dating to 1462) and Frascati's Festa della Cortesia celebrating the wine harvest. Among the most spectacular are Genzano di Roma's Infiorata, where streets transform into intricate floral carpets, and Ronciglione's Carnival, a vibrant tradition since 1538.

While Catholic traditions shape many Italian festivals, these celebrations welcome everyone, regardless of faith. They're joyful expressions of history, tradition, and community spirit where all can create lasting memories.

A sagra (plural: sagre), by contrast, springs from ancient harvest celebrations. The word itself derives from "sacro," meaning "sacred" in Latin. Originally held in temple yards to thank Roman gods for bountiful harvests, these festivals live on in small towns and villages as community fundraisers for schools and local projects, powered entirely by volunteers.

While feste celebrate various aspects of culture, sagre focus specifically on local cuisine. From Nemi's Sagra delle Fragole showcasing strawberries grown in the rich Castelli Romani soil to festivals honoring chestnuts, sausages, gnocchi, wild rabbit, fish, and wine: there's a celebration for every palate.

Here's my essential sagra tip: arrive hungry. Purchase your meal ticket at the event booth: for 12 to 15 euros, you'll enjoy an exceptional zero kilometro meal with local wine. ("Zero kilometro" refers to food produced within roughly 150 kilometers, ensuring peak freshness and supporting local farmers.)

For feste, I recommend staying two to three nights minimum, as celebrations often continue into the late evening. (You'll find specific accommodation recommendations in each chapter.) Sagre, however, work perfectly as day trips, since they often occur in tiny villages that may not even have hotels. Many visitors base themselves in larger nearby towns and venture out to experience these local food festivals.

Whether you're traveling solo, with family, or planning a multi-generational trip, these festivals offer rich experiences for everyone. Photographers, influencers, and creatives discover endless possibilities, from vibrant processions to intimate cultural moments. Music festivals showcase Italy's performing arts, while markets built around the festivals highlight local artisans creating unique treasures. Many festivals offer hands-on experiences with traditional crafts or cooking techniques.

Families particularly appreciate the child-friendly atmosphere, complete with puppet shows, parades, and special treats. Importantly, these events support sustainable tourism and directly benefit local communities, helping to preserve these cherished traditions for future generations. Consider this guide your personal festival planner for creating authentic experiences beyond the typical tourist path.

Why Festival Travel?

- Experience cities at their most alive and authentic, when streets pulse with music, color, and celebration.

- Join in centuries-old traditions that most tourists never witness, from solemn processions to joyous feasts.

- Savor once-a-year delicacies and festival-specific dishes that rarely appear on restaurant menus.

- Discover the fascinating stories and cultural significance behind each celebration, passed down through generations.

- Connect meaningfully with local communities as they welcome visitors into their cherished traditions.

- Capture extraordinary moments, from elaborate costumes to

breathtaking ceremonial displays.

- Share in activities that delight all ages, making these festivals perfect for family memories.

- Support and help preserve local traditions while contributing directly to community economies.

An Insider's Perspective

Because of my love for Italy and our goal to move there one day, I started studying Italian in 2020 when our son Augustus left for university. I don't do anything halfway, so when I decided to learn Italian, I really committed myself to it and became fluent quickly (somewhat thanks to lockdowns). What began as a personal challenge soon opened up a whole extra dimension of Italian culture to me.

Every morning, I tune into Di Buon Mattino on TV2000. What started as a simple language immersion exercise blossomed into a genuine passion. The show, broadcasting from Rome, goes beyond typical news coverage; it journeys across Italy, discovering festivals, traditions, and local specialties. Between watching Italian TV series, chatting with Italian friends, reading Italian newspapers, and my daily dose of Di Buon Mattino, I kept discovering one fascinating festival after another. Even now, each day the show transports me to a new celebration somewhere in Italy, revealing another region's unique culture. It's a daily way to learn about new cities, regions, saints, or celebrated foods.

As I explored deeper, I realized these festivals truly embody Italian culture; they're living celebrations of community, history, folklore, and tradition. This sparked an idea: why not experience these festivals firsthand? When I began planning our travels around them several years ago, I was thrilled that my husband, son, cousins, and friends were just as excited to join the adventure.

While we have cultural festivals in the U.S., they're different. Italian festivals are lifelong commitments, drawing people back year after year, even from far away. These aren't just celebrations; they are cherished reunions with family and friends.

A huge part of what makes these festivals special is the food, dishes and desserts you can only find during these celebrations, flavors that stay hidden from restaurant menus the rest of the year. As I researched these festivals for our trips, the cuisine emerged as a crucial part of the story, deeply woven into local traditions and memorable experiences.

I'll never forget hunting down the Testa del Turco at the Festa della Madonna delle Milizie in Scicli. Following the enticing aromas through the centro storico, my anticipation grew with each step. That first bite, the delicate, crisp pastry with its rich, creamy filling, was unlike anything I had tasted before. It was not just delicious; it was a gateway into the festival's spirit, a flavor that captured the essence of celebration and tradition. Don't worry, I have included all these special festival foods in the chapters.

My friend Annalisa's story perfectly captures this festival spirit. Like many Italians, she moved to Rome for work but returns to her hometown every year for her patron saint's festival. When I asked to join her one year, she laughed and said, "Katerina, you wouldn't be able to keep up! I run all over town just to see the procession of Sant'Ambogio at every important viewpoint!" Her enthusiasm showed me how deeply these festivals are woven into Italian life.

What to Expect in This Unique Travel Guide

In the chapters ahead, you'll find in-depth profiles of the most captivating festivals in Rome and Lazio. Each chapter includes:

- The story behind the celebration and what makes it special

- Key details: location, date, temperature, website

- Cultural context: from saints to seasonal foods

- Walking tours and local highlights

- Travel tips: how to get there, where to stay, where to eat

- Immersion experiences to enrich your trip

Festival travel transforms tourism into a shared human experience. Whether you plan a weekend around a village sagra or time your Rome visit to coincide with a saint's feast day, this book will help you create deeper connections and unforgettable moments.

Let me welcome you to the world of festival travel. Your most extraordinary Italian adventures are about to begin.

Worried about crowds?

Don't be. While major events like the Natale di Roma, Easter and Holy Week, Carnivale, and Viterbo's Macchina di Santa Rosa draw large numbers, most festivals in this book are intimate affairs, primarily attended by locals. These relaxed, laid-back celebrations let you soak in the culture without the tourist rush. Yes, I hope to inspire more travelers to become Festival Followers, but you won't find yourself lost in crowds. In fact, many of these festivals are far less crowded than a typical morning at St. Peter's Basilica, offering a more authentic and personal experience. At many events, we've been the only tourists present, making each discovery feel special.

This guide to Rome's festivals marks just the beginning of our journey through Italy's rich cultural landscape. As the third book in the Travel Italy series, it joins our mission to explore the festivals and traditions of all 20 Italian regions. Each book delves deep into a different region, uncovering its unique celebrations, local customs, and hidden gems.

Festival Travel transforms ordinary tourism into extraordinary experiences. Instead of viewing Rome through the lens of a guidebook, you'll experience it through the joy of its celebrations, the warmth of its communities, and the depth of its traditions.

Join me in discovering the real Italy: one festival at a time. Let's embark on this journey together, where every cobblestone street echoes with history, every local dish tells a story, and every celebration invites you to become part of Europe's living heritage.

Festivals in Rome and Lazio (Rome's Enchanting Region)

Rome: The Eternal City of Celebrations

Picture yourself standing in the Colosseum's shadow as a centuries-old procession weaves through ancient cobblestone streets, where past and present dance together in vibrant celebration. As both Italy's capital and the heart of Catholicism, Rome has cultivated these festivals for nearly two millennia. From the Festa dei Santi Pietro e Paolo, celebrated since the earliest Christian days, to Natale di Roma marking the city's 2,700-year legacy, each festival writes a new chapter in Rome's endless story.

These celebrations unfold against a backdrop of some of the world's most iconic landmarks, lending each event a unique majesty. Many festivals trace their roots to ancient Roman customs; some religious processions still follow medieval routes unchanged by time, creating living bridges between today's Romans and their ancestors.

Lazio: Beyond the City Walls

Step away from Rome, the region of Lazio's capital, and you'll discover the true essence of Italian festival culture in these regions towns and villages. Here, each community carefully guards its unique traditions, whether they honor local saints, celebrate harvest seasons, or commemorate historic battles. You might find yourself in a medieval piazza where locals, dressed in traditional costume, gather for a sagra celebrating the fall's first chestnuts or the season's freshly pressed olive oil. Festivals like Marino's Sagra dell'Uva or Tivoli's Festa del Sant'Antonio Abate offer intimate glimpses into small-town life while celebrating Lazio's rich heritage.

The Magic of Lazio's Festivals

Rome may be the jewel in Lazio's crown, but the region's soul truly awakens in its festival-filled towns and villages. Picture yourself here: following flickering torches through the medieval streets of Ciociaria as ancient traditions come alive, swaying to music under a star-filled sky at a summer festival in the Castelli Romani, or raising a glass of just-pressed wine at a centuries-old hill town sagra. These are moments most travelers never experience. The pulse of Italian life reaches its peak during its celebrations.

This guide opens doors most visitors never know exist. Beyond just telling you when and where festivals happen, I'll share the secrets that transform you from observer to participant: the hidden piazzas where locals gather for the best views of processions, the family-run kitchens where festival specialties have been perfected over generations, and the timeless traditions that welcome visitors into their ancient rhythms.

Let me invite you to venture beyond the guidebook landmarks and into living history. Here, every festival writes a new chapter in stories centuries old, every feast celebrates the flavors of heritage, and every celebration offers the chance to become part of something extraordinary. From Rome's grand spectacles echoing imperial times to intimate village festivals where everyone feels like family, these experiences will transform your Italian journey into a treasured memory.

Welcome to Festival Travel. Your most extraordinary Italian adventures are about to begin.

Be sure and stay for the fireworks!

CHAPTER TWO

How Plan an Unforgettable Journey

Organize Your Travel, Explore with Curiosity, Enjoy Every Moment

While festivals are the vibrant heart of this guide, its purpose is much broader. This book is your gateway to exploring **Rome and the Lazio region** with depth, ease, and cultural insight. Whether you are planning your first trip or returning to uncover hidden layers of the Eternal City, this book is designed to be useful year-round. Festivals set the rhythm of the calendar, but the guide offers value throughout the year, with immersive city descriptions, local traditions, practical tips, and honest recommendations.

Each chapter takes you beyond the surface and into the living fabric of Lazio's towns and cities. You will find historical background, walking tours, restaurant and accommodation suggestions, transportation tips, and cultural insights. Even if you are not planning your visit around a specific festival, you can use this guide to experience Rome and the surrounding region like a well-prepared traveler.

If you are interested in festivals, you will find a comprehensive festival calendar, chapters organized by date, and a full alphabetical index of towns. These tools help you align your travel plans with local events. Festival chapters include detailed descriptions of what to expect, from processions and fireworks to rare seasonal foods and centuries-old traditions.

Use the book however it suits your style. You might build a full itinerary, plan one memorable day, or simply browse through it with a cappuccino for inspiration.

Quick Start Guide

Want to include a festival? Try this:

1. Check the Festival Calendar chapter to see what is happening during your visit

2. Read the Joy of Festival Travel chapter to understand why festivals offer a deeper connection to Italian culture

3. Use the maps and transportation chapters to visualize where festivals are located and how to get there

4. Choose one or two festivals to start with. Keep your itinerary light.

5. Book accommodations early, especially for major events like Natale di Roma or the Feast of Saints Peter and Paul

6. Arrive the evening before a festival for the best experience

7. Already know the towns you want to visit? Use the Index of Locations to see if festivals align with your plans.

Bonus Tip: The travel blogs on my website are updated regularly, and I send out a free monthly newsletter packed with travel tips, itinerary ideas, and insider festival info.

Visit https://katerinaferrara.com to sign up.

Chapter Organization

Chapters are organized to get you everything you need to attend the festival as well as enjoy the town:

1. Town and Main Festival Information

2. Must-See Sights in Walking Tour order

3. Logistics, how to arrive and get around

4. Restaurant Recommendations

5. Accommodation Recommendations

6. Day Trips, Nearby Sights to See

7. Events in Town throughout the Year

Maximize Your Festival Experience with FestaFusion

Why experience just one festival when you can enjoy several? With careful planning, you can attend multiple celebrations during a single trip. Throughout this guide, you will find **FestaFusion** combinations that let you experience overlapping festivals in nearby towns.

Examples in Lazio include:

- FestaFusion Rome: Celebrate Ferragosto alongside the Feast of the Assumption

- FestaFusion Frascati: Experience both the Feast of Saints Philip and James and the local grape harvest festival

- FestaFusion Castelli Romani: Attend wine and chestnut celebrations in the same week

These combinations help you uncover surprising cultural connections and deepen your experience of Italian life and traditions.

Immersion Experiences: Beyond the Festivals

Italy's spirit is not limited to its celebrations. In this guide, you will also find **Immersion Experience chapters** that introduce you to authentic adventures near each festival location.

These year-round experiences invite you to:

- Get Your Hands Dirty: Make pasta with a Roman nonna or learn pottery in Civita Castellana

- Embrace Nature: Hike through Ciociaria's hills or boat across Lake Bolsena

- Live the History: Walk an ancient Roman road or attend a performance in a historic theater

- Go Behind the Scenes: Visit a vineyard, press olives, or craft cheese in a local workshop

- Be a Local: Stay in an agriturismo, take part in a seasonal harvest, or stroll a local market

Each chapter includes:

- The Full Story: What makes the experience special

- Making It Happen: When to go, how to book, and what to bring

- Insider Secrets: Tips to elevate your experience

Planning Your Festival Travel

Arrive the night before. This allows time to explore the town, enjoy the local rhythm, and locate the main piazza and church, which are usually the center of festivities.

How Long to Stay

For major festivals, I recommend two to three nights. Don't let accommodation costs worry you: outside major cities, Italian hotels are surprisingly affordable. (One of my favorite stays was right in Piazza Duomo in Ragusa for just $100 a night!) Longer stays let you fully immerse yourself in evening events, especially during those magical summer festivals, without worrying about late-night drives. Plus, festival schedules can be delightfully unpredictable: having extra time lets you go with the flow.

For food festivals (sagre), you can often make it a day trip. These typically happen in smaller towns that might not have many accommodation options.

Early Bird Benefits

Arrived with time to spare? Perfect! Use these precious hours to:

- Follow my walking tour to uncover the town's hidden gems.

- Sample regional specialties at local restaurants.

- Stop by cafes to chat with locals. They often share insider festival tips and stories that you won't find in any guide.

Consider a local guide: While I've crafted over 30 self-guided walking adventures for you, there's something special about exploring with a local guide. If your budget allows and you have extra time, I recommend booking through Tours By Locals or With Locals, especially in smaller towns where local knowledge is invaluable. Locals can offer in-depth festival background and history, share their own families' experiences, show you where events occur, and ensure you see the festival information flyers that are posted around town.

As the festival draws near, keep an eye out for event programs yourself as well. In my experience, they're usually posted on cathedral doors and other prominent spots around town. Check if there are any traditional dress codes or color schemes. Taking part in these customs not only shows respect but makes you feel part of the celebration.

Feel the Rhythm of the Festival

Once the festival begins, let yourself be swept up in the experience. Join in the activities, savor those once-a-year festival treats, and connect with the community.

While capturing memories is important, remember that some of the most magical moments happen when you put the camera down and simply participate.

Festival Categories and Flexibility

Italian festivals usually fall into two types:

- Fixed-date events, like April 21 for Natale di Roma or June 29 for Saints Peter and Paul

- Movable feasts, tied to the liturgical calendar, local harvests, or community traditions

Each listing in this guide includes timing details to help you plan. Always leave room for flexibility. Festival schedules may shift, especially in small towns.

Complete Travel Companion

This book serves just as well for general travel. Even without attending a festival, you will find:

- Historical context and cultural insight

- Walking routes designed for ease and discovery

- Practical guidance on food, lodging, and transportation

While other travel guides simply list attractions and leave you to figure out the logistics, this book is designed differently. Each town includes a carefully crafted walking tour with sites presented in a logical, walkable order, complete with practical tips to help you plan efficiently and make the most of your time.

Though festivals are at the heart of this guide, it also serves as a complete travel companion for Rome and the Lazio region. Whether or not your trip includes a celebration, you'll find detailed city profiles, walking routes, cultural insights, and honest advice on food, lodging, and transportation. From major monuments to hidden corners, this guide helps you travel with confidence.

To support your planning even further, my website offers sample itineraries that combine festival experiences with broader regional exploration, making it easier to design your ideal Italian journey. You'll also find regularly updated travel blogs and a free monthly newsletter with tips, inspiration, and the latest festival news. Visit https://katerinaferrara.com to sign up.

Whether you're coming for the vibrant festivals or to explore the region's timeless towns, let this guide lead you beyond the typical tourist trail. Let yourself be swept up in warm hospitality, savor the flavors of local cuisine, and discover the living traditions that make this region of Italy so unforgettable.

A Note on Roman Festival Chapters

Unlike the chapters covering festivals outside Rome, this and other Roman festival chapters focus solely on the celebrations, their history, events, and cultural significance. But Rome, with its vast number of festivals and endless travel possibilities, required a different structure. To avoid repeating where to stay, eat, and explore in Rome across multiple chapters, I've created dedicated sections under the Navigating Rome portion toward the back of the book. These include:

- Arrive and Explore

- Savoring the Flavors of Rome

- Dining in Rome: A Neighborhood Guide

- Smart, Walkable Itineraries

- Securing Tickets for Rome's Busiest Sights

- Accommodation Detail Rome

This organization allows you to plan your Roman holiday as a complete experience, while still appreciating the distinct character and traditions of each festival. It also avoids repeating essential travel details in every Rome-based chapter.

CHAPTER THREE

Discover Lazio, Rome's Enchanting Region

A Tapestry of Ancient Traditions and Timeless Beauty

Exploring Rome and Beyond: Hidden Treasures of Lazio

There's a saying in Italian: "Roma non basta una vita": a lifetime isn't enough for Rome. But during our years of exploring this remarkable region, we've discovered that the same could be said for the entire region of Lazio. While millions flock to the Eternal City's iconic landmarks, some of our most cherished memories come from ventures beyond Rome's ancient walls.

I'll never forget that crisp summer morning in 2017 when we joined the audience with Pope Benedict at Castel Gandolfo. The papal summer residence, perched above Lake Albano, felt worlds away from Rome's tourist crowds. As sunlight filtered through the courtyard's Renaissance arches, the intimate gathering created a sense of connection that would have been impossible in St. Peter's Square.

These unexpected moments of magic define Lazio. Like the afternoon we stumbled upon Nemi, a tiny town crowned by a medieval castle. The local strawberries, grown in rich volcanic soil beside a crater lake, were a revelation: tiny, intensely flavored jewels that put supermarket berries to shame. The vendor told us her family had been cultivating these fragole di bosco for generations, using methods passed down through centuries.

This is the Lazio we've come to love: a land where ancient traditions live on in daily life. In the towns surrounding Rome, you won't find tourist menus or souvenir shops. Instead, you'll see Italian grandmothers scrutinizing produce at morning markets, 8-year-olds playing soccer in centuries-old piazzas (with no parents in sight), and locals gathering for their ritual evening passeggiata (stroll). Time moves differently here, following rhythms established long ago.

Understanding Lazio: Rome's Cradle and Crown

Imagine Rome as a brilliant jewel, and Lazio as the intricate setting that both showcases and nurtures it. One of Italy's 20 regions, Lazio was not just the birthplace of Rome, it was the heartland that sustained an empire. The region's volcanic soil provided the fertile foundation for Roman agriculture, its quarries supplied the travertine stone that built the Colosseum, and its hills offered escape from summer heat for emperors and popes alike.

Today, Lazio continues in this supporting role while maintaining its own distinct identity. The region unfolds like chapters in an ancient story: the wine-growing hills of the Castelli Romani, where Romans have retreated for summer leisure since imperial times; the wild Ciociaria, where medieval towns cling to mountainsides; and the Etruscan coast, where pre-Roman mysteries still linger in seaside caves and necropoli.

Why Venture Beyond Rome?

"But why leave Rome? There's so much to see!" This is the question we hear most often from first-time visitors. I remember asking myself the same thing on my first trip. Then, one sweltering August afternoon, following a local friend's advice, we escaped to the hills of Frascati. As we sat in a family-run trattoria, sipping crisp local wine while looking out over Rome in the distance, I finally understood - this was the Rome that Romans themselves have loved for centuries.

I call it "the beyond": all those varied landscapes and towns of Lazio that lie outside Rome's borders. This region offers something increasingly rare in our modern world: authenticity. Here, traditions aren't maintained for tourists; they're simply the fabric of daily life. During the olive harvest in Sabina, we watched three generations of a family working together, collecting olives just as their ancestors did. At a festival in Viterbo, we found ourselves swept into a medieval parade, alongside locals in Renaissance costumes who have participated in this ritual since birth.

What makes these experiences so special is their accessibility. Unlike many of Italy's more remote regions, Lazio's treasures are remarkably easy to reach. Efficient trains and buses connect Rome to countless historic towns, making it possible to step from a modern train into a medieval village in under an hour.

Concise History of Rome and Lazio

Walking through Lazio is like turning pages in a living history book. Each layer reveals another chapter in this remarkable story.

Ancient Lazio: The Etruscans and Early Rome

The mysterious Etruscans left their mark in the necropoli of Tarquinia and Cerveteri. The painted tombs of Tarquinia reveal intricate details that illuminate ancient life: from dancers' gestures reflecting religious beliefs to banquet scenes depicting the cuisine and fashion of the era. These archaeological treasures serve as windows into the lives of the people who inhabited these hills thousands of years ago. The careful preservation of these tomb paintings allows modern visitors to glimpse the vibrancy of Etruscan civilization, transforming abstract history into a tangible human experience.

The Roman Empire: Lazio at the Heart of an Empire

When Rome emerged from its humble beginnings on the Palatine Hill, it transformed Lazio forever. The Romans weren't just empire builders; they were master engineers who reshaped the landscape itself. Standing on the ancient Appian Way today, you can still see their genius at work. The road's massive paving stones have supported travelers for over two thousand years, while overhead, broken aqueducts march across the countryside like ancient giants.

Via Appia

During the height of the Roman Empire, Lazio was the epicenter of political, cultural, and military power. Rome became the capital of an empire that stretched from Britain to North Africa and from Spain to the Middle East. The region's landscape was transformed by monumental architecture, including aqueducts, roads, and grand temples.

Lazio's towns also flourished during this time, serving as retreats for Roman elites or strategic military outposts. Tivoli, for example, became a favorite destination for emperors and aristocrats, who built lavish villas such as Hadrian's Villa.

The Castelli Romani, towns of the countryside around Rome offered fresh air and cool breezes in the summer heat. This volcanic crater lake near the Alban Hills offered a cool retreat. The Roman aristocracy constructed lavish summer homes along its shores, and the site later became the location of the papal summer residence. Meanwhile, the port city of Ostia was a vital hub for trade and commerce.

The Appian Way of Ancient Rome

The Fall of Rome and the Medieval Era

The 5th century AD brought profound changes to Lazio as the Western Roman Empire crumbled. Successive waves of Visigoth and Vandal invasions swept through the region, repeatedly sacking Rome itself. Yet despite this turmoil, Lazio maintained its significance as a cultural and spiritual hub, anchored by the continued presence of the papacy in Rome.

As the medieval period unfolded, the Papal States emerged with Rome as their heart, serving both as a spiritual beacon and administrative capital. Under the Catholic Church's stewardship, Lazio flourished as a guardian of ancient knowledge and artworks, while also evolving into a major destination for religious pilgrims. The region's importance in Church affairs was further cemented by towns like Anagni, which earned the title "City of Popes" for its role as both a papal residence and a center of ecclesiastical authority.

The Renaissance and Baroque Periods

The Renaissance transformed Lazio into a grand artistic canvas. Under the patronage of powerful popes and cardinals, Rome became Europe's cultural heart. Master artists like Michelangelo, Raphael, and Bernini turned the city into a living museum; their masterpieces still take our breath away today. Standing beneath the soaring dome of St. Peter's or gazing up at the Sistine Chapel ceiling, you're experiencing the same sense of wonder that visitors have felt for centuries.

But what I find most fascinating is how the Renaissance spirit spread beyond Rome's walls. The Castelli Romani hills became a playground for papal nobility, who built magnificent villas to escape the city's summer heat. The Palazzo Comunale anchors Velletri's historic center, its medieval tower rising above the city's rooftops. In the evening, locals gather in Piazza Cairoli, where you might sample Velletri's renowned red wine at a traditional osteria while admiring views of the Alban Hills.

Modern Lazio: Where Past Meets Present

The story of modern Lazio begins with Italian unification in 1871, when Rome became the capital of the new nation. You can still sense this pivotal moment in the grand boulevards and government buildings around Piazza della Repubblica: a sharp contrast to the medieval alleys of Trastevere.

Lazio's Provinces and Cultural Regions

Though Lazio has five official provinces, each holds cherished local areas, such as the Castelli Romani and Ciociaria, which maintain their own identities and cultural uniqueness. These traditional zones offer a deeper sense of place and are celebrated throughout this guide.

Lazio

Subregions of Lazio

Rome (Province and Metropolitan City of the Capital)

The heart of the region and of Italy itself, this area includes not just the Eternal City but also surrounding towns like Tivoli, Frascati, and Castel Gandolfo, blending imperial grandeur with vineyard-covered hills and papal retreats.

Castelli Romani: Rome's Enchanted Hills

The first time I drove up the winding road to the Castelli Romani, emerging from the urban sprawl of Rome into a world of vineyard-covered slopes and medieval towers, I understood why Romans have been escaping here for two millennia. These hill towns, including Tivoli, aren't just places: they are portals to another Italy, one that moves to the rhythm of church bells and long lunches.

Papal Palace in Castel Gandolfo

Each town has its own magic. Frascati, with its elegant Renaissance villas and wine cellars carved deep into volcanic rock, draws you in with the promise of its famous white wine. I remember ducking into a family-run enoteca one autumn afternoon, where the owner insisted we try his grandfather's wine while showing us black-and-white photos of grape harvests from the 1950s.

Castel Gandolfo, the pope's summer residence, perches like a white jewel above Lake Albano. The view from its main square stretches across the countryside - the same view that has refreshed papal eyes for centuries. In spring, the town's gardens burst with camellias and azaleas, their colors reflected in the deep blue volcanic lake below.

Viterbo

Often referred to as Tuscia, this northern province preserves Etruscan sites, medieval hill towns, and volcanic lakes. Highlights include Tarquinia, Cerveteri, and Viterbo's papal quarter.

Viterbo, the "City of Popes," guards Italy's best-preserved medieval quarter. Walking through the San Pellegrino district at dusk, when lanterns cast a golden light on ancient stones and cats doze in Gothic doorways, feels like stepping into a living museum.

Palazzo dei Papi di Viterbo

During the Macchina di Santa Rosa festival, this medieval setting becomes the backdrop for one of Italy's most spectacular traditions: an illuminated tower carried through torch-lit streets by hundreds of porters.

Rieti

The most mountainous and pastoral of Lazio's provinces, Rieti is home to the Sabine Hills and sacred Franciscan sites like Greccio. It's a place of olive groves, medieval abbeys, and spiritual retreats.

Frosinone

Also known as part of Ciociaria, this southern inland province is known for its rugged terrain, pre-Roman ruins, and towns like Anagni and Alatri, which retain deep medieval and papal connections.

Ciociaria: Land of Ancient Footsteps

South of Rome lies a region that even many Italians haven't discovered. The Ciociaria takes its name from the ciocie, distinctive sandals once worn by local shepherds, bound to their legs with leather straps. Today, these sandals are mainly seen during festivals, but they symbolize the region's proud, independent spirit.

Fontana Pio IX in Alatri

Here, mountain towns like Alatri and Anagni rise from hilltops, their massive stone walls testifying to over two thousand years of history. Anagni, the "City of Popes," whispers tales of medieval power and intrigue. Its frescoed papal palace witnessed some of the Church's most dramatic moments - walking through its halls, you can almost hear the echoes of centuries-old footsteps.

Latina

Stretching along the Tyrrhenian coast, Latina includes seaside towns like Sperlonga and Gaeta, as well as inland archaeological parks and the reclaimed Pontine Marshes, turned into farmland during the 20th century.

The south offers yet another face of Lazio. Here, dramatic cliffs plunge into the Tyrrhenian Sea, and whitewashed towns like Sperlonga seem to float between blue sky and bluer water. The beach where Emperor Tiberius built his seaside villa still attracts sun-seekers today, though now they're more likely to be enjoying fresh seafood at a beachside restaurant than plotting imperial politics.

Grotto of Tiberius, Sperlonga

The Magic Beyond the Walls

There's a phrase Italians use that perfectly captures the essence of Lazio: "Il bello della provincia": the beauty of the provinces. Beyond Rome's ancient walls lies an Italy that few tourists experience, but every traveler dreams of finding.

Why Journey Beyond?

In these towns and villages, you'll discover treasures that even Rome, with all its imperial splendor, cannot match. Here, history isn't displayed behind glass;

it's woven into daily life. In Anagni, shopkeepers arrange their modern wares in medieval storefronts, while in Marino, wine still flows from the town fountain during the annual Sagra dell'Uva, just as it has for centuries. Each stone step worn smooth by centuries of footsteps tells a story.

The rhythm of life moves to an older, gentler beat. Imagine joining an evening passeggiata (evening stroll) in Viterbo, where the golden light makes the medieval quarter glow like honey. Or finding yourself invited to a family's vendemmia (grape harvest) in Montefiascone, where families and neighbors work together, sharing stories and traditions as ancient as the gnarled vines themselves.

Top Experiences in Lazio Beyond Rome

Savor & Sip: Taste Frascati wine in volcanic cave cellars, and dine seaside in Sperlonga.

Step into the Past: Walk through Etruscan tombs in Tarquinia, and take part in medieval celebrations in Anagni.

Live the Tradition: Join the Macchina di Santa Rosa procession, harvest olives in the Sabine Hills, and lose yourself in the rhythm of village festivals.

Your Journey Begins

After years of exploring these festivals and towns, I have discovered that the true magic of Lazio lies in unexpected moments of connection. This book is not just a guide; it is an invitation to become part of something ancient and alive.

Whether it is the thunder of hooves during the Santa Rosa festival in Viterbo, the echo of a choir in a twelfth-century cathedral, the joy of village wine shared at harvest, or the rhythm of tamburi drums pulsing through medieval streets, these are the moments that stay with you.

Beyond the gates of Rome lies a world that does not just welcome visitors, it embraces them like family. Let this book be your key to festivals, traditions, and stories waiting to become part of your own. Rome may take a lifetime to explore, but Lazio makes you want to live that lifetime to the fullest.

Adventure is calling. Are you ready?

CHAPTER FOUR

Arrive & Explore

A Quick Guide to Transportation and Accommodation

Arriving in Rome: A Visitor's Guide

Rome is a city where history, culture, and spirituality converge, making it an incredible destination. Whether you're arriving from abroad or planning your daily excursions, this guide will help you navigate the Eternal City with ease.

Getting to Rome

Rome welcomes visitors through two major airports. Leonardo da Vinci–Fiumicino Airport (FCO) is the primary international gateway, located 32 kilometers (20 miles) from the city center. For those flying with low-cost carriers, Ciampino Airport (CIA) offers a closer alternative at just 15 kilometers (9 miles) from central Rome.

From Fiumicino Airport, you have several transfer options to reach the city center. The Leonardo Express train provides the most efficient route, running every 15-30 minutes directly to Termini Station in just 32 minutes for €14.

Budget-conscious travelers might prefer the shuttle bus services, which cost between €6-8 and take about an hour. Official white taxis offer a fixed-rate service to the center, while private transfers provide door-to-door convenience for €60-80.

Ciampino Airport connects to the city via Terravision or SIT shuttle buses, reaching Termini Station in approximately 40 minutes for €6. Alternatively, taxis charge a flat rate of €31 to the center.

Choosing Your Base in Rome

When selecting accommodation, the historic center of Rome offers unparalleled advantages that justify the higher costs. The neighborhoods of Centro Storico, Trastevere, and Monti place you at the heart of Rome's cultural tapestry, allowing you to fully immerse yourself in the city's rhythm. From these central locations, you can easily walk to major attractions, enjoy early morning or late evening strolls, and take afternoon breaks at your hotel when needed.

The benefits of central accommodation extend beyond convenience. You'll find yourself steps away from authentic trattorias, historic landmarks, and vibrant piazzas. During my last visit, I logged 16 miles (25 kilometers) in a single day of sightseeing: having a central hotel provided the flexibility to rest and recharge between explorations.

See Accommodation Detail Chapter for more information, guidance, and hotel recommendations by neighborhood.

Getting Around Rome

Rome unfolds as an open-air museum, best experienced on foot once you've settled into your accommodations. Walking through the city's piazzas reveals magnificent historical architecture, while the gentle sounds of clinking cups from sidewalk cafes create the perfect backdrop for exploration.

We prefer staying near Campo dei Fiori or Piazza Navona, as these central locations provide an ideal base for discovering the city. Though we typically walk everywhere, careful pre-trip planning helps organize our sightseeing route to minimize unnecessary distances. The walking tours detailed in later chapters offer efficiently planned routes through the city's highlights.

When longer distances call for public transportation, Rome's comprehensive metro system serves as a convenient option. Three lines crisscross the city: the orange Line A, connecting major sites like the Spanish Steps and Vatican; the blue Line B, stopping near the Colosseum; and the green Line C. At €1.50 for 100 minutes of travel, the metro provides an economical choice for covering greater distances.

The extensive bus and tram network, enhanced in 2025 for the Jubilee Year, complements the underground system, reaching areas beyond metro coverage.

For added convenience, official white taxis can be hailed on streets or booked through apps like FreeNow. While Uber operates in Rome, only the premium Uber Black service is available: I recommend this for scheduling airport returns in advance.

Those seeking eco-friendly alternatives might enjoy exploring Rome's narrow streets via electric scooters and bikes. The Roma Pass (available at www.romapass.it) offers excellent value by combining public transport access with museum entry benefits, making it worth considering for extended stays.

Andiamo!

Enough with the introductions! Let's dive into the heart of Italy and explore the vibrant traditions. Together we'll discover the festivals, sagre, and unforgettable events that make this island come alive throughout the year. Ready? Andiamo (Let's Go)!

CHAPTER FIVE

Map of Must-See Celebrations

Explore Lazio's Festivals & Sagre with Our Interactive Map

Festival & Sagra Map: Your Essential Guide

Immerse yourself in Lazio's most cherished traditions! Our detailed festival map pinpoints every vibrant celebration across the region, from ancient religious processions to mouthwatering food sagre. Each marker reveals event dates and locations, making it easy to weave these authentic Italian experiences into your journey. Find the map here:

https://katerinaferrara.com/ultimate-festival-and-travel-guide-rome-and-beyond/

Interactive Google Map: Plan Your Adventure

Take your exploration further with our comprehensive Google Map! This dynamic tool brings Lazio's festival cities to life, helping you visualize your route, estimate travel times, and preview each destination through local photos. From Rome to Lazio's hidden corners, plan your journey here: https://maps.app.goo.gl/BpABrVRM2hMJ3tsu6

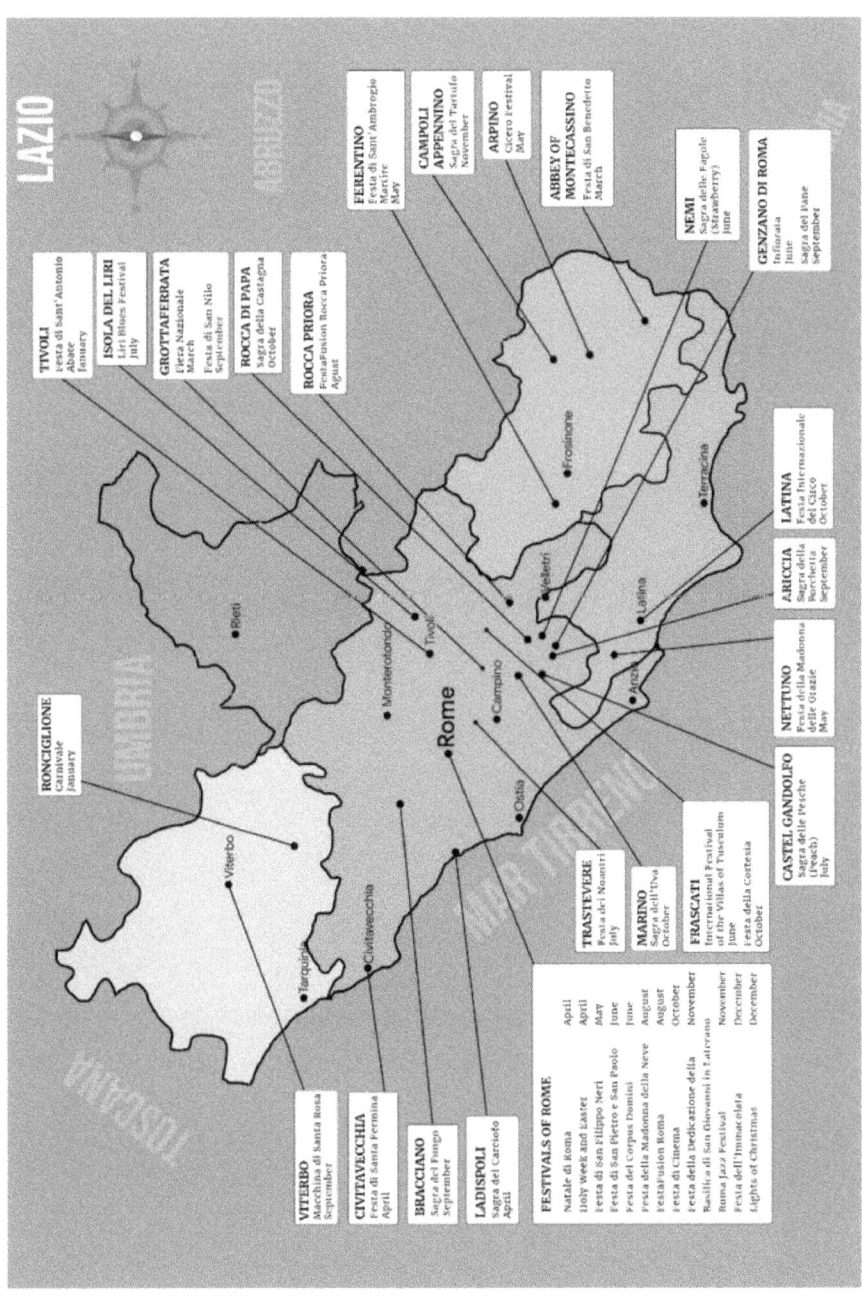

Summer Celebrations

May through August

CHAPTER SIX

Ferentino's Twin Tributes to Sant'Ambrogio

From Ciociaria's Pastoral Charm to its Festive Present

Festa di Sant'Ambrogio Martire

Where: Ferentino

When: May 1 (Principal Celebration) and August 16 (Memorial of the Martyrdom of St. Ambrose).

Average Festival Temperatures: High: 21°C (70°F). Low: 10°C (50°F).

Ferentino Events on Instagram: @citta_di_ferentino

Ferentino: A Historical Gem in the Heart of Ciociaria

Nestled within the province of Frosinone in the Lazio region, Ferentino is a historic town with a legacy dating back to ancient times. In the heart of Ciociaria, this area is known for its lush landscapes, rich traditions, and unique cultural identity. Ciociaria, a term used to describe the region of southern Lazio, boasts a fascinating blend of history, folklore, and cuisine.

Ferentino itself is perched on a hill overlooking the picturesque Sacco Valley, approximately 65 kilometers (40 miles) southeast of Rome and 20 kilometers from Frosinone, the provincial capital. The town's strategic location along ancient trade routes contributed to its significance throughout history, serving as a crucial hub for communication and commerce.

Ferentino became a thriving Roman colony with its inclusion in the Roman Republic around the 4th century BC. Evidence of this period is visible in the well-preserved polygonal walls (opus poligonale), a hallmark of ancient engineering. The town played a pivotal role in the Roman road network, being along the Via Latina, a major thoroughfare connecting Rome with southern Italy.

Throughout the medieval period, Ferentino maintained its importance as a religious and administrative center. Its affiliation with the Papal States brought both prosperity and conflict, as it became a contested site during political and military struggles. The town's ecclesiastical prominence is underscored by its cathedral, the Basilica of Saints John and Paul, which stands on the site of the ancient acropolis.

Ferentino occupies a hilly terrain typical of Ciociaria, offering breathtaking views of the surrounding countryside, dotted with olive groves and vineyards. The town is at an elevation of approximately 400 meters (1300 feet) above sea level, which provides a mild climate throughout the year. Its position in the Apennine foothills also places it close to natural parks and reserves, making it a gateway to outdoor adventures in central Italy.

The town has a population of 20,000 residents, known as ferentinati. While many embrace modern lifestyles, Ferentino retains its rural charm and traditional customs, which are celebrated at local festivals and community events.

The Province of Frosinone and Ciociaria

Ferentino is one of many historic towns in the Province of Frosinone, a region renowned for its scenic beauty and cultural significance. Frosinone serves as the administrative and cultural hub of Ciociaria, which extends across the valleys and hills south of Rome. Known for its hearty cuisine, traditional music, and artisanal crafts, Ciociaria offers visitors a glimpse into an Italy untouched by mass tourism.

Festival of Saint Ambrose

The Festival of Sant'Ambrogio in Ferentino is a deeply rooted tradition that honors the town's patron saint, Saint Ambrose. The devotion to Sant'Ambrogio dates back to the early 4th century when he was martyred for his Christian faith. Over the centuries, the citizens of Ferentino have commemorated his sacrifice through annual celebrations, with records indicating that organized festivities have been held since at least the 17th century.

Who is Sant'Ambrogio

Saint Ambrose is the patron saint of Ferentino and a Roman centurion who became a Christian martyr in the early 4th century AD. Originally from Liguria, he served in the Roman army during Emperor Diocletian's reign.

While stationed in Ferentino, Ambrose converted to Christianity during a time of severe persecution. He openly defied imperial orders to worship Roman gods, choosing instead to proclaim his Christian faith. Despite torture and threats, he remained unwavering in his beliefs.

In 304 AD, Ambrose was beheaded at Monticchio, an area in Ferentino, for refusing to renounce Christianity. His remains were initially buried in a local church and later transferred to the Cathedral of Saint John and Saint Paul in Ferentino, where they remain a focus of devotion today.

Important distinction: Sant'Ambrogio Martire (the martyr of Ferentino) should not be confused with Sant'Ambrogio of Milan, who was a prominent 4th-century bishop and theologian known as one of the Doctors of the Church.

Festival Events during the May Celebration

Festival Timeline and Events

April 30

Noon

The festivities reach a pivotal moment on April 30th, when at precisely noon, the normally concealed statue of the saint is unveiled for public veneration.

1:00 p.m.

The solemn Procession of the Relics of Sant'Ambrogio begins.

During this sacred ceremony, the faithful join with clergy and local dignitaries to carry the saint's cherished relic through Ferentino's streets, expressing their profound devotion and seeking his divine intercession.

This procession marks the culmination of a nine-day novena period, during which the community gathers daily for dedicated prayers and masses, spiritually preparing themselves for the upcoming feast day on May 1st.

May 1

9:00 a.m.

The day begins with a solemn Mass at the Cathedral of Saint John and Saint Paul, where the relics are enshrined. Following the service, a grand procession winds through the historic streets of Ferentino.

The silver statue of Sant'Ambrogio, crafted in 1641 by Roman silversmith Fantino Taglietti, is carried by devoted parishioners, accompanied by clergy, local officials, and townspeople. The procession is marked by hymns, prayers, and the ringing of church bells, creating a profound sense of community and reverence.

Post-Procession Festivities: After the religious ceremonies, the town comes alive with various cultural events, including traditional music performances, folk dances, and local craft exhibitions. Stalls line the streets, offering regional delicacies and artisanal products, fostering a festive atmosphere that extends into the evening.

May 2

8:00 p.m.

The statue is hidden again until the next festival, and the celebration ends with a fireworks display.

Feast of St. Ambrose – August Celebration

The Feast of Sant'Ambrogio on August 16th in Ferentino commemorates the martyrdom of the town's patron saint, Saint Ambrose.

In the days leading up to August 16th, the faithful engage in spiritual preparations, including novenas and special masses dedicated to Sant'Ambrogio. These practices foster a reflective atmosphere, allowing participants to honor the saint's legacy and seek his intercession.

August 15

1:00 p.m.

The hidden statue of Sant'Ambrogio is revealed and available to the congregation for prayer.

August 16th

Feast Day Events

9:00 a.m.

The day begins with a solemn Eucharistic celebration at the Cathedral of Saint John and Saint Paul, where the relics of the saint are preserved. This mass draws congregants from Ferentino and neighboring regions, united in their reverence for the patron saint.

10:00 a.m.

Following the mass, a grand procession unfolds through the historic streets of Ferentino. The silver statue, an exquisite piece crafted in 1641 by the Roman silversmith Fantino Taglietti, is borne aloft by devoted parishioners. Accompanied by clergy, civic leaders, and the faithful, the procession is a moving display of communal faith and tradition. The route is often adorned with floral decorations, and the air resonates with hymns and prayers, creating a profound spiritual ambiance. Note to check local information as the August Procession does not happen each year.

Cultural Events: The evening typically features various cultural activities, including musical performances, folk dances, and exhibitions that showcase Ferentino's rich heritage. Local artisans may display their crafts, and traditional Ciociarian music adds to the festive atmosphere.

Fiera: A market featuring various stalls with vendors, including food and drink stands.

The Feast of Sant'Ambrogio on August 16th is a testament to Ferentino's enduring devotion to its patron saint. Through a blend of solemn religious observance and vibrant cultural expression, the festival encapsulates the spirit and heritage of this historic town.

Special Festival Food
Tronchetto di Sant'Ambrogio

A highlight of the festival is the "Tronchetto di Sant'Ambrogio," an artisanal cake inspired by the legend of the saint. According to tradition, Saint Ambrose was tied to a tree trunk and condemned to be burned alive, but the trunk did not catch fire, and he emerged unharmed. This event was interpreted as a divine sign of his sanctity.

The cake, named after this miraculous event, is made from a mixture of flour, sugar, eggs, honey, and milk, with additions of walnuts, hazelnuts, pistachios, sultanas, and pine nuts. It is characterized by its bulbous shape, brown color, and grains of sugar sprinkled on its surface. The flavor profile includes pronounced notes of egg, butter, dried fruit, honey, and vanilla, offering a sweet treat that embodies the town's rich culinary heritage.

Additionally, the festival showcases other regional specialties, such as:

Fettuccine alla Ciociara: A hearty pasta dish featuring a sauce made with tomatoes, pancetta, and pecorino cheese.

Ciambelle al Vino: Wine-infused ring-shaped cookies, perfect for dipping.

Local Wines: Selections from the surrounding vineyards, reflecting the area's viticultural traditions.

These culinary offerings provide festival-goers with an authentic taste of Ferentino's delights.

The Cathedral of Saint John not only honors the town's patron saint but also serves as a vibrant expression of Ferentino's historical and cultural identity, bringing together the community in a celebration of faith, tradition, and local heritage.

Walking Tour of Ferentino

#1. Porta Montana

Begin at Porta Montana, an impressive ancient gate that once served as a primary entrance to the city. Built with massive rectangular blocks of volcanic stone called tuff (a light, porous rock formed from volcanic ash), it exemplifies the engineering prowess of the time. Passing through this gate offers a tangible connection to Ferentino's storied past.

#2. Porta Sanguinaria

From Porta Montana, head to Porta Sanguinaria, a short walk away. This gate's evocative name, "Blood Gate," and its arched stone blocks (voussoirs) made of volcanic tuff stone offer a glimpse into Ferentino's storied past.

#3. Arimi di Casamare

Walk along the ancient walls known as Arimi di Casamare, located near Porta Sanguinaria. This section showcases the remarkable defensive structures that once protected the city.

#4. Porta Pentagonale

Continue to the Porta Pentagonale, another fascinating element of the ancient fortifications. Its unique five-sided design is a standout feature that underscores Ferentino's strategic ingenuity.

#5. Porta Sant'Agata

Next, visit Porta Sant'Agata, named after the nearby Church of Sant'Agata. This gate reflects a blend of Roman and medieval influences, along a well-preserved section of the city's walls.

#6. Acropolis of Ferentinum

Proceed to the Acropolis, the highest point in Ferentino, fortified with ancient walls dating back to the 2nd and 1st centuries BC. This area, once the religious and political hub, provides insights into the town's historic significance and offers panoramic views of the surrounding landscape.

Ancient Roman Walls of the Acropolis

#7. Cathedral of Saint John and Saint Paul

Perched majestically atop Ferentino's ancient acropolis, this stunning Romanesque cathedral commands attention against the sky. Its weathered stone facade tells the story of centuries, from its founding by Pope Paschal I in the early 9th century to its grand 12th-century renovation. The cathedral's strategic position on the acropolis, built atop ancient Roman foundations, offers sweeping views across the Lazio countryside.

As you approach, notice the intricate medieval stonework and the cathedral's imposing bell tower rising above the town. The main portal features elaborately carved medieval reliefs, while the rose window above bathes the interior in ethereal light. Inside, your eyes are drawn to the breathtaking 12th-century Cosmati mosaic floors, masterworks of geometric precision created by the renowned Cosmati family studio. These intricate patterns of colored marble and precious stones form mesmerizing designs that seem to flow through the nave.

The cathedral's crowning jewel is its 13th-century ciborium, crafted by the master artist Trudo de Trivio. This ornate marble canopy over the altar showcases the height of medieval craftsmanship with its delicate carvings and architectural detail. The most sacred treasure here are the relics of Saint Ambrose, Ferentino's beloved patron saint, held in an ornate reliquary that takes center stage during the town's twice-yearly festivals honoring the saint.

#8. Porta San Francesco

Descend slightly to Porta San Francesco, near the Church of San Francesco. This gate reflects Ferentino's layered history, blending Roman and medieval elements.

#9. Chiesa di Santa Maria Maggiore

Next, explore the Church of Santa Maria Maggiore, a Gothic church dating from the 13th to 14th centuries. Its exterior showcases exquisite medieval architecture, while the interior, despite restorations, retains elements that reflect its historical significance.

Arch and Campanile

After your walking tour, consider an appointment at the spa!

Terme Pompeo

Terme Pompeo is a renowned thermal spa complex with a rich history dating back to 1854. The facility uses natural sulfurous-bicarbonate-calcium waters, emerging at a temperature of 18°C (64.4°F), known for their therapeutic properties beneficial in treating respiratory, vascular, rheumatic, dermatological, and other conditions.

Facilities and Services:

Thermal Treatments: Offering a variety of treatments, including balneotherapy, fango therapy (mud), inhalation therapies, and hydrotherapy, all aimed at promoting health and well-being.

Nature Spa: The spa features a modern thermal pool equipped with hydromassage stations and relaxation areas set within a serene garden of ancient trees, providing a holistic wellness experience.

Logistics

Train: Ferentino has a train station located just outside the town center, offering convenient connections to Rome and other towns in the Lazio region. Regional trains are frequent and provide a quick and affordable option for reaching Ferentino. From the station, local buses or taxis can take visitors to the historic center.

Bus: Ferentino is served by regional bus services that connect it to nearby towns and cities, including Frosinone and Rome. The principal bus stop is centrally located, making it a convenient option for those traveling without a car.

Car: To arrive by car from Rome, take the A1 Autostrada del Sole southbound toward Naples and exit at Frosinone. From there, follow signs to Ferentino, which is just a short drive away. The journey typically takes about an hour and fifteen minutes, depending on traffic.

Parking: Free and paid parking areas are available just outside the city center, allowing easy access to the town.

Restaurant Recommendations

Trattoria Consolare. Address: Via Consolare, 59
Near the heart of Ferentino's historic center, Trattoria Consolare offers a cozy and authentic dining experience. The restaurant is known for its traditional Italian and Mediterranean cuisine, with a menu that features local specialties and fresh ingredients. The warm atmosphere and attentive service make it a favorite among both locals and visitors.

Il Giardino Pizzeria Restaurant. Address: Via Casilina Sud, 96
Though slightly outside the immediate historic center, this restaurant is celebrated for its extensive variety of calzones, each generously sized and filled with fresh, high-quality ingredients. The menu caters to diverse tastes, including options for vegetarians and those requiring gluten-free preparations. Beyond calzones, Il Giardino offers a range of Italian dishes, including pizzas and desserts. The establishment is known for its welcoming atmosphere and attentive service, making it a popular choice for both locals and visitors.

Accommodation

For the Festa di Sant'Ambrogio, I would recommend two or three nights in town.

Hotel Bassetto. Address: Via Casilina Km 74
A 3-star hotel offering comfortable accommodations with modern amenities. Near the historic center, it provides easy access to local attractions and is known for its hospitable service.

Hotel Fontana Olente. Address: Via Casilina Nord Km 76
A 3-star hotel located close to the historic center, it offers a relaxing stay with convenient access to Ferentino's cultural sites. For those seeking an extended stay at the Terme Pompeo, the on-site hotel offers comfortable accommodations, allowing guests to fully immerse themselves in the therapeutic and relaxing environment of the Terme.

Day Trips: Nearby Sites, Cities and Towns

Lago di Canterno. Lago di Canterno, located about 15 kilometers or 9.3 miles from Ferentino, is often called the "floating lake" and is nestled within the Regional Natural Park of Monti Simbruini. This picturesque and tranquil destination offers a peaceful escape into nature, surrounded by rolling hills and lush greenery. The lake's unique geological formation adds to its appeal, having been created by the collapse of underground caves that resulted in a water-filled sinkhole.

Visitors can enjoy walking and hiking along scenic paths that wind around the lake, offering both leisurely strolls and more invigorating hikes through the park. The area is also rich in wildlife, with waterfowl and small mammals inhabiting the region, making it a rewarding spot for nature lovers. Photographers will find plenty to capture, from the still reflections on the lake's surface to the warm light of sunrise and sunset. The lakeside is also perfect for a relaxing picnic or simply unwinding while taking in the serene atmosphere.

Lago di Canterno makes for an ideal day trip for anyone seeking natural beauty, tranquility, and an easy getaway from Ferentino.

Abbey of Montecassino. A 65 kilometer (40 mile) drive from Ferentino, this iconic Benedictine monastery is one of the most significant religious sites in Italy. Founded in 529 AD by Saint Benedict, it has been rebuilt several times after destruction, most notably during World War II. Today, visitors can explore its beautiful cloisters, museum, and panoramic views of the Liri Valley.

Reggia di Caserta. Located 110 kilometers (68 miles) southeast of Ferentino. Known as the "Italian Versailles," this UNESCO World Heritage Site is a magnificent 18th-century royal palace and gardens. About an hour from Ferentino, the Reggia offers opulent interiors, stunning fountains, and a grand park for exploration.

Parco Nazionale d'Abruzzo, Lazio e Molise. This national park, 90 kilometers (56 miles) east of Ferentino, about an hour and a half away, is a haven for nature lovers. Renowned for its breathtaking landscapes, it's home to wildlife like wolves, bears, and chamois. Visitors can enjoy hiking, birdwatching, or simply soaking in the serene beauty of the mountains and forests.

Fiuggi. 20 kilometers (12 miles) north of Ferentino, this charming spa town, is famed for its natural mineral springs and wellness centers. Visitors can stroll through its medieval old town, enjoy spa treatments, or savor local dishes at traditional trattorias.

Alatri and its Cyclopean Walls. Only a 15-minute drive (15 kilometers, 9 miles) from Ferentino, Alatri boasts an impressive historical site: the Cyclopean Walls, massive stone fortifications from the 6th century BC. The picturesque town also features a beautiful cathedral and quaint streets perfect for a leisurely visit.

Ferentino Festivals and Sagre Throughout the Year

Historical Reenactment Festival
Spring
This event immerses visitors in Ferentino's storied past with reenactments of historical periods. Participants don period costumes, and various activities highlight the town's ancient heritage and traditions.

Ferentino Music Festival and Ferentino Estate
July / August
A vibrant summer event that brings together musicians from diverse genres. Concerts are held in picturesque settings around Ferentino, promoting cultural exchange and celebrating music.

Ferentino È
September
A cultural festival that fills the town with music, theater performances, art exhibitions, and local foods. The streets of the Santa Lucia district and other areas come alive with celebrations, showcasing the creativity and traditions of Ferentino.

Wine and Food Festival
October
This festival celebrates the culinary and viticultural heritage of Ferentino. Visitors can enjoy tastings of local wines, traditional dishes, and artisanal products, offering a true taste of the region.

CHAPTER SEVEN

Rome's Festival of Faith and Joy

Celebrating San Filippo Neri and the Giro delle Sette Chiese

F esta di San Filippo Neri

Where: Rome

When: May 26 -27

Average Festival Temperatures: High 31°C (88°F). Low 18°C (64°F).

Festival of San Filippo Neri, the Apostle of Rome

Having spent time in Rome over the years, I understand why the Festival of San Filippo Neri holds such a special place in Roman hearts. Celebrated annually on May 26, its origins trace back to 1622 - when Filippo was canonized just 27 years after his death, reflecting his profound impact on Roman spiritual life.

The festival's roots intertwine with the Congregation of the Oratory, founded in 1575. While ancient celebrations centered on traditional observances, what fascinates me is how they maintained Filippo's distinctive blend of reverence and joy even in formal ceremonies.

The Giro delle Sette Chiese remains a powerful tradition that I've witnessed firsthand. Walking these ancient paths, you can still feel how Filippo transformed what was once a solemn duty into a celebration of community.

The pilgrimage route connects seven of Rome's most significant churches: Basilica di San Pietro (St. Peter's Basilica), Basilica di San Paolo fuori le Mura (St. Paul Outside the Walls), Basilica di San Sebastiano fuori le Mura (St. Sebastian Outside the Walls), Basilica di San Giovanni in Laterano (St. John Lateran), Basilica di Santa Croce in Gerusalemme (Holy Cross in Jerusalem), Basilica di San Lorenzo fuori le Mura (St. Lawrence Outside the Walls), and Basilica di Santa Maria Maggiore (St. Mary Major).

What strikes me most about this festival is how perfectly it balances reverence and joy. Dawn at Chiesa Nuova brings the solemn Mass, where Filippo's remains rest in a crystal urn beneath Ciro Ferri's masterful altar. By afternoon, the streets fill with the same spirit of community that Filippo fostered - children playing, families sharing meals, music drifting from church doorways.

Who Was San Filippo Neri?

Walking through Rome's streets today, I'm often reminded of how Filippo moved through these same spaces. He arrived from Florence in 1533 as an unassuming eighteen-year-old, carrying little more than his faith and an extraordinary gift for connecting with people. Where we now see established churches and formal traditions, he saw opportunities for connection. His decision to teach in markets and shops rather than cloistered spaces was radical - imagine a priest today setting up a card game to keep young people from gambling halls.

Known for his infectious laughter and practical jokes, Filippo shattered the stereotype of the stern, distant priest. He engaged merchants in spiritual conversations at their shops and organized musical gatherings that would later evolve into the oratorio music form. His unconventional methods earned him the affectionate nickname "Pippo Buono" (Good Filippo) from the Roman people.

Among the many stories that capture his spirit, one of my favorites involves a woman who left Mass immediately after communion. Before enough time had passed for the host to dissolve, Filippo dispatched two altar boys to follow her home with lit ceremonial candles. When she asked why they were escorting her, they explained that Father Filippo had sent them to accompany the Blessed Sacrament, still physically present within her. The lesson about proper Eucharistic procedures was delivered with his characteristic wit rather than stern lectures, and reportedly, she never again left Mass early.

A Personal Note

When writing about the festivals of Rome, I was delighted to discover that the Festival of San Filippo Neri would be one of our first celebrations to explore in this book, and our first in Rome. His presence is woven into the fabric of this city; his name graces churches, streets, and even neighborhoods, while his cheerful, welcoming approach to faith still resonates in modern Rome. Writing about him feels like paying homage to a saint whose heart was so intricately tied to the Eternal City, and I'm thrilled to start this book with his story.

Festival Events

Santa Maria in Vallicella, also referred to simply as the Chiesa Nuova (New Church), stands at the very heart of San Filippo Neri's legacy. This church was built under his guidance and became the principal home of the Congregation of the Oratory, the community of priests and brothers he founded.

Besides housing his remains and preserving the personal artifacts of the saint, it also embodies the spirit of joyous devotion that he promoted. Because of these deep historical and spiritual ties, Santa Maria in Vallicella naturally serves as the central location for celebrating San Filippo's festival, offering pilgrims and devotees a direct connection to the life and mission of Rome's "Apostle of Joy."

The Novena (May 17 – May 25)

In the days leading up to San Filippo Neri's feast, a solemn novena takes place at Santa Maria in Vallicella. Each evening, Mass is celebrated at 7:00 p.m, followed by the traditional novena prayers. During this period, worshippers gather to reflect on the saint's life, offer personal intentions, and immerse themselves in the joyful spirit he inspired. The novena acts both as a spiritual preparation for the feast and as a communal reminder of San Filippo's enduring message of joy and humility.

Giro Alle Sette Chiese (More detail below)

A highlight of the festival is the Visit to the Seven Churches, which takes place one evening during the novena. Participants walk on a pilgrimage to seven historically significant churches in Rome, a tradition that San Filippo revitalized in the 16th century. This nocturnal journey includes moments of prayer, singing, and fellowship, recalling the saint's trademark blend of devotion and lively companionship.

Opening the Rooms of San Filippo

On Saturday, May 25, and Sunday, May 26, visitors are invited to tour the rooms of San Filippo, the private living quarters in which he prayed, counseled guests, and nurtured his spiritual life. Stepping into these spaces allows pilgrims and history-lovers alike to connect with the saint on a personal level, seeing firsthand where he spent his days in service and contemplation.

Feast Day Celebrations (May 26)

8:00 a.m. Mass at the Altar of the Saint

An early morning Mass is offered in the church's dedicated altar space for San Filippo. Parishioners and visitors gather in quiet gratitude to begin the day in prayer.

9:00 a.m. "Messa dei Ragazzi" (Children's Mass)

A special Mass focuses on children, reflecting Filippo's joyful spirit and his love for teaching and guiding the young. Local authorities frequently pay tribute to the saint, and after that, families and parishioners sometimes have breakfast, which is similar to the community Filippo encouraged.

11:00 a.m. Late Morning Mass

Another Mass provides an opportunity for those who prefer a slightly later service. The atmosphere remains festive, with hymns, readings, and homilies that highlight San Filippo's enduring impact on Rome.

7:00 p.m. Evening Solemn Concelebration

In the early evening, another Solemn Concelebration takes place.

A Living Legacy

Beyond the official ceremonies, Rome's neighborhoods celebrate San Filippo through music, shared meals, and charitable works. These local festivities embody his spirit of joy and inclusivity, welcoming both residents and visitors to participate in concerts, community dinners, and service projects.

*The Giro alle Sette Chiese (Night Pilgrimage)

One of the most memorable experiences during the Festival of San Filippo Neri is the Giro alle Sette Chiese, literally the "Tour of the Seven Churches." This pilgrimage, traditionally walked by night during the novena period, is deeply intertwined with the history of San Filippo and the spiritual heritage of Rome. The custom of visiting seven notable churches in Rome dates back to the Middle Ages. Pilgrims to Rome, especially in Holy Years, often followed a set path to earn indulgences and worship at the city's most sacred sites.

In the mid-16th century, San Filippo Neri re-energized this practice, infusing it with his characteristic warmth and camaraderie. He encouraged not just solemn prayer but also lively conversation, singing, and even shared meals along the route. It was Filippo's way of bringing people closer to God while fostering a sense of fellowship in an uplifting atmosphere.

Filippo's joyful pilgrimage, blending prayer and play, mirrored his faith. The Giro soon became one of the hallmark traditions of his Oratory community and a testament to his belief that religion should be celebrated in both solemn and lighthearted ways.

The Seven Churches and Their Significance

The journey begins at Basilica di San Pietro in Vaticano, the heart of the Catholic Church built over St. Peter's tomb. Here, Michelangelo's dome soars overhead while Bernini's magnificent bronze canopy (baldachin) - a towering 95-foot tall bronze canopy supported by twisted columns - marks the papal altar. Standing under that vast dome, pilgrims from around the world gather to honor the first pope and witness the universal reach of their faith.

The path then leads to Basilica di San Paolo Fuori le Mura, erected over the burial place of the "Apostle to the Gentiles." Its serene colonnaded courtyard and intricate apse mosaics create an atmosphere of majesty and contemplation. Along its walls, medallion portraits of every pope throughout history tell the story of the Church's continuity.

At Basilica di San Giovanni in Laterano, the "Mother of All Churches" and official cathedral of Rome, ancient Christianity comes alive. As the oldest of the major basilicas, its medieval cloister and ancient baptistery whisper stories of the early Church, while imposing statues of the Apostles line its central nave with solemn dignity.

The Basilica di Santa Maria Maggiore stands as a testament to Rome's devotion to the Virgin Mary. Its 5th-century mosaics glitter overhead, while the basilica's own "Sistine Chapel" (distinct from the Vatican's) houses treasured artwork. Here, the beloved icon "Salus Populi Romani" draws the faithful seeking Mary's intercession.

San Lorenzo Fuori le Mura honors one of the Church's most beloved deacons and martyrs. Its Romanesque architecture and ancient mosaics create an atmosphere of timeless devotion, while below, the crypt houses St. Lawrence's tomb, commemorating his ultimate sacrifice for the faith.

At Santa Croce in Gerusalemme, pilgrims encounter tangible connections to Christ's Passion through relics brought to Rome by Emperor Constantine's mother, St. Helena. The Chapel of the Relics and serene gardens provide space for contemplation of Christianity's deepest mysteries.

The pilgrimage concludes at San Sebastiano Fuori le Mura, built above catacombs once thought to shelter the remains of Saints Peter and Paul. Today, pilgrims venerate St. Sebastian's relics and explore the peaceful grounds and ancient underground passages that speak to Christianity's earliest days in Rome.

In the days before San Filippo Neri's feast (May 26), groups gather at dusk to embark on the Giro alle Sette Chiese, often led by priests or members of the Oratory. The route covers all seven churches, typically concluding in the early morning. At each church, the group pauses for a brief prayer service or hymn singing. These moments of reflection ensure that the focus remains on pilgrimage rather than sightseeing—something dear to Filippo's heart.

Optional Routes: For those with time or physical constraints, shorter routes can be arranged. Some pilgrims select a few key churches instead of the entire seven, embracing the spirit of the Giro while adapting to their personal circumstances.

A Note on Roman Festival Chapters

Unlike the chapters covering festivals outside Rome, this and other Roman festival chapters focus solely on the celebrations, their history, events, and cultural significance.

But Rome, with its vast number of festivals and endless travel possibilities, required a different structure. To avoid repeating where to stay, eat, and explore in Rome across multiple chapters, I've created dedicated sections under the Navigating Rome portion toward the back of the book. These include:

- Arrive and Explore

- Savoring the Flavors of Rome

- Dining in Rome: A Neighborhood Guide

- Smart, Walkable Itineraries

- Securing Tickets for Rome's Busiest Sights

- Accommodation Detail Rome

This organization allows you to plan your Roman holiday as a complete experience, while still appreciating the distinct character and traditions of each festival. It also avoids repeating essential travel details in every Rome-based chapter.

CHAPTER EIGHT

Nettuno, Anchored in Faith and Tradition

Feast of Our Lady of Grace and the People of the Sea

Festa della Madonna delle Grazie e delle Genti di Mare

Where: Nettuno

When: First Two Weeks in May

Average Festival Temperatures: High 20°C (68°F). Low 14°C (58°F).

Nettuno: A Coastal Jewel Rooted in Time

Nettuno, a picturesque coastal town in the Lazio region, boasts a history that intertwines with ancient Rome, medieval fortifications, and modern maritime life. Located 60 kilometers (37 miles) south of Rome, Nettuno has long been a strategic settlement, given its proximity to the Tyrrhenian Sea and fertile inland plains.

In Roman times, Nettuno was part of the territory of Antium (modern-day Anzio), a flourishing port and elite resort. Though less prominent than its neighbor, Nettuno likely served as a supporting settlement for the bustling Roman trade routes and maritime activity. The area was known for its luxurious villas and estates, owned by wealthy Romans who sought refuge from the bustling capital. Artifacts and ruins suggest the town played a role in Rome's expansive network of ports and coastal defense.

Medieval and Renaissance Eras

Nettuno rose to greater prominence during the medieval period. Its strategic location made it a fortified town, with strong walls and a protective castle. The Forte Sangallo, built in the late 15th century by Pope Alexander VI and designed by Giuliano da Sangallo, remains a defining feature of the town, highlighting its importance in regional defense. During the Renaissance, Nettuno developed as a thriving fishing community and religious hub.

In the 20th century, Nettuno became widely known for its religious significance and its proximity to key World War II events, particularly the Allied Anzio-Nettuno landings in 1944. The town's Sicily-Rome American Cemetery, a solemn site, honors thousands of American soldiers who fought during the Italian Campaign.

Nettuno lies on the Tyrrhenian Sea, with its coastline featuring sandy beaches and small coves. The town's mild Mediterranean climate and scenic location make it a popular destination for both locals and tourists.

Nettuno has 50,000 residents, a number that swells during the summer months as visitors flock to its beaches and historical sites. The town is a blend of old and new, with a well-preserved medieval quarter and modern amenities.

One of Italy's largest marinas, showcasing Nettuno's enduring relationship with the sea.

Beyond the coast, Nettuno is surrounded by fertile plains, vineyards, and olive groves, contributing to its agricultural significance.

Feast of Our Lady of Grace and the People of the Sea

The Festa della Madonna delle Grazie e delle Genti di Mare in Nettuno is a centuries-old celebration deeply rooted in the town's maritime heritage and devotion to the Virgin Mary.

The festival commemorates the arrival of the sacred statue of Our Lady of Grace, which, according to tradition, reached Nettuno's shores in 1550. This event marked the beginning of a profound devotion among the townspeople, leading to the Madonna delle Grazie being proclaimed the patron saint of Nettuno in 1854.

Key Festival Events

The festival takes place in early May, with a series of religious and cultural events:

May 1

Rievocazione dell'Approdo (Reenactment of the Landing)

A historical reenactment commemorates the 1550 arrival of the Madonna's statue. Participants in period costumes recreate the event along the waterfront, bringing history to life.

First Saturday in May

Processione di Andata (Procession from the Church)

On the first Saturday of May, the statue is carried from the Sanctuary of Nostra Signora delle Grazie e Santa Maria Goretti to the Church of San Giovanni. This solemn procession is accompanied by prayers and hymns.

Blessing of the Boats: As part of the maritime traditions, local fishing boats are blessed, seeking protection and bountiful harvests from the sea. This event underscores Nettuno's deep connection to maritime life.

Second Sunday in May

Processione di Ritorno (Return Procession)

On the second Sunday of May, the statue is returned to its sanctuary, concluding the religious observances.

Festival Activities

Historical Parades: Colorful parades featuring traditional costumes and performances celebrate Nettuno's rich history and cultural heritage.

Markets and Food Stalls: Local markets offer traditional foods, crafts, and souvenirs, allowing visitors to immerse themselves in the local culture.

Concerts and Performances: Live music and theatrical performances are held in various venues, adding to the festive atmosphere.

Fireworks Display: The celebrations often culminate with a spectacular fireworks show over the sea, symbolizing joy and communal unity.

This festival not only honors Nettuno's patron saint but also reinforces the town's identity, blending faith, history, and community spirit in a vibrant tapestry of events.

Walking Tour of Nettuno

#1: Sanctuary of Nostra Signora delle Grazie e Santa Maria Goretti

This beautiful sanctuary is the spiritual heart of Nettuno and houses the revered statue of Our Lady of Grace. It is also dedicated to Saint Maria Goretti, a young martyr whose remains rest here. Built in the 16th century, the sanctuary became a pilgrimage site after the arrival of the Madonna delle Grazie statue in 1550. The addition of Maria Goretti's remains in the 20th century reinforced its religious significance. A serene and sacred space, it offers an opportunity to reflect on Nettuno's spiritual heritage and admire its stunning architecture.

#2: Forte Sangallo

A Renaissance-era fortress constructed to protect Nettuno from pirate attacks, Forte Sangallo was designed by Giuliano da Sangallo under Pope Alexander VI. Completed in 1503, it played a key defensive role during its time and today houses cultural exhibitions and events. Its well-preserved structure and panoramic views of the sea make it a highlight of Nettuno's historical landscape.

Forte Sangallo, Nettuno

#3: Marina di Nettuno

One of the largest marinas in Italy, the harbor is home to a variety of boats, from fishing vessels to luxury yachts. The marina has long been a hub of Nettuno's maritime activity, reflecting its deep connection to the sea. Visitors can stroll along the harbor, enjoy waterfront cafes, and take in the lively atmosphere.

#4: Medieval Quarter (Borgo Medievale)

A charming maze of narrow streets, stone houses, and quaint piazzas, the medieval quarter transports visitors back in time. This historic area dates back to the Middle Ages and showcases Nettuno's legacy as a fortified town. Wander through picturesque alleyways, visit artisan shops, and enjoy the ambiance of a bygone era.

#5: Sicily-Rome American Cemetery and Memorial

If you are interested, this memorial is a 20-minute walk from the historic center. This solemn memorial site is dedicated to the American soldiers who lost their lives during the Allied campaigns in World War II. Established in 1944, the cemetery features meticulously maintained grounds, rows of white headstones, and a serene chapel. It serves as a moving tribute to history and sacrifice, offering an opportunity for quiet reflection.

Logistics

Train: Nettuno is well-connected to Rome via the regional train line. The Nettuno Train Station is centrally located, and trains to Rome Termini Station take approximately 1 hour and 10 minutes. Trains run frequently throughout the day, providing a convenient option for both locals and visitors.

Bus: Several Cotral buses connect Nettuno to nearby towns like Anzio, Latina, and other destinations within the Lazio region. The main bus station is close to the train station, and buses typically run hourly, with schedules varying by destination.

Car: Driving from Rome to Nettuno is straightforward. Take the SS148 Pontina highway south, then follow the signs to Nettuno. The distance is approximately 60 kilometers (37 miles), and the drive takes about 1 hour, depending on traffic. Nettuno is also accessible from other towns in the Lazio region via well-maintained regional roads.

Parking: Nettuno offers several parking options, including free and paid parking lots near the city center and seafront. Popular spots include parking areas near the train station and Forte Sangallo. Visitors should avoid parking in ZTL (Zona a Traffico Limitato) areas in the medieval quarter, which are restricted to residents. Clearly marked parking areas outside the ZTL provide easy access to major attractions.

Restaurant Recommendations

Le Sirene 2. Address: Via Giacomo Matteotti, 37

A beachfront restaurant specializing in Mediterranean cuisine with an emphasis on seafood. Popular dishes include fried calamari, seafood risotto, and a variety of antipasti. Perfect for a relaxed meal with sea views (closed during winter).

Ristorante Dal Folle Spadarao 1974. Address: Piazza Marcantonio Colonna, 13/14

A contemporary restaurant offering a mix of traditional and modern dishes. Highlights include innovative takes on seafood and locally sourced ingredients. The chic interior and creative menu make it a standout dining option.

Accommodation

For the festival, I recommend two to three nights in town.

Astura Palace Hotel. Address: Via G. Matteotti, 75

A 4-star seafront hotel offering elegant rooms with modern amenities. Guests can enjoy panoramic sea views, an on-site restaurant, and easy access to the historic center and marina.

Day Trip Options: Nearby Sites, Cities, and Towns

Anzio. 7 kilometers (4 miles) from Nettuno. Anzio, Nettuno's neighbor, was a significant port city in ancient Rome and is famous for its connection to Emperor Nero and the Allied landings during World War II. Visitors can explore the ruins of Nero's Villa, the Anzio War Museum, and the stunning beaches. Anzio's harbor is bustling with seafood restaurants and vibrant local markets.

Cisterna di Latina. 20 kilometers (12 miles). Known for the beautiful Garden of Ninfa, Cisterna di Latina offers a serene escape into one of Italy's most romantic gardens, filled with medieval ruins, lush plants, and flowing streams. The town itself has a charming historical center and connections to Roman and medieval history.

Latina. 32 kilometers (20 miles) from Nettuno. Founded during the 1930s as part of Mussolini's reclamation of the Pontine Marshes, Latina is a modern city with a unique architectural style. Highlights include the Piazza del Popolo, museums, and nearby coastal areas like Sabaudia for beach lovers.

Sermoneta. 35 kilometers (22 miles). A well-preserved medieval hill town, Sermoneta is home to the Caetani Castle, offering stunning views of the countryside. Stroll through cobblestone streets, visit the ancient churches, and enjoy its artistic heritage. Sermoneta is also near the Abbey of Valvisciolo, a tranquil spiritual site.

Ardea. 40 kilometers (25 miles) from Nettuno.Ardea, a town with roots in ancient Latium, is known for its archaeological remains and art collections. The Giuliano Vangi Museum and ancient fortifications attract history and art enthusiasts. Its proximity to the coast adds scenic charm to the experience.

Cori. 50 kilometers (31 miles). Cori is a picturesque hilltop town renowned for its Temple of Hercules, Roman walls, and Renaissance architecture. Its wine production and olive oil make it a destination for food lovers, while its festivals showcase local traditions.

Nettuno Festivals and Sagre Throughout the Year

Holy Week Events

Week leading up to Easter

During Holy Week, Nettuno hosts religious ceremonies, including processions, reenactments of the Passion of Christ, and traditional masses. These deeply spiritual events highlight the town's strong Catholic traditions and draw locals and visitors alike.

Rievocando La Nostra Storia

April

This April celebration transforms the historic center into a living museum, with particular focus on three pivotal periods: the medieval maritime republic era, the Renaissance when Nettuno's iconic Forte Sangallo was built, and the dramatic World War II landing at nearby Anzio-Nettuno.

Local residents spend months preparing authentic period costumes, from medieval merchants' robes to 16th-century nobles' attire. The streets come alive with historically accurate craft demonstrations - blacksmiths forge medieval tools using traditional techniques, women weave on period-correct looms, and artisans demonstrate the art of crafting the distinctive "butteri" (local cowboys) leather goods.

A highlight is the evening torchlight procession representing the arrival of Vittoria Colonna, the famed Renaissance poet who frequented the Forte

Sangallo. Participants carry banners of historic Nettuno families while drummers play medieval rhythms that echo off the ancient stone walls.

Sagra della Rana (Frog Festival)

June (date varies)

The Sagra della Rana emerged from Nettuno's relationship with its surrounding wetlands, which historically provided an abundant source of frogs. The preparation of frog legs became a symbol of resourcefulness during leaner times when coastal families would supplement their seafood diet with this inland protein source.

During the festival, local chefs compete to present innovative interpretations of traditional frog leg recipes. The most celebrated dish is "rane fritte alla nettunese" - frog legs that are marinated in white wine, herbs, and garlic, then lightly dusted with flour and fried until golden. Other preparations include "rane in guazzetto" (frog legs in a tomato and herb sauce) and "zuppa di rane" (frog leg soup with local vegetables).

Festa di San Rocco (St. Roch)

August 16

Dedicated to Saint Roch, this festival includes religious processions, traditional music performances, and community gatherings. Saint Roch is venerated as a protector against plagues and diseases, making this a deeply significant celebration for Nettuno.

Nettuno Wine Festival

September (date varies)

This festival celebrates the region's winemaking heritage and grape cultivation (viticulture), with wine tastings, vineyard tours, and the pairing of local wines with traditional dishes. It highlights Nettuno's agricultural and culinary traditions, attracting wine enthusiasts and food lovers.

CHAPTER NINE

Arpino, In the Footsteps of Cicero

The Vibrant Spirit of Rome's Greatest Orator

Certamen Ciceronianum Arpinas / The Cicero Festival

Where: Arpino

When: 2nd Weekend in May

Average Festival Temperatures: High: 20.7°C (69.3°F). Low: 9.7°C (49.5°F).

Festival Website: https://certamenciceronianum.it/it/

A History of Cicero's Hometown

Nestled in the hills of southern Lazio, Arpino is a town steeped in ancient history, offering visitors a chance to step back in time and walk in the footsteps of one of Rome's greatest orators, Marcus Tullius Cicero. About 100 kilometers (62 miles) southeast of Rome, Arpino sits at an elevation of 450 meters, providing stunning views of the surrounding Liri Valley. With a population of just over 7,000, the town keeps a quiet charm and offers a picturesque setting with its narrow, cobbled streets and historic stone buildings.

The history of Arpino dates back to pre-Roman times, when it was settled by the Volsci, an ancient Italic tribe. Later absorbed into the Roman Republic, Arpino became a prominent town, especially known for producing figures of exceptional intellect, such as Cicero and Gaius Marius, a famous Roman general. The town's historical significance is further highlighted by its ancient acropolis, which is crowned by a massive wall built with enormous limestone blocks fitted together without mortar (known as cyclopean masonry), a rare architectural feature that dates back to the 7th century BC. Arpino was a center of Roman culture and politics, leaving a lasting legacy in its ruins and historical sites.

Geographically, Arpino's position in the Liri Valley places it in a strategic and fertile area that has supported agriculture for centuries. The landscape is dotted with olive groves and vineyards, adding to the rustic beauty of the region. Its hilly terrain makes for stunning panoramas, and the nearby Fibreno River offers opportunities for nature walks and outdoor activities. The climate is mild, with warm summers and cool winters, making it a pleasant destination year-round.

In modern times, Arpino has maintained much of its historical character, with well-preserved Roman and medieval architecture visible throughout the town. The town center revolves around the Piazza Municipio, where locals and visitors gather to enjoy cafés and admire the town's 15th-century clock tower. The annual Certamen Ciceronianum is one of the most significant events in the town, drawing international attention and transforming this small hilltop village into a hub for classical scholars and Latin enthusiasts.

The Certamen Ciceronianum Arpinas—A Celebration of Classical Legacy

Every May, the hill town of Arpino, birthplace of Marcus Tullius Cicero, hosts one of the world's most prestigious Latin competitions. The Certamen Ciceronianum Arpinas brings together top students and scholars from across the globe to celebrate Cicero's enduring legacy.

Founded in 1980, the event centers on a rigorous contest where students translate and interpret passages from Cicero's works, exploring his philosophy, rhetoric, and political thought. What began as a local tribute has become an international gathering that connects young minds with the classical world.

Cicero's influence on law, oratory, and philosophy remains foundational to Western thought, and this festival honors that legacy in the very place he once called home. For a few remarkable days, Arpino becomes the beating heart of classical scholarship.

Day-by-Day Breakdown of the Festival

Day 1: Opening Ceremonies and Welcome Events

The festival begins in Arpino's central piazza with welcoming speeches from local officials and scholars celebrating Cicero's legacy. Medieval streets come alive with music, parades, and flag-throwers as visitors and students explore the town and meet fellow participants. The atmosphere is festive, warm, and steeped in tradition.

Day 2: The Latin Competition

Students gather at the historic Liceo Classico Tulliano to translate and analyze a selected text from Cicero. This prestigious exam challenges both Latin skills and philosophical understanding. Meanwhile, non-competitors can attend lectures, workshops, and guided tours of Arpino's Roman sites, including the Cicero Museum and ancient acropolis.

Day 3: Awards Ceremony and Cultural Celebrations

Winners are honored in a formal ceremony that highlights the value of classical education. The day continues with a lively street festival featuring traditional food, crafts, reenactments of Roman scenes, and a grand procession. Music and fireworks close out the celebration, blending scholarship with joyful community spirit.

Walking Tour of Arpino

#1. Gates of Arpino

Arpino's ancient defensive walls, known as Cyclopean walls, are among the oldest in Italy and include several gates that served as key entrances to the town.

The gates of Arpino are remarkable historical landmarks, showcasing the town's ancient and medieval heritage.

Porta Saturno, also called Porta Napoletana, is the most iconic, with its Cyclopean construction and rare keyhole-shaped (ogival) arch, dating back to pre-Roman times. It symbolizes Arpino's connection to southern Italy, with its orientation toward Naples.

Entry Gate in Cyclopean Walls of Arpino

Similarly, the Porta dell'Arco, or Porta dell'Acropoli, leads to the ancient Acropolis of Arpino and is a masterpiece of Italic craftsmanship, offering access to the town's most elevated and historically significant area. Other gates, such as Porta Sant'Agata, reflect Arpino's strengthening fortifications, blending medieval modifications with ancient walls, while Porta Romana served as a key entrance for travelers arriving from Rome, highlighting the town's connection to the Roman Empire.

Lastly, Porta Civita Falconara links to another significant section of Arpino's walls, reflecting the layered history of this ancient settlement. Together, these gates tell the story of Arpino's strategic importance and its enduring architectural legacy.

#2. Acropolis of Civitavecchia (Civita Vecchia)

The Acropolis, also known as Civita Vecchia, is a must-visit for its fascinating cyclopean walls, which date back to pre-Roman times. It's one of the most significant historical and archeological sites in Arpino, offering sweeping views over the Liri Valley. The walls, built with massive limestone blocks, are a testament to the ancient Italic tribes that inhabited this region.

#3. Tower of Cicerone (Torre di Cicerone)

Standing atop the Acropolis, this medieval tower is said to be named after the famous Roman orator Cicero, who was born in Arpino. Although the connection to Cicero is debated, the tower is an excellent example of medieval fortifications and offers panoramic of the area's natural beauty and historic depth.

#4. Piazza Municipio and Palazzo Boncompagni

The heart of Arpino's civic life, this square houses the Palazzo Boncompagni, the former residence of Pope Boniface VIII. The building, now the town hall, has beautiful architecture and a rich historical background. Visitors can admire its Renaissance style and learn about its importance in both the town's political and religious history.

#5. Chiesa di San Michaele (Church of San Michele Arcangelo)

In the historic center, the Church of San Michele Arcangelo is a stunning example of Baroque architecture. Its interior is richly decorated, and it houses important works of art, including frescoes and sculptures. The church has been a religious center for centuries and is known for its beautiful altar and spiritual significance.

#6. Museo della Liuteria e degli Strumenti Musicali Popolari (Museum of Luthiery and Popular Musical Instruments)

This unique museum showcases traditional craftsmanship and musical heritage in the form of string instruments like violins, lutes, and mandolins. The museum preserves the art of luthiery, a craft with deep roots in Arpino. It offers a fascinating glimpse into the history of music and instrument-making in the region.

#7. Santuario di Santa Maria di Civita

This ancient church, built on the Acropolis, is one of the oldest in Arpino. Its origins date back to the early Middle Ages, and it features a beautiful Romanesque façade. Inside, visitors can find stunning frescoes and artifacts from the early Christian era. The church is also tied to local religious traditions and is an important stop on the town's spiritual journey.

#8. Cicero's Birthplace Memorial

A site dedicated to the memory of Arpino's most famous historical figure, Marcus Tullius Cicero, this memorial marks the birthplace of the skilled orator and philosopher. Though the exact location is debated, this spot pays homage to his legacy and contributions to Roman law and rhetoric. It's a meaningful visit for history enthusiasts.

#9. Mercato Sano e Genuino di Arpino

Explore the local farmers' market for fresh, locally produced goods.

#10. Museo di Archeologia di Arpino (Archaeological Museum of Arpino)

This small but impressive museum displays artifacts from Arpino's rich past, including Roman, Italic, and pre-Roman relics. Visitors can explore exhibits featuring ceramics, sculptures, and inscriptions that highlight the town's historical importance. It's a perfect stop for those interested in the ancient civilizations that once inhabited the area.

Logistics

Train: The nearest train station to Arpino is the Roccasecca Station, located 20 kilometers (12 miles) away. Travelers from Rome can take a train from Roma Termini to Roccasecca, with the journey typically taking around 1 hour and 45 minutes, including transfers. From Roccasecca, you can reach Arpino by local bus or taxi.

Alternatively, the Sora Station is about 17 kilometers (11 miles) from Arpino. However, train services to Sora may require more connections and longer travel times compared with Roccasecca.

Bus: Cotral is the bus service operator with services connecting Rome and the towns in Frosinone.

Car: From Rome, take the A1 Autostrada del Sole towards Naples. Exit at Frosinone, then follow signs to Arpino via the SS156 and SP11 roads.

Parking: Area di Parcheggio. Address: 03033 Arpino, Italy.

Dining Recommendations

Trattoria Del Corso. Address: Corso Tulliano 23

A cozy trattoria offering traditional Italian dishes with a modern twist. Known for its fresh pasta and local specialties, it's a favorite among both locals and visitors.

I Giardini dell'Acropoli. Address: Via Acropoli 12

This charming restaurant provides a delightful dining experience with a menu that highlights seasonal ingredients and classic Italian recipes. The ambiance is warm and inviting, making it perfect for intimate dinners.

Ristorante La Perla. Address: Via Colle Bianco 11

Specializing in seafood and Mediterranean cuisine, La Perla is renowned for its elegant presentations and high-quality ingredients. The sophisticated atmosphere complements the exquisite dishes, offering a memorable dining experience.

Accommodation

For the festival, I recommend two nights in town.

Hotel Il Cavalier D'Arpino. Address: Via Vittoria Colonna 21

Housed in a meticulously restored 16th-century wool mill, this 4-star hotel combines historic charm with modern amenities. Guests can enjoy elegantly appointed rooms and a serene park-like setting.

Agritourismo / B&B La Pietra. Address: Via Caio Mario 14

Set in a tranquil rural location, this bed-and-breakfast offers comfortable rooms and a hearty breakfast featuring local produce. It's an ideal spot for those seeking peace and proximity to nature.

Albergo Ristorante Il Ciclope. Address: Via San Francesco 23

This 3-star hotel provides cozy accommodations alongside an acclaimed restaurant known for its traditional Italian fare. Its convenient location makes it a preferred choice for travelers exploring the region.

Day Trips: Nearby Sites, Cities and Towns

Veroli. Distance from Arpino: 25 kilometers (16 miles). Veroli is an ancient hilltop town with a history that dates back to the pre-Roman era, having been a significant settlement for the Hernici people. Its well-preserved medieval center and rich cultural heritage make it a charming day-trip destination. Visitors can stroll through its narrow streets, admire its ancient churches, and visit important landmarks such as the Cathedral of Sant'Andrea, which contains beautiful artworks and relics. Veroli is also known for the Church of Santa Maria Salome, which houses the Scala Santa, a replica of the Holy Staircase in Rome.

Sora. Distance from Arpino: 17 kilometers (11 miles). Nestled in the Liri Valley, Sora is a town with a rich Roman and medieval past. It is home to the remains of ancient Roman structures, including walls and bridges, and has a charming historic center that invites visitors to explore its narrow streets and piazzas. The Church of San Bartolomeo, a stunning example of Baroque architecture, is a must-visit, along with the scenic view from the medieval Sora castle that overlooks the town. Sora is also known for its connection to Cicero, as it was once part of his homeland.

Arpino Festivals and Sagre Throughout the Year

Il Faone di San Giovanni (Fire of St. John)

June 23rd

An ancient tradition marking the summer solstice, where an enormous bonfire is lit to symbolize purification and the triumph of light over darkness. This festival has its roots in pagan customs tied to agricultural cycles and the celebration of summer.

Le Cantine d'Estate (Summer Festival)

Early July

This summer festival transforms Arpino's historic center into a lively hub of street food, local wines, and live music. Visitors can stroll through the artisan markets while enjoying regional delicacies.

Sagra delle Fettuccine con Funghi Porcini e Tartufo (Fettuccine and Mushroom Festival)

August 9th

A popular culinary event celebrating fettuccine with porcini mushrooms and truffles, two highly prized ingredients in the region. The festival draws food enthusiasts eager to savor this traditional pasta dish alongside other local specialties.

Il Gonfalone di Arpino

Sunday after Ferragosto

A historical and folkloric event where the town's districts (contradas) compete in traditional games and performances. Highlights include the "Corsa con la Cannata," a race with water jugs, and other lively contests that showcase Arpino's cultural traditions.

Arpino Locals in Traditional Ciociari Dress

Sagra degli Gnocchi

Third weekend in August

This festival celebrates one of Italy's favorite dishes, gnocchi, served in various traditional preparations. Visitors can enjoy the food while listening to live music and enjoying the festive atmosphere in the Oasi del Vallone area.

CHAPTER TEN

Nemi's Strawberry Spectacular

From Ancient Ships to Berry Lips

S agra delle Fragole

Where: Nemi

When: First Sunday of June, with some events spanning the weekend.

Average Festival Temperatures: High 25°C (77°F), Low 14°C (57°F).

Nemi: A Timeless Grove of Legends and Legacy

Nemi is a picturesque town in the Lazio region of central Italy, 30 kilometers (18 miles) southeast of Rome. Perched at an elevation of 521 meters (1,700 feet) above sea level, it overlooks the serene Lake Nemi, a volcanic crater lake nestled within the Alban Hills.

The name "Nemi" derives from the Latin word *nemus*, meaning "holy wood," reflecting the area's ancient sacred groves. In antiquity, Nemi was renowned for the Temple of Diana Nemorensis, a sanctuary dedicated to the goddess Diana.

Established around 300 BC, the temple was a significant pilgrimage site for centuries, attracting worshippers from across the Italian peninsula.

During the Roman Empire, Emperor Caligula constructed elaborate pleasure barges on Lake Nemi, possibly linked to the cult of Diana. These ships were later scuttled and remained submerged until their recovery in the early 20th century. Unfortunately, they were destroyed by fire during World War II, with remnants now displayed in the Museo delle Navi Romane in Nemi.

In the medieval period, Nemi came under the dominion of various noble families, including the Colonna, Cesarini, and Orsini. The Castello Ruspoli, dating back to the 10th century, stands as a testament to this era, dominating both the town and the surrounding landscape.

Nemi is within the Castelli Romani, a group of communes in the Alban Hills known for their natural beauty and historical significance. The town's proximity to Lake Nemi provides a unique microclimate, fostering the growth of wild strawberries for which the area is famous. The volcanic origins of the lake and surrounding hills contribute to the fertile soil and lush vegetation that characterize the region.

Nemi has a population of 1,851 residents. Despite its small size, the town attracts visitors with its rich history, scenic views, and cultural traditions. Nemi's blend of historical depth, natural beauty, and cultural heritage makes it a noteworthy destination in the Lazio region, offering insights into both ancient and medieval Italy.

The Strawberry Festival

Sweet Delights of Nemi: The Centennial Sagra delle Fragole

My first visit to Nemi was nothing short of enchanting. Nestled in the hills, this small town captivated me with its picturesque historic center, offering breathtaking views that swept across the sparkling waters of Lake Nemi and rolled over the lush strawberry fields beyond. As I wandered through Nemi's narrow, winding streets, I was struck by how this tiny hilltop town preserved its medieval charm while embracing its most famous modern tradition - the cultivation of its prized strawberries.

The Sagra delle Fragole has been a highlight of Nemi's calendar since 1922. This centennial celebration centers around the fragoline di bosco, small wild strawberries known for their intense flavor and aroma. While my visit coincided with the festival weekend, I discovered the celebration perfectly balances tradition with festive energy.

Lago di Nemi

The festival unfolds over a full weekend, with Saturday morning bringing the opening ceremony and parade. Throughout the weekend, local farms and shops transform the town into a strawberry lover's paradise, offering everything from fresh berries to homemade jams and creative strawberry-themed products. I particularly enjoyed watching local chefs demonstrate their strawberry-based recipes, sharing techniques that blend traditional and modern approaches.

The undisputed centerpiece of the festival is the Giant Strawberry Goblet, where fresh strawberries meet spumante fragolino (strawberry-flavored sparkling wine) in a massive vessel. Sampling this effervescent treat while watching traditional dancers perform in period costumes made me feel deeply connected to Nemi's rich cultural heritage. Live music fills the air throughout the town, creating a joyful atmosphere that's impossible to resist.

A more recent addition to the festival is the Flower Exhibition, which culminates in Sunday afternoon's Golden Strawberry Award ceremony. The winning florist receives a precious jewel containing a real gold-plated strawberry - a fitting tribute to the town's favorite fruit. Beyond the festival itself, I discovered Nemi offers year-round attractions that shouldn't be missed. The Diana's Mirror Museum houses fascinating artifacts from Emperor Caligula's ancient ships, once submerged in Lake Nemi. Peaceful walks with stunning views are found on the lakeside paths, with great hiking in the reserves. The local trattorias serve delicious regional specialties that showcase why this area is a food lover's paradise.

As I left Nemi, with the taste of sun-ripened strawberries still on my lips (and baskets of strawberries in the trunk) and the memory of that stunning lake view etched in my mind, I knew I'd discovered a special corner of Italy - one that I'd be eager to revisit, especially when the strawberries are in full bloom and the town comes alive with the joy of its sweetest celebration.

The Berries of Nemi

Walking Tour of Nemi

#1. Start at Piazza Umberto I

Begin your tour in the heart of Nemi at Piazza Umberto I. This charming square offers your first glimpse of Lake Nemi and is a perfect spot to orient yourself.

#2. Palazzo Ruspoli

From the piazza, head to Palazzo Ruspoli, a 16th-century palace that now houses the town hall. Its distinctive clock tower is one of Nemi's most recognizable landmarks.

#3. Church of Santa Maria del Pozzo

Walk to this 16th-century church, known for its beautiful frescoes and a well (pozzo) that gives the church its name. Legend has it that the well is connected to Lake Nemi by underground passages.

Santa Maria del Pozzo

#4. Diana's Mirror Terrace

Walk along the lake to this viewpoint, named after the ancient Romans who called Lake Nemi "Diana's Mirror". Enjoy panoramic views of the lake and surrounding hills.

#5. Strawberry Fields Viewpoint

Climb back up into town and find a good vantage point to view the famous strawberry fields that surround Nemi. The exact location may vary, but locals can point you to the best spots.

#6. Temple of Diana

While the temple itself no longer stands, you can visit the archaeological site where the famous Temple of Diana once stood. This was one of the most important sanctuaries in ancient Latium.

#7. Nemi Castle Ruins

Conclude your tour at the ruins of Nemi's medieval castle. While little remains of the structure, the site offers stunning views over the lake and town.

Museo delle Navi Romane (Museum of Roman Ships)

Consider a visit the fascinating lakeside museum. It houses artifacts recovered from two enormous ships built by Emperor Caligula and sunk in Lake Nemi. The museum tells the story of these ships and their recovery in the 1930s. This walking tour allows you to experience Nemi's rich history, from ancient Roman times through the medieval period to the present day, all while enjoying its natural beauty and famous strawberries.

Logistics

Train: No direct train routes to Nemi exist. However, you can take a train from Rome's Termini Station to Velletri or Albano Laziale, which are nearby towns. Rome to Albano Laziale by Train: Trains from Roma Termini to Albano Laziale run frequently (roughly every 30 minutes), with a journey time of around 50 minutes. From Albano Laziale, COTRAL buses to Nemi take around 15–20 minutes.

Bus: COTRAL Bus. Direct buses run from Anagnina Metro Station (Rome's Line A) to Nemi, with a journey time of approximately 1 hour. Anagnina is about a 30-minute metro ride from the center of Rome, and the buses are a convenient option for travelers not wishing to drive.

Car: The most direct route is via Via Appia Nuova (SS7), passing through Albano Laziale and then taking the SP18b towards Nemi. The drive typically takes around 45 minutes to an hour, depending on traffic.

Parking: Nemi offers various parking areas near the town center. Since Nemi is a small town with narrow streets, it's best to park in designated areas outside the historic center and explore the town on foot.

Restaurant Recommendations

Il Ramo D'oro. Address: Corso Vittorio Emanuele, 9/11-13

Il Ramo D'oro is a popular Italian restaurant in Nemi, known for its cozy atmosphere and friendly service. It offers a variety of classic Roman pasta dishes, pizzas, and Mediterranean cuisine. The restaurant is praised for its homemade pasta, especially the pappardelle with wild boar sauce. The beautiful terrace overlooking the lake provides a stunning view, making it a perfect spot for a relaxing meal.

La Rosa. Address: Corso Vittorio Emanuele 41

La Rosa is a charming Italian restaurant that serves traditional dishes with a focus on fresh, local ingredients. It is known for its homey atmosphere and accommodating staff. Popular dishes include pasta with mushrooms, wild boar antipasto, and homemade pasta with truffles. The restaurant also offers a delightful selection of desserts, including strawberry gelato and panna cotta.

La Sirena del Lago. Address: Via del Plebiscito 26

Near the lake, this restaurant offers stunning views and a menu featuring seafood and Italian cuisine. The restaurant is perfect for a scenic dining experience, with its picturesque setting and delicious seafood dishes. It's a brilliant spot to enjoy a meal with family or friends while taking in the beautiful lake views.

Ristorante Le Scalette. Address: Salita Garibaldi, 8

In the heart of the historic center, the restaurant features local specialties with a focus on strawberries. The restaurant is known for its cozy ambiance and excellent service. It offers a variety of dishes featuring strawberries, such as strawberry risotto and strawberry desserts. The restaurant is a must-visit for those looking to experience the local flavors of Nemi.

Accomodation

Staying overnight is unnecessary for sagre. There are no hotels in Nemi. It is a tiny town. It is close enough to the other Castelli Romani cities that accommodations from those chapters can be used.

Day Trip Options: Nearby Sites, Cities and Towns

Tarquinia. 100 km (62 miles) from Nemi. This UNESCO World Heritage site features a remarkable Etruscan necropolis with beautifully frescoed tombs. The National Etruscan Museum is housed in the 15th-century Palazzo Vitelleschi, and the medieval old town offers beautiful churches and palaces to explore.

Subiaco. 70 km (43 miles). Home to the Sacro Speco (Sacred Cave) where St. Benedict lived as a hermit, and Santa Scolastica Monastery, the oldest Benedictine monastery in the world. The medieval walled town (borgo) with its narrow stone streets and well-preserved historic center, features picturesque streets and stunning views.

Sperlonga. 120 km (75 miles) west of Nemi. A stunning, white-washed old town perched dramatically on a cliff overlooking the Tyrrhenian Sea. Visitors can enjoy beautiful beaches, explore the Archeological Museum, and visit the historic Grotto of Tiberius.

Towns of the Castelli Romani. 0-15 km (0-9 miles) from Nemi. The picturesque hill towns of the Castelli Romani include Castel Gandolfo, the Pope's summer residence overlooking Lake Albano; Frascati, famous for its historic villas and white wine; Ariccia, known for its monumental Chigi Palace and traditional porchetta; and Genzano di Roma, renowned for its Infiorata flower festival and artisanal bread. These towns, set among volcanic lakes and chestnut forests, share a rich history as ancient Roman resort towns and Renaissance noble retreats.

Nemi's Other Festival

Festa dei Santi Filippo e Giacomo

May 1

This religious festival honors Saints Philip and James, who are celebrated together in the Catholic tradition. The highlight of the festa patronale is a solemn procession through Nemi's streets, carrying relics and standards of the saints.

The procession begins at the Church of Santa Maria del Pozzo and winds through the historic center, accompanied by prayers, hymns, and a palpable sense of reverence and community.

CHAPTER ELEVEN

Immersion Experience: Wine, Oil, and Tradition

Tasting the Essence of the Castelli Romani

The Castelli Romani region is not only stunningly beautiful but also brimming with centuries-old traditions in winemaking and olive oil production. Unlike the bustling streets of Rome, the towns of Frascati, Ariccia, Grottaferrata, and others offer a peaceful retreat into Italy's countryside. This immersion experience is perfect for those seeking to go beyond sightseeing and engage deeply with Italy's culinary heritage.

World-Class Wine: The region has been producing wine since ancient times, with Frascati DOCG being its most renowned white wine. Known as the "Wine of the Popes," Frascati has been cherished for its refreshing flavors and ties to Roman history.

Premium Olive Oil: The olive groves of the Castelli Romani produce some of the finest extra virgin olive oils, celebrated for their rich flavor and health benefits. Sampling freshly pressed olive oil is a sensory experience like no other.

Workshops and Tastings: Many wineries and farms in the region offer guided tastings, where you can sample wines and oils while learning about their production. Workshops often include pairing sessions with local delicacies, enhancing your appreciation for regional dishes.

A Suggested Itinerary for Wine and Olive Oil Tasting

Start in Frascati

Begin your day in Frascati, the wine capital of the Castelli Romani. Visit a family-run vineyard to learn about the Frascati DOCG production process, from vine to glass. Sample a selection of wines paired with local cheeses, cured meats, and freshly baked bread.

Grottaferrata and Olive Oil Tasting

Head to a traditional olive grove in Grottaferrata, where you can learn about the harvesting and pressing process. Taste different varieties of olive oil, noting their flavors and aromas, and discover how the oil complements regional dishes.

Lunch in Ariccia

Stop in Ariccia, known for its porchetta (slow-roasted pork), and enjoy a farm-to-table meal at a local trattoria. Pair your meal with wines from the region, and don't forget to drizzle olive oil over your bread or vegetables for a true taste of the area.

End the Day in Castel Gandolfo

Conclude your experience in the scenic town of Castel Gandolfo, overlooking Lake Albano. Enjoy a glass of wine at a lakeside café or visit another vineyard to end your day surrounded by breathtaking views.

Websites for Booking Tastings and Workshops

Here are some great places to book wine and olive oil tastings in the Castelli Romani.

Casale Marchese (Frascati)

A family-owned vineyard offering wine tastings, cellar tours, and olive oil workshops.

Website: www.casalemarchese.it

Poggio Le Volpi (Monte Porzio Catone)

A modern winery offering guided tastings and food pairings in a stunning setting.

Website: www.poggiolevolpi.com

Tenuta di Pietra Porzia (Frascati)

A historic estate offering tours, tastings, and accommodations.

Website: www.tenutadipietraporzia.com

Azienda Agricola Principe Pallavicini (Colonna)

One of the oldest wine estates in the area, with guided tours and tastings.

Website: www.principepallavicini.com

Frascati Wine Tour

A comprehensive tour company that organizes half-day or full-day wine experiences in the region. Search Frascati Wine Tour–offered by many tour operators out of Rome.

Logistics: How to Get to the Castelli Romani

By Car: Drive along the Via Appia Nuova or Via Tuscolana for a scenic journey through the countryside. Parking is available in most towns.

By Tour: Join a guided wine and olive oil tasting tour departing from Rome, which often includes transportation, tastings, and a knowledgeable guide.

CHAPTER TWELVE

Rome's Sacred Procession and Celebration of Corpus Domini

A Radiant Path of Light and Devotion

Festa del Corpus Domini

Where: Rome

When: June (The Thursday after Trinity Sunday, often celebrated on the following Sunday in Italy.)

Average Festival Temperatures: High 31°C (88°F). Low 18°C (64°F).

The Feast of Corpus Christi / Corpus Domini

I've witnessed other festivals in Rome, but the Feast of Corpus Christi (Festa del Corpus Domini) stands out as something truly special. During this sacred evening that celebrates the body of Christ, the Eternal City transforms in a way distinct from any other celebration I've experienced.

As the warm early summer evening settles over Rome, the city prepares for one of its most profound and visually stunning religious events. The Festa del Corpus Domini, also known as Corpus Christi, isn't just another festival - it's a powerful display of faith that turns Rome's bustling streets into a solemn pathway of devotion.

The Essence of Corpus Domini

The Feast of Corpus Domini, also known as the Solemnity of the Most Holy Body and Blood of Christ, is a significant Christian observance in Rome. It honors the Holy Eucharist and celebrates the real presence of Christ in the Eucharist. The feast is observed by the Roman Catholic Church, as well as certain Western Orthodox, Lutheran, and Anglican churches. The feast is celebrated on the Thursday after Trinity Sunday, which falls 60 days after Easter. In 2025, it will be observed on June 19th. In 2026, the Feast of Corpus Domini will be observed on June 4th.

Corpus Domini, meaning "The Body of the Lord" in Latin, surpasses a mere date on the liturgical calendar. It's a powerful reaffirmation of one of the central mysteries of the Catholic faith: the real presence of Christ in the Eucharist. This feast day, instituted in the 13th century, celebrates the Catholic belief in transubstantiation - the miraculous transformation of bread and wine into what Catholics believe to be the actual Body and Blood of Christ during the Mass, while retaining their physical appearance. The feast was proposed by Thomas Aquinas and established by Pope Urban IV in 1264, following the Eucharistic Miracle of Bolsena.

In Rome, the celebration takes on an extraordinary dimension. Christianity's epicenter for 2000 years, the city hosts an unparalleled procession. Led by the Pope himself, this event offers a unique opportunity to witness the convergence of ancient tradition and devout belief.

The Papal Mass at the Basilica of San Giovanni in Laterano (St. John Lateran)

The day begins as the sun climbs high over the city's seven hills. Thousands of pilgrims and locals stream towards the Basilica of St. John Lateran, Rome's cathedral and the ecclesiastical seat of the Pope. Here, amidst the splendor of gilt and marble, the Pontiff celebrates a solemn Mass, setting the tone for the profound events to follow.

The basilica itself is a testament to Rome's long Christian history. Founded in the 4th century by Constantine the Great, it has witnessed centuries of papal coronations and councils. As the Mass concludes and the faithful spill out onto the piazza, there's a palpable sense of anticipation for what comes next.

A Procession Steeped in History and Symbolism

The highlight of Corpus Domini in Rome is undoubtedly the grand Eucharistic march that winds its way through the city's historic streets. This procession is not merely a religious parade; it's a moving tableau of faith, history, and Roman culture.

Facade of the Basilica di San Giovanni in Laterano

The Procession: A River of Faith Through Roman Streets

As evening approaches and the heat of the day begins to soften, the march begins its journey from the Basilica di San Giovanni to the Basilica of Santa Maria Maggiore. This route, along the Via Merulana, becomes a river of flickering candlelight and murmured prayers.

The Pope, holding the consecrated Host, leads the procession. This golden vessel, centuries old and adorned with precious gems, gleams in the fading daylight. The Pope walks beneath a ceremonial canopy known as a baldacchino, a symbol of honor that has its roots in ancient Roman customs.

Following the leader of the church are cardinals in their distinctive red robes, bishops in purple, priests in white, and religious orders in their various habits. Behind them come the lay faithful, a diverse tapestry of humanity united in their devotion. The air is filled with the scent of incense, the sound of hymns, and the glow of thousands of candles.

As the procession moves through the streets, Romans and visitors alike line the route. Many kneel as the Blessed Sacrament passes, while others make the sign of the cross or bow their heads in reverence. Flower petals are often strewn in the procession's path, a beautiful gesture of devotion that dates back centuries.

Involvement of Confraternities

Rome's historic confraternities, lay brotherhoods that date back centuries, often take part in the procession in their ceremonial garb. Carrying banners and candles, they march in orderly ranks to honor the Blessed Sacrament. Their presence brings a striking sense of continuity, linking modern-day celebrations to Rome's deep Catholic heritage.

The Culmination at Santa Maria Maggiore

The procession's final destination is the Basilica of Santa Maria Maggiore, one of Rome's four major papal basilicas. This magnificent church, with its soaring ceilings and glittering mosaics, provides a fitting conclusion for the evening's events.

With the fading light and the candles shining brighter, the Pope concludes with a final benediction using the Blessed Sacrament. Thousands of faithful receive this blessing in profound silence and reverence, near one of Christianity's oldest shrines.

Evening Benediction and Festive Gatherings

At the close of the procession, many faithful linger in the piazza outside Santa Maria Maggiore, where they sometimes enjoy informal gatherings or visit nearby cafés and restaurants. Even after the religious ceremonies end, the festive atmosphere continues into the night, uniquely blending Roman spirituality and community.

Facade of the Basilica di Santa Maria Maggiore

Experiencing Corpus Domini as a Visitor

For those fortunate enough to be in Rome during Corpus Domini, the experience can be deeply moving, regardless of one's personal faith. Optimize this unique event using these tips.

1. Plan Ahead: The exact date of Corpus Domini changes each year, so check the Vatican's official calendar when planning your trip.

2. Arrive Early: The best viewing spots along the Via Merulana fill up quickly. Consider arriving a few hours before the procession to secure an excellent position.

3. Dress Appropriately: Rome in June can be quite warm, but modest dress is required for entering the basilicas. Bring a light scarf or shawl to cover shoulders if needed.

4. Be Prepared for Crowds: While the atmosphere is reverent, the event draws sizeable crowds. Stay hydrated and be patient with security checks.

5. Respect the Solemnity: Whether you're a devout Catholic or a curious observer, remember that this is a deeply significant religious event for many participants.

A Timeless Tradition in the Eternal City

The Festa del Corpus Domini in Rome is more than just a religious celebration; As the procession winds its way through streets that have seen emperors and pilgrims, saints and sinners, it offers a unique window into the soul of the Eternal City.

Whether you're drawn by faith, fascinated by history, or simply in awe of Rome's ability to blend the ancient and the modern, the Corpus Domini celebration is an unforgettable experience. In Rome, the past lingers close, and sacredness is ever-present.

Layers of Faith and History: Key Locations Along the Corpus Domini Route

I thought I would suggest some key sites that are either along the procession route or nearby in case you can spend a day in the area.

Scala Santa; These holy stairs near St. John Lateran are said to be the very steps Jesus climbed during his trial before Pontius Pilate, brought to Rome by St. Helena in the 4th century.

Basilica di San Clemente; This fascinating three-tiered complex reveals Rome's layers - a 12th-century basilica built over a 4th-century church, itself standing above a 1st-century Roman house and Mithraic temple.

Santi Quattro Coronati; This 4th-century fortress-church is renowned for its serene medieval cloister and remarkable frescoes.

Villa Wolkonsky; Now serving as the British Ambassador's residence, its gardens incorporate fragments of an ancient Roman aqueduct.

Basilica di Santa Prassede; This 9th-century church houses stunning Byzantine mosaics and a segment believed to be from the pillar of Christ's flagellation.

Arch of Gallienus; This 3rd-century Roman arch, once part of the Servian Wall, stands near Santa Maria Maggiore as a testament to Rome's ancient defenses.

Restaurant Recommendations Near the Procession Route

If you're looking to enjoy a meal before or after the Corpus Domini procession, there are several excellent options near the route. From casual trattorias to upscale dining experiences, these restaurants offer a taste of Roman cuisine while keeping you close to the action.

Trattoria Monti. Address: Via di San Vito, 13A (near Santa Maria Maggiore)

Known for traditional Roman cuisine with a modern twist. Try the egg-based dishes like their famous "tortino", homemade pasta. Small, family-run trattoria with a cozy, authentic feel.

Hostaria da Nerone. Address: Via delle Terme di Tito, 96 (close to the Colosseum, close to San Clemente).

Renouned for classic Roman dishes in a traditional setting. Roman specialities include carbonara, amatriciana, and grilled meats. Rustic and welcoming atmosphere, popular with locals and tourists alike.

Aroma Restaurant. Address: Palazzo Manfredi, Via Labicana, 125 (near the Colosseum)

Upscale dining with a stunning view of the Colosseum. Contemporary Italian cuisine and tasting menus. Elegant rooftop setting, perfect for a special meal.

CHAPTER THIRTEEN

Blooming Streets: The Art of the Infiorata in Genzano

Petal Perfection

Infiorata di Genzano

Where: Genzano di Roma, Italy

When: Mid-to-late June (exact Sunday varies yearly based on Easter date).

Average Festival Temperatures: High 28°C (82°F), Low 16°C (61°F).

Festival Website: https://www.infioratadigenzano.it/

Roots of Roses: The Rich History of Genzano di Roma

Genzano di Roma, a picturesque town in the Lazio region of central Italy, boasts a rich heritage intertwined with the cultural and religious traditions of the Roman countryside. Its origins trace back to ancient times, with evidence of settlements in the area during the Roman Republic. The town's name is believed to derive from the Latin term "Gentianum," referencing the Roman deity Janus or the Gentian flower that once grew abundantly in the region.

During the Roman era, Genzano lay along the famous Appian Way ("Via Appia Antica"), one of the most important roads of the empire. The area was known for its fertile soil, thanks to the nearby volcanic activity of the Alban Hills, which supported agriculture and viticulture. Roman villas and farmsteads dotted the landscape, serving as retreats for the Roman elite.

In the medieval period, the town came under the control of various noble families, including the Savelli and Colonna, as part of the Papal States. These families contributed to the construction of significant buildings and infrastructure, including churches, palaces, and fountains, that remain integral to Genzano's charm.

The Baroque period saw the growth of Genzano as a center of religious and cultural significance, particularly with the establishment of the Infiorata tradition in the 18th century. This iconic floral festival, tied to the Catholic celebration of Corpus Domini, became a hallmark of the town's identity.

Genzano di Roma is in the heart of the Castelli Romani, a region characterized by its lush landscapes, volcanic lakes, and proximity to Rome. The town sits on the slopes of the ancient volcanic crater that now forms Lake Nemi, providing breathtaking views of the surrounding countryside. The fertile volcanic soil supports the cultivation of grapes and olives, contributing to the town's reputation for producing excellent wines and olive oils.

Genzano is 30 kilometers (18 miles) southeast of the Italian capital. Its elevation of about 435 meters (1,427 feet) above sea level gives it a temperate climate, making it a pleasant destination for visitors year-round.

As of the latest census, Genzano di Roma has a population of 24,000 residents. The town keeps its small-community charm while benefiting from its proximity to Rome, which provides economic opportunities and access to urban amenities. Its economy is largely based on agriculture, small-scale industry, and tourism, with the Infiorata playing a significant role in attracting visitors.

The town's streets, particularly the central Via Italo Belardi, come alive during the Infiorata, when intricate carpets of flower petals create stunning designs that blend religious, historical, and artistic themes. This festival, combined with Genzano's scenic beauty, vibrant local markets, and culinary delights, ensures its place as a beloved destination in Lazio.

In recent years, Genzano di Roma has made efforts to preserve its historical and cultural heritage while promoting sustainable tourism. The local government works to maintain the town's traditional character, ensuring that events like the Infiorata continue to captivate both residents and visitors.

Genzano di Roma's rich history, strategic geography, and vibrant traditions make it a fascinating subject for exploration. Its legacy as a Roman retreat, its Baroque cultural revival, and its enduring Infiorata tradition highlight the town's unique place in Italian heritage.

The Infiorata Festival

In the charming town of Genzano di Roma a breathtaking transformation occurs each year following the feast of Corpus Domini (see previous chapter, Rome's Sacred Procession for more detail on Corpus Domini and the 2025, 2026 dates.)

The Infiorata di Genzano, a spectacular flower festival, turns the town's streets into a canvas of vibrant colors and intricate designs. This centuries-old tradition sees skilled artisans and residents create elaborate floral carpets, offering visitors a unique blend of art, faith, and community spirit.

Flower Art of the Infiorata

Infiorata History

The Infiorata di Genzano, deeply rooted in the town's religious and cultural heritage, transforms streets into magnificent carpets of flower petal "paintings" each year. This artistic tradition began as part of the Catholic feast of Corpus

Domini, which celebrates the belief in the real presence of Jesus Christ in the Eucharist.

While decorating processional paths with flowers was a common practice across Italy, Genzano elevated this custom into a unique art form in the 18th century, with the first documented celebration in 1778. Though it originated as a religious observance, the Infiorata has evolved into a significant cultural and artistic event while preserving its spiritual essence.

Eucharistic Procession Genzano

The festival has survived various historical challenges, including wars and social changes, strengthening from a purely religious observance to a broader cultural celebration. Today, it stands as a testament to the town's ability to preserve its traditions while adapting to modern times, serving as a point of pride for locals and a major attraction for visitors.

The Infiorata di Genzano is more than just a beautiful display of floral art; it's a living testament to the town's rich cultural heritage, community spirit, and artistic prowess. As you walk along the petal-strewn streets, marveling at the intricate designs beneath your feet, you'll be taking part in a tradition that has captivated visitors for centuries. Whether you're an art enthusiast, a culture lover, or simply someone seeking a unique Italian experience, the Infiorata di Genzano offers a feast for the senses and a window into the heart of Italian tradition. From the painstaking creation of the floral carpets to the symbolic procession that marks their end, every moment of this festival is infused with passion, creativity, and a deep sense of community that will leave a lasting impression long after the last petal has fallen.

Today, the Infiorata di Genzano is renowned as one of the most beautiful and well-preserved flower festivals in Italy, attracting visitors from around the world and playing a crucial role in preserving local traditions and fostering community bonds.

Key Events and Highlights

Petal Preparation: The preparation of flower petals is a cherished tradition involving families and community groups. This collaborative effort fosters a strong sense of community pride and unity.

Design Competition: Local artists compete to have their designs selected for the main carpet sections. This friendly rivalry elevates the artistic quality of the festival and ensures a diverse range of designs.

Community Participation: Residents of all ages actively take part in creating the floral carpets, from laying petals to assisting with logistics. This hands-on involvement strengthens the town's communal bonds.

Artistic Exhibitions: Alongside the floral carpets, various exhibitions showcase the history of the Infiorata and related artworks, offering visitors a deeper understanding of this cherished tradition.

Cultural Performances: Music, dance, and theatrical performances highlight the rich cultural heritage of Genzano, creating a festive atmosphere that complements the visual splendor of the flower carpets.

Food Stands: The festival also celebrates the culinary traditions of the Castelli Romani region. Visitors can sample local specialties and traditional foods at various food stands, adding a delicious dimension to their experience.

Walking Tour of Genzano di Roma

#1. Piazza Tommaso Frasconi

Start your tour at the heart of Genzano in Piazza Tommaso Frasconi, the main square and hub of local activity. The square is often bustling with locals enjoying coffee or running errands, offering a great introduction to the town's atmosphere. The square is also home to the Monument to the Fallen Soldiers, which commemorates those who lost their lives in past wars.

#2. Chiesa della Santissima Trinità (Holy Trinity)

Just a few minutes from Piazza Tommaso Frasconi, visit the Chiesa della Santissima Trinità, a beautiful 18th-century church that's an essential stop for those interested in religious architecture. The church features a Baroque façade and houses several notable works of religious art inside, giving visitors a peaceful spot to reflect and admire its serene atmosphere.

#3. Via Italo Belardi

Stroll along Via Italo Belardi, the street famous for hosting Genzano's annual Infiorata. Even when the festival is not occurring, the street is still worth visiting for its historical charm and significance.

#4. Palazzo Sforza Cesarini

A short walk from Via Italo Belardi brings you to Palazzo Sforza Cesarini, a historic palace dating back to the 16th century. This impressive building once belonged to the powerful Sforza Cesarini family and is now home to cultural events and exhibitions. Be sure to explore the palace's gardens, which overlook Lake Nemi and offer stunning views of the surrounding countryside.

#5. Parco Sforza Cesarini

Next, head to the adjacent Parco Sforza Cesarini, a large public park with beautiful walking paths, lush greenery, and panoramic views. The park is perfect for a relaxing stroll and offers a tranquil escape from the bustle of the town center.

#6. Chiesa di Santa Maria della Cima

Walk up to the Chiesa di Santa Maria della Cima, on a hill offering fantastic views of the town and the surrounding landscape. This church, built in the 17th century, has a simple yet elegant design and is a key religious site in Genzano. From its elevated position, it's a brilliant spot for taking in the vistas over the Alban Hills.

#7. Visit a Forno (Bread Shop)

End your tour with a visit to a bakery, one of Genzano's historic brick kilns, which played a crucial role in the town's industrial history. Nearby, you can also explore the small workshops and bakeries producing the town's famous Pane di Genzano, traditional bread with PGI status.

Logistics

Train: From Roma Termini: You can take a train from Roma Termini to the nearby town of Albano Laziale or Velletri, both of which are about 15 minutes by bus or taxi to Genzano. The train ride takes about 40 minutes to Albano or Velletri, and local buses or taxis are readily available to complete the journey.

Bus: From Rome (Anagnina Metro Station): Regular COTRAL buses leave from the Anagnina Metro Station (Line A) in Rome to Genzano di Roma. The journey takes approximately 45 minutes and offers scenic views of the Alban Hills along the way.

Car: From Rome: Genzano di Roma is about 30 km southeast of Rome, and the journey by car takes roughly 40-45 minutes. Take the SS7 (Via Appia) from Rome, which passes through the Castelli Romani region.

Parking: In Genzano di Roma, the Zona a Traffico Limitato (ZTL) restricts vehicle access to certain central areas during specific times to reduce congestion and pollution. To avoid fines, it's essential to park outside these zones. Parcheggio Via Ercole Imbastari: A public parking area offering convenient access to the town center while remaining outside the ZTL boundaries. Parcheggio Via Dottore Catalano: An open-air parking lot near local amenities, providing easy access without entering restricted zones.

Restaurant Recommendations

For the Infiorata, I recommend three to four nights in town. Genzano is in the Castelli Romani with several beautiful towns very nearby.

Osteria Pelliccione dal 1954. Address: Via Sebastiano Silvestri, 13

This historic osteria, established in 1954, is a favorite among locals for its authentic Roman and regional dishes. Osteria Pelliccione is known for its rustic, hearty meals, including traditional pasta dishes like cacio e pepe and amatriciana, as well as grilled meats and local specialties. The restaurant offers a true taste of the area's culinary traditions, all served in a welcoming, no-frills setting.

Accommodation

Monte Due Torri Agriturismo. Address: Via Montegiove Nuovo, 77

Nestled in the scenic hills of Genzano di Roma, Agriturismo Montegiove offers a tranquil retreat surrounded by lush landscapes. This charming accommodation combines modern comforts with traditional Italian hospitality, providing guests with a relaxing atmosphere.

Day Trip Options: Nearby Sites, Cities, and Towns

Lanuvio. Distance from Genzano di Rome, 6 kilometers (2 miles). Step into the timeless beauty of Lanuvio, a small hilltop town with a history as rich as its views. Famous in ancient times for its Temple of Juno Sospita, Lanuvio still whispers its Roman heritage through remnants scattered across the landscape. Meander through the narrow lanes of the historic center, where quiet charm meets stories of the past. Be sure to visit the Fountain of Hercules, a symbol of the town's enduring legacy.

Lariano. 11 kilometers (6 miles) from Genzano. Lariano is a cozy town tucked into the lush greenery of the Castelli Romani, renowned for its culinary prowess and stunning natural surroundings. Take a leisurely walk through the town's charming streets or venture into the surrounding woodlands for a taste of the great outdoors. Lariano's warmth lies in its simplicity, friendly locals, authentic cuisine, and a deep connection to the land. It's the perfect destination for those who want to savor both nature and tradition.

Genzano Festivals and Sagre Throughout the Year

Mercatus Cynthianus (antique market)

Last Sunday of each month

Step into a treasure hunter's paradise at Genzano di Roma's atmospheric antique market, where the historic Piazza Dante Alighieri and Via Veneto transform into a bustling bazaar of yesteryear. Winding through the charming stalls, visitors discover an eclectic collection of timeless pieces - from intricate handcrafted artifacts and rare numismatic collections to vintage paintings that tell stories of the past.

Passionate collectors and casual browsers alike can explore an impressive array of curiosities, each with its own history to tell. Local dealers proudly display their carefully curated selections of antique books, while artisans showcase traditional craftsmanship. The market has become a beloved meeting point where the thrill of discovering unique pieces mingles with the pleasure of exchanging stories and knowledge with fellow enthusiasts.

La Festa del Pane Casareccio (Traditional Bread Festival)

September

*See Breaking Bread with Saint Thomas in Genzano di Roma Chapter. Each September, Genzano celebrates its famous Pane Casareccio, their local bread. The streets are lined with stalls offering wine, food, and local products, while guided tours around Lake Nemi and Slow Food tastings are held to highlight the region's culinary excellence.

La Festa del Vino Novello (New Wine Festival)

November

Celebrate the vibrant flavors of Genzano di Roma at this enchanting new wine festival, where local winemakers showcase their latest wines in the heart of the historic town. This community-driven event, organized by the town council, puts the spotlight on the region's emerging wine producers and their fresh, young wines.

Beyond the exceptional wine tastings and delectable local cuisine, festival-goers can immerse themselves in the town's rich cultural heritage. Live musical performances create a festive atmosphere throughout the event, while expert-led tours wind through Genzano's charming historical center. A special feature is touring the grand Sforza-Cesarini Palace, letting visitors explore this historic landmark that has stood guard over the town for centuries.

CHAPTER FOURTEEN

Rome's Celebration of the Pillars of Faith

A Feast of Tradition, Unity, and Devotion Honoring Rome's Patron Saints

Festa di San Pietro e San Paolo

Where: Rome

When: June 29 (Events June 28-30).

Average Festival Temperatures: High 28°C (82°F). Low 18°C (64°F).

The Feast of Saints Peter and Paul

The Feast of Saints Peter and Paul, celebrated on June 29th, honors the two apostles who are considered the spiritual founders and protectors of the Church in Rome.

Both saints were martyred in Rome during Emperor Nero's persecution of Christians in the first century, around 64-67 AD, and their lives and sacrifices are deeply intertwined with the city's Christian identity.

Who is Saint Peter?

Saint Peter, originally named Simon, was one of Jesus Christ's twelve apostles and a central figure in the foundation of the Christian Church. A fisherman from Galilee, he was called by Jesus to leave his nets and follow Him, becoming one of His closest disciples. Jesus gave Simon the name "Peter," meaning "rock," and proclaimed, "Upon this rock, I will build my church" (Matthew 16:18), signifying Peter's foundational role in the establishment of Christianity.

Known for his fervent, if sometimes impulsive, faith, Peter witnessed key moments in Jesus' ministry, including the Transfiguration and the agony in the Garden of Gethsemane. Despite denying Christ three times before the Crucifixion, Peter's deep repentance and subsequent leadership cemented his role as a pillar of the Church.

After Christ's resurrection and ascension, Peter became the leader of the apostles and the first bishop of Rome, often regarded as the first pope. His missionary work took him across the ancient world, spreading the Gospel and strengthening early Christian communities.

According to tradition, Peter was martyred in Rome under Emperor Nero, crucified upside down because he felt unworthy to die in the same manner as Christ. His tomb lies beneath St. Peter's Basilica in Vatican City, making it one of the most sacred sites in Christianity. Saint Peter is venerated as the patron saint of fishermen, the papacy, and Rome itself. His legacy endures as a cornerstone of Christian faith and leadership.

Who Is St. Paul?

Saint Paul, originally known as Saul of Tarsus, was a devout Jew and a Roman citizen who initially persecuted Christians. However, his life changed dramatically after a profound encounter with Jesus Christ on the road to Damascus, where he was struck blind and heard Christ's voice asking, "Saul, why do you persecute me?" (Acts 9:4). This transformative experience led to his conversion to Christianity and his baptism as Paul.

Known as the "Apostle to the Gentiles," Paul dedicated his life to spreading the Gospel beyond Jewish communities, embarking on extensive missionary journeys across the Roman Empire. His letters (epistles) to early Christian communities, such as those in Corinth, Rome, and Galatia, form a significant part of the New Testament and continue to guide Christian theology and practice.

Paul's work was instrumental in shaping the early Church, particularly his emphasis on faith, grace, and the universality of salvation. Despite facing constant persecution, imprisonment, and hardships, Paul remained steadfast in his mission, ultimately traveling to Rome, where he was martyred under Emperor Nero around 64-67 AD. He was beheaded, a death considered honorable for a Roman citizen, and his remains are interred at the Basilica of Saint Paul Outside the Walls in Rome.

Saint Paul is venerated as a patron saint of missionaries, theologians, and writers. His life and teachings remain a testament to the transformative power of faith and the resilience of the human spirit in service to God.

History of the Festival

The festival has been celebrated since at least the 4th century, when Christianity became the official religion of the Roman Empire under Emperor Constantine. The earliest recorded commemorations included pilgrimages to the tombs of the saints, which became key sites for Christian worship.

By the 8th century, the feast was firmly established as one of the most important solemnities of the liturgical calendar in Rome, with elaborate liturgies and public celebrations. Over the centuries, it has evolved into a unifying event for the city, emphasizing the enduring influence of these two apostles on the global Catholic Church.

Festival Events

June 28: Prayer Vigil
9:00 p.m.

Prayer Vigil at St. Peter's Basilica: A solemn gathering for prayer and reflection.

June 29: Traditional Celebrations
7:00 a.m.

Early Masses: Local churches across Rome hold morning Masses in honor of Saints Peter and Paul, focusing on their lives and martyrdom.

9:30 a.m.

Papal Mass at St. Peter's Basilica: The Pope celebrates a solemn Mass at St. Peter's Basilica, attended by pilgrims, clergy, and dignitaries. This is the spiritual highlight of the day and includes the blessing of the palliums - white wool bands worn around archbishops' shoulders as symbols of their authority and connection to Rome.

Infiorata: The area in front of St. Peter's Square is decorated with beautiful pictures made from flower petals, known as the "Infiorata." These intricate designs are created by associations from all over Italy.

11:00 a.m.

Quo Vadis Walking Event: A special urban pilgrimage following two routes (long and short) through historic sites connected to Saints Peter and Paul. Highlights include:

- San Sebastiano fuori le Mura

- Santa Prisca

- Mamertine Prison

- Santa Maria in Via Lata

- Exclusive free access to the Colosseum Archaeological Park
  **Participants receive a commemorative cobblestone, symbolizing their journey through Rome's sacred history.

Afternoon: Cultural Activities and Processions

1:00 p.m.

Lunch Break: Restaurants and trattorias near the Vatican and in Trastevere fill up as people enjoy traditional Roman dishes, such as cacio e pepe or carbonara.

3:00 p.m.

Procession Preparations

Traditional Fair at St. Paul's Outside the Walls: St. Paul's Church hosts a traditional fair with street food, entertainment, games, and various stalls selling items.

Canoe Regatta on the Tiber River: There is a canoe regatta on the Tiber River near the Ponte Margherita bridge.

4:00 p.m.

Procession Begins: The statues of Saints Peter and Paul are carried through the streets of Rome. The procession takes around two hours.

The Procession begins at the Basilica di San Paolo Fuori le Mura (Saint Paul Outside the Walls)

St. Paul Outside the Walls

The Procession ends at the Basilica di San Pietro (Vatican).

Evening: Festive Atmosphere and Fireworks

6:00 p.m.

Evening Mass: Additional Masses are held for those unable to attend earlier services, often accompanied by choral music and prayers.

7:30 p.m.

Public Gatherings and Concerts: Squares such as Piazza San Pietro or Piazza Navona host musical performances, food stalls, and communal gatherings. Many locals and tourists enjoy the festive atmosphere.

9:00 p.m.

Fireworks Preparations at Castel Sant'Angelo: Crowds gather along the Tiber River and near Castel Sant'Angelo for the traditional fireworks display, known as La Girandola.

9:30 p.m.

Fireworks Show: The spectacular Girandola illuminates the night sky, accompanied by music and cheers from the audience. This tradition dates back centuries and remains a festival highlight.

Castel Sant'Angelo

Night: Wrapping Up the Celebrations

10:30 p.m.

Late-Night Strolls: Many people take evening walks through Rome's historic streets, enjoying the festive lights and ambiance.

11:00 p.m.

Informal Gatherings: Not wanting the night to end, families and friends gather in homes or local cafes for desserts like gelato or tiramisu, reflecting on the day's celebrations.

Additional Information

Traffic and Closures: The city is generally less crowded as many Romans take advantage of the long weekend to travel. This day is a National Holiday in honor of the saints. Museums in Rome are usually open, except for the Vatican Muscums, which arc closed.

Infiorata Preparations: The preparations for the Infiorata begin the evening before, and you can watch the artists at work as they create the flower designs in Piazza San Pietro.

June 30: Theatrical Performance
9:00 p.m.

"Peter and Paul in Rome": A theatrical performance in the atrium of St. Peter's Basilica. The performance brings to life the period when both apostles walked the streets of Rome, combining profound spiritual themes with authentic Roman culture.

CHAPTER FIFTEEN

Frascati's Celebration of Tuscolum's Grand Estates

Courtyards of Culture

Festival Internazionale delle Ville Tuscolane

Where: Frascati

When: End of June.

Average Festival Temperatures: High 26°C (79°F). Low 17°C (63°F).

Town History: Frascati and Its Noble Villas

Frascati, a jewel in the Castelli Romani region, is famous for its villas, wine, and proximity to Rome. The town's scenic landscape, rich cultural history, and the construction of magnificent Renaissance and Baroque villas have made it a cultural hub for centuries.

Frascati's elite villas, known as the Ville Tuscolane, were built primarily between the 16th and 17th centuries by prominent Roman families seeking a countryside retreat. These estates were more than just grand homes—they were symbols of power, wealth, and artistic achievement. As centers of artistic, cultural, and political influence, the villas housed many of the period's greatest artists, sculptors, and intellectuals, contributing to the richness of Italy's Renaissance heritage. Many of these villas are still owned by families of Rome today.

International Festival of the Villas of Tusculum

The Festival Internazionale delle Ville Tuscolane (International Festival of the Villas of Tusculum) is a modern celebration of this incredible legacy. Held annually in June, the festival brings together theater, music, dance, and visual arts, set against the stunning backdrop of Frascati's historical villas.

History of the Festival and the Villas of Tusculum

The villas of Tusculum, or Ville Tuscolane, represent the height of Renaissance and Baroque architecture in Italy. Each villa is a testament to the artistic ambitions of the Roman nobility, who sought to create countryside estates that reflected their wealth, status, and cultural patronage.

Some of the most important families, such as the Aldobrandini and Colonna, constructed these grand estates as places of leisure, diplomacy, and artistic exploration. The villas are famous for their elegant gardens, fountains, and frescoes, many of which were created by some of Italy's most celebrated artists, including Annibale Carracci, Domenichino, and Caravaggio.

The Festival Internazionale delle Ville Tuscolane was founded in the 1980s to promote the cultural and historical significance of these villas while providing a platform for artistic expression. The festival celebrates the town's role as a center of art, music, and theater, and it has grown into one of the most prestigious cultural events in the Castelli Romani region.

Over the years, the festival has attracted internationally renowned artists, musicians, directors, and politicians, who come to experience the unique combination of historic beauty and contemporary performances.

What Happens During the Festival?

The Festival Internazionale delle Ville Tuscolane is a multi-day celebration that takes place at the end of June. The events are held in the gardens and grounds of some of the most famous villas in Frascati, including Villa Torlonia, Villa Aldobrandini, and Villa Mondragone.

Highlights of the Festival:

Theater Performances: One of the principal attractions of the festival is the theater performances held in the open-air spaces of the villas. Productions often include Shakespearean plays, Italian classics, and modern theater pieces, performed by both Italian and international theater companies.

The performances are staged in the gardens and courtyards of the villas, creating a magical ambiance, with the historical architecture serving as a stunning backdrop. Past editions of the festival have featured famous actors and directors, making it one of the most expected cultural events of the year.

Music Concerts and Dance Performances: The festival also features a series of classical music concerts, which take place in the villas' gardens. Renowned orchestras and soloists perform works by Beethoven, Mozart, Vivaldi, and other great composers, adding to the elegant setting.

Besides classical music, the festival often includes dance performances, ranging from ballet to contemporary dance, showcasing the talents of Italian and international dancers. The blend of music and movement, set in the tranquil gardens of the villas, makes for an unforgettable experience.

Art Exhibitions and Tours of the Villas: One of the unique aspects of the festival is the opportunity for visitors to explore the villas of Tusculum, many of which are not always open to the public. Guided tours are offered, providing an in-depth look at the architecture, art, and history of these grand estates.

The tours highlight the gardens, designed by some of the most famous landscape architects of the time, as well as the villas' interiors, which are adorned with frescoes, sculptures, and other priceless works of art. In addition to the tours, the villas often host art exhibitions, showcasing works by both contemporary artists and historical collections from the villas' archives.

Cultural Workshops and Lectures: The festival includes a series of workshops and lectures on topics such as Renaissance art, landscape architecture, and the history of the Ville Tuscolane. These educational events are a great way for visitors to deepen their understanding of the artistic and cultural heritage of the region.

Experts in the field give talks on art restoration, Renaissance garden design, and the lives of the noble families who built the villas, providing valuable insight into the significance of these estates.

Gastronomy and Wine Tastings: As with many festivals in the Castelli Romani region, food and wine play an important role in the Festival Internazionale delle Ville Tuscolane. During the festival, visitors can enjoy wine tastings featuring the famous Frascati wines, which have been produced in the area for centuries.

Local wineries set up booths offering samples of their best vintages, often paired with traditional Roman dishes such as porchetta, cheese, and olive oil. Special gala dinners are sometimes held in the villas' gardens, offering a unique opportunity to dine in the same spaces where Renaissance aristocrats once indulged in lavish banquets.

Other Important Things to Know

- What to Bring: Since many of the events are held outdoors, it's a good idea to bring a hat, sunscreen, a blanket to settle on the lawn, and water for daytime activities. For evening performances, a light jacket is recommended, as the temperature can drop after sunset. Most performances require tickets, so be sure to purchase them in advance if possible.

- Best Time to Visit: The evening concerts and theater performances are some of the most popular events, and they sell out quickly. If you're interested in the guided tours of the villas, the early morning or late afternoon is the best time to go, as these are the quietest hours for exploration.

- Getting There: Frascati is about 20 kilometers (12 miles) southeast of Rome and is easily accessible by train. The train ride from Roma Termini to Frascati Station takes about 30 minutes, and the villas are within walking distance of the station. If you're driving, there are parking areas near the town, but spaces can fill up quickly during the festival, so it's best to arrive early.

Why Visit the Festival Internazionale delle Ville Tuscolane?

The Festival Internazionale delle Ville Tuscolane offers a unique blend of history, art, and entertainment, set in some of Italy's most beautiful Renaissance villas. Whether you're a lover of theater, classical music, dance, or art, the festival provides an immersive cultural experience that brings together the past and present in a stunning natural setting.

Visitors can explore the rich history of Frascati's villas, enjoy world-class performances, and sample some of the best wines and cuisine that the Castelli Romani region offers. For anyone interested in Italian art, architecture, or culture, this festival is not to be missed.

*See Frascati's Toast to Tradition, Chapter 35, for Frascati Logistics, Day Trip Options, Restaurant Recommendations and Accommodation. For this festival, I recommend two to three nights in town.

CHAPTER SIXTEEN

Isola del Liri's Harmonic Journey

Where Blues Music Echoes Through the Waterfalls

Liri Blues Festival

Where: Isola del Liri

When: First two weeks in July.

Average Festival Temperatures: High: 31°C (87°F). Low: 18°C (64°F).

Festival Website: https://en.wikipedia.org/wiki/Liri_Blues_Festival

Isola del Liri: The Enchanting Island of Waterfalls

Isola del Liri, a picturesque town in the province of Frosinone, is renowned for its unique setting and captivating waterfalls.

As its name suggests, Isola del Liri is on an island formed by two branches of the Liri River. This distinctive location features two notable waterfalls, the Cascata Grande and the Cascata del Valcatoio, each approximately 30 meters high, right in the town center. The surrounding landscape is characterized by rolling hills and lush greenery, typical of the Ciociaria region.

The town's origins date back to the Volsci, an ancient Italic tribe. Throughout history, Isola del Liri has been under various dominations, including the Byzantines and Lombards. In the Middle Ages, it became part of the County of Sora and was later ruled by noble families such as the dell'Isola, Cantelmo, and Boncompagni. The Boncompagni family, in particular, left a significant mark by transforming the local castle into a luxurious palace in the 17th century.

Isola del Liri has a population of 10,760 residents. The town's unique combination of natural wonders, historical heritage, and cultural vibrancy makes Isola del Liri a captivating destination for visitors seeking an authentic Italian experience.

Liri Blues Festival

Established in 1988 in Isola del Liri, the Liri Blues Festival emerged as a cultural response to the town's industrial decline, particularly the closure of its paper mills. Luciano Duro, the festival's founder, aimed to revitalize the community by introducing international blues artists to this central Italian locale. The inaugural event featured performances by notable musicians such as Albert King, Pinetop Perkins, and Buddy Guy, setting a high standard for future editions.

Over the years, the festival expanded its musical scope, incorporating diverse genres and artists, including Jorma Kaukonen of Jefferson Airplane, Canned Heat, and the Art Ensemble of Chicago. Despite this diversification, the festival maintained a strong blues identity, hosting legends like Luther Allison, Son Seals, and Jimmy Rogers. A significant milestone occurred in 1997 when Isola del Liri was twinned with New Orleans, strengthening the festival's international ties and cultural significance.

The festival has shown a commitment to social causes. Following Hurricane Katrina in 2005, the Liri Blues Festival organized a charity concert to support affected musicians from New Orleans, exemplifying its solidarity with the global blues community.

Traditionally held in early July, the Liri Blues Festival transforms Isola del Liri into a vibrant hub for blues enthusiasts. The event spans several days, featuring free concerts by both renowned international artists and emerging talents. Performances are typically staged in the town's historic center, with the picturesque Cascata Grande waterfall providing a stunning backdrop. The festival fosters a communal atmosphere, attracting visitors from across Europe who come to enjoy high-quality blues music in a unique setting.

Day-by-Day Schedule

Day 1: Opening Night
The festival kicks off with performances by local blues bands, setting the tone for the days ahead. The evening culminates with a headline act by an internationally acclaimed artist.

Day 2: Blues and Beyond
This day features a mix of traditional blues and fusion genres, showcasing the versatility of blues music. Workshops and jam sessions may be held during the afternoon, offering interactive experiences for attendees.

Day 3: Tribute Performances
Artists pay homage to blues legends, performing classic tracks that have shaped the genre. The night often includes special collaborations between musicians.

Day 4: Emerging Artists Showcase
Dedicated to up-and-coming blues musicians, this day provides a platform for new talent to perform before an appreciative audience.

Day 5: Grand Finale
The festival concludes with performances by top-tier blues artists, delivering high-energy sets that leave a lasting impression. A closing ceremony may follow, celebrating the success of the event and the communal spirit it fosters.

Walking Tour Isola del Liri

#1. Cascata Grande
Begin your tour at the heart of Isola del Liri, where the Liri River dramatically plunges over a 27-meter (88 foot) drop, creating the stunning Cascata Grande. This rare urban waterfall provides a picturesque backdrop and is a central feature

of the town's charm. In the late 16th century, the energy from the Liri River's waterfalls was harnessed to power various industries, including paper mills and wool manufacturing. This utilization marked the beginning of Isola del Liri's transformation into an industrial hub.

By the 19th century, advancements led to the establishment of hydroelectric plants, further leveraging the waterfalls' power for industrial purposes. The Cascata Grande played a central role in this development, providing a reliable energy source that attracted and sustained various manufacturing activities in the region.

Waterfall in Liri's Town Center

#2. Castello Boncompagni-Viscogliosi
Next to the waterfall stands the historic Castello Boncompagni-Viscogliosi. Dating back to the 12th century, this castle has witnessed various historical events and architectural transformations. While the interior may not always be open to the public, the exterior and its gardens offer a glimpse into the town's noble past.

#3. Chiesa di San Lorenzo Martire (St. Lawrence)
A short walk from the castle leads you to the Church of San Lorenzo Martire. This 13th-century church showcases a blend of Gothic and Baroque architectural styles, with notable frescoes and artworks adorning its interior.

#4. Museo della Media Valle del Liri

Continue to the Museum of the Media Valle del Liri, housed in a historic building. The museum offers insights into the region's archaeological finds, industrial heritage, and cultural evolution, providing context to Isola del Liri's development over the centuries.

#5. Cascata del Valcatoio

Proceed to the second waterfall, Cascata del Valcatoio, on the opposite side of the island. Though smaller than Cascata Grande, it offers a serene spot for reflection and photography, highlighting the town's unique relationship with water.

#6. Piazza Boncompagni

Conclude your tour at Piazza Boncompagni, the town's central square. Surrounded by historic buildings, cafes, and shops, it's an ideal place to relax, enjoy local cuisine, and immerse yourself in the daily life of Isola del Liri.

Logistics

Train: The nearest train station to Isola del Liri is in Sora, located approximately 7 kilometers (4 miles) away. Regional trains connect Sora to Rome and other major cities in Lazio. From the Sora train station, visitors can take a short bus or taxi ride to reach Isola del Liri.

Bus: Isola del Liri is well-connected by regional bus services operated by Cotral. These buses provide regular connections to nearby towns such as Sora, Arpino, and Frosinone, as well as to Rome. The principal bus stop is centrally located in the town, making it a convenient option for travelers.

Car: To arrive by car from Rome, take the A1 Autostrada del Sole northbound and exit at Frosinone. From Frosinone, follow the SR82 road toward Isola del Liri. The journey is approximately 100 kilometers (62 miles) and takes around 1 hour and 30 minutes, depending on traffic. The scenic drive through the Ciociaria countryside adds to the experience.

Parking: Isola del Liri offers several parking options just outside the historic center to accommodate visitors. Public parking lots are available near the main entrances to the town, such as those along Via Cascata and Piazza Boncompagni.

Parking areas are clearly marked, and it is advisable to use these facilities to avoid restricted zones (ZTL) within the historic center.

Restaurant Recommendations

Osteria da Mauretto. Address: Via San Lorenzo Colle 4
This Italian and seafood restaurant is praised for its friendly service and great location. Dishes like calamari and mussels are highly recommended.

La Taverna. Address: Via Largo Bernardo 6
Specializing in Italian and seafood dishes, La Taverna is appreciated for its high-quality food and pleasant dining experience. It's a great place for lunch or dinner.

Accommodation

For the festival I recommend two or three nights in town.

Hotel Scala alla Cascata. Address: Corso Vittorio Emanuele, 9/11-13
Hotel Scala alla Cascata is a charming hotel near the waterfall in Isola del Liri. It offers cozy accommodations with a touch of local charm. Guests can enjoy the beautiful views of the waterfall and the surrounding area.

Day Trips: Nearby Sites, Cities, and Towns

Fumone. Distance from Isola del Liri: 40 kilometers (25 miles). Fumone is a picturesque hilltop town dominated by the Castello di Fumone, a medieval castle famous for its panoramic roof garden and historical significance. The castle once served as a papal prison and offers fascinating guided tours. The town's narrow cobblestone streets, stone houses, and breathtaking views of the surrounding countryside make it a charming destination for history and nature enthusiasts alike.

Pico. 30 kilometers (19 miles) from Isola del Liri. Pico is a small town listed among "The Most Beautiful Villages of Italy." Its medieval charm is evident in the well-preserved historic center, with narrow alleys, stone houses, and the ancient Farnese Castle, which offers insights into the region's feudal past. Surrounded by rolling hills and natural beauty, Pico provides a tranquil escape and an authentic Italian village experience.

Anagni. 35 kilometers (22 miles) from Isola del Liri. Known as the "City of Popes," Anagni is steeped in medieval history and was the residence of several popes. The town is famous for its magnificent Anagni Cathedral, featuring stunning frescoes and a crypt often referred to as the "Sistine Chapel of the Middle Ages." The historic center is a treasure trove of medieval architecture, with charming piazzas and palaces that transport visitors back in time.

Isola del Liri Festivals and Sagre Throughout the Year

Festa del Santissimo Crocifisso

2nd Sunday in July

This religious festival honors the Holy Crucifix with solemn processions, liturgical ceremonies, and community gatherings, highlighting the town's deep-rooted faith and traditions.

Sagra degli Gnocchi

Early September

A culinary celebration dedicated to gnocchi, this sagra offers visitors the chance to savor traditional handmade potato dumplings prepared according to local recipes. The event typically includes live music, dancing, and other entertainment, fostering a festive community ambiance.

L'Isola del Natale

December to January

During the Christmas season, Isola del Liri transforms into a winter wonderland with festive decorations, a large ice-skating rink, and various holiday-themed attractions. The event aims to create a magical atmosphere for families and visitors, featuring markets, entertainment, and opportunities to experience the holiday spirit in a unique setting.

CHAPTER SEVENTEEN

Immersion Experience: Steps of Serenity

Walking the Cammino di San Benedetto

The Cammino di San Benedetto: A Journey Through Faith and History

Website: https://www.ilcamminodisanbenedetto.it/home

If you've read my other travel guides, you'll know I have a special fondness for Italy's Cammini. I make sure to include these extraordinary pilgrimage routes because they always steal my heart. These are not your average hiking trails, but gateways to an Italy that few tourists ever see. And among these remarkable paths, the Cammino di San Benedetto holds a place all its own.

Picture this: you're walking in the footsteps of St. Benedict himself, the remarkable monk who shaped Western monasticism, through some of Italy's most soul-stirring landscapes. This journey weaves through three incredible regions, Umbria, Lazio, and Abruzzo, each with its own distinct character and charm. I've found that there's something almost magical about how this route combines magnificent Benedictine monasteries, drowsy medieval towns that seem frozen in time, and natural vistas that will literally stop you in your tracks.

Whether you're drawn to the spiritual significance of walking in the footsteps of St. Benedict or simply looking for an unforgettable way to explore Italy off the beaten path, the Cammino di San Benedetto is a transformative experience. From the birthplace of St. Benedict in Norcia to the majestic Abbey of Montecassino, this journey is an invitation to rediscover balance, purpose, and connection with nature, history, and perhaps yourself.

The Walk of St. Benedict

The Cammino di San Benedetto (The Way of St. Benedict) is a pilgrimage route that spans over 300 kilometers (186 miles), connecting some of the most significant locations in the life of St. Benedict of Nursia, the founder of Western monasticism. This inspiring journey begins in Norcia, his birthplace, winds through central Italy's picturesque countryside, and culminates at the Abbey of Montecassino, where he founded his most famous monastery and where his earthly life ended.

You do not have to walk all 186 miles! The route is divided into 16 stages, taking pilgrims through enchanting villages, serene forests, and ancient Benedictine monasteries. Each stop reflects the profound spiritual and historical impact of St. Benedict's life and teachings. The trail immerses travelers in the beauty of Umbria, Lazio, and Abruzzo, offering breathtaking views, peaceful paths, and opportunities for deep reflection and connection with nature.

Key Stops Along the Way

The pilgrimage includes key Benedictine sites, such as:

Norcia: The journey begins at St. Benedict's birthplace, marked by the stunning Basilica of San Benedetto.

Subiaco: Known as the cradle of Benedictine monasticism, Subiaco is home to the Sacro Speco (Holy Cave) where St. Benedict lived as a hermit, and the Monastery of St. Scholastica, the oldest surviving Benedictine monastery.

Abbey of Montecassino: The final destination and crowning jewel of the Cammino, Montecassino is where St. Benedict wrote the Rule of St. Benedict and established the foundations of Western monastic life.

A Pilgrimage of Body, Mind, and Soul

The Cammino di San Benedetto is not just a physical journey but a deeply spiritual experience. Pilgrims follow in the footsteps of St. Benedict, embracing his philosophy of "ora et labora" (prayer and work). Each step along the path is an invitation to reflect on his teachings of balance, humility, and faith.

Travelers encounter warm hospitality in monasteries, small inns, and family-run accommodations, fostering a sense of community that echoes Benedict's emphasis on shared living. The trail is accessible to both experienced hikers and casual walkers, with stages ranging from 10 to 25 kilometers per day. Pilgrims can earn a testimonial, a certificate of completion, by collecting stamps at key locations along the route.

Why Walk the Cammino di San Benedetto?

For those seeking spiritual renewal, historical insights, or simply the joy of traversing Italy's stunning landscapes, the Cammino di San Benedetto offers a unique and enriching experience. It combines history, faith, and nature into a journey of discovery, tracing the life and legacy of one of Christianity's most influential figures. Whether undertaken as a full pilgrimage or explored in smaller sections, the Cammino invites travelers to slow down, reflect, and rediscover the essence of Benedictine spirituality.

The Cammino website offers a comprehensive suite of resources for pilgrims and travelers interested in the Cammino di San Benedetto.

CHAPTER EIGHTEEN

Trastevere's Timeless Festa dei Noantri

Five Centuries of Devotion, Community, and Celebration

Festa dei Neoantri

Where: Rome in the Trastevere Neighborhood

When: July 16 (the Feast of Our Lady of Mount Carmel) to July 31.

Average temperatures: High 31°C (88°F). Low 18°C (64°F).

Website: https://www.festadenoantri.it/

Trastevere: Rome's Timeless Neighborhood

Trastevere, one of Rome's most enchanting districts, sits on the west bank of the Tiber River, its name derived from the Latin *trans Tiberim* "beyond the Tiber." This historic quarter has always been a place of contrasts: a haven for the working-class and immigrants, a vibrant cultural hub, and a favorite retreat for emperors and popes alike.

From Ancient Rome to the Middle Ages

In the early days of Rome, Trastevere lay outside the city's walls, making it an ideal refuge for populations who didn't belong to the heart of Roman society. Etruscans, Syrians, and Jews settled here, transforming Trastevere into a multicultural enclave. Over time, Emperor Augustus formally included Trastevere within the city boundaries, connecting it to central Rome with bridges like the Pons Sublicius (the city's oldest wooden bridge) and later the more durable Ponte Cestio and Ponte Fabricio, which still stand today.

In antiquity, Trastevere became a vibrant neighborhood, home to artisans, sailors, and merchants who depended on the Tiber River for trade. It also played host to grand villas belonging to the Roman elite, including Julius Caesar's gardens and residences owned by powerful families.

During the early Christian era, the neighborhood embraced its role as a religious center. Trastevere is home to Santa Maria in Trastevere, one of the oldest churches in Rome, dating back to the 3rd century AD. Its iconic golden mosaics and serene piazza anchor the district in both history and faith.

By the Middle Ages, Trastevere had developed into a lively working-class neighborhood. Its narrow, winding cobblestone streets—many unchanged to this day, formed a labyrinth of humble dwellings, workshops, and taverns. The Tiber's constant flooding often isolated the district, fostering a unique community spirit. Its residents, known as *Trasteverini*, developed a fierce pride in their identity, maintaining a distinct dialect and traditions that set them apart from central Rome.

The medieval period also saw Trastevere as a religious and artistic hub. Churches like San Crisogono and Santa Cecilia in Trastevere were constructed and decorated with stunning frescoes and mosaics, reflecting both spiritual devotion and artistic achievement.

The Renaissance and Baroque eras brought renewed attention to Trastevere. Wealthy Roman families commissioned grand palazzi and adorned the churches with art from the likes of Pietro Cavallini and Gian Lorenzo Bernini. The neighborhood balanced its humble roots with elegant residences and cultural landmarks. During this time, Trastevere's iconic character emerged: a mix of Roman grit, artistic splendor, and timeless beauty.

Throughout the 19th and early 20th centuries, Trastevere kept its working-class character, even as Rome expanded and modernized. In recent decades, Trastevere has undergone a renaissance of its own. Its bohemian atmosphere, charming piazzas, and trattorias have drawn artists, intellectuals, and travelers, transforming the neighborhood into one of Rome's most beloved districts.

Festival of Trastevere

Each July, the Trastevere neighborhood comes alive for the Festa dei Noantri, one of Rome's oldest and most cherished festivals. Celebrated for over 500 years, its name means "of us others" in the Roman dialect, reflecting the strong identity and community spirit of Trastevere.

The tradition began in 1535 when local fishermen discovered a statue of the Madonna del Carmine in the Tiber River after a storm. Believed to be miraculous, the statue was brought to the Church of Sant'Agata, where it remains today. Since then, the community has honored it with a grand religious procession through the cobbled streets, accompanied by music, celebrations, and neighborhood pride. What began as a devotional act has become a vibrant expression of Trastevere's deep cultural and spiritual roots.

Events of the Festa dei Noantri

The Festa dei Noantri is a two-week celebration filled with religious processions, cultural events, and festivities.

Saturday after July 16th (the Feast of Our Lady of Mount Carmel)

The Procession of the Madonna del Carmine

6:00 p.m.

During the Festa dei Noantri, the statue of the Madonna del Carmine, dressed in rich robes and adorned with jewels is carried in a grand procession through the heart of Trastevere. Starting at the Church of Sant'Agata, her usual home, the statue is paraded along the neighborhood's narrow cobblestone streets to the music of the Capital Police band.

The procession winds through key streets and piazzas, eventually reaching the Church of San Crisogono, where the Madonna remains for a week before returning to Sant'Agata. Accompanied by prayers, hymns, clergy, and city officials, the event draws hundreds of locals and pilgrims, creating a powerful expression of faith and neighborhood unity.

Last Sunday in July

The River Procession (Processione Fiumarola)

7:30 p.m.

One of the most striking moments of the Festa dei Noantri is the river procession. Honoring the legend of the Madonna's discovery in the Tiber, her statue is placed on a boat and gently carried down the river, accompanied by a flotilla of vessels. Locals and visitors line the riverbanks to watch, creating a magical, festive atmosphere along the water.

On land, the procession continues through Trastevere's storied streets, following a route that includes Calata degli Anguillara, Piazza Gioacchino Belli, Viale di Trastevere, and ends with fireworks and final prayers at the Basilica of Santa Maria in Trastevere.

Final Procession

Monday 7:30 a.m.

Procession Route: Basilica S. Maria in Trastevere-Via della Paglia-Piazza di S. Egidio-Via della Scala-Piazza della Scala-Via di S. Dorotea-Via Benedetta-Via del Moro-Piazza di S. Apollonia-Via della Lungaretta-Largo S. Giovanni de' Matha. The procession ends at the Chiesa Sant'Agata.

Street Festivals, Concerts, and Cultural Events

Alongside the religious observances, the Festa dei Noantri is a time for community celebration. The streets of Trastevere are filled with stalls, food vendors, and musicians, giving the neighborhood a festive atmosphere.

Open-air concerts, ranging from traditional Roman music to more contemporary performances, take place throughout the festival. Street markets offer everything from local food specialties to handcrafted goods, adding a lively cultural and social element to the festivities. The festival often concludes with a spectacular fireworks display, lighting up the skies over Trastevere.

Attending the Festa dei Noantri

The Festa dei Noantri is a wonderful way to experience the deep-rooted traditions of Trastevere and immerse yourself in local Roman culture. Whether attending the religious processions or enjoying the lively street fairs, visitors are welcomed to take part in the festivities. Arriving early for the processions in Trastevere is a good idea to ensure a good view of the Madonna, as the streets can get crowded.

Trastevere is famous for its Roman cuisine, and the festival brings out street vendors selling traditional dishes like supplì (fried rice balls, a favorite of mine) and porchetta (roast pork), along with sweet treats like maritozzi (cream-filled buns, I might eat them two in one sitting, no judgement!). Beyond the festival, Trastevere offers a labyrinth of charming streets, cafes, and piazzas, perfect for exploring between events.

Walking Tour of Trastevere

#1. Basilica di Santa Maria in Trastevere

Santa Maria in Trastevere, one of Rome's oldest and most revered churches, is a treasure trove of art, history, and spirituality. Founded in the 3rd century and later reconstructed in the 12th century under Pope Innocent II, the basilica boasts a stunning collection of mosaics, frescoes, and religious artifacts that reflect the rich cultural tapestry of the city.

The façade, adorned with golden mosaics by Pietro Cavallini, depicts the Virgin Mary and Child flanked by ten women holding lamps, symbolizing the virtues of faith and purity. Inside, the basilica's ceiling, crafted by Domenichino in the 17th century, features a gilded depiction of the Assumption of Mary, complemented by intricate carvings and detailing.

Facade of the Basilica di Santa Maria

The apse is the true highlight of Santa Maria in Trastevere, showcasing breathtaking mosaics from the 12th century that narrate scenes from the life of the Virgin Mary and Christ. These mosaics, glowing in gold and vivid hues, include the central image of Mary and Christ enthroned, surrounded by saints. Visitors should also note of the 22 granite columns that line the nave, believed to have been repurposed from ancient Roman temples.

Additionally, the Chapel of Altemps houses a 15th-century tabernacle, while the serene atmosphere of the piazza outside the church, with its central fountain, offers a perfect place to reflect on the artistic and spiritual wonders within. Santa Maria in Trastevere is not just a church but a profound journey into Rome's layered history and artistic legacy.

#2. Chiesa di San Francesco a Ripa

Walk 10 minutes to a charming Baroque church deeply connected to the legacy of Saint Francis of Assisi, who stayed in the adjoining convent during his visits to Rome. The church, built in the 17th century, holds remarkable artistic and spiritual significance. Its most celebrated treasure is Gian Lorenzo Bernini's masterpiece, the Blessed Ludovica Albertoni, a stunning marble sculpture housed in the Altieri Chapel. This dynamic and emotive work captures Ludovica's ecstatic vision and is one of Bernini's finest expressions of spiritual intensity.

The interior of the church is adorned with richly detailed chapels, frescoes, and altars that reflect the artistic wealth of the Baroque period, while the relics and artifacts associated with Saint Francis add a sense of reverence and history. This hidden gem in Trastevere invites visitors to explore its artistic marvels while offering a peaceful space for contemplation.

#3. Santa Cecilia in Trastevere

Continue with a 15-minute walk to this church dedicated to St. Cecilia, the patron saint of music. Santa Cecilia in Trastevere is a Roman church steeped in history and devotion, dedicated to Saint Cecilia, the patron saint of music. In the heart of Trastevere, the church stands on the site of Cecilia's house, where she was martyred in the 3rd century.

The basilica's façade, redesigned in the 18th century by Ferdinando Fuga, exudes a neoclassical charm and welcomes visitors to a space that beautifully intertwines spirituality and art. A notable feature is the striking sculpture of Saint Cecilia beneath the altar, crafted by Stefano Maderno. This poignant work depicts the saint's body in the position in which it was found when her tomb was opened in 1599, emphasizing her serenity and faith even in death.

Inside, the church dazzles with its 9th-century apse mosaics depicting Christ and Saint Cecilia alongside other saints, radiating golden hues that symbolize divine glory. Visitors should not miss the crypt, which contains the archaeological remains of Cecilia's original house and ancient Roman structures.

Visitors can go down into the crypt of Santa Cecilia in Trastevere, which adds another layer of historical and spiritual significance to the church. The crypt houses the remains of Saint Cecilia and offers a fascinating glimpse into the early Christian history of Rome. This sacred space is believed to have been part of Cecilia's original house, where she lived and was martyred. Archaeological excavations have uncovered Roman-era structures, including walls and ancient mosaics, further connecting the site to its origins as a place of worship and refuge for early Christians.

#4. Villa Farnesina

Just a 10-minute walk from Santa Cecilia, Villa Farnesina is a Renaissance jewel built for banker Agostino Chigi in the early 1500s. Designed by Baldassare Peruzzi, the villa is famed for its richly frescoed interiors by masters such as Raphael, Sebastiano del Piombo, and Peruzzi himself.

Highlights include Raphael's Triumph of Galatea, a vivid mythological seascape, and the Loggia of Cupid and Psyche, adorned with romantic scenes full of color and grace. With its elegant architecture and celebration of classical myths, Villa Farnesina offers a window into the humanist ideals and artistic brilliance of Rome's Golden Age.

#5. Porta Portese Flea Market

If visiting on a Sunday, head to the Porta Portese Flea Market, one of the largest and most eclectic markets in Rome. Situated just outside the ancient Porta Portese gate, this sprawling market stretches through the streets and offers an incredible variety of goods, from antiques, vintage clothing, and books to homeware and curiosities. Held every Sunday morning, the market is a treasure trove for bargain hunters and those seeking a vibrant Roman experience.

Restaurant Recommendations in Trastevere

Trattoria Da Enzo al 29. Address: Via dei Vascellari, 29

Trattoria Da Enzo al 29 is a beloved, small Roman trattoria that is well known for its traditional Roman comfort food. On every visit, we prioritize choosing this place when I can reserve a spot. Despite its simple and unassuming decor, the restaurant is celebrated for its authentic flavors and top-quality ingredients.

Tonnarello. Address: Via della Paglia, 1/2/3

Tonnarello is a popular dining spot in Trastevere, offering both indoor and outdoor seating in a lively, trendy atmosphere. Known for its Roman cuisine, the restaurant is particularly praised for its generous portions and quality ingredients. It's a great place to enjoy classics like cacio e pepe, carbonara, and their namesake tonnarelli pasta. With its vibrant setting, Tonnarello attracts a young crowd looking for a flavorful and affordable Roman dining experience.

Appetito Pizza Gourmet. Address: P.za di Sant'Apollonia, 7/8

Try the Suppli here! Supplì are a beloved Italian street food (fast food, Roman style) and a quintessential part of Roman cuisine. These delicious snacks are fried rice balls, typically served as an appetizer or snack. Grab one on your way to the Basilica di Santa Maria in Trastevere. This spot is practically in the piazza in front of the church.

Accommodation: See the Accommodation Detail Chapter for information on hotels in Rome.

Trastevere Festivals Throughout the Year

Feast of Santa Cecilia

November 22

This feast day honors Saint Cecilia, the patron saint of musicians. The Basilica of Santa Cecilia in Trastevere holds special masses and musical events, reflecting her association with music.

Feast of Santa Maria in Trastevere

August 15, December 8

*See FestaFusion Rome Chapter 22. While there isn't a specific feast day solely dedicated to Santa Maria in Trastevere, the basilica plays a central role in various Marian celebrations throughout the year, including the Feast of the Assumption on August 15 and the Feast of the Immaculate Conception on December 8. These events feature special liturgies and community gatherings.

CHAPTER NINETEEN

Immersion Experience: Walk the Streets of Ancient Rome

Exploring Ostia Antica

V isiting Ostia Antica, the ancient harbor city of Rome, is like stepping back in time to walk the very streets where Romans lived, worked, and thrived nearly 2,000 years ago. This well-preserved archaeological site offers a glimpse into the daily life of ancient Rome, from bustling marketplaces to grand temples and cozy taverns. More than just a tour, Ostia Antica offers a deep connection to Italy's history, art, and culture.

Unlike the crowds of Rome's Colosseum or Forum (or Pompeii further south), Ostia Antica provides a quieter, more personal experience, making it ideal for travelers seeking to explore Italy beyond the beaten path. Every mosaic, fresco, and ruin tells a story, and walking these streets allows you to imagine the lives of the people who built the Roman Empire.

While Pompeii may be more famous, Ostia Antica offers an equally fascinating look at ancient Roman life, with the added advantage of being much closer to Rome. Located just 30 minutes by train, it's a convenient day trip for those based in the capital, eliminating the need for long travel to southern Italy. Unlike

Pompeii, which was frozen in time by the catastrophic eruption of Mount Vesuvius, Ostia Antica showcases a thriving Roman port city in its prime, preserved through gradual abandonment rather than disaster. This difference gives Ostia a unique charm, offering a more organic glimpse into daily Roman life, complete with well-preserved apartment buildings, bathhouses, and taverns.

For travelers short on time or looking for a more accessible alternative, Ostia Antica provides an exceptional immersion into ancient Roman history without the long journey or sizeable crowds often associated with Pompeii. It's a hidden gem waiting to be explored, just a stone's throw from Rome.

Roman Main Road at Ostia

What to See: A Walking Tour of Ostia Antica

Your visit to Ostia Antica begins at the Porta Romana, the ancient city gate. From here, you'll walk through the decumanus (main street) and explore a mix of impressive public buildings, temples, and residential areas.

#1. The Baths of Neptune

Admire the stunning black-and-white mosaics of Neptune and Amphitrite that decorate this ancient bath complex. The baths were a social hub for the citizens of Ostia, showcasing the grandeur of Roman public spaces.

#2. The Theater

Built in the late 1st century BC and expanded by Emperor Commodus, this amphitheater once held 4,000 spectators. Climb the steps for a stunning view of the surrounding ruins and imagine the lively performances that once entertained the crowds.

#3. The Piazzale delle Corporazioni

Behind the theater, this square was the commercial heart of Ostia. Its mosaics depict symbols of ancient trade guilds, illustrating the city's bustling economy and its importance as Rome's port.

#4. The Forum and the Capitolium

The political and religious center of Ostia, the Forum features the towering Capitolium, a temple dedicated to Jupiter, Juno, and Minerva. The structure provides a glimpse into the religious life of the city.

#5. The House of Diana

Step into one of the best-preserved Roman apartment buildings, complete with multiple floors and courtyards. This residence offers a peek into how ordinary citizens lived in ancient Rome.

#6. The Thermopolium

Visit this ancient tavern, complete with a stone counter and niches for storing food and drinks. It's a remarkable reminder of the social life and dining culture of the Romans.

#7. The Synagogue

One of the oldest synagogues in the Western world, this site highlights the diverse religious and cultural communities that thrived in Ostia.

8. The Necropolis

Near the Porta Marina, this burial site features fascinating funerary monuments, providing insight into Roman burial customs and beliefs about the afterlife.

More than a tour, exploring Ostia Antica transports you to ancient Rome. Walking through its streets, sitting in its theater, and standing inside its houses allows you to feel the rhythm of life in an ancient Roman city. You'll see where people worked, worshipped, and relaxed, making history come alive in a tangible way.

Logistics: How to Get to Ostia Antica from Rome

Getting to Ostia Antica from Rome is straightforward, making it an ideal day trip. Here's how to plan your journey:

Train: Take the Roma-Lido line from Piramide Station (connected to Rome's Metro Line B). Disembark at the Ostia Antica station. The journey takes about 30 minutes.

From the station, it's a 5-10 minute walk to the archaeological site.

Car: Drive along the Via del Mare (SS8) toward Ostia. Parking is available near the site. The drive takes approximately 45 minutes from central Rome, depending on traffic.

Guided Tour: Many operators in Rome offer half- or full-day tours to Ostia Antica, including transportation and a guided experience.

Tips for Your Visit

Timing: Arrive early to make the most of your visit, especially during warmer months. The site opens at 8:30 a.m. and closes in the late afternoon, with seasonal variations.

Tickets: Purchase tickets online or at the entrance. Consider booking a guided tour or downloading an audio guide for added insights. The tickets are available through the Coop Culture website.

https://www.coopculture.it/en/products/ticket-for-archaeological-area-of-ostia -antica

CHAPTER TWENTY

Castel Gandolfo: Papal Palace & Peach Festival

Blending Legacy with Local Delights

Sagra delle Pesche

Where: Castel Gandolfo

When: Last Sunday of July.

Average Festival Temperatures: 30°C (86°F). Low 17°C (63°F).

From Roman Villa to Papal Refuge: The History of Castel Gandolfo

Welcome to Castel Gandolfo, a town steeped in history and beauty, perched above the stunning Lake Albano. The history of Castel Gandolfo stretches back to ancient times. The area was originally home to Alba Longa, a legendary Latin city said to be the birthplace of Romulus and Remus, the founders of Rome. Archaeological evidence suggests that the region was inhabited as far back as the 5th century BC.

During the Roman Empire, the area became a favorite retreat for patrician families and emperors. Emperor Domitian (81-96 AD) built an extensive villa here, parts of which can still be seen today. The remains of this villa, including the Ninfeo Bergantino, form an important part of Castel Gandolfo's archaeological heritage.

After the fall of the Roman Empire, the area went through a period of decline. In the 12th century, the Gandolfi family from Genoa gained the territory and built a castle, from which the town derives its name. The castle changed hands several times over the centuries, belonging to various noble Roman families.

In 1596, Pope Clement VIII acquired Castel Gandolfo for the Apostolic See, marking the beginning of its history as a papal residence. However, it was Pope Urban VIII who, in 1628, designated it as the summer residence of the Pope, a tradition that continues to this day.

The 17th century saw a significant development in Castel Gandolfo. The Papal Palace was constructed, and the Church of St. Thomas of Villanova was built under the direction of Gian Lorenzo Bernini. Over the centuries, successive Popes added to and improved the palace and its grounds.

During World War II, Castel Gandolfo played a crucial role as a refuge. Pope Pius XII opened the Papal Palace to thousands of residents and refugees, protecting them from the conflict that raged around Rome.

Today, Castel Gandolfo is known not only for its papal connection but also for its picturesque beauty. In 2014, it was voted one of the most beautiful towns in Italy. In 2016, Pope Francis opened the Papal Palace to the public as a museum, allowing visitors to explore this historic site. The town is home to 8,600 residents.

Personal Experience: Our first visit to Castel Gandolfo in 2012 started as a happy accident. We had only five days in Rome, and my husband Mike, my son Augustus, and I had originally planned to attend a Papal Audience with Pope Benedict XVI at the Vatican. Instead, we learned the pontiff was spending the summer in this beautiful town perched above Lake Albano and that the Papal Audience would be held there.

Back then, access to the Papal Palace at Castel Gandolfo was quite limited quite different from today, when Pope Francis has opened both the site and the Papal train route from the Vatican to visitors. We felt incredibly lucky to secure tickets, and with growing excitement, we arranged a taxi from Rome to take us to the Papal Palace.The moment we arrived, the magnificent Swiss Guard escorted us into the palace courtyard. What followed was unforgettable: we stood among nuns from around the world who filled the air with beautiful hymns, surrounded by other fortunate families sharing in our anticipation. While Pope Benedict's balcony address was certainly special, what made the day truly extraordinary was being inside the usually restricted palace grounds a rare privilege few visitors ever experienced.

After the audience, we spent a perfect morning soaking in the spectacular views of Lake Albano, wandering through Castel Gandolfo's charming local shops, and lingering over lunch in town. As afternoon approached, we caught a taxi back to central Rome, knowing we'd just experienced something truly special the kind of unexpected adventure that makes traveling so magical.

Lago Albano from Castel Gandolfo

The Peach Festival

The Sagre delle Pesche, or Peach Festival, is a cherished tradition in Castel Gandolfo that celebrates the town's rich agricultural heritage. While the exact origins of the festival are not provided in our source material, many believe it has roots that stretch back centuries.

In Castel Gandolfo, the festival has likely developed over time, intertwining with the town's unique status as the Pope's summer residence. The tradition of offering peaches to the Holy Father suggests a long-standing connection between the local agriculture and the papal presence, possibly dating back to the 17th century when Castel Gandolfo became the property of the Holy See.

Festival Events

The Sagre delle Pesche is a vibrant celebration that engages the entire community and welcomes visitors from near and far.

Peach Tastings: The heart of the festival is the celebration of the peach itself. Throughout the old town center, visitors can sample a variety of peach-based delicacies, including:

- Fresh peaches

- Peach drinks

- Peach marmalades

- Peach cakes

- Peach fruit salads

- Peach Gelato

Traditional Costume Parade: One of the festival's highlights occurs in the morning when local youth, dressed in traditional costumes, participate in a colorful parade. This procession begins in the town and makes its way up to the Pontifical Palace.

Offering to the Pope: Upon reaching the Pontifical Palace, the costumed participants present baskets of peaches as an offering to the Holy Father. This ceremony symbolizes the deep connection between the town's agricultural bounty and its spiritual significance.

Cultural Events: Throughout the day, various cultural activities take place, showcasing local traditions, music, and arts.

Sporting Events: The festival includes sporting competitions, adding an element of friendly rivalry to the celebrations.

Recreational Activities: A range of fun activities for all ages ensure that there's never a dull moment during the festival.

Where the Festival Takes Place

The Sagre delle Pesche unfolds across various locations in Castel Gandolfo:

- Old Town Center: The heart of the festival is in the historic center of Castel Gandolfo. The narrow streets and picturesque squares come alive with stalls, tastings, and activities. This area, known for its elegant architecture and charm, provides a stunning backdrop for the celebrations.

- Route to the Pontifical Palace: The traditional costume parade travels from the town center up to the Pontifical Palace. This route likely winds through some of Castel Gandolfo's most scenic areas, offering spectacular views of Lake Albano along the way.

- Pontifical Palace: While the public doesn't enter the palace, the surrounding area becomes a focal point during the offering ceremony.

The festival essentially transforms the entire town of Castel Gandolfo into a celebration of peaches, local culture, and community spirit. The unique setting of this historic papal retreat, perched above the stunning Lake Albano, adds an extra layer of magic to the festivities.

Significance of the Festival

The Sagre delle Pesche is more than just a food festival; it's a celebration of Castel Gandolfo's identity:

Agricultural Heritage: It highlights the importance of peach cultivation in the local economy and culture.

Papal Connection: The offering to the Pope underscores the town's unique status as a papal retreat.

Community Cohesion: The festival brings together locals and visitors, strengthening community bonds.

Cultural Preservation: Through traditional costumes and ceremonies, it helps preserve local customs and history.

Tourism: As one of the town's major events, it attracts visitors, boosting the local economy.

The Sagre delle Pesche embodies the spirit of Castel Gandolfo, blending its agricultural roots, spiritual significance, and vibrant community life into a joyous celebration that captivates all who attend.

Walking Tour of Castel Gandolfo

#1. Papal Palace (Palazzo Apostolico)

The tour begins at the crown jewel of Castel Gandolfo, the Papal Palace. Known formally as the Apostolic Palace of Castel Gandolfo, this grand residence served as the summer retreat for the Pope from the 17th century until Pope Francis opened it to the public in 2016.

Construction began in 1624 under Pope Urban VIII atop the ruins of the Savelli family castle. Designed by Carlo Maderno and completed in 1629, the palace showcases a refined blend of Renaissance and Baroque architecture. Its clean white and yellow façade, arched windows, and balustrade lined with statues give it a commanding presence above Lake Albano.

Over the centuries, popes expanded the complex. In the 1930s, Pope Pius XI added a villa and working farms to make it more self-sufficient. Today the palace spans 55 hectares, even larger than Vatican City. Its many rooms, though not officially counted, include the Pope's private chapel, bedroom, study, and library, as well as grand reception halls, staff quarters, and museum galleries now open to visitors.

More than a historic residence, the Papal Palace is a living monument to the legacy of the papacy, offering a rare glimpse into the private, political, and spiritual worlds of those who once lived here.

The palace reveals its splendor through remarkable spaces, each reflecting its layered history. Visitors are greeted by frescoes of alpine landscapes in the Swiss Hall, which pays tribute to the Swiss Guard's service. The grand Throne Room, once used to receive diplomats and religious leaders, reflects its role in international affairs. In contrast, the Papal Chapel offers a quiet space for private worship, while the Papal Bedroom, with its lakefront balcony, brings you closer to the human side of papal life.

Outside, the Barberini Gardens stretch across 30 hectares, blending formal landscaping with the ruins of Emperor Domitian's villa, a harmonious mix of nature, history, and faith. The palace also includes the Vatican Observatory, founded by Pope Leo XIII in 1891, and a farm that provides fresh produce to the Vatican. The private train station, built under Pius XI in the 1930s, now occasionally welcomes public visitors thanks to Pope Francis.

Standing before this extraordinary complex, you encounter more than architectural beauty. You are witnessing centuries of devotion, diplomacy, and cultural legacy in one unforgettable place.

#2. Church of St. Thomas of Villanova

Just a short walk through the winding streets of Castel Gandolfo leads to the Church of St. Thomas of Villanova, a stunning work by Gian Lorenzo Bernini, the master of Roman Baroque architecture. Built between 1658 and 1661 under Pope Alexander VII, the church features a graceful dome that defines the town's skyline and a perfectly balanced facade that blends classical harmony with Baroque drama.

Inside, the church follows a Greek cross plan and reveals Bernini's flair for theatrical beauty. Visitors are greeted by an impressive main altar with a painting of St. Thomas of Villanova, intricate ceiling frescoes, richly decorated side chapels, and marble craftsmanship that reflects the grandeur of the era.

Still serving as the main parish church, it has welcomed popes for centuries during their summer retreats at the nearby Papal Palace. For the best experience, visit in the morning when soft light filters through the dome and the church is peaceful.

#3. Piazza della Libertà

From the church, we'll walk to the main square of Castel Gandolfo, Piazza della Libertà.

This charming square is the heart of the town's social life. Here, you can find cafes, restaurants, and shops. It's an excellent place to pause for a coffee or gelato and watch local life unfold.

#4. Belvedere (Viewpoint)

Just off the square, you'll find a scenic viewpoint offering breathtaking views over Lake Albano. This is a perfect spot for photos and for appreciating the natural beauty of the area.

Lago di Albano from Castel Gandolfo

#5. Porta Romana

Next, we'll walk to Porta Romana, one of the main gates of the old town walls.

This 17th-century gate marks the entrance to the historic center of Castel Gandolfo. It's adorned with the coat of arms of Pope Alexander VII, who had it built.

#6. Villa Barberini Gardens

If open to the public (check current access), we'll visit the Villa Barberini Gardens.

Part of the Papal Palace complex, these gardens offer a mix of manicured lawns, flower beds, and ancient Roman ruins. The ruins are part of Emperor Domitian's villa, dating back to the 1st century AD.

Logistics

Train: Castel Gandolfo is easily accessible by train from Rome. Direct connections to Castel Gandolfo are available from the Roma Termini station.

The journey takes about 45 minutes, with the Roma-Velletri line being the most common route. The Castel Gandolfo station is a short 10-minute walk to the town center and the Papal Palace.

Bus: COTRAL buses run frequently from Anagnina metro station (Rome, Line A) to Castel Gandolfo. The trip takes around 50 minutes and offers scenic views as you head towards the Alban Hills.

Car: Castel Gandolfo is roughly 25 kilometers from Rome, with a drive taking about 45 minutes depending on traffic. Take the Via Appia Nuova (SS7) heading south and follow the signs towards the Castelli Romani.

Parking: Parcheggio Belvedere Giovanni XXIII: A parking facility at Belvedere Giovanni XXIII, offering scenic views and proximity to local attractions.

Restaurant Recommendations

Antico Ristorante Pagnanelli dal 1882. Address: Via A. Gramsci 4

Established in 1882, Antico Ristorante Pagnanelli offers a refined dining experience with breathtaking views of Lake Albano. The menu features elegantly presented Italian dishes, including fresh seafood and classic meat options, all complemented by an extensive wine cellar housed in ancient caves beneath the restaurant.

Ristorante Bucci. Address: Via De Zecchini, 31

In the historic center of Castel Gandolfo, Ristorante Bucci specializes in traditional Roman cuisine served in a warm and inviting atmosphere. Guests can enjoy home-cooked specialties on the terrace overlooking Lake Albano, making it a favorite spot for both locals and visitors.

Accommodation

Overnight stays are unnecessary for sagre (food festivals) but the area is beautiful so I would recommend two to four nights in town.

Hotel Castel Gandolfo. Address: Via de Zecchini, 27

Nestled in the heart of Castel Gandolfo, the 4-star Hotel Castel Vecchio is a refined Liberty-style building offering panoramic views of Lake Albano. The hotel features 44 elegantly furnished rooms equipped with modern comforts, two restaurants serving exquisite cuisine, meeting rooms for business gatherings, and a splendid roof garden with an outdoor swimming pool. Guests can also enjoy the convenience of a private parking, subject to availability. The historic center of Castel Gandolfo is just 500 meters away, allowing easy access to local attractions and the Papal Palace.

Day Trip Options: Nearby Sites, Cities, and Towns

Cerveteri. 65 kilometers (40 miles). Immerse yourself in Etruscan history at this UNESCO World Heritage Site. The Banditaccia Necropolis, with its thousands of tombs, offers a fascinating look into ancient burial practices.

Orvieto. 130 kilometers (81 miles). Experience this stunning hill town in Umbria, known for its magnificent cathedral and underground cave network. Highlights include the Orvieto Cathedral, St. Patrick's Well, and the underground city tour.

Gaeta. 140 kilometers (87 miles). Enjoy this coastal town's mix of beaches, history, and beautiful scenery. Key attractions include the Montagna Spaccata (Split Mountain), the medieval old town, and pristine beaches.

Sabine Hills. 80 kilometers (50 miles). Explore this rural area known for its olive oil production and medieval hill towns. Visit the historic Farfa Abbey and charming towns like Fara in Sabina and Poggio Mirteto.

Castel Gandolfo Festivals Throughout the Year

Palio del Drago (Boat Race)

June

The Palio del Drago, established in 2003, is a thrilling boat race held among the towns of the Castelli Romani. This summer event takes place on Lake Albano, showcasing the competitive spirit of the region. Beyond the excitement of the race, visitors can enjoy a food fair on the lake's banks, featuring typical and homemade products from Castel Gandolfo. It's a perfect blend of sport, culinary delights, and local culture.

Mercatino Profumo di Antico per le vie del Borgo (Antique Fair)

Last Sunday of each month

On the last Sunday of every month, Castel Gandolfo's town center transforms into a treasure trove for antique enthusiasts and collectors. The Mercatino Profumo di Antico per le vie del Borgo features stalls selling antiques, collector's items, second-hand goods, handicrafts, and unique objects. This regular event adds a touch of nostalgia and charm to the town's calendar, attracting both locals and visitors looking for special finds.

Festa del Santo Patrono (Patron Saint's Day)

First Sunday of September

The Festa del Santo Patrono honors St. Sebastian, Castel Gandolfo's patron saint, on the first Sunday of September. This traditional celebration includes a solemn procession through the town, accompanied by music and various cultural events. The day culminates in a spectacular fireworks display, lighting up the night sky over Lake Albano. It's a day of spiritual significance, community bonding, and joyous festivities.

CHAPTER TWENTY-ONE

Summer Snowfall: Rome's Miraculous Feast

Honoring the Basilica di Santa Maria Maggiore

Festa della Madonna della Neve

Where: Rome, Basilica di Santa Maria Maggiore

When: August 5

Average Festival Temperatures: Highs 31°C (88°F). Lows 19°C (66°F).

Festival of Our Lady of the Snows

On August 5th each year, Rome witnesses a unique spectacle that blends faith, history, and legend. The Feast of Our Lady of the Snows (Festa della Madonna della Neve) at the Basilica of Santa Maria Maggiore commemorates a miraculous summer snowfall that occurred over 1600 years ago. This celebration offers visitors a chance to experience a beautiful tradition that has captivated Romans and pilgrims alike for centuries.

The festival commemorates a legendary miraculous snowfall that occurred on August 5th, 352 AD, at the height of summer. According to tradition, a wealthy Roman couple, John and his wife, prayed for guidance on how to use their fortune. The Virgin Mary appeared to them in a dream, instructing them to build a church on the site where snow would fall the next day.

To everyone's astonishment, snow fell on the Esquiline Hill on August 5th, outlining the perimeter of the future church. It is said that Pope Liberius marked the outlined the church, then construction began. This event is considered the foundation miracle of Santa Maria Maggiore, one of Rome's four major papal basilicas.

Timeline of Events

10:00 a.m.

Morning Mass

A solemn Mass celebrated by a high-ranking church official, often the Pope's vicar for Rome.

2:00 - 6:00 p.m.

Afternoon Prayers and Reflections

Various prayer services and reflections are held throughout the afternoon.

9:00 p.m.

"Snowfall" Ceremony

The highlight of the day, featuring an artificial "snowfall" of white rose petals both inside and outside the basilica. Tickets are not needed to attend the event, but it is best to arrive early.

10:00 p.m.

Evening Procession

A procession carrying an icon or statue of the Virgin Mary through the surrounding streets.

The "Snowfall" Ceremony: A Closer Look

The evening "snowfall" celebration is the most anticipated event of the feast. As darkness falls, the basilica and the area surrounding the piazza are illuminated with special lighting. At precisely 9:00 p.m., white rose petals begin to fall from the ceiling inside the basilica and from a raised platform outside in the piazza.

The petals descend slowly, creating the illusion of gently falling snow. This visual spectacle is accompanied by music and hymns, creating a truly magical atmosphere. The ritual lasts about 20 minutes, during which the interior of the basilica and the piazza are carpeted with a layer of white petals.

This re-enactment is not just a beautiful sight, but a powerful symbol of the miracle that led to the basilica's construction. Witnessing it brings wonder and serves as a reminder of the legend.

Local Customs and Traditions

- **Flower Offerings**: Many locals bring white flowers to the basilica as offerings to the Virgin Mary.

- **Candle Lighting:** It's customary for visitors to light candles in the basilica, offering prayers or intentions.

- **White Clothing:** Some attendees wear white clothing to symbolize the snow and the purity associated with the Virgin Mary.

- **Special Gelato:** Local gelaterias often offer special white-colored flavors on this day, such as fior di latte or white chocolate.

Historical Context of the Celebration

The Feast of Our Lady of the Snows has been celebrated at Santa Maria Maggiore for centuries. The first recorded "snowfall" re-enactment dates back to the 14th century, making it one of Rome's oldest continuing traditions.

The feast day is also significant because Santa Maria Maggiore houses several important relics, including pieces of wood said to be from Christ's manger. Relics displayed today add spiritual significance to the celebration.

In medieval times, the feast was marked by a grand procession from the Lateran Palace to Santa Maria Maggiore. Over the centuries, the celebration has evolved, with the "snowfall" ceremony becoming increasingly elaborate.

The Basilica

Santa Maria Maggiore stands as one of Rome's four major papal basilicas, its majestic presence dominating the Esquiline Hill. The church's architectural evolution spans nearly 1500 years, creating a harmonious blend of styles from Early Christian to Baroque. The imposing façade, added in the 18th century, features both Romanesque and Baroque elements, crowned by an elegant loggia that offers sweeping views of the piazza below.

Stepping inside, visitors are immediately struck by the basilica's remarkable 5th-century nave, where 36 marble and granite columns support walls adorned with some of the oldest Christian mosaics in Rome. These spectacular mosaics narrate Old Testament stories in vivid detail, from Abraham and Isaac to Moses and Joshua. Above the columns, the glittering triumphal arch presents scenes from Christ's early life, centered on the Annunciation and the Adoration of the Magi.

The church's crowning glory is its coffered ceiling, said to be gilded with the first gold brought from the Americas, a gift from Ferdinand and Isabella of Spain to Pope Alexander VI. Below this magnificent ceiling, the Borghese Chapel houses the famous icon of Salus Populi Romani, one of Rome's most venerated images of the Virgin Mary, believed to have been painted by St. Luke himself. In contrast, the Sistine Chapel (not to be confused with its Vatican namesake) houses the tombs of Popes Sixtus V and Pius V, its dome adorned with frescoes celebrating the Virgin Mary.

The basilica's most precious relic, displayed in the confessio beneath the high altar, is the crystal reliquary containing what tradition holds to be pieces of the Christ child's manger. During the Christmas season, these relics are displayed in an elaborate silver reliquary designed by Giuseppe Valadier, drawing pilgrims from around the world.

Walking Tour from Santa Maria Maggiore

Let me highlight some remarkable churches you won't want to miss during your walk through the area.

#1. Basilica di Santa Prassede

A short walk from Santa Maria Maggiore, Santa Prassede is a hidden gem known for its dazzling Byzantine mosaics. Built in the 9th century, it was commissioned by Pope Paschal I to honor Saint Praxedes, a Roman martyr. The mosaics in the apse and the Chapel of St. Zeno are extraordinary examples of medieval art, illustrating heavenly visions and biblical scenes. What to see:

- The Chapel of St. Zeno, also known as the "Garden of Paradise".

- Stunning mosaics depicting Christ, the Virgin Mary, and saints.

- The ancient well is said to have been used by Saint Praxedes to collect the blood of martyrs.

#2. Basilica di Santa Pudenziana

Located a short distance from Santa Prassede, Santa Pudenziana is one of the oldest churches in Rome, dating back to the 4th century. Dedicated to Saint Pudentiana, the sister of Saint Praxedes, the basilica sits on the site of an ancient Roman house church. Its mosaics, considered the oldest in Rome, depict Christ enthroned among the apostles in a Roman architectural setting, blending Christian and Roman iconography. What to see:

- The 4th-century mosaic in the apse, featuring Christ surrounded by apostles.

- The relics of Saint Pudenziana.

- Ancient Roman architectural elements incorporated into the structure.

#3. Church of San Martino ai Monti

Just a short walk from Santa Maria Maggiore, this ancient church, officially known as Santi Silvestro e Martino ai Monti, was built in the 4th century. It features early Christian and Baroque elements, with a richly decorated interior. The church also has an underground crypt with fascinating remains of earlier structures. Why visit:

- The stunning frescoes by 17th-century painter Pietro Testa.

- The underground crypt and remnants of an earlier basilica.

- The relics of Saints Silvester and Martin of Tours.

#4. Basilica di San Clemente al Laterano

Located on the way to San Pietro in Vincoli, San Clemente is a fascinating multi-layered site. The current 12th-century basilica sits atop a 4th-century church, which in turn was built over a 1st-century Roman house. Each layer unveils a chapter of Roman history, from early Christianity to Mithraic worship. Why visit:

- Magnificent 12th-century mosaics in the apse.

- The frescoes of Masolino da Panicale.

- The Mithraeum and ancient Roman house beneath the church.

#5. Arch of Gallienus

This lesser-known ancient Roman arch is a short detour from Santa Prassede. Originally part of a Roman city gate, it was repurposed in the 3rd century to honor Emperor Gallienus. Though simple, it is an interesting historical relic that adds depth to the tour. Look for:

- The inscription is dedicated to Emperor Gallienus.

- The preserved structure of the ancient Roman city gate.

#6. Basilica di San Pietro in Vincoli (St. Peter in Chains)

A slightly longer walk but worth the detour, San Pietro in Vincoli is renowned for housing the chains that held Saint Peter during his imprisonment. The basilica, built in the 5th century, also features Michelangelo's magnificent statue of Moses, part of the tomb of Pope Julius II. This church is a harmonious blend of art, history, and faith. What you will find:

- Michelangelo's Moses.

- The relics of St. Peter's chains, displayed under the main altar.

- Frescoes and statues are throughout the basilica.

Dining Recommendations in the Area:

- L'Angolo di Napoli (Pizza) Address: Via Agostino Depretis, 77. My favorite for delicious Neapolitan pizza, perfect for a quick and authentic lunch.

- Tosca Trattoria Pinseria Address: Via del Viminale, 31. Specializes in pinsa, an ancient Roman-style flatbread similar to pizza.

- The Gelatist Address: Via Nazionale, 19. Top-notch artisanal gelato, offering a variety of flavors.

Apse and Rear Facade of Santa Maria Maggiore

Accommodation

See Accommodation Detail chapter for Rome hotel information. I always recommend a minimum of four nights for any visit to Rome.

CHAPTER TWENTY-TWO

Festa Fusion Rome

The Assumption and Ferragosto: A Harmonious Blend of Faith and Festivity in Rome

FestaFusion Rome

#1 Festa dell'Assunta. A national holiday, this festival commemorates the moment when the Virgin Mary, mother of Jesus, was taken up, body and soul, into heaven.

#2 Ferragosto. Originating in 18 BC under Emperor Augustus as *Feriae Augusti*, this ancient Roman festival celebrated the harvest and honored the emperor with feasts, games, and public festivities.

#TuttoItalia - A festival throughout all of Italy, not just in Rome.

#FestaFusion means two or more festivals happen at around the same time in the same town, so visitors can enjoy multiple events during their visit.

Where: Rome, Basilica of Santa Maria in Trastevere

When: August 15

Average Festival Temperatures: High 31°C (88°F). Low 19°C (66°F).

#1. Feast of the Assumption: A Midsummer's Magic in Rome

On August 15th, Rome offers visitors an extraordinary treat - two celebrations woven into one vibrant tapestry. Imagine standing in the heart of Trastevere as church bells ring out across the city, marking both the sacred Feast of the Assumption and the joyous summer festival of Ferragosto. This unique fusion creates one of Rome's most captivating days, when ancient traditions blend seamlessly with modern celebrations.

The story begins centuries ago, when Emperor Augustus established Ferragosto in 18 BC as Feriae Augusti, a harvest celebration filled with feasts and public festivities. Over time, this pagan festival merged with the Catholic Feast of the Assumption - the celebration of the Virgin Mary's ascension into heaven. Today, this dual celebration transforms Rome, especially the historic neighborhood of Trastevere and its beautiful Basilica of Santa Maria.

Timeline of Events – Santa Maria Assunta

10:00 a.m.

The day begins at 10:00 a.m. with the Solemn Mass at the Basilica, forming the spiritual heart of the festival. This central celebration draws both local parishioners and pilgrims from afar, filling the ancient church with prayer and song beneath its gleaming golden mosaics.

2:00-4:00 p.m.

The afternoon hours from 2:00 to 4:00 p.m. are dedicated to contemplation and community, with successive prayer services and guided reflections taking place in different spaces throughout the basilica. These intimate gatherings allow participants to engage more deeply with the day's spiritual significance.

5:00 p.m.

As evening approaches, the Vespers service transitions into a traditional procession through the winding streets of Trastevere. Following these formal observances, the neighborhood transforms into a celebration of community spirit, with local families and visitors alike sharing in street performances, communal meals at neighborhood restaurants, and spontaneous gatherings that often continue well into the evening.

Local Customs and Traditions

Flower Offerings: Many locals bring flowers to the church as offerings to the Virgin Mary.

Family Gatherings: It's common for families to have large lunches or dinners together after the morning Mass.

Street Decorations: The streets of Trastevere are often decorated with lights and religious symbols.

Special Foods: Look out for 'pizza di Ferragosto', a traditional savory pie, and 'gelato al fior di latte', a popular ice cream flavor during this time.

The Procession: A Closer Look

The evening parade is a highlight of the celebrations. Starting from Santa Maria in Trastevere, it winds through the narrow alleys of the neighborhood. The route typically includes:

- Via della Lungaretta

- Piazza in Piscinula

- Via dei Genovesi

- Returning to the basilica on Via della Luce

The procession lasts about 1.5 hours. Participants carry a statue of the Virgin Mary, and the streets are lined with candles and flowers. Local confraternities, dressed in traditional robes, lead the march, followed by clergy and the faithful. The air is filled with hymns and prayers, creating a deeply moving experience.

#2. Ferragosto in Rome: A City Transformed

While many Romans leave the city during Ferragosto, those who stay - and visitors lucky enough to be here - discover a different side of Rome. The usually bustling streets take on a more relaxed pace, and the city reveals itself in a new light, offering a perfect blend of spiritual devotion and summer celebration. Whether you're drawn by religious significance, cultural curiosity, or simply the magic of a Roman summer evening, August 15th in Rome promises an unforgettable experience where sacred and secular traditions dance together under the Mediterranean sky.

Ferragosto Celebrations

Religious Observance

The religious aspect of Ferragosto centers on the Feast of the Assumption, marked by special masses and processions, particularly in Trastevere. The Church of Santa Maria in Trastevere is a focal point, with events highlighting the spiritual significance of the day.

Papal Events

The Pope gives a speech at 12 o'clock and prays the Angelus at St. Peter's Square, which is open to the public without a reservation.

Lungo il Tevere

This summer festival along the Tiber River is a Ferragosto highlight. Stroll through food stalls offering Roman and international cuisine, explore artisan markets, and enjoy live performances ranging from music to theater. The festival ambiance is perfect for both families and solo travelers.

Live Performances

Lungo il Tevere is known for its lively atmosphere, with various performances throughout the evening:

Music: From jazz to rock, you'll find a range of musical genres performed by both local bands and touring artists.

Theater and Dance: Enjoy theatrical productions and dance performances that add to the cultural richness of the festival.

Street Performers: Jugglers, magicians, and acrobats entertain all ages.

Ambiance and Atmosphere

The festival creates a festive and relaxed ambiance, perfect for an evening stroll. The Tiber River, illuminated by lights and lanterns, provides a picturesque backdrop for the festivities. Stalls line the pathways, and music and laughter echo.

Outdoor Markets and Food Stalls

Various markets pop up offering local produce, handmade crafts, and traditional Italian street food. It's a great opportunity to taste delicacies like gelato, arrosticini (grilled skewers), and porchetta (roast pork).

Gran Ballo di Ferragosto

On Ferragosto evening, various piazzas across Rome transform into open-air dance floors. Each square celebrates a distinct style of dance, salsa in one, waltz in another, allowing visitors to experience diverse rhythms and connect with locals in a joyous celebration.

Outdoor Cinema

Several parks in Rome, including Villa Borghese and Villa Ada, host open-air film screenings during Ferragosto evenings. With the backdrop of a Roman summer night, watching classic or contemporary films becomes an unforgettable experience.

CHAPTER TWENTY-THREE

FestaFusion Rocca Priora

Food, Faith, and Festivity

FestaFusion Rocca Priora

#1 Festa di San Rocco. A religious festival honoring Saint Rocco with processions, music, and community celebrations, deeply rooted in the traditions of Rocca Priora.

#2 Sagra della Bruschetta. A lively celebration of Rocca Priora's culinary heritage, featuring delicious bruschetta prepared with local bread, olive oil, and fresh toppings.

Where: Rocca Priora

When: August 16

Average Temperatures: High 31°C (88°F), Low 19°C (66°F).

#FestaFusion means two or more festivals happen at around the same time in the same town, so visitors can enjoy multiple events during their visit.

Rocca Priora: A Pinnacle of History and Tradition

Perched atop the Alban Hills, Rocca Priora stands as the highest town in the Castelli Romani, at an elevation of nearly 800 meters (2,625 feet). This lofty position once made it a crucial lookout point for ancient inhabitants, offering strategic advantages for monitoring the surrounding areas. Today, the town provides breathtaking panoramic views of the countryside, including the Roman Campagna and, on clear days, even glimpses of Rome.

Rocca Priora's deep-rooted agricultural traditions, particularly in olive cultivation and wine production, trace back to ancient Roman times.

Rocca Priora is located 30 kilometers (18 miles) southeast of Rome, making it a serene escape from the bustling capital. Nestled within the Castelli Romani Regional Park, it is surrounded by lush forests and rolling hills that contribute to its picturesque charm and unique ecosystem.

As of recent estimates, Rocca Priora has a population of 12,000 residents, maintaining its status as a small yet vibrant community within the Lazio region. The town's combination of natural beauty, historical significance, and traditional festivals makes it a notable destination in the Castelli Romani.

#1. Festa di San Rocco / Feast of Saint Roch

Who is San Rocco?

San Rocco, known as Saint Roch in English, was a Christian saint born in 1295 in Montpellier, France. He is venerated as the patron saint of the sick, particularly those suffering from infectious diseases, and is also associated with dogs.

According to tradition, San Rocco devoted his life to caring for plague victims across Italy. After contracting the disease himself, he retreated to a forest, where a dog miraculously brought him bread and tended to his wounds. He recovered and continued his mission until his death on August 16, 1327, which is now commemorated as his feast day.

History of the Festival

The Festa di San Rocco in Rocca Priora has deep historical roots, reflecting the town's enduring devotion to its patron saint. Celebrated annually on August 16th, the festival combines religious observance with communal festivities, fostering a sense of unity and cultural heritage among residents and visitors.

While the exact inception date of the festival is not precisely documented, it has been an integral part of the town's cultural and religious life for many centuries.

Festival Events

10:00 a.m.

Religious Procession: The day begins with a solemn procession through the streets of Rocca Priora, where the statue of San Rocco is carried by devotees, accompanied by prayers and hymns. This ritual symbolizes the town's reverence and seeks the saint's protection.

- Starting Point: The procession begins at the Parrocchia Maria Assunta in Cielo and winds its way through the vicoli del Centro Storico (the narrow streets of the historic center). The procession is a beautiful and solemn event, symbolizing the town's reverence for its patron saint and fostering a sense of community and shared heritage.

- Participants: The statue of San Rocco, along with his relic, is carried by devotees through the streets. The Banda Musicale Corbium accompanies the procession with hymns and prayers.

- Route: The procession covers various streets in the historic center of Rocca Priora, allowing residents and visitors to join and participate.

Food Trucks: Following the procession, various food stands are open, offering local delicacies and traditional dishes. This aspect of the festival celebrates the region's culinary heritage and provides an opportunity for communal dining.

Evening Entertainment: The festivities often continue into the evening with musical performances, comedy acts, and other entertainment, creating a lively atmosphere.

9:00 p.m.

Fireworks Display: The celebration typically concludes with a spectacular fireworks display, illuminating the night sky and marking the culmination of the day's events.

#2. Bruschetta Festival

The fertile volcanic soil of the Alban Hills made the area ideal for growing olives and vines, and these traditions have continued through the centuries. This agricultural heritage is celebrated annually with the Bruschetta Festival, which highlights the town's high-quality olive oil and its culinary significance.

Bruschetta is a traditional Italian appetizer consisting of grilled or toasted bread that is rubbed with garlic, drizzled with olive oil, and often topped with various ingredients. The most common and well-known version is topped with diced fresh tomatoes, basil, and a sprinkle of salt, making it a refreshing and flavorful dish.

Bruschetta originated as a way to make use of stale bread and showcase high-quality olive oil. The term comes from the Italian word "bruscare," which means "to toast" or "to char." While the tomato-topped variety is the most iconic, other regional variations include toppings like roasted vegetables, cheeses, cured meats, or even anchovies.

It's a simple yet versatile dish that highlights the freshness of its ingredients and is often served as a starter or snack.

History and Significance

The Sagra della Bruschetta pays homage to one of Italy's most beloved and simple dishes. Bruschetta, with its origins in ancient Rome, began as a clever way to make stale bread palatable. The festival, inaugurated in the 1970s, serves a dual purpose: showcasing Rocca Priora's exceptional olive oil and celebrating the town's rich agricultural heritage.

Bruschetta's history is intertwined with that of olive oil production in the region, a practice that has continued unbroken since Roman times. The festival highlights not only this historical continuity but also emphasizes the importance of traditional food preparation methods in Italian culture.

Events at the Sagra della Bruschetta

The Sagra della Bruschetta fills the streets with enticing aromas during the first half of August. The festivities begin with an opening ceremony on the first evening, where local dignitaries inaugurate the celebration amid the sounds of traditional music echoing through the medieval streets.

Throughout each day of the festival, the town center transforms into a culinary showcase, with vendors offering endless variations of bruschetta from morning until night. Expert cooks conduct regular demonstrations, revealing the secrets behind creating the perfect bruschetta while sharing traditional recipes and techniques passed down through generations. Running parallel to these demonstrations, olive oil exhibitions celebrate the region's liquid gold, with producers offering tastings and explaining the nuances of different varieties.

As daylight fades, the atmosphere shifts from culinary education to entertainment, with evening concerts featuring local and regional musicians filling the piazzas with music. The festival reaches its crescendo on the final evening with a grand community dinner that brings together residents and visitors alike, culminating in a spectacular fireworks display that illuminates the town's historic skyline.

Bruschetta Tastings: The festival's centerpiece, offering a wide variety of bruschetta, from traditional to innovative recipes.

Olive Oil Exhibitions and Tastings: Local producers showcase their extra virgin olive oils, offering samples and sales.

Cooking Demonstrations: Chefs and local cooks share bruschetta-making techniques and tips.

Live Music and Dance: Folk music performances and traditional dances enliven the town's main square.

Street Performances: Jugglers and other entertainers add to the festive atmosphere.

Historical Reenactments: Showcasing the town's medieval past and the history of olive cultivation in the region.

Local Customs and Traditions

- Bread Blessing: A local priest often blesses the bread used for bruschetta at the festival's opening.

- Olive Oil Pressing Demonstration: Using traditional methods to showcase the oil-making process.

- Bruschetta Competition: Locals compete to create the most innovative or delicious bruschetta recipe.

- Community Oven: A large communal oven is often used to toast bread for the festival.

It's a celebration of Italian culinary tradition, agricultural heritage, and community spirit. As you wander through the town's medieval streets, sampling delicious bruschetta and taking in panoramic views of the Alban Hills, you'll be taking part in a festival that encapsulates the essence of Italian food culture. Whether you're a food enthusiast, history buff, or simply looking for an authentic Italian experience, the Bruschetta Festival offers a delightful taste of Rocca Priora's charm and hospitality.

Walking Tour of Rocca Priora

#1. Piazza Zanardelli

This central square is the heart of Rocca Priora, offering breathtaking views of the surrounding valleys and hills. It's an excellent spot to start your exploration and enjoy the tranquil ambiance of the town. The piazza often hosts local events and markets, making it a lively gathering place for residents and visitors alike.

#2. Historical Center

Wander through the narrow cobblestone streets of Rocca Priora's historic center, lined with charming homes adorned with colorful flower pots. The area is dotted with local shops, cafes, and artisan boutiques, where you can experience the town's unique character and warmth.

#3. Chiesa di Santa Maria Assunta in Cielo

Dating back to the 13th century, this medieval church is a must-see for history and architecture enthusiasts. Its simple yet elegant facade gives way to a richly adorned interior, showcasing frescoes and religious artifacts that speak to Rocca Priora's spiritual heritage. The church remains a central point for the town's religious celebrations and festivals.

#4. Quaint Squares

As you navigate the historic center, you'll encounter several small, picturesque squares, such as Piazza della Madonna della Neve. These squares provide perfect opportunities to pause, admire the surroundings, and take in the slow pace of life that defines Rocca Priora.

#5. Rocca Priora Castle (Rocca Savelli)

The castle's strategic importance made it a frequent target during medieval conflicts, leading to several significant sieges and battles throughout its history. One of the most notable confrontations occurred in 1436 when tensions erupted between the Savelli family and Pope Eugene IV, resulting in substantial damage to the fortress. The castle suffered further destruction during the regional wars of 1484, though its sturdy construction allowed it to maintain its defensive capabilities. Throughout the 15th and 16th centuries, the fortress played a crucial role in the ongoing power struggles between noble Roman families, serving as both a military stronghold and a symbol of political authority in the region.

Visitors today can still appreciate several well-preserved elements of the original structure that offer insights into its medieval architecture and defensive design. The remaining portions of the defensive walls showcase the impressive engineering capabilities of medieval builders, while the base of the main tower stands as a testament to the fortress's once-imposing presence. Carefully restored medieval stonework allows visitors to observe authentic construction techniques, while architectural details throughout the site reveal different phases of construction and modification over the centuries. The surviving remnants of the castle's residential quarters provide glimpses into the daily life of its noble inhabitants.

From its commanding position, the castle site rewards visitors with breathtaking panoramic views that demonstrate why this location was so strategically valuable. The sprawling Roman countryside stretches out below, creating a stunning vista that encompasses both historical and modern landscapes. The peaks of the Alban Hills, including the prominent Monte Cavo, dominate the horizon and showcase the region's volcanic history. On particularly clear days, visitors can catch glimpses of the Mediterranean Sea in the distance, while the modern town of Rocca Priora spreads out below, offering a striking contrast between medieval and contemporary architecture.

#6. Olive Groves

Just a short walk from the town center, these nearby olive groves offer a glimpse into Rocca Priora's agricultural heritage. The groves have been cultivated for centuries, producing high-quality olive oil that is a staple of local cuisine. This peaceful detour allows visitors to connect with the town's deep-rooted traditions and natural beauty.

Logistics

Train: The closest train stations are in Frascati and Colleferro, both offering regular services to Rome's Termini Station. From either of these towns, a local bus or taxi will take you to Rocca Priora. The train journey from Rome to Frascati takes about 30 minutes.

Bus: Direct bus routes from Rome's Anagnina Metro Station (on Line A) to Rocca Priora are available and take about 40-50 minutes.

Car: Located 40 kilometers (25 miles) from Rome, Rocca Priora is accessible by either the Via Tuscolana or the A1 motorway.

Parking: Parking is available throughout town, including Via Roma, 28. The public parking area is at: Piazza Umberto I.

Restaurant Recommendations

La Taverna di Bacco. Piazza Umberto I, 14

In the heart of Rocca Priora, this cozy eatery is renowned for its variety of bruschetta, available year-round with toppings that showcase the region's fresh produce and flavors. La Taverna di Bacco also offers other local favorites, including hearty pasta dishes and grilled meats. The outdoor seating in Piazza Umberto I provides a delightful spot to enjoy a meal while soaking in the town's historic charm.

Accommodations

Normally for a festival I say a minimum of two nights in town. Rocca Priora has some hotels, but none that I can recommend.

Day Trip Options: Nearby Sites, Cities, and Towns

Monte Compatri. Monte Compatri, located 5 kilometers (3.1 miles) from Rocca Priora, has a rich history dating back to ancient times. The town originated on a hill believed to have been the site of the ancient pre-Roman city of Labicum. Over the centuries, it has been a fief of various noble families, including the Counts of Tusculum, the Annibaldi, the Altemps, and the Borghese. The Borghese family, in particular, played a significant role in the town's development, turning it into a summer residence and a center of classical art.

One notable site is the Monastero di San Silvestro, a hermitage perched on the hill that offers a peaceful retreat and stunning views of the surrounding countryside. The Church of Santa Maria Assunta in Cielo, built between 1630 and 1633, features beautiful frescoes and a historic campanile that adds to the town's charm. The Palazzo Borghese, originally built by Cardinal Scipione Borghese and now serving as the town hall, showcases Monte Compatri's architectural heritage. Visitors should also explore the underground cellars carved into the tuff rock, which are open to the public during special events, particularly around Christmas.

Tusculum. Tusculum, about 8 kilometers (5 miles) from Rocca Priora, was once one of the most important cities of the Latin League and later became a favored summer retreat for Roman emperors, senators, and writers. Although the city was destroyed in 1191, it remains a significant archaeological site that continues to reveal the grandeur of ancient Roman life.

Among the ruins is the Roman Theatre, built around 75 BC, which is remarkably well preserved and offers insight into the entertainment of the period. Outside the city walls lies the Roman Amphitheatre, partially concealed by vegetation but still visible and evocative of Tusculum's past. The forum, at the heart of the ancient city, contains ruins of important public buildings and offers a window into the daily life of its Roman inhabitants. The Via dei Sepolcri, an ancient road that once connected the residential area to the amphitheater, can still be seen in some sections and provides a tangible link to the past.

Rocca Priora Festivals Throughout the Year

Festa di Sant'Antonio Abate (St. Anthony Abbot)

January 17

This festival honors the patron saint of animals. Locals bring their pets to the church for a special blessing. The event often includes a parade of farm animals, traditional bonfires (falò), and the distribution of panini benedetti (blessed bread rolls).

Sagra dello Scottone (Cheese Festival)

Late January

Coinciding with the close of the St. Antonio Abate festival, this event celebrates "Scottone," a local ricotta cheese made by boiling milk twice. The hot ricotta is served in earthenware bowls, often paired with local honey or chestnut jam. The festival also features demonstrations of traditional cheese-making techniques.

Carnevale Rocchiciano

February

Rocca Priora's carnival celebration features colorful parades with elaborate floats and costumed performers. Street parties, mask-making workshops for children, and traditional sweet treats like frappe and castagnole are all part of the festivities.

Festa Madonna della Neve

Late July / Early August

This unique religious festival commemorates a miraculous summer snowfall in 352 AD. It includes a solemn procession with the statue of the Madonna, followed by the children's song concert "Bimbincanto". The highlight is an artificial snowfall in the town square, creating a magical summer "winter wonderland" experience.

"Ti presento il Galletto" (Sagra del Fungo Porcino -Porcini Mushroom Festival)

September

This chanterelle mushroom festival, organized by the local Cultural Association "Amici del Fungo Galletto," celebrates the delicate flavors of this prized fungus. Visitors can enjoy mushroom-themed menus, attend cooking classes, and purchase fresh chanterelles. The event also features music performances, artisanal craft stalls, and educational talks on sustainable foraging practices.

Fall Celebrations

September through October

CHAPTER TWENTY-FOUR

The Macchina di Santa Rosa in Viterbo

A Spectacular Night of Faith, Fire, and Human Strength

Macchina di Santa Rosa

Where: Viterbo

When: September 3

Average Festival Temperatures: High 25°C (77°F). Low: 12°C (55°F).

Website: http://www.macchinadisantarosa.viterbo.it/

Viterbo: The City of Popes

In the northern part of the Lazio region, Viterbo is a city steeped in history and medieval charm. Known as the City of Popes, it served as the papal seat during the 13th century and continues to captivate visitors with its well-preserved medieval architecture, cultural events, and thermal springs.

Viterbo lies 80 kilometers (50 miles) north of Rome and sits at an altitude of about 326 meters (1,070 feet) above sea level. Nestled in the Cimini Hills, the city enjoys a picturesque setting surrounded by lush forests, olive groves, and vineyards. Its strategic location historically made it a hub for travelers moving between Rome and Tuscany.

Viterbo's origins date back to Etruscan times, though its prominence grew during the Roman era when it became a vital stop on the Via Cassia. By the Middle Ages, Viterbo rose to prominence as a fortified city under the control of the Papal States. In the 13th century, Viterbo became the residence of several popes, earning its nickname as the City of Popes. The Palazzo dei Papi (Palace of the Popes) remains a symbol of this era, where important ecclesiastical councils and the first-ever papal conclave were held.

Viterbo also played a significant role during the Renaissance, with noble families commissioning elegant palaces and artworks. The city later endured damage during World War II but kept much of its medieval core. Viterbo has a population of 65,000 residents, giving it a lively yet relaxed small-town atmosphere. The city blends its rich history with modern amenities, offering a vibrant cultural scene, bustling markets, and a variety of dining and shopping options.

The Macchina, A Towering Tradition in Viterbo

In the heart of ancient Viterbo, as September's evening shadows lengthen, an extraordinary spectacle unfolds that has captivated audiences for centuries. Rising an astounding thirty meters into the night sky taller than a three-story building the Macchina di Santa Rosa illuminates the medieval streets with thousands of twinkling lights and dancing flames, creating a mesmerizing tower of light that seems to float through the darkness.

Who is Santa Rosa?

The Macchina di Santa Rosa is a centuries-old religious festival dedicated to Santa Rosa, the patron saint of Viterbo. Born in 1233, Santa Rosa devoted her brief life to prayer, charity, and aiding the poor. Following her death in 1251, she was canonized by popular acclaim. Her remains were interred in the Sanctuary of Santa Rosa, where they continue to be venerated.

La Macchina di Santa Rosa

History of the Festival

The origins of the festival date back to the 13th century when, in 1258, Pope Alexander IV ordered the transfer of her relics to a safer location within Viterbo's walls. To mark the occasion, a grand procession was held, inspiring the tradition of carrying an illuminated structure, known as the *Macchina*, through the streets in her honor. Over the years, this structure strengthened into a towering, intricate tower adorned with lights, sculptures, and religious imagery.

In 2013, the Macchina di Santa Rosa was recognized by UNESCO as an Intangible Cultural Heritage of Humanity, cementing its status as a symbol of Viterbo's faith, tradition, and community spirit.

Festival Events

The Macchina di Santa Rosa festival unfolds over several days, culminating in the spectacular procession on the evening of September 3rd.

September 1st–2nd: Preparatory Events

In the days leading up to the main event, Viterbo comes alive with religious services, public events, and cultural performances. The Facchini di Santa Rosa, the 100 men who carry the Macchina, undergo blessings and final preparations. The city is adorned with festive lights, banners, and decorations.

September 2

In the afternoon, the celebration begins with a solemn procession carrying a silver reliquary that contains the heart of Santa Rosa. This reliquary, a gift from Pope Pius XI in 1929, is normally housed in the Monastery of Santa Rosa in Viterbo. As it is carried through the city, people dressed in period costumes from the 14th to the 19th centuries accompany it, adding to the historical and religious significance of the event.

September 3rd: The Procession of the Macchina

8:00 p.m.

On September 3rd each year, a breathtaking display of human strength and devotion takes place as 100 chosen men, known as the Facchini, shoulder this five-ton masterpiece through Viterbo's historic center. These bearers, selected for their extraordinary strength and unwavering coordination, carry this towering tribute to Santa Rosa along torch-lit streets lined with ancient stones that have witnessed this tradition for generations.

9:00 p.m.

The procession begins at Piazza San Sisto, where the magnificent structure has been meticulously assembled over the preceding weeks. As darkness falls, the Macchina comes alive with a brilliant combination of electric lights and open flames, transforming into a beacon of faith and tradition that draws thousands of spectators from across the globe.

The kilometer-long journey through Viterbo's historic center is marked by five ceremonial stops, each a moment of intense anticipation and collective breath-holding:

1. The ancient Fontana Grande, where water has flowed since medieval times

2. The majestic Piazza del Plebiscito, before the watchful eyes of the Town Hall

3. The bustling Piazza delle Erbe, alive with the energy of countless past celebrations

4. The solemn pause before the Church of Suffragio on Corso Italia

5. The grand finale at Piazza Verdi, where history and present day merge in celebration

---

Festival Foods

The Macchina di Santa Rosa is not just a spiritual and cultural event, but also an opportunity to celebrate Viterbo's culinary traditions. Special festival foods include:

Frittelle di Santa Rosa: These sweet fritters are made in honor of the saint. Lightly fried and dusted with sugar, they are a favorite among locals and visitors during the festival.

Tozzetti with Hazelnuts: A type of biscotti crafted with local hazelnuts, reflecting the region's agricultural heritage. These are often enjoyed with *Vinsanto*, a sweet dessert wine.

Porchetta Sandwiches: While not exclusive to this festival, porchetta (roast pork) is a popular street food during the celebrations. Vendors set up stalls throughout the city, offering savory options to hungry festival-goers.

This feat of engineering, artistry, and human determination culminates at the Sanctuary of Santa Rosa, where the illuminated tower stands as a testament to Viterbo's enduring spirit. Every five years, a new design is commissioned, ensuring that each generation adds its own chapter to this living tradition.

The Macchina di Santa Rosa is more than just a procession; it's a symphony of light and shadow, strength and grace, faith and community. As the tower moves through the narrow streets, the cheers of the crowd blend with ancient chants, creating an atmosphere that transforms a September night into an unforgettable celebration of Viterbo's cultural heritage. This UNESCO-recognized spectacle continues to enchant visitors and locals alike, proving that some traditions don't just survive through time; they thrive and become more magical with each passing year.

Viterbo Walking Tours

Viterbo Walking Tour Day One

#1. Palazzo dei Papi (Papal Palace)

The Palazzo dei Papi stands as the crown jewel of Viterbo, and I never tire of watching visitors' faces when they first encounter this magnificent structure. Constructed in the 1200s, this palace is significant because of its connection to interesting moments in the Catholic Church's past.

Picture this: it's 1257, and Pope Alexander IV has fled Rome due to political unrest. He chose Viterbo as his haven, beginning what would become a remarkable period in the city's history. For over two decades (1257-1281), the palace served as the heart of the Catholic Church, hosting five different popes and becoming the site of the first papal conclave in history.

The architecture tells its own story of power and beauty. The palace's most striking feature is its elegant covered gallery, known as a loggia, supported by seven delicate arches that seem to float above the Piazza San Lorenzo. Look closely at the columns they're actually spolia (repurposed materials) from an ancient Roman temple, a common medieval practice that literally built new power on old foundations. This stunning loggia became the blueprint for many civic buildings throughout Italy.

Inside, you'll find the Aula del Conclave, where the term "conclave" was born. After the death of Pope Clement IV in 1268, the cardinals took so long to elect a new pope that the city's residents eventually locked them in and reduced their food to bread and water to speed up the decision! The result was the election of

Pope Gregory X after nearly three years and the establishment of strict rules for future papal elections.

Don't miss the Sala del Trono (Throne Room), with its impressive curved stone bench where cardinals once sat during consistories, formal meetings of the College of Cardinals with the Pope. The Great Hall features original 13th-century floor tiles and remnants of medieval frescoes that hint at its former splendor.

#2. Cathedral of San Lorenzo and Bell Tower

Built on the site of an ancient Roman temple dedicated to Hercules, this Romanesque cathedral was constructed by Lombard architects. It was later rebuilt in the 16th century but sustained significant damage during World War II. The 14th-century Gothic bell tower showcases Sienese influence. Inside, visitors can admire the sarcophagus of Pope John XXI and the masterpiece *Christ Blessing* (1472) by Girolamo da Cremona.

#3. San Pellegrino Quarter

Explore the medieval heart of Viterbo, known for its abundance of profferli, external staircases typical of the region's medieval architecture. Stroll through its narrow cobblestone streets, admire the well-preserved buildings, and soak in the ambiance of one of Italy's best-preserved medieval quarters.

#4. Fontana Grande

This medieval fountain, constructed in 1206, is one of the oldest and most significant public fountains in Viterbo. Its design reflects the town's rich history and is a popular spot for photos and relaxation.

#5. Sanctuary of Santa Rosa

Dedicated to Viterbo's patron saint, Santa Rosa, this church is a reconstruction from the 19th century. Each year, it becomes the focal point for the Macchina di Santa Rosa festival, during which a towering illuminated structure is paraded through the city.

Viterbo Walking Tour Day Two

#1. Museo Civico

The Museo Civico is an excellent starting point for understanding Viterbo's history. The museum houses archaeological artifacts from prehistoric to Roman times, as well as a Pinacoteca with works by renowned artists such as Sebastiano del Piombo and Salvator Rosa.

#2. Basilica di San Francesco (St. Francis)Built over a pre-existing Lombard fortress, this Gothic-style church features a Latin cross plan and a single nave. It houses the sepulcher of Pope Adrian V, considered to be the first monument by Arnolfo di Cambio.

#3. Piazza del Plebiscito and Civic Palaces

This central square is surrounded by important civic buildings, including the Palazzo Comunale, Palazzo del Podestà, and Palazzo della Prefettura. The frescoes inside the Palazzo Comunale, created by artists like Tarquinio Ligustri and Bartolomeo Cavarozzi, are worth seeing.

#4. Santa Maria Nuova Church

This Romanesque church, dating back to the 11th century, is one of Viterbo's oldest. Its simple yet elegant design reflects the architectural style of the period, and its serene atmosphere makes it a lovely spot to end your tour.

Logistics

Train. Viterbo Porta Romana or Viterbo Porta Fiorentina (two main stations in the city). Trains depart regularly from Roma Termini or Roma Tiburtina stations to Viterbo.

Bus. COTRAL buses provide direct connections from Saxa Rubra station in Rome to Viterbo. The journey takes approximately 1 hour and 40 minutes. Tickets can be purchased at the station or online. The bus terminus in Viterbo is near the city center, providing easy access to the festival sites.

Car: The drive from Rome to Viterbo is approximately 90 kilometers (56 miles) and takes about 1 hour and 30 minutes via the A1 Autostrada (Rome-Florence) and SS675 (Superstrada Orte-Viterbo). Follow the signs to Viterbo Centro. Note that the historic center has a ZTL (Zona a Traffico Limitato), and access is restricted to authorized vehicles.

Parking: For visitors driving to the festival, there are several parking options outside the ZTL:

- Parking Valle Faul. Near Porta Faul, just below the historic center. Large parking area with shuttle service or a short uphill walk to the city center.

- Parking Sacrario. Adjacent to Piazza del Sacrario. Underground parking facility with elevators leading to the city center.

- Parking Piazza della Rocca. Near Porta Fiorentina. Convenient for accessing the festival route.

- Parking Riello. Near the shopping area outside the historic center. Free parking with a slightly longer walk to the festival area or shuttle service during major events.

Restaurant Recommendations

Ristorante Taverna Etrusca. Address: Via Annio 8/10

In the heart of Viterbo's medieval quarter, Taverna Etrusca offers a cozy and authentic dining experience.

Il Richiastro. Address: Via della Marrocca 16/18

Nestled in the iconic San Pellegrino quarter, Il Richiastro combines history and fine dining in a charming medieval setting. The restaurant is housed in a historic building with stone walls and vaulted ceilings, offering a memorable atmosphere.

Accommodation

For the festival, I would recommend three to four nights in town.

Hotel Salus Terme. Address: Strada Tuscanese, 26/28

While slightly outside the immediate historic center, this 4-star hotel offers luxurious accommodations and a renowned spa. Ideal for visitors who want to combine festival excitement with relaxation, Hotel Salus Terme provides amenities such as thermal pools, wellness treatments, and fine dining. A short drive or taxi ride connects guests to the festival area and procession route.

Hotel Centrale. Address: Via del Corso, 2

This hotel is conveniently located near the historic center of Viterbo and offers comfortable accommodations. It's just a short walk from the procession route, making it an ideal choice for witnessing the festivities.

Hotel Tuscia Hotel. Address: Via della Repubblica, 1

Another excellent option, Hotel Tuscia is also close to the procession route. It provides modern amenities and a welcoming atmosphere, ensuring a pleasant stay during the festival.

Day Trips: Nearby Sites, Cities and Towns

Civita di Bagnoregio. 25 kilometers (15 miles) from Viterbo. Civita di Bagnoregio is a stunning hilltop village accessible only by a pedestrian bridge. Founded by the Etruscans more than 2,500 years ago, the town is renowned for its striking beauty, charming streets, and panoramic views of the surrounding valleys. Highlights include the Church of San Donato, quaint artisan shops, and the unique atmosphere of a town frozen in time. It's a perfect visit for history lovers and photographers.

Sutri. 20 kilometers (12 miles) from Viterbo. Sutri is a small town with an oversized history, featuring a well-preserved Roman amphitheater carved directly into the rock and an Etruscan necropolis. The Mitreo, a cave used as a Mithraic temple and later converted into a Christian church, is a fascinating site. Sutri's picturesque streets and historical significance make it an excellent half-day excursion.

Bagnaia and Villa Lante. Distance from Viterbo: 6 kilometers (4 miles). A quick trip from Viterbo, Bagnaia is home to Villa Lante, one of Italy's finest examples of Renaissance garden design. The villa features intricate fountains, terraces, and manicured gardens that reflect the era's emphasis on harmony and beauty. Pair your visit with a leisurely stroll through Bagnaia's charming historic center.

Montefiascone. Distance from Viterbo: 17 kilometers (10 miles). Famous for its Est! Est!! Est!!! wine, Montefiascone sits atop a hill overlooking Lake Bolsena. The town features the Rocca dei Papi, offering stunning views of the surrounding countryside, and the Church of San Flaviano, known for its unique architecture and connection to the legendary wine.

Viterbo Festivals and Sagre Throughout the Year

Sagra del Biscotto di Sant'Anselmo (Bomarzo)

April

This festival honors Bomarzo's patron saint, Sant'Anselmo, and features the traditional "biscotto," a sweet bread resembling a ciambella. The event includes the Palio di Sant'Anselmo, a historic horse race among the town's five districts, along with processions, historical reenactments, and the distribution of the biscotto to attendees.

Sagra dell'Asparago Verde (Canino)

Early April

This food festival showcases the locally grown green asparagus, known as "mangiatutto" for its entirely edible nature. The event features culinary stands offering asparagus-based dishes, live music, artisan markets, and activities like preparing a massive asparagus frittata, highlighting the town's agricultural traditions.

San Pellegrino in Fiore

Late April to Early May

This floral festival celebrates the arrival of spring and showcases the medieval quarter of San Pellegrino in vibrant flower displays. Dating back several decades, the festival is a modern celebration that highlights Viterbo's connection to nature and beauty. Visitors can enjoy walking tours through the decorated streets, with floral art installations created by local and international artists. The event also includes markets, performances, and cultural activities.

Ludika 1243

July

Ludika 1243 is a medieval reenactment festival held in the historic San Pellegrino district. It commemorates events from the year 1243, a time of political and social upheaval in Viterbo's history. Participants dress in period costumes, and the festival includes historical games, theater performances, and artisan markets. Visitors can immerse themselves in the medieval atmosphere, learning about the city's heritage while enjoying lively entertainment.

Wine Fair in Montefiascone (Fiera del Vino)

August

This wine festival, held in the nearby town of Montefiascone, celebrates the famous local wine, Est! Est!! Est!!! According to legend, a German bishop in the 12th century was so enamored by the wine that he exclaimed "Est! Est!! Est!!!" to describe its excellence. The event features wine tastings, food stalls, and parades, attracting wine lovers from all over Italy.

Chestnut Festival (Sagra della Castagna)

October

The chestnut harvest is celebrated in Viterbo and its surrounding areas with this festival, which features roasted chestnuts, traditional dishes, and local wines. The tradition of honoring the chestnut, a staple of the region's economy and cuisine, dates back centuries. Music, performances, and artisan markets create a festive atmosphere, while visitors can enjoy the culinary delights of the season.

Co-Patron Saints Festival: St. Ilario and St. Valentino

November 3

In Viterbo, the feast day of Saints Valentino and Ilario, the city's co-patrons, is observed annually on November 3rd. While this celebration is not as widely recognized as some of Viterbo's other festivals, it holds significant historical and religious importance for the local community.

Saints Valentino, a priest, and Ilario, a deacon, are venerated as martyrs by the Catholic Church. According to tradition, they played a pivotal role in converting the Viterbo area to Christianity during the early 4th century. Their missionary activities led to their arrest and execution in 303 AD during the Diocletian persecution. The site of their martyrdom is believed to be near an ancient Roman bridge called Camillario, located a few kilometers from Viterbo's current city walls. Their relics were initially moved to the Abbey of Farfa in the 9th century and later, in 1303, brought back to Viterbo, where they are now preserved.

The primary venue for the commemoration is the Church of Saints Valentino and Ilario in the Villanova district of Viterbo. The day's events typically include:

Solemn Mass: A Eucharistic celebration is held, often presided over by prominent clergy. For instance, in 2021, Cardinal Angelo Comastri, former Vicar General for Vatican City, led the mass, accompanied by the Bishop of Viterbo and other religious and civil authorities.

Processions and Liturgical Activities: The faithful take part in processions and other religious observances, reflecting on the lives and sacrifices of the saints.

Community Gatherings: The event fosters a sense of community, with parishioners and visitors coming together to honor the legacy of Saints Valentino and Ilario.

While the feast day may not attract large crowds or extensive festivities compared to other events in Viterbo, it remains a meaningful occasion for residents, particularly those in the Villanova neighborhood, to celebrate their spiritual heritage and the enduring legacy of their patron saints.

CHAPTER TWENTY-FIVE

Immersion Experience: The Thermal Baths of Viterbo

A Journey through History and Relaxation

Terme di Viterbo

The thermal baths of Viterbo, known as the Terme di Viterbo, offer a unique blend of ancient history and rejuvenating relaxation. These natural hot springs have been celebrated for their therapeutic properties since antiquity. The Etruscans were among the first to utilize these thermal waters, believing in their healing and spiritual benefits. Later, the Romans fully embraced the baths, incorporating them into their culture of public bathing and health. Roman aristocracy and even emperors visited the Viterbo baths, which were seen as places for both physical restoration and social gathering. The waters were praised by ancient authors, including Pliny the Elder, for their ability to treat ailments ranging from arthritis to skin conditions.

During the Middle Ages, the baths retained their popularity, with legends connecting them to figures such as Saint Catherine of Siena, who is said to have used the thermal waters for meditation and healing. In the Renaissance, the baths were further developed under papal influence, particularly during the pontificate of Pope Nicholas V, who sought to revive their grandeur. Today, the thermal baths of Viterbo continue to attract visitors seeking relaxation and wellness amidst the historical backdrop of this charming medieval city.

What to Expect at the Terme di Viterbo

Visitors to the baths can enjoy modern spa facilities alongside the natural hot springs that have bubbled up for millennia. The Terme dei Papi, one of the most famous establishments, boasts a massive thermal pool fed by the Bullicame spring, mentioned by Dante in The Divine Comedy. The sulfur-rich waters, averaging around 58°C (136°F), are reputed to soothe muscles, improve circulation, and rejuvenate the skin.

In addition to the main pools, private grottoes and therapeutic treatments such as mud baths and massages are available, offering a truly immersive experience. Walking through these facilities, guests can feel the echoes of history, knowing they are partaking in a tradition cherished for centuries.

Making the Most of Your Visit

Spend a day indulging in the thermal baths, but also take time to explore the medieval town of Viterbo itself, known as the "City of Popes" for its historical significance. The town's well-preserved medieval quarters, such as San Pellegrino, provide a picturesque backdrop to your relaxation. Conclude your day with a meal at a local trattoria, savoring the flavors of Tuscia cuisine, including dishes like acquacotta or wild boar stew, to complete your immersive experience. Whether for history enthusiasts or wellness seekers, the thermal baths of Viterbo offer a captivating journey through time and tranquility.

Viterbo, renowned for its rich thermal heritage, offers several notable thermal bath locations where visitors can indulge in the healing properties of its natural hot springs. Here are some of the top thermal baths in the area:

Terme dei Papi: A luxurious spa complex featuring a monumental thermal pool fed by the Bullicame spring, offering therapeutic treatments such as mud baths and massage.

Website: termedeipapi.it

Il Bagnaccio: An open-air thermal area with both free and paid sections, featuring multiple pools of varying temperatures, set in a natural environment ideal for relaxation.

Piscine Carletti: A free-access thermal site with several pools of differing temperatures, popular among locals and travelers seeking a natural bathing experience. These outdoor thermal pools are about 2.5 kilometers (1 mile) from the center of Viterbo and are always open.

CHAPTER TWENTY-SIX

Pigging Out in Ariccia

A Celebration of Porchetta, Tradition, History, and Flavor in Lazio's Culinary Heart

S agra della Porchetta

Where: Ariccia

When: First weekend of September.

Average Festival Temperatures: High: 25°C (77°F). Low: 15°C (59°F).

Ancient Ariccia: A Religious and Strategic Hub

Ariccia is a historic town located 25 kilometers (15 miles) southeast of Rome in the Alban Hills, part of the Castelli Romani area. Nestled above a scenic valley and overlooking volcanic lakes and vineyards, it enjoys a picturesque position along the ancient Via Appia, the Roman road that connected the capital to southern Italy. With a population of approximately 18,000 residents, Ariccia retains a small-town feel while offering deep historical and cultural appeal.

The town flourished during the Roman Republic and Empire, benefiting from its position as a key stop for traders and pilgrims along the Via Appia. Its religious importance was amplified by its proximity to Lake Nemi and the Sanctuary of Diana Nemorensis, one of the most important centers of worship in ancient Italy. Devoted to the goddess Diana, the sanctuary drew countless pilgrims and inspired myths and rituals that shaped Roman religious life.

Ariccia's fortunes declined after the fall of the Roman Empire and during the early medieval period, but the seventeenth century brought a dramatic revival. The influential Chigi family, based in Rome, took control of the town and transformed it into a jewel of Baroque architecture. They commissioned Gian Lorenzo Bernini and Carlo Fontana to redesign Ariccia's urban core, resulting in a stunning ensemble of buildings that still define the town today. These include the Piazza di Corte, known for its harmonious layout; the Church of Santa Maria Assunta in Cielo, with its graceful dome; and the grand Palazzo Chigi, once the family's residence and now a museum filled with art and artifacts.

The Porchetta Festival

Ariccia comes alive each September with the sizzling aromas and festive atmosphere of the Sagra della Porchetta. This beloved festival celebrates the town's claim to fame: porchetta, a succulent, slow-roasted pork dish seasoned with herbs and garlic.

Ariccia is widely regarded as the birthplace of porchetta, a culinary tradition that traces its roots back to ancient Rome. This savory delicacy was a favorite among both emperors and commoners, solidifying its place in Italian gastronomic heritage. The Sagra della Porchetta, started in the 1950s, was conceived as a way to honor Ariccia's rich culinary heritage and its centuries-old custom of porchetta-making.

Over the decades, the event has grown from a community celebration into one of Italy's most renowned food festivals. It not only showcases the town's culinary prowess but also serves as a testament to the enduring appeal of traditional Italian cuisine. The event plays a crucial role in preserving age-old cooking techniques and recipes, passed down through generations of Ariccia's families.

The festival's significance extends beyond gastronomy. It serves as a cultural touchstone, bringing together locals and visitors in a celebration of regional identity. The Sagra della Porchetta has become a platform for Ariccia to showcase its Baroque architecture, historical sites, and the warm hospitality of its people, all while centered on the star of the show - the perfectly roasted porchetta.

Timeline of Events

Friday

On Friday evening, the festivities begin with an opening ceremony in Piazza di Corte, where local dignitaries give speeches and musicians perform. Traditional flag-wavers and a parade of the Bersaglieri, Italy's famed military corps, make their way through Piazza della Repubblica, setting the stage for the weekend.

Saturday

Morning: Start of porchetta tastings and opening of food stalls throughout the center.

Afternoon: Cooking demonstrations and competitions begin. Throughout the celebration, skilled local butchers demonstrate their mastery of knife work, showcasing the precise art of carving porchetta to appreciative crowds.

Evening: Live music performances and cultural dance shows.

Sunday

Sunday begins with a special Mass at the Church of Santa Maria Assunta in Cielo, blessing the celebration and honoring the town's traditions. Later in the afternoon, the most anticipated event takes place in Piazza della Repubblica: the porchetta panini launch. At 6:30 p.m., 3,000 sandwiches filled with freshly roasted porchetta are launched into the crowd, creating a joyful frenzy as people scramble to catch one.

The fun continues with a live music performance at 9 p.m. and the festival concludes with a spectacular fireworks display at midnight, lighting up the skies above Ariccia and bringing the weekend to a festive close.

Key Sagra Events

Porchetta Tastings: The heart of the festival, featuring various vendors offering their unique versions of porchetta.

Cooking Demonstrations: Master chefs showcase the art of preparing and roasting the perfect porchetta.

Porchetta-Making Contest: Producers compete for the title of best porchetta in Ariccia.

Wine Pairings: Tastings of local wines from the Castelli Romani region, perfectly complementing the rich flavors of porchetta.

Roman Food Stalls: Offering a variety of regional specialties beyond porchetta, such as supplì and carciofi alla giudia.

Live Music and Dance: Performances of traditional Roman songs and folk dances.

Historical Reenactments: Actors in period costumes showcase the ancient Roman origins of porchetta.

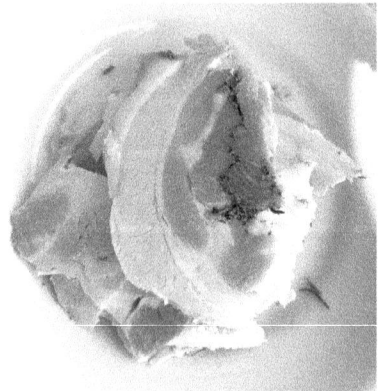

Porchetta in Ariccia

Whether you're a dedicated foodie or simply looking to enjoy the festive atmosphere, the Sagra della Porchetta offers a delicious slice of Italian culture that will leave you with lasting memories - and a very satisfied appetite.

Walking Tour of Ariccia

#1. Piazza di Corte

Start your walking tour at the heart of Ariccia in Piazza di Corte, designed by renowned Baroque architect Gian Lorenzo Bernini. This elegant square is surrounded by significant landmarks, including Palazzo Chigi and Santa Maria Assunta. Admire the architectural harmony of this central space.

#2. Palazzo Chigi

Right off Piazza di Corte, visit the Palazzo Chigi, a stunning Baroque palace that served as a residence for the Chigi family. The palace provides an engaging historical experience with its lavish rooms and a beautiful garden. It is also a filming location for several famous Italian films, making it culturally significant.

#3. Church of Santa Maria Assunta in Cielo

Across from the palace, the Church of Santa Maria Assunta is a Baroque masterpiece also designed by Bernini. Its symmetrical design and elegant façade make it a prominent feature of the. Inside, admire the beautifully crafted altars and paintings.

Collegiata di Santa Maria Assunta

#4. Parco Chigi

A short walk from the center, head to Parco Chigi, a lush park once part of the Chigi family estate. The park is filled with scenic walking paths, ancient oak trees, and lovely views of the surrounding countryside. It's the perfect spot for a peaceful stroll.

#5. Ponte di Ariccia

End your walking tour at the Ponte di Ariccia, an impressive bridge that connects Ariccia to neighboring towns. The bridge presents panoramic views of the Castelli Romani region and the countryside below. It's a glorious spot for photography and to appreciate the scale of this engineering marvel. Interestingly, the bridge was initially nicknamed the "Ponte del Suicidio" (Bridge of Suicide) because of its height and the tragic history of some individuals who jumped from it. Protective barriers were later added to prevent such incidents.

The bridge has undergone several restorations, especially after damage during World War II and a partial collapse in 1969. Today, it stands as a safe and picturesque spot, offering stunning views of Ariccia and its surrounding.

Logistics

Train: Take the train from Rome Termini to Albano Laziale (approximately 45 minutes), then transfer to a local bus or taxi for the short ride to Ariccia.

Bus: From Rome's Anagnina Metro Station, you can take a COTRAL bus directly to Ariccia. The journey takes about an hour, depending on the traffic.

Car: Ariccia is easily accessible by car, located 25 (15 miles) kilometers southeast of Rome.

Parking: Parking is available near the center. Parcheggio Bernini; A free parking lot located at Via del Pometo, 26. It provides convenient access to the town center via a nearby inclined elevator (funicular) that operates daily from 6:00 a.m. to 1:00 a.m., costing €1 per person each way.

Dining Recommendations

Osteria di Corte. Address: Via Dell'Uccelliera, 30

Near Piazza di Corte, this osteria offers a traditional menu with a focus on regional ingredients. Their famous porchetta is a must-try, alongside other classic Roman dishes. The cozy atmosphere and outdoor seating make it an excellent choice for a meal in the heart of Ariccia.

Osteria L'Ariccierola. Address: Via Borgo San Rocco, 9

Known for its exceptional porchetta and other regional specialties, L'Ariccierola is a popular spot for both locals and tourists. The menu allows visitors to experience the genuine flavors of Castelli Romani through roasted meats, pasta dishes, and a variety of antipasti.

Accommodation

Overnight stays are unnecessary for sagre, but here are some options in Ariccia.

Hotel California. Address: Via Appia Nuova, km 21

A 3-star hotel offering classic-style accommodations with air conditioning and free Wi-Fi. Guests appreciate its proximity to the town center and the availability of free parking.

Hotel Villa Aricia. Address: Via Appia Nuova, 1

Set in a historic villa surrounded by a park, this hotel provides elegant rooms and an on-site restaurant. It's conveniently near the town's principal attractions and offers free private parking.

Day Trip Options: Nearby Sites, Cities, and Towns

Palestrina: 30 kilometers (18.6 miles). Ancient Praeneste was one of the most powerful cities in Latium, and its crowning achievement was the massive Sanctuary of Fortuna Primigenia, built in the 2nd century BCE. This architectural marvel was one of the largest religious complexes in the ancient world, rising in a series of dramatic terraces up the hillside. The design influenced Renaissance architecture and continues to impress visitors today.

Calcata: 70 kilometers (43.5 miles) from Ariccia. This dramatic village, perched on an isolated cliff of volcanic rock, seems frozen in time. After being abandoned in the 1960s because of concerns about the stability of the cliff, it was gradually rediscovered by artists and craftspeople who transformed it into a unique creative community. The medieval architecture remains remarkably intact.

Thick stone walls, worn steps, and ancient doorways create an incredibly atmospheric setting. The narrow streets wind past artisan workshops, small galleries, and bohemian cafes. You'll find everything from traditional crafts to contemporary installations.

Ariccia Festivals and Sagre Throughout the Year

Festa di Santa Apollonia (Patron Saint's Day)

February 9th

This event honors St. Apollonia, the town's patron saint. A procession carries a golden statue of the saint through the streets of Ariccia, creating a spiritual and communal atmosphere throughout the town.

Festa della Madonna di Galloro

Pentecost (May/June)

This celebration, established in 1661 by Pope Alexander VII, takes place during Pentecost (May or June) and honors Mary's Immaculate Conception. In the evening, the statue is returned to the Sanctuary of Galloro.

The festival now features a lively market where handcrafted products are sold, as well as domestic animals like ducks, cows, and goats. The festivities conclude with a dazzling fireworks display.

Festa della Signorina

December 8th

Held in honor of the Immaculate Conception, this celebration commemorates the miracle attributed to the Virgin of Galloro, believed to have saved the people of Ariccia from the plague that affected neighboring towns. During the event, following a solemn procession, the statue of the Holy Mary is ceremoniously entrusted to one of the youngest girls in the city, continuing a beloved tradition.

CHAPTER TWENTY-SEVEN

Breaking Bread in Genzano di Roma

The Festa del Pane Experience

Festa Festa del Pane Casareccio IGP e Del Santo Padrono

Where: Genzano di Roma

When: Third Weekend in September incorporating St. Thomas' Feast day of September 22.

Average Festival Temperatures: High: 27°C (81°F). Low 15°C (59°F).

Event Website:

https://www.comune.genzanodiroma.roma.it/vivere-il-comune/eventi/festa-del-pane-casareccio-igp-di-genzano-di-roma-e-del-santo-patrono-2024

Genzano di Roma

Perched on the rim of an extinct volcano in the Alban Hills, Genzano di Roma has been perfecting the art of bread-making since the 16th century. The town's signature creation, Pane Casareccio di Genzano IGP is a testament to centuries of tradition. This rustic loaf is instantly recognizable by its dark, textured crust dusted with wheat flour and its soft, airy interior, a result of slow fermentation and baking in wood-fired ovens.

What makes Genzano's bread so special isn't just its texture or taste; it's the entire process. Local bakers still use pure spring water from the volcanic hills, specially selected flour, and natural sourdough starters passed down through generations. In 2004, this dedication to tradition earned Pane di Genzano the prestigious IGP (Protected Geographical Indication) status, making it the first bread in Europe to receive this recognition.

Each year, the town celebrates this living heritage with a multi-day festival that transforms Genzano's medieval streets into a celebration of bread culture. The festival brings together centuries-old baking traditions with modern culinary techniques, turning the spotlight on the bakers who continue to craft this remarkable bread just as their ancestors did. It's a time when the whole town comes alive with the aroma of fresh-baked bread, and visitors can experience firsthand why Genzano has earned its reputation as "La Città del Pane", The City of Bread.

The Bread Festival and Feast Day of St. Thomas Villanova

The aroma of freshly baked bread has always been my weakness. So when I heard about the bread festival in Genzano, I couldn't resist. This small Italian town's bread-making heritage stretches back centuries, with its signature Pane di Genzano standing as one of Italy's most celebrated breads. It's so special that it is protected by a PGI (Protected Geographical Indication) status[1], joining an elite group of Europe's protected food traditions.

What makes Pane di Genzano extraordinary is its perfect contrast: a dark, crackling crust that gives way to a cloud-like interior. Local bakers still use

---

1. The PGI label protects both producers and consumers by ensuring that products are genuine and produced according to traditional methods in specific areas. For consumers, it guarantees the quality and authenticity of a product, while for producers, it helps maintain the reputation and economic value of traditional products tied to their region. It also helps safeguard against imitations or counterfeit products that could damage the reputation of the authentic items.

traditional wood-fired ovens, a method that infuses each loaf with a subtle smokiness and creates that characteristic crispy exterior. The bread's texture and flavor are a testament to generations of bakers who have preserved these time-honored techniques.

History of the Festa del Pane

The Festa del Pane (Bread Festival) in Genzano di Roma celebrates the town's long-standing tradition of bread-making and the importance of Pane di Genzano in Italian cuisine. This festival was established in the 1980s to promote the unique qualities of Genzano's bread and to honor the bakers who have kept the town's baking traditions alive. The festival has grown in popularity over the years and is now a major event in the Castelli Romani region.

The festival is held in Piazza Tommaso Frasconi and in the surrounding streets. The town's location near Lago di Nemi adds to the picturesque setting of the festival.

What Happens During the Festival?

The Festa del Pane is a multi-day event that brings together bakers, food lovers, and locals to celebrate one of Italy's most beloved foods:

Bread Tastings and Market Stalls: Visitors can sample freshly baked Pane di Genzano, known for its crunchy crust and soft interior. Stalls throughout the town offer bread in various forms, including ciabatta, focaccia, and whole wheat varieties. Bread is served with a variety of toppings, from olive oil and tomato to cheese and cured meats.

Bread-Making Demonstrations: Local bakers set up wood-fired ovens in the square, demonstrating how Pane di Genzano is made. These demonstrations are a great way to learn about the traditional techniques used to bake this bread, including the special fermentation process that gives it its unique texture.

Traditional Roman Foods: The festival offers a wide range of Roman dishes, such as coda alla vaccinara (oxtail stew), carciofi alla giudia (fried artichokes), and porchetta, all served with slices of Pane di Genzano.

Music, Dance, and Entertainment: Throughout the festival, there are performances by local musicians and folk dancers, celebrating the town's rich cultural heritage. Street performers and jugglers entertain the crowds, adding to the festive atmosphere.

Artisan Markets: Local artisans display and sell their handcrafted goods, including pottery, wooden utensils, and textiles. These markets provide visitors with an opportunity to purchase unique, locally made souvenirs.

Festival Food: Try the local porchetta sandwich, which pairs perfectly with Pane di Genzano.

The Genzano Festival: A Four-Day Celebration

Day 1

Day One centers on spiritual traditions and community heritage. The festival opens with a Solemn Eucharistic Celebration at the Church of the Holy Trinity, presided over by the Bishop of the Diocese of Albano. As evening falls, a grand procession winds through the historic streets, accompanied by the town band.

The highlight comes at Annunziata Square, where visitors witness a historical reenactment of Genzano choosing Saint Thomas of Villanova as its patron saint, followed by the blessing and sharing of Saint Thomas's bread from local bakeries.

Day 2

Day Two shifts focus to the culinary arts with exclusive wine and bread tastings at the magnificent Palazzo Sforza Cesarini. Expert-guided sessions pair regional wines with fresh creations from Genzano's renowned bakeries, offering visitors a taste of local excellence.

Day 3

Day Three brings together culture and community. The day begins with children's activities, including storytelling and bread-making workshops. International perspectives are shared through "Bread from the World" presentations, highlighting the cultural significance of bread across Mediterranean traditions.

The evening comes alive with music competitions and entertainment, including comedy shows and live performances.

Day 4

The final day marks the festival's grand finale, featuring the breathtaking Infiorata di Pane, where master artisans transform Via Nazario Sauro into an artistic canvas using bread as their medium. The day's events include:

- The traditional Bread Race through town streets

- Bruschetta-making competitions between local chefs

- Guided palace tours and art exhibitions

- Street markets and artistic performances

- The spectacular creation of "The Longest Bruschetta in the World"

- Evening concerts and a closing fireworks display

Throughout the festival, Palazzo Sforza Cesarini hosts evening wine and bread tastings, offering visitors the chance to experience the finest local products. The streets fill with markets, music, and the irresistible aroma of fresh-baked bread, while classic Italian films celebrating food culture are screened under the stars.

*See June Blooming Streets, Chapter 13: The Art of the Infiorata of Genzano Chapter for a more detailed history of Genzano di Roma and the information on logistics, day trips, restaurant recommendations, and accommodation. For this festival, I recommend two to three nights in town.

CHAPTER TWENTY-EIGHT

Celebrating San Nilo in Grottaferrata

Monks, Miracles, and Merriment

Festa Patronale di San Nilo da Rossano

Where: Grottaferrata

When: September 24-27

Average Festival Temperatures: High 24°C (75°F). Low 14°C (57°F).

Grottaferrata: A Byzantine Gem in the Castelli Romani

Grottaferrata, nestled in the Castelli Romani hills 20 kilometers (12 miles) southeast of Rome, has a history as rich as its wine and as layered as its volcanic soil. The town's name comes from the Greek crypta ferrata, meaning "iron crypt," referring to the fortified gate of the ancient abbey that remains its centerpiece.

In 1004, Saint Nilus of Rossano, a Byzantine monk, founded the Abbey of Santa Maria di Grottaferrata, establishing a spiritual and cultural hub that would define the town's character. Built on Roman villa ruins, the abbey uniquely blends

Greek and Latin traditions, following the Byzantine Rite while maintaining communion with the Catholic Church. Over centuries, it has served as a sanctuary of faith, art, and scholarship.

During the Middle Ages, Grottaferrata flourished as a religious center, later becoming part of the Papal States. Its strategic location, serene beauty, and proximity to Rome made it a favored retreat for clergy and nobles alike.

Grottaferrata captured our hearts from our first visit. The town's fortress and abbey immediately draw you in. They are an incredible medieval surprise in a town of this size.

Today, the town's 21,000 residents maintain their rich heritage while keeping a vibrant community spirit alive. Ancient Byzantine treasures sit comfortably alongside bustling cafes and shops, while the surrounding Castelli Romani parkland cradles the town in greenery, perfect for local vineyards.

The Feast of San Nilo

The annual Feast of San Nilo on September 26th celebrates the town's patron saint and the abbey's founder. More than just a religious observance, it's a vibrant celebration of cultural heritage and community spirit, offering visitors a glimpse into the Byzantine-Greek traditions that have thrived here for over a millennium.

Who is San Nilo?

San Nilo lived during turbulent times, facing Saracen raids and political upheaval. After being widowed young, he devoted himself to monastic life, initially as a hermit in Calabria. His reputation for wisdom and miracles spread throughout medieval Italy. Among his famous miracles was healing a possessed boy, saving Rossano from Saracen invasion through prayer, and reportedly writing perfect manuscripts even while sleeping.

His final miracle came near life's end when the Virgin Mary appeared to him near a fern-covered grotto, instructing him to build an abbey uniting Eastern and Western Christian traditions. Though he died before its completion, his disciples finished what became one of Italy's last active Greek Byzantine monasteries.

The festival stands as a testament to cultural preservation and interfaith dialogue, celebrating a tradition that has survived for over a thousand years. Whether drawn by religious devotion, cultural curiosity, or simply the charm of an Italian festival, visitors find themselves part of a living tradition that continues to shape this unique corner of Italy.

Timeline of Events

September 24th: Opening Ceremony

Evening: The festival begins with an official opening ceremony, held in the town square or near the Abbey of Santa Maria di Grottaferrata. This event often features a concert or cultural performance, setting the tone for the celebrations to come. Residents and visitors gather to enjoy music, speeches, and a lively atmosphere.

September 25th: Vespers and Cultural Events

Daytime: Cultural events begin, including exhibitions, lectures, and guided tours of the Abbey. Visitors can explore Byzantine-inspired art displays, take part in workshops on traditional crafts, or learn about the life of San Nilo through historical presentations.

Evening: Solemn Vespers are sung in the Abbey church, marking the eve of the feast day. The service, steeped in Byzantine tradition, is a spiritual highlight and a moment of reflection for attendees.

Solemn Procession: On September 25th, the traditional Solemn Procession takes place, with the icon of the Patron Saint carried through Corso del Popolo, followed by the saint's relic.

September 26th: Feast Day of San Nilo

Morning: The day begins with a Solemn Mass, usually celebrated in the Byzantine Rite, at the Abbey of Santa Maria di Grottaferrata. The service, held around 10:00 AM, features hymns, prayers, and blessings in the breathtaking setting of the Abbey, adorned with frescoes and mosaics.

Procession: A procession with the relics of San Nilo takes place, starting from the Abbey and winding through the streets of Grottaferrata. The relics are carried in an ornate reliquary, accompanied by participants dressed in traditional costumes, prayers, hymns, and often musicians playing Byzantine or local instruments. The procession begins around 5:00 PM and is a deeply spiritual and communal event.

Evening: The festival concludes with a spectacular (silent) fireworks display, lighting up the skies over Grottaferrata. This event marks the joyous culmination of the celebrations, bringing together locals and visitors to celebrate the legacy of San Nilo.

September 27th and Beyond: Extended Cultural Activities

In some years, cultural events continue after the feast day, providing opportunities for further exploration of Grottaferrata's heritage. Activities may include concerts of Byzantine chant, theatrical performances, and additional guided tours of the Abbey, including areas usually closed to the public.

Local Customs and Traditions

Town Decorations: Grottaferrata is beautifully adorned with lights, banners, and flowers in honor of San Nilo.

Religious Items: Stalls selling religious artifacts, particularly those related to San Nilo and the Byzantine tradition, are set up around the town.

Local Crafts: Artisans display and sell traditional local crafts, offering unique souvenirs for visitors.

Food Stalls: Local specialties, particularly those with Greek influences, are available throughout the festival.

Music and Dance: Performances of traditional music and dance in Piazzale San Nilo, both Italian and Greek-inspired, add to the festive atmosphere.

Walking Tour of Grottaferrata

#1. Abbey of Santa Maria di Grottaferrata

Begin your visit at the Abbey of Santa Maria di Grottaferrata, founded in 1004 by Saint Nilo. One of the last active Byzantine monasteries in Italy, it stands as a spiritual and architectural landmark, blending Roman, Byzantine, and Baroque traditions.

The basilica's Romanesque exterior features a towering bell tower, ceramic inlays, and a rose window framed by Gothic arches. Enter through carved cedar doors to discover a sacred space filled with centuries of art and devotion. A mosaic above the entrance from the 11th century shows Christ with Mary and John the Baptist. Inside, the sanctuary preserves its early Byzantine character, with a 12th-century mosaic of the Apostles and a richly colored Cosmatesque floor.

A highlight is the iconostasis designed by Bernini in 1665, a marble screen adorned with lapis lazuli, angels, and a revered 10th or 11th-century icon of the Virgin and Child. Believed to be miraculous, this icon inspired Grottaferrata's major religious festivals: the Annunciation on March 25 and the Nativity of the Virgin Mary on September 8. Pilgrims, saints, and popes, including John XXIII and John Paul II, have come to venerate it.

Sangallo Cloister of the Abbey

Nearby, the Farnesian Chapel holds relics of Saint Nilo and Saint Bartholomew. Its frescoes by Domenichino depict key moments from Saint Nilo's life, including his encounter with Emperor Otto III. The blue and gold coffered ceiling adds to its beauty.

Do not miss the Sangallo Cloister, designed by Giuliano Sangallo. A quiet, open-air space lined with relics from the Roman villa that once stood on this site, it offers a reflective pause with ancient columns, mosaic fragments, and peaceful arcades. Surrounding the abbey is a 15th-century fortress designed by Baccio Pontelli, complete with towers and battlements, built to defend this sacred site.

#2. Grottaferrata Fortress and Walls

After leaving the abbey, walk towards the fortress surrounding the abbey grounds. This imposing structure, with its towers, battlements, and moat, was built in the 15th century under the direction of Cardinal Giuliano della Rovere (later Pope Julius II). The walls were raised to protect the abbey from military invasions, giving it the grand and fortified appearance it retains today.

Beautiful views from the Fortress

#3. Piazza Cavour

From the abbey, make your way to Piazza Cavour, the main square of Grottaferrata. This vibrant square is the heart of town life, surrounded by cafes, shops, and restaurants. It's an ideal spot to pause and enjoy a coffee or light snack while soaking in the local atmosphere. The square is often lively, especially during market days and festivals, and serves as a hub for community gatherings.

#4. Chiesa del sacro Cuore di Gesù

A short walk from Piazza Cavour takes you to the Chiesa del sacro Cuore di Gesù (Church of the Sacred Heart of Jesus), a more modern building that contrasts with the ancient abbey. Built in the early 20th century, this church offers insight into developing religious architecture in Grottaferrata. Its neoclassical style and beautiful interiors make it worth a visit.

#5. Villa Cavalletti

Continue your walk to Villa Cavalletti, a historical villa nestled among the rolling hills of Grottaferrata. The villa is known for its expansive gardens, which offer stunning views of the Castelli Romani and Rome in the distance. Enjoy the serene gardens, a peaceful retreat from the bustling town.

#6. Church of San Pio X

Next, walk over to the Church of San Pio X, another gorgeous church built in the mid-20th century. Though it's a more recent addition to Grottaferrata's architectural landscape, it offers a contrast to the older structures and serves as a community focal point for religious life.

#7. Walk Along Via Roma

Take a stroll along Via Roma, Grottaferrata's main street. This charming road is lined with shops, cafes, and small boutiques, making it perfect for a leisurely walk. You can find local products, including wine and olive oil from the Castelli Romani region, as well as artisan crafts that reflect the area's cultural heritage.

#8. Parco Patmos

End your walking tour with a visit to Parco Patmos, a public park near the town center. The park offers a peaceful environment, perfect for relaxation after your walking tour. With its green spaces and shaded benches, it's an ideal spot to sit and reflect on your visit to Grottaferrata.

Logistics

Train: From Rome (Termini Station): While Grottaferrata doesn't have its own train station, nearby towns like Frascati or Ciampino do. Trains from Roma

Termini to Frascati or Ciampino take 30 minutes, and from there, it's a 15 minute bus ride or taxi to Grottaferrata.

Bus: From Rome (Anagnina Metro Station): Regular COTRAL buses depart from the Anagnina Metro Station (Line A) in Rome to Grottaferrata. The journey takes about 30 minutes, offering a scenic ride through the Castelli Romani region.

From Frascati or Marino: Local bus services connect Grottaferrata with nearby towns such as Frascati and Marino, which are also well connected by regional trains from Rome. The bus ride between Grottaferrata and these towns is short, taking 10-15 minutes.

Car: From Rome: Grottaferrata is approximately 20 kilometers (12 miles) southeast of Rome. The most convenient way to reach it by car is via the SS7 (Via Appia) or the A1 highway, which takes around 30 minutes depending on traffic.

Parking: There are public parking areas near the Abbey of Santa Maria and throughout the town, though availability can be limited during festivals or weekends.

Restaurant Recommendations

Da Leo. Address: Viale San Nilo

Known for authentic Italian dishes, fresh seafood, and homemade pasta. The warm atmosphere and attentive staff make it a popular choice.

Fatto in Casa. Address: Via Gabriele d'Annunzio 20

A cozy spot specializing in home-cooked Italian meals made with fresh, local ingredients. Perfect for families and casual dining.

Accommodation

For the festival I recommend two to three nights in Grottaferrata.

Park Hotel Villa Grazioli. Address: Via Umberto Pavoni, 19

A 4-star hotel set in a restored 16th-century villa, offering elegant rooms with panoramic views of Rome and the surrounding countryside. Guests can enjoy the historic architecture, beautiful gardens, and an on-site restaurant serving Italian cuisine.

Locanda dello Spuntino. Address: Via Cicerone, 22

This charming 4-star boutique hotel features rustic-style rooms with modern amenities. Known for its warm hospitality and an excellent on-site restaurant specializing in local dishes.

Hotel Verdeborgo. Address: Via Anagnina, 10

A 3-star hotel surrounded by a lush garden, offering comfortable rooms with classic décor. Guests appreciate the peaceful atmosphere and proximity to Rome, making it suitable for both relaxation and exploration.

Tenuta Cusmano. Address: Via Anagnina, 20

A family-run 4-star country house hotel set amidst vineyards and olive groves. It offers spacious rooms with terraces, an outdoor pool, and stunning views of the Roman countryside.

Day Trip Options: Nearby Sites, Cities, and Towns

Cycling the Castelli Romani Wine Roads. Round trip from Grottaferrata (25–40 kilometers (15 to 25 miles) depending on route).

The Castelli Romani is one of the most beautiful areas in Lazio for cycling. This scenic loop takes you through a string of historic towns including Frascati, Grottaferrata, Monte Porzio Catone, Marino, and Castel Gandolfo, with panoramic views, vineyard-lined roads, and shaded stretches through forested hills. Riders can pause to explore local cantinas, taste wines such as Frascati Superiore, or enjoy a lakeside gelato at Lake Albano.

The terrain is gently rolling, but an e-bike makes the route accessible to all skill levels. Trails such as Via dei Laghi and country roads around Monte Cavo and Lake Nemi offer quiet, bike-friendly paths with very little traffic and sweeping countryside views. This is also a favorite route among local Roman cyclists on weekends.

E-Bike Rental and Guided Tours:

- Castelli Romani Bike Tour (Frascati) offers guided and self-guided tours with e-bike rentals. Located in central Frascati, it's easily accessible from Grottaferrata. They offer half-day and full-day packages. Website: www.castelliromani.bike

- e-Bike Rent Albano Laziale provides e-bike rentals and routes around Lake Albano and the surrounding parks. Great for those wanting a lakeside ride or to explore the slopes of Monte Cavo.

Cerveteri. 50 kilometers (31 miles) from Grottaferrata. Cerveteri is home to the Necropolis of Banditaccia, a UNESCO World Heritage Site that offers an immersive look at Etruscan history. This extensive network of ancient tombs is one of the most important archaeological sites in Italy. Visit the Etruscan Museum in Cerveteri's town center, or explore the surrounding countryside known for its wine and olive oil production.

Palestrina. 30 kilometers (19 miles) from Grottaferrata. Set dramatically on a hillside overlooking the Roman countryside, Palestrina is built atop the ancient city of Praeneste, once a powerful Latin center. The town's crown jewel is the Sanctuary of Fortuna Primigenia, an immense terraced temple complex from the 2nd century BC dedicated to the goddess of fortune. Much of the sanctuary now forms part of the National Archaeological Museum of Palestrina, housed in the Palazzo Colonna Barberini. Highlights include exquisite Roman mosaics, sculptures, and one of the oldest known world maps, the Nile Mosaic of Palestrina.

After exploring the ruins and museum, stroll through Palestrina's charming medieval streets or hike the surrounding trails for panoramic views over the Lazio countryside. The area also offers quiet natural spots perfect for walking or picnicking, with trails that connect to regional parks nearby.

Grottaferrata Festivals and Sagre Throughout the Year

Mostra Mercato di Antiquariato ed Artigianato (Antiques and Artisan Market)

Every third Sunday of the month

Grottaferrata's antiques and artisan market takes place on the third Sunday of every month. The streets of the town fill with stalls selling handcrafted items, antiques, and curiosities, making it a must-visit for those looking for unique souvenirs or artisan crafts.

Fiera Grottaferratta

Last week in March / First Week in April (dates can vary based on Easter)

The fair showcases a wide range of artisanal and culinary products, including local wines and foods, from across Italy. Over 100 exhibitors from 19 regions take part, offering everything from handmade crafts, jewelry, and furniture to gourmet foods and local specialties. The event also features workshops, seminars, and cultural performances, making it a vibrant celebration of Italian craftsmanship and culinary traditions.

The origins of the fair date back to the Middle Ages, when it provided pilgrims visiting the Abbey of Santa Maria di Grottaferrata with essential supplies. Over time, it strengthened into a significant commercial and cultural event.

Estate Grottaferratese (Grottaferrata Summer Festival)

June-August

The Estate Grottaferratese is a summer-long festival that features concerts, theatrical performances, and outdoor events such as movie screenings. The festival takes place in Piazza Cavour and other venues around town, entertaining both locals and visitors during the warmer months.

CHAPTER TWENTY-NINE

Bracciano's Flavorful Harvest

The Sagra del Fungo and Lakeside Traditions

S agra del Fungo

Where: Bracciano

When: Last Week in September and First Week in October.

Average Festival Temperatures: High 26°C (79°F). Low 18°C (64°F).

Bracciano: A Lakeside Gem with Timeless Charm

Bracciano is a picturesque town located approximately 40 kilometers (25 miles) northwest of Rome. The town overlooks the stunning Lake Bracciano, one of the largest and cleanest volcanic lakes in Italy. Surrounded by rolling hills and lush greenery, Bracciano offers visitors a harmonious blend of natural beauty and historical allure. The lake, with its pristine waters, is a protected area within the Bracciano-Martignano Regional Park, making it a popular destination for swimming, sailing, and hiking.

Bracciano's history dates back to ancient times, with evidence of Etruscan settlements around Lake Bracciano. During the Middle Ages, the town gained prominence under the Orsini family, who constructed the magnificent Castello Orsini-Odescalchi in the 15th century. This imposing Renaissance fortress, perched on a hilltop, became a symbol of the town's strategic and political importance. Over the centuries, the castle has hosted notable figures, including popes, kings, and celebrities. Today, it serves as a museum and a venue for events, offering panoramic views of the lake and the surrounding countryside.

Lake Bracciano, formed over 100,000 years ago within a volcanic crater, is the lifeblood of the region. With a circumference of 32 kilometers (20 miles), it is Italy's eighth-largest lake. The lake's crystal-clear waters are maintained by strict environmental regulations, prohibiting motorboats to preserve its tranquility and ecological balance. Along its shores lie charming villages such as Trevignano Romano and Anguillara Sabazia, each offering unique cultural and culinary experiences.

Bracciano is home to 19,000 residents, many of whom are deeply connected to the town's traditions and natural environment. The community thrives on tourism, agriculture, and fishing, with local festivals and sagre playing a central role in preserving its cultural identity. The town's strategic location, combined with its historical significance and scenic beauty, makes Bracciano a beloved destination for both local and international travelers.

Bracciano offers a perfect blend of history, culture, and outdoor activities. Visitors can explore the majestic Castello Orsini-Odescalchi, stroll through the medieval streets of the historic center, or relax by the serene shores of Lake Bracciano. Whether enjoying a meal at a lakeside trattoria or taking part in one of the town's vibrant festivals, Bracciano provides an unforgettable experience that captures the essence of Lazio's rich heritage.

The Mushroom Festival

The Sagra del Fungo in Bracciano is a relatively recent addition to the town's cultural calendar, with its inaugural edition in 2018. Despite its young age, the festival has quickly become a cherished tradition, celebrating the rich flavors of autumn and the local culinary heritage. Organized by the Associazione Rione Monti in collaboration with the Gruppo Ecologico Micologico Alto

Lazio (G.E.M.A.L.), the event aims to promote traditional cuisine, highlighting mushrooms as the star ingredient.

The festival not only offers culinary delights but also serves as a platform for cultural exchange and community engagement. It attracts both locals and visitors, fostering a sense of unity and pride in Bracciano's natural and culinary resources.

Festival Timeline

Saturdays (Last Weekend September / First Weekend October)

7:30 p.m.

Opening of the gastronomic stands in Piazza IV Novembre. Visitors can enjoy a variety of mushroom-based dishes, including Fettuccine ai Funghi Porcini, Zuppa di Funghi (soup), Funghi Porcini Fritti Dorati (golden fried), Spezzatino di Carne con Misto Funghi, and Bruschetta Misto Funghi.

Sundays (Last Weekend September / First Weekend October)

12:30 p.m.

Lunch service begins, allowing visitors to enjoy mushroom dishes for lunch.

7:30 p.m.

Dinner service begins, offering another opportunity to savor mushroom-based cuisine.

Throughout the festival, Piazza IV Novembre transforms into a vibrant hub featuring:

- Food Stalls: A gastronomic stand serving traditional dishes with mushrooms as the central ingredient.

- Artisan Market: A market showcasing local artisanal crafts and agro-food products.

- Cultural Performances: Live music and entertainment, enhancing the festive atmosphere.

Additionally, the festival offers take-away menus for those who prefer to enjoy the delicacies elsewhere.

Mostra del Fungo e delle Erbe Spontanee

Following the Sagra del Fungo, Bracciano hosts the Mostra del Fungo e delle Erbe Spontanee. This exhibition features over 200 species of fungi, educational displays about wild herbs, and a recreated woodland environment, providing an immersive experience into the region's natural biodiversity.

The Sagra del Fungo and its associated events offer a delightful immersion into Bracciano's autumnal traditions, combining culinary excellence with cultural enrichment.

Walking Tour Bracciano

#1. Castello Orsini-Odescalchi

Begin at this majestic 15th-century castle, a masterpiece of Renaissance military architecture. Castello Orsini-Odescalchi is the crown jewel of Bracciano, standing majestically on a hill overlooking Lake Bracciano. Built in the 15th century by the powerful Orsini family, the castle is an extraordinary example of Renaissance military architecture combined with opulent residential design.

The castle was constructed by Napoleone Orsini and his descendants as both a fortress and a noble residence. It later passed to the Odescalchi family in the 17th century, who further enhanced its elegance. Over the centuries, the castle has hosted many notable figures, including popes, kings, and artists. One of its most famous events was the 1494 marriage of Virginio Orsini and Felice della Rovere, the illegitimate daughter of Pope Julius II.

Visitors can explore its six towers, massive walls, and intricately designed courtyards. The castle's interior houses an array of treasures, including antique furniture, frescoes, and a remarkable armory. Some highlights include:

The Hall of Arms: Displaying medieval weapons and armor.

The Papal Apartment: Featuring lavish furnishings and frescoes from the Renaissance period.

The Noble Hall: Adorned with a painted ceiling depicting mythological themes.

Beyond its historical and artistic significance, the castle offers unparalleled panoramic views of Lake Bracciano and the surrounding countryside. The serene beauty of the lake and the lush greenery of the Bracciano-Martignano Regional Park make it a photographer's dream. The castle is also a popular venue for weddings and cultural events, adding to its allure.

#2. Historic Center (Centro Storico)
Wander through narrow, cobblestone streets lined with medieval buildings, charming boutiques, and traditional trattorias. The historic center reflects Bracciano's rich past and vibrant present, providing a glimpse into local life.

#3. Piazza IV Novembre
This central square serves as a hub for community gatherings and events, including the Sagra del Fungo. Surrounded by historic architecture, it's an ideal spot to relax and observe daily life.

#4. Duomo di Santo Stefano

The Cathedral of Santo Stefano Protomartire, also known as the Duomo di Santo Stefano, is a stunning example of medieval architecture. The church was originally built around the year 1200 and underwent significant expansions in the 17th century. A beautiful blend of Romanesque and Baroque styles characterizes the current structure. Inside, you'll find a gilded wood reliquary and an impressive baptismal font.

The cathedral also houses a painting depicting the martyrdom of Saint Stephen, created by the Modenese painter Giacomo Zoboli in 1696. The exterior facade, completed between 1758 and 1760, is adorned with the symbols of the Orsini and Odescalchi families, who played significant roles in the church's history.

#5. Chiesa di Santa Maria Novella
The Church of Santa Maria Novella was founded in 1436 by Cardinal Giordano Orsini and originally belonged to the Augustinian order. The church showcases a mix of Renaissance and Gothic architectural elements. Inside, you'll find beautiful frescoes and artworks, including an impressive altarpiece depicting the Assumption of Mary by Taddeo Kuntze. The church also features three paintings by Giuseppe Tori, a friar and student of Kuntze, which depict saints

of the Augustinian order. The convent next to the church now houses the Civic Museum and the Historical Archives of Bracciano.

#6. Belvedere della Sentinella
The Belvedere della Sentinella is a scenic viewpoint offering breathtaking vistas of Lake Bracciano and the surrounding hills. It's the perfect spot to end your walking tour, providing a panoramic view of the natural beauty of the area. The viewpoint is ideal for taking photos, enjoying a picnic, or simply reflecting on the rich history and culture you've experienced during your visit to Bracciano.

Logistics

Train: Bracciano has its own train station, which is part of the regional FL3 railway line connecting Rome to Viterbo. Trains run frequently, making it convenient for travelers from Rome (approximately 50 minutes) and Viterbo (around 1 hour). The station is within walking distance of the town center and Lake Bracciano.

Bus: Regional bus services, operated by Cotral, provide connections to nearby towns such as Anguillara Sabazia, Trevignano Romano, and Cerveteri. There are also buses linking Bracciano to Rome and Civitavecchia. The main bus stop is in the town center, ensuring easy access to public transportation.

Car: To reach Bracciano by car from Rome, take the A90 (Grande Raccordo Anulare) and exit onto Via Aurelia (SS1) or Via Cassia (SR2), depending on your starting point. Follow the signs for Bracciano, approximately 40 kilometers (25 miles) from the capital. The drive offers scenic views of the Lazio countryside.

Parking: Bracciano provides ample parking options, including public parking lots near the town center and the castle. Popular parking areas include those along Via Claudia and Piazza IV Novembre. During festivals or peak tourist seasons, parking can be limited, so it's advisable to arrive early. Note that the historic center may have ZTL (Limited Traffic Zone) restrictions, so park outside these areas and enjoy the short walk into town.

Restaurant Recommendations

Ristorantino del Castello. Address: Via Agostino Fausti, 28
This Italian and seafood restaurant is praised for its great location near the castle and very kind staff. The food is really delicious, offering a journey into the authentic flavors of Bracciano.

Trattoria Del Castello. Address: Via della Collegiata, 9
Known for its great location near the castle, this Italian and seafood restaurant offers delicious food, making it a journey into the authentic flavors of Bracciano.

Accommodation

There is a lot to see in the area, so I would recommend two to three nights in town.

Albergo Della Posta. Address: Via Agostino Fausti, 29
This 3-star hotel is in the heart of Bracciano, offering easy access to the town's attractions, including the Castello Orsini-Odescalchi. Guests appreciate its comfortable rooms, friendly service, and proximity to local restaurants and shops.

Hotel Villa Clementina. Address: Via Traversa Quarto Del Lago, 12
Near the shores of Lake Bracciano, this boutique hotel offers elegant rooms with lake views. The property features a spa, swimming pool, and a restaurant serving local cuisine. Its tranquil setting and proximity to the lake make it a popular choice for travelers seeking relaxation.

Vigna Caio Relais & Spa. Address: Via Baglione, 13
Situated a short distance from the town center, this hotel offers luxurious accommodations with panoramic views of Lake Bracciano. Amenities include a spa, outdoor swimming pool, and beautifully landscaped gardens. Guests praise the serene atmosphere and attentive service.

Day Trip Options: Nearby Sites, Cities, and Towns

Anguillara Sabazia. 9 kilometers (5.6 miles) from Bracciano. Nestled on the southern shore of Lake Bracciano, Anguillara Sabazia is a charming lakeside town with a medieval atmosphere. Stroll through its narrow cobblestone streets, admire historic buildings like the Church of San Francesco, and enjoy lakeside dining with stunning views. Its proximity to the lake makes it a hub for water sports and relaxing boat trips.

Trevignano Romano. 13 kilometers (8 miles) north of Bracciano. On the northern shore of Lake Bracciano, Trevignano Romano is a picturesque town renowned for its peaceful ambiance. Visitors can explore the ruins of the 12th-century Orsini Castle, visit the Romanesque Church of Santa Maria Assunta, and enjoy the waterfront promenade lined with cafes and restaurants. The town is also a gateway to hiking trails in the Bracciano-Martignano Regional Park.

Ceri. 25 kilometers (16 miles) from Bracciano. A small medieval village perched on a hilltop, Ceri is known for its enchanting atmosphere and the Sanctuary of the Madonna di Ceri. The village's single narrow street leads visitors through its historic heart, offering breathtaking views of the surrounding countryside.

Assisi. 249 kilometers (155 miles) from Bracciano (2.5 hours). Okay, I know that this is a stretch for a day trip, but it's Assisi, and in this guide, this is the closest we will be!

Perched on the slopes of Mount Subasio in Umbria, Assisi rises like a dream in pink stone, its medieval architecture glowing warmly in the Italian sun. This hill town, forever linked to Saint Francis and Saint Clare, offers visitors more than just religious significance. Light and space fill the soaring Upper Church, where vibrant frescoes adorn the walls. Their naturalistic style and emotional depth revolutionized Western art. It's a journey through time, art, and spirituality.

The heart of any visit is the magnificent Basilica of Saint Francis, a 13th-century architectural marvel that's actually two churches in one. The Lower Church, dim and contemplative, houses some of Italy's most precious frescoes by Giotto and Cimabue, depicting scenes from Saint Francis's life. Light and space fill the soaring Upper Church, its walls adorned with vibrant frescoes that revolutionized Western art with their naturalistic style and emotional depth.

Beyond the basilica, Assisi reveals itself through winding medieval streets and quiet corners. The San Damiano Monastery, tucked away down a cypress-lined path, offers a more intimate connection to the town's spiritual heritage. This is where Saint Francis heard the crucifix speak to him, commanding him to "rebuild my church," and where Saint Clare later established her order of nuns. The simple chapel and peaceful gardens provide a moment of reflection away from the busier sites.

Bracciano Festivals and Sagre Throughout the Year

Feast of San Sebastiano

January 20

Bracciano honors its patron saint, San Sebastiano, with religious ceremonies, processions, and community gatherings, reflecting the town's deep-rooted traditions and spiritual heritage.

International Dance and Music Festival "Bracciano's Castle"

August 24–27

This international folklore festival features dance and music groups from various countries, showcasing traditional, folklore, and modern performances near the historic Castello Orsini-Odescalchi.

CHAPTER THIRTY

The Vibrant Harvest Festival of Marino

Fountains of Wine

S agra dell'Uva

Where: Marino, Italy

When: First Sunday in October

Average Festival Temperatures: High 22°C (72°F). Low 12°C (54°F).

From Latins to Lepanto: The Story of Marino

Marino is a historic town in the Lazio region, 21 kilometers (13 miles) southeast of Rome. On the Alban Hills, it stands at an elevation of 360 meters above sea level.

Marino's origins date back to ancient times, with evidence suggesting it was inhabited by the Latins before becoming part of the Roman Empire. The town's Latin name, *Castrimoenium*, reflects its ancient history. During the Middle Ages, Marino gained prominence under the control of various noble families, notably the Orsini and Colonna families. The Colonna family, in particular, left a significant mark on Marino's history, with Marcantonio Colonna, a notable figure, leading the papal fleet to victory in the Battle of Lepanto in 1571. This victory is celebrated annually in Marino during the Sagra dell'Uva (Grape Festival), which began in 1925 and has become one of Italy's most famous wine festivals.

Marino is part of the Castelli Romani, a group of communes in the Alban Hills known for their picturesque landscapes and wine production. The town's elevated position offers panoramic views of the surrounding countryside and proximity to Lake Albano, a volcanic crater lake. The fertile volcanic soil and favorable climate contribute to the area's renowned viticulture, particularly the production of white wines.

Grape and Wine Festival

In the picturesque town of Marino the first Sunday of October brings a unique celebration that has captivated locals and visitors alike for nearly a century. The Sagra dell'Uva, or Grape and Wine Festival, is a vibrant tribute to Marino's rich winemaking heritage, blending historical commemoration, religious devotion, and joyous festivity. This event, **where fountains flow with wine instead of water,** offers a truly unique experience that embodies the spirit of Italian harvest celebrations.

History and Significance

Established in 1925 by local poet and public figure Leone Ciprelli, the Sagra dell'Uva was created to honor Marino's longstanding tradition of winemaking and to celebrate the town's harvest. The event coincides with the community's religious devotion to the Madonna del Rosario, combining both sacred and profane elements.

The occasion is also closely tied to the Battle of Lepanto in 1571, in which the Christian naval forces, under the command of Marcantonio Colonna (a nobleman from Marino), defeated the Ottoman fleet. This historical connection adds a layer of cultural significance to the festivities, with parades and reenactments commemorating this victory.

Timeline of Events: Sagra dell'Uva

While the primary focus of the celebration occurs on the first Sunday of October, festivities extend over several days.

Friday Evening

Opening Ceremony marks the official start of the festival with traditional speeches and musical performances that set the tone for the weekend ahead.

Saturday Morning

The Blessing of the Grapes takes place in the main square, a solemn ceremony honoring the harvest and continuing centuries-old traditions.

Saturday Afternoon

5:00 P.M.

The cobblestone streets of Marino transform into a living theater as hundreds of costumed performers bring one of Italy's most pivotal naval battles to life. Watch in awe as locals, dressed in meticulously crafted 16th-century attire, reenact the Battle of Lepanto and the triumphant return of hometown hero Marcantonio Colonna.

Sunday Events

Historical Reenactments: The day starts with more historical reenactments, including scenes from the Battle of Lepanto and Marcantonio Colonna's triumphant return. These performances take place in the historic center, particularly around Piazza Giuseppe Mazzini and Corso Vittoria Colonna.

The Miracle of the Fountains: One of the most anticipated moments is the "miracle of the fountains that pour wine." During this event, the town's historic fountains flow with wine instead of water, offering visitors a truly unique and memorable experience.

Cultural Performances: Throughout the day, there are various cultural performances, including concerts, theatrical shows, and traditional dances. These performances are held in different locations within the historic center.

Wine Tastings: Visitors can enjoy wine tastings of local wines produced in the Castelli Romani region. There are several stands and tents set up for this purpose, allowing you to sample a variety of wines.

Market and Exhibitions: The festival also features a market with artisanal products, local crafts, and traditional foods. There are exhibitions showcasing the history and culture of Marino, providing a deeper understanding of the town's heritage.

Children's Activities: There are special activities and games for children, ensuring that the festival is enjoyable for the whole family.

Concerts and Shows: In the evening, there are concerts and shows to entertain visitors. The day concludes with a grand finale, often including a spectacular fireworks display.

Local Customs and Traditions

Grape Decoration: The town is adorned with grape-themed decorations and bunches of fresh grapes.

Traditional Costumes: Many locals dress in historical costumes, particularly for the reenactments.

Winemaking Demonstrations: Some local wineries offer demonstrations of traditional winemaking techniques.

Grape Stomping: A fun, traditional activity where participants crush grapes with their feet.

Walking Tour of Marino

#1. Piazza Giuseppe Mazzini

This central square is indeed a focal point in Marino, surrounded by historic architecture and offering a vibrant atmosphere.

#2. Duomo di San Barnaba (Cathedral of Saint Barnabus)

Standing proudly near Marino's main square, the Duomo di San Barnaba is much more than just another Italian church. Built in the 17th century at the behest of the powerful Colonna family, this Baroque masterpiece tells the story of both faith and nobility in the Castelli Romani. The cathedral's facade immediately catches your eye with its harmonious proportions and elegant design, but it's the interior that truly showcases its unique artistic heritage.

Inside, you'll discover Guercino's masterpiece *The Martyrdom of Saint Bartholomew* (1618), which demonstrates the artist's mastery of dramatic lighting and emotional depth. The church also houses a beloved brass statue of Christ entering Jerusalem by local artist Paulino Petrucci, which plays a central role in Easter celebrations. The elaborately decorated ceiling features scenes from Saint Barnabas's life, while side chapels display works from various 17th and 18th-century artists. Ancient Roman artifacts, including repurposed columns, are incorporated throughout the structure, complementing the ornate marble high altar. The cathedral holds special significance during Marino's famous Sagra dell'Uva (Grape Festival), serving as a focal point for religious ceremonies associated with the harvest celebrations.

#3. Palazzo Colonna

The Palazzo Colonna perfectly embodies the town's rich history and the enduring legacy of one of Italy's most influential noble families. Built in the 16th century, this remarkable structure masterfully balances defensive architecture with Renaissance elegance, serving today as Marino's town hall while preserving its historical grandeur.

The palazzo's story is woven deeply into the fabric of Marino's history. Originally constructed as both a fortress and residence for the Colonna family, it has weathered centuries of change, including significant damage during World War II, before being transformed into the town hall in the early 20th century. Despite its modern administrative role, the building retains much of its Renaissance splendor, from its impressive courtyard with a beautiful central fountain to the original 16th-century frescoes depicting the Colonna family's military triumphs.

What makes this palazzo particularly fascinating is its architectural details. The elegant stone balconies offer commanding views over the town, while the family's coat of arms proudly adorns the facade, a reminder of their centuries-long influence.

#5. Church of Santissima Trinità

Dating back to 1640, this church is known for its serene ambiance and artistic interior. It's a peaceful spot to visit and admire the local art and architecture.

#6. Villa Desideri

Tucked away in Marino's historic center, Villa Desideri stands as an elegant testament to the refined lifestyle of the region's noble families. Built in the late 18th century, this charming villa and its surrounding gardens offer visitors a serene escape from the bustling town streets. The property showcases classic Italian garden design with its symmetrical layouts, ornamental fountains, and carefully manicured hedges. Inside, the villa houses Marino's public library and cultural center, breathing new life into this historic space while preserving its architectural character. The real magic of Villa Desideri lies in its elevated position, offering breathtaking views across the surrounding countryside and distant glimpses of Rome on clear days.

Logistics

Train. Trains depart from Rome Termini Station towards Marino Laziale on the Rome-Albano Laziale railway. Journey time is around 30-35 minutes. From Marino Laziale Station, it's a 10-minute walk to the town center.

Bus. Regional buses depart from Anagnina Metro Station (Line A) in Rome. The bus journey takes around 45 minutes.

Car: Take the Via Appia or the Via dei Laghi for scenic routes through the Castelli Romani hills.

Parking: When visiting Marino, Italy, it's important to be aware of the Zona a Traffico Limitato (ZTL), or Limited Traffic Zone, which restricts vehicle access to certain parts of the town, particularly the historic center. Parcheggio Piazzale degli Eroi. Address: Piazzale degli Eroi. This parking area is conveniently located near the town center but outside the ZTL, making it an ideal spot for visitors.

Dining Recommendations

Ristorante Adriano Address: Via San Giovanni, 37

Ristorante Adriano is a celebrated spot in Marino for traditional Roman and Castelli Romani cuisine. The restaurant prides itself on using locally sourced ingredients to prepare classic dishes such as cacio e pepe, amatriciana, and roasted lamb.

La Cantina di Bacco Address: Via Giuseppe Garibaldi

This traditional wine bar is a must-visit for wine enthusiasts. La Cantina di Bacco offers tastings of local Marino wines, such as the crisp white Frascati and other specialties from the Castelli Romani area. The menu includes light bites and small plates, such as cured meats, cheeses, and bruschetta, perfectly complementing the wine offerings.

Accommodation

For sagre normally I tell you that an overnight stay is unnecessary. However, since this is a wine festival, here are some hotel options. I think three nights would be nice; there are many sites to see nearby.

LH Hotel Domus Caesari. Address: Via Romana, 23

A 4-star hotel offering elegant rooms with panoramic views of Rome's skyline, in the Castelli Romani countryside.

Grand Hotel Helio Cabala. Address: Via Spinabella, 13/15

A 4-star hotel featuring comfortable accommodations, a restaurant, and proximity to local attractions.

Day Trip Options: Nearby Sites, Cities, and Towns

Ardea. Distance from Marino: 45 kilometers (28 miles) southwest. Ardea is an ancient town with roots stretching back to the 9th century BC, when it was a prominent settlement of the Rutulians, a pre-Roman Italic people. The town played a significant role during the early Roman Republic. Visitors can explore the remnants of the original acropolis and marvel at the archaeological sites that highlight its ancient history.

Pomezia. 35 kilometers (22 miles) southwest of Marino. Established in the 1930s, Pomezia is another example of a Fascist-era planned town. Despite its modern origins, the town boasts several historical and recreational highlights. The Torre Maggiore, a medieval watchtower, stands as a reminder of its strategic importance in earlier centuries. Selva dei Pini park offers green spaces for relaxation, and nearby, the Zoomarine water park in Torvaianica provides family-friendly entertainment. Pomezia's blend of history, leisure, and modernity makes it a versatile destination.

Marino Festivals Throughout the Year

Festa Patronale di San Barnaba

June 11

The celebration pays tribute to San Barnaba, Marino's patron saint since 1619. The celebration includes a livestock trade fair and various exhibition stands, continuing a centuries-old tradition. The festival commemorates the town's appeal to San Barnaba for protection against hailstorms that struck Marino on June 11th between 1615 and 1618.

Festa della Compatronale di Santa Lucia

December 13

This festival honors Santa Lucia, Marino's original patron saint. The celebration includes religious ceremonies and a procession of young girls dressed in white, symbolizing Santa Lucia's role as the bearer of light. The procession moves from the Civic Museum to the Church of San Barnaba, where a girl representing Santa Lucia lights a candle, marking her association with vision and light.

Mercatino dell'Antiquariato

Last Sunday of every month

This monthly antique market brings both locals and tourists to the charming streets of Marino's old town. Visitors can browse a wide variety of stalls offering antiques, curiosities, and collectibles.

CHAPTER THIRTY-ONE

Lights, Camera, Roma!

Celebrating the Magic of the Cinema at the Eternal City's International Film Festival

Festa di Cinema del Roma

Where: Rome

When: 10 days in mid-October.

Average Festival Temperatures: Highs 23°C (73°F). Lows of 12°C (54°F).

Event Website: https://www.romacinemafest.it/it/

The Rome Film Festival

The Rome Film Festival, known locally as Festa del Cinema di Roma, is one of Italy's premier film festivals, showcasing both international and Italian films. This festival has quickly become an influential event on the global film circuit. Held annually, the festival brings together filmmakers, actors, and film enthusiasts from around the world, celebrating cinema in the heart of Italy's capital.

History

Since its inception in 2006, the Rome Film Festival has evolved into a major player in the international film festival scene. Initially created to bring more cultural events to Rome in the fall, it has grown to attract world-renowned directors, actors, and industry professionals. Over the years, the festival has expanded its program to include more diverse film categories, industry events, and public engagement initiatives, cementing its place as a significant date on the global film calendar.

The Rome Film Festival typically takes place in October. Specific dates vary year to year. The festival usually spans the second half of October, providing a mix of autumnal weather and a vibrant cultural atmosphere in the city.

Where Is the Rome Film Festival Held?

The primary hub of the festival is the Auditorium Parco della Musica, a stunning complex designed by renowned architect Renzo Piano, in the northern part of Rome. Most of the festival's screenings, red carpet events, and panel discussions are held at the venue, which boasts multiple screening rooms.

Besides the Auditorium Parco della Musica, screenings and special events also take place at other iconic locations across the city, including:

- MAXXI Museum: A contemporary art museum that often hosts special events and screenings.

- Casa del Cinema: In Villa Borghese, this cinema offers a more intimate setting for select films.

- Centrale Montemartini: A fascinating venue combining ancient Roman art and modern cinema, adding a unique atmosphere to the screenings.

What You Need to Know to Attend

1. Tickets and Passes

Single Tickets: You can purchase individual tickets for specific films or events online or at the festival box office. It's highly recommended to buy tickets in advance, especially for popular screenings or red-carpet events, as these sell out quickly.

Festival Pass: If you plan to go to multiple screenings, consider purchasing a festival pass, which provides access to a selection of films throughout the festival. The pass offers more flexibility and is perfect for dedicated cinema enthusiasts.

2. Language

Films are screened in their original language, with Italian subtitles. Many international films will have English subtitles, making it accessible for non-Italian-speaking visitors. However, be sure to check the language and subtitle details when selecting films to attend.

3. Getting There

The Auditorium Parco della Musica is easily accessible by public transport. You are able to reach it by taking the Metro A to Flaminio station, then switching to tram Line 2 to the Apollodoro stop, which is a short walk from the venue.

Rome's public transportation system will also get you to the other screening locations, such as MAXXI and the Casa del Cinema, which are scattered across the city but accessible via bus or tram.

For those who prefer more direct transportation, taxis and ride-sharing services like Uber are readily available in Rome. If you're planning to explore beyond the festival venues, consider renting a car, but be aware that parking in central Rome can be challenging.

4. What to Expect

Red Carpet Events: The festival hosts glamorous red-carpet events featuring international and Italian stars. While access to these events is limited to ticket holders, spectators can watch the arrivals from outside the designated area at the Auditorium Parco della Musica.

Panels and Masterclasses: Besides screenings, the festival offers panels, workshops, and masterclasses with industry professionals, which are great for aspiring filmmakers and those interested in behind-the-scenes cinema.

Film Categories and Awards

The Rome Film Festival showcases a diverse range of films across various categories:

- Feature Films: The main competition section, featuring recent works from established and emerging directors.

- Documentaries: A selection of non-fiction films covering various subjects and styles.

- Short Films: A platform for up-and-coming filmmakers to showcase their talent.

- Retrospectives: Screenings of classic films or tributes to specific directors or actors.

The festival also presents several awards, including:

- Golden Marcus Aurelius Award for Best Film

- Best Director Award

- Best Actor and Actress Awards

- Special Jury Prize

Festival Etiquette

- Arrive on time: Latecomers may not be admitted to screenings.

- No photography or recording: This is strictly prohibited during film screenings.

- Q&A session: If you attend a Q&A, keep questions brief and relevant to the film.

Dining Recommendations Near the Events

After a day of film screenings, you'll likely want to experience some of Rome's famous cuisine. Here are a few recommendations near the main festival venues:

Ristorante Rinaldi al Quirinale. Address: Via Parma, 11

It's a brilliant choice for an upscale dining experience with traditional Roman cuisine, ideal for a relaxing evening after a full day of screenings.

Taverna Rossini. Address: Viale Gioacchino Rossini, 54

A more casual option where you may enjoy a comforting Italian meal without a high price tag, making it ideal for a quicker yet satisfying meal between events.

Fatamorgana. Address: Via Aosta, 3

Ideal for a sweet break, this artisanal gelato spot will give you a refreshing treat between screenings.

Accommodation: See Accommodation Detail Chapter for information on Rome hotels. I would recommend a minimum of four nights in Rome for the festival.

CHAPTER THIRTY-TWO

Immersion Experience Game: The Great Obelisk Hunt

Discovering Ancient Rome's Egyptian Treasures

Transform your Roman holiday into an extraordinary treasure hunt through the heart of the Eternal City.

In "Find the Ancient Obelisks," you (or your kids) can become modern-day explorers on a quest to discover eight magnificent Egyptian obelisks that stand as silent sentinels throughout Rome's historic streets.

We played this game with our ten-year-old son Augustus during our visit to Rome. It really kept him engaged, as we gradually discovered most of the obelisks while exploring Rome's principal sites. The following year, when his teacher assigned an "Ancient Rome Project," Augustus built a 3-D model featuring all eight obelisks. His teacher was impressed and amazed, she hadn't known about these ancient treasures!

These towering monuments, each transported thousands of miles from the banks of the Nile centuries ago, represent one of history's most ambitious acts of art collection. Armed with your map and camera, you'll weave through Renaissance piazzas, past baroque fountains, and across ancient forums to locate these majestic stone pillars.

While the obelisks themselves tower openly in Rome's squares, the adventure lies in crafting your route, uncovering their stories, and enjoying their grandeur during your visit.

Lateran Obelisk

Location: Piazza San Giovanni in Laterano

The tallest obelisk in Rome, this one also originated in Karnak, Egypt, and was commissioned by Pharaoh Thutmose III. It was transported to Rome by Emperor Constantine II in the 4th century CE and erected in the Circus Maximus. Pope Sixtus V relocated it to its current site in 1588. It stands 32 meters (45 meters (147 feet) including the base).

Fun Fact: It is the largest standing ancient Egyptian obelisk in the world.

Minerveo (Minerva Obelisk)

Location: Piazza della Minerva

Standing at 5.47 meters (12.69 meters, 41 feet with its base), this obelisk was originally from Sais and was brought to Rome by Diocletian. The Egyptian hieroglyphs on the obelisk praise the pharaoh Apries, who ruled during the 26th dynasty. The unique combination of ancient Egyptian art and Baroque creativity makes this monument a perfect example of Rome's ability to blend different cultural elements.

Bernini completed the elephant base design in 1667 under Pope Alexander VII's patronage, and the statue quickly became a beloved landmark among Romans who affectionately nicknamed it "il pulcino" (the little chicken). Local legend says that Bernini deliberately positioned the elephant so that its rear end faces the Dominican monastery nearby, as a subtle jest toward his critics among the Dominican priests.

Fun Fact: The obelisk rests upon one of Bernini's most whimsical designs: an elephant base known as "Pulcino della Minerva" ("Minerva's Little Chicken"), where the elephant appears to carry the ancient monument on its back with a playful, almost smiling expression. Romans gave it this affectionate nickname because of its small, stocky proportions compared to typical majestic elephant statues.

Minerva Obelsk

Flaminio (Flaminian Obelisk)

Location: Piazza del Popolo

The obelisk was initially erected at the Circus Maximus, where it stood as a monument to Roman triumph and power. After centuries buried in debris, it was rediscovered in 1587 and moved to its current location under the direction of Pope Sixtus V. The hieroglyphic inscriptions celebrate the glory of Ramses II and the sun god Ra, while the Latin inscriptions added to its base proclaim Christian triumph.

Today, it serves as the centerpiece of one of Rome's most elegant squares, where three main streets, the "trident", converge, creating a masterpiece of urban planning. The obelisk's placement transformed what was once the main northern entrance to Rome into a grand architectural statement about papal authority and urban renewal.

Fun Fact: Originally from Heliopolis and commissioned by Pharaohs Seti I and Ramses II, this 24-meter (36.50 meters, 119 feet with its base) obelisk was brought to Rome by Augustus in 10 BC.

Obelisk of Ramesses II from Heliopolis, Piazza del Popolo

Macuteo (Pantheon Obelisk)

Location: Piazza della Rotonda (in front of the Pantheon)

This 6.34-meter (14.52 meters, 48 feet with its base) obelisk was originally one of a pair at the Temple of Ra in Heliopolis, commissioned by Ramses II.

Fun Fact: It was moved to its current location in 1711.

Solare (Sundial Obelisk)

Location: Piazza di Montecitorio

Commissioned by Pharaoh Psammetichus II, this 21.79-meter (33.97 meters, 112 feet with its base) obelisk was brought to Rome by Augustus in 10 BC to serve as the gnomon of the Solarium Augusti, a giant sundial.

Fun Fact: It was rediscovered and erected in its current location in 1792.

Dogali Obelisk

Location: Near the Baths of Diocletian

Originally one of a pair from Heliopolis, this obelisk was moved to the Temple of Isis in Rome.

Fun Fact: It now commemorates the Battle of Dogali.

Matteiano (Villa Celimontana Obelisk)

Location: Villa Celimontana

At 2.68 meters (12.23 meters, 40 feet with its base), it's the smallest of Rome's ancient Egyptian obelisks. Originally one of a pair at the Temple of Ra in Heliopolis, it was moved to the Temple of Isis in Rome.

Fun Fact: It was re-erected in its current location in 1820.

Esquiline Obelisk

Location: Piazza dell'Esquilino (near Santa Maria Maggiore)

The twin to the Quirinal Obelisk, this monument was carved in the late 1st century AD and originally stood at the entrance to the Mausoleum of Augustus. It was re-erected here by Pope Sixtus V in 1587 as part of his grand urban plan. Height: 14.5 meters (25 meters/82 feet including the base).

Fun Fact: Although it appears Egyptian, this obelisk is a Roman creation carved in the Egyptian style to honor Augustus's fascination with Egypt after his conquest.

CHAPTER THIRTY-THREE

The Heart of Autumn in Rocca di Papa

Chestnuts Roasting on an Open Fire

S agra della Castagna

Where: Rocca di Papa

When: Third Weekend in October

Average Festival Temperatures: High: 18°C (64°F). Low: 10°C (50°F).

In Defense of the Papacy: The History of Rocca di Papa

Rocca di Papa, nestled in the Alban Hills of the Castelli Romani, has a rich history dating back to ancient times. It was once part of the Latin League, a confederation of Latin cities that opposed the early expansion of Rome. The town's strategic location on the slopes of Monte Cavo made it an important defensive point throughout history. In the Middle Ages, Rocca di Papa became a fortified stronghold, and its name ("Rock of the Pope") reflects its long-standing ties to the papacy. During the 13th century, the town was controlled by various noble families and played a role in the region's medieval power struggles.

In later centuries, Rocca di Papa developed into a popular summer retreat because of its cooler climate and scenic views of the Roman countryside. During the 19th century, it became a refuge for artists, writers, and intellectuals who sought inspiration in its natural beauty and historic charm. Today, Rocca di Papa is known for its panoramic views from Monte Cavo, as well as its quaint streets, religious festivals, and peaceful atmosphere, all of which preserve its historical identity as a significant cultural and religious center in the region.

The Chestnut Festival

Rocca di Papa comes alive each October with the aroma of roasting chestnuts and the vibrant colors of autumn. The Sagra della Castagna, or Chestnut Festival, is a beloved celebration that draws visitors from across Italy to this picturesque town in the Castelli Romani region.

Festival History

The Sagra della Castagna in Rocca di Papa has deep roots in the agricultural traditions of the Alban Hills. Chestnuts have been a staple food in this region for centuries, thriving in the volcanic soil that characterizes the area. The festival's origins can be traced back to medieval harvest celebrations, where communities would gather to give thanks for the bountiful chestnut crop.

The modern incarnation of the festival began in the 1930s, developing from a simple harvest celebration into a major cultural event. Over the decades, it has grown to encompass not just the celebration of chestnuts, but also the rich culinary, artistic, and historical heritage of Rocca di Papa and the surrounding Castelli Romani region.

The festival's significance extends beyond mere culinary appreciation. It serves as a vital link to the town's past, preserving traditional methods of chestnut cultivation and preparation. It plays a crucial role in the local economy, providing a platform for artisans, farmers, and food producers to showcase their products to a wider audience.

Ancient Roots of the Chestnut Tree in Italy

Chestnuts have been cultivated in Italy since ancient times. The tree is believed to have been introduced to the Italian peninsula by the Greeks around 5th-6th century BC, but some evidence suggests that chestnuts might have been present even earlier, growing wild in Italy's mountainous regions. Later, the Romans played a key role in spreading chestnut cultivation throughout their empire, including Italy, because of its versatility as a food source.

During the Middle Ages, chestnuts became a crucial staple food for people living in Italy's mountainous and forested regions. These areas often had poor soil that was unsuitable for growing grains, but chestnut trees thrived. Chestnuts were ground into flour to make bread, polenta, and pasta, sustaining rural populations during harsh winters when other food sources were scarce. For this reason, chestnuts were often referred to as "the bread of the poor."

Key Events

The festival's centerpiece is the tasting of freshly roasted chestnuts (caldarroste) and an array of sweet and savory chestnut based dishes. A colorful historical parade winds through the cobblestone streets, featuring participants in medieval costume, flag throwing displays, drummers, and musicians. An artisan market offers chestnut wood carvings, pottery, and leather goods, with live demonstrations of traditional crafts.

Cooking demonstrations by local nonnas and chefs reveal time-honored secrets for roasting chestnuts and preparing chestnut flour pasta, while folk music and dances like the saltarello invite audience participation. Visitors can join chestnut-themed competitions, from peeling contests to culinary challenges, and sample regional wines from the Castelli Romani at guided tastings.

Festival Timeline

The Sagra della Castagna fills Rocca di Papa with autumn energy each October.

Friday: Opening ceremony with music in the town's historic center.

Saturday: Artisan markets, food stalls, historical procession, street performances, and evening folk music capped by fireworks from the medieval fortress.

Sunday: Grand historical parade, chestnut competitions, wine tastings, and closing festivities with music and a final fireworks display.

Local Customs

Highlights include the ceremonial first roasting of chestnuts by the town's most senior resident and the blessing of the harvest by the parish priest. Traditional costumes, often family heirlooms, bring history to life, and seasonal workshops teach the art of autumn wreath making using chestnuts, leaves, and berries from the Alban Hills.

Special Festival Treat
Monte Cavo Cake

No visit to the festival would be complete without sampling the renowned "Monte Cavo" cake, a beloved local delicacy that pays homage to the volcanic peak towering above the town. This rich dessert masterfully combines ground chestnuts with high-quality chocolate, creating a dense, moist cake that captures the essence of the region.

The recipe, closely guarded by local families, is said to have originated in the kitchens of noble families who once summered in the area. Today, each bakery in Rocca di Papa offers its own subtle variation of this classic, leading to friendly debates among locals about which version best represents the traditional recipe.

Walking Tour of Rocca di Papa

#1. Piazza della Repubblica

Begin your tour at Piazza della Repubblica, the main square of Rocca di Papa. This bustling square is the heart of Rocca di Papa. Surrounded by pastel-colored buildings, it's a perfect example of a traditional Italian piazza. The square is often filled with locals chatting, children playing, and visitors soaking in the atmosphere. Notice the 19th-century clock tower that dominates one side of the square, a symbol of the town's civic pride.

#2. Historic Center

From the square, venture into the narrow cobblestone streets of the historic center.

As you wander through these winding alleys, you'll be transported back in time. The historic center dates back to medieval times, with some structures even older. Admire the charming houses with their colorful shutters and flower-filled balconies. The streets themselves tell a story, with worn cobblestones that have seen centuries of footsteps. Keep an eye out for local artisans selling handcrafted goods, a tradition that has been kept alive for generations.

#3. Duomo di Santa Maria Assunta

This beautiful Baroque church, dating back to the 17th century, is a jewel of Rocca di Papa. Its elegant facade features intricate stonework and a central rose window. Step inside to discover a world of artistic treasures. The interior is adorned with stunning frescoes, including works by the renowned painter Taddeo Zuccari. Pay special attention to the main altar, a masterpiece of marble inlay. The church also houses several important religious relics, making it a significant pilgrimage site.

#4. Via del Tuscolo

This street offers some of the best views in Rocca di Papa. As you stroll, you'll notice how the town is built on a steep slope, with houses seeming to cascade down the hill. The street provides breathtaking vistas of the surrounding Alban Hills and, on clear days, you might even glimpse Rome in the distance. The gardens and terraces along this street are beautiful in spring when they burst into bloom.

#5. Belvedere della Fortezza

The Belvedere della Fortezza is the crown jewel of Rocca di Papa. These ruins remain of a medieval fortress that once guarded the town. Built in the 12th century, it played a crucial role in the area's defense for centuries. Today, it offers the most spectacular panoramic views of the Castelli Romani area and Lake Albano. On a clear day, you can see as far as the Mediterranean Sea. The site also includes informative panels that detail the fortress's history and significance.

#6. Geophysical Museum

Housed in a former seismic station, this unique museum offers insight into the geological forces that shaped the region. Interactive exhibits explain concepts like plate tectonics and volcanic activity, with a focus on the local Alban Hills volcanic complex. The museum also features a seismograph that records real-time earthquake activity, offering a fascinating glimpse into the Earth's constant movements.

#7. Via dei Castelli Romani

Make your way back towards the town center on Via dei Castelli Romani.

This street offers a different perspective of Rocca di Papa and the surrounding landscape. As you descend, enjoy views of the lush forests that carpet the hillsides. The road is lined with chestnut trees, which have been economically important to the region for centuries. In autumn, the changing colors of the leaves create a spectacular display.

Logistics

Train: The nearest train station is in Frascati, about 9 km from Rocca di Papa. From Rome Termini, the journey to Frascati takes around 30 minutes. From there, you can take a bus or taxi to Rocca di Papa, which is a quick ride away.

Bus: Direct buses run from Anagnina Metro Station (Rome's Line A) to Rocca di Papa, with a journey time of approximately 40 minutes.

Car: Driving from Rome to Rocca di Papa is a straightforward journey of approximately 26 kilometers (16 miles) and typically takes around 30 to 40 minutes, depending on traffic.

Parking: Rocca di Papa has a ZTL to preserve its historic center, restricting vehicle access during certain hours. To avoid entering the ZTL and potential fines, consider these parking options: Via delle Barozze, 55 Parking: An open-air parking area located at Via delle Barozze, 55 or Piazza Giuseppe di Vittorio Parking.

Restaurant Recommendations

La Locanda nel Bosco. Address: Via Rocca Priora 39

Tucked away in a forested area near Rocca di Papa, this restaurant is renowned for its cozy atmosphere and traditional dishes made with local ingredients. Their menu features seasonal dishes, homemade pasta, and a variety of meats, offering a true taste of the region.

Osteria Dei Colli. Address: Via dei Colli 17

A family-run trattoria in the heart of Rocca di Papa, this restaurant serves up classic Roman cuisine with a focus on regional flavors. Their warm hospitality and hearty dishes, like porchetta and fettuccine al ragù, make it a favorite among locals.

Accommodation

Overnight stays are unnecessary for sagre, but if you would like to stay here is a hotel option near Rocca di Papa. I believe two nights would be nice to see the town and enjoy the sagra.

Villa Palazzola. Address: V. dei Laghi, Km 10,800

Villa Palazzola is set in the hills south of Rome, high above the extinct volcanic Lago Albano. It is an ideal resort for travelers who want to get away from the hubbub and maelstrom of urban life, while still keeping close to all that Rome offers.

Day Trip Options: Nearby Sites, Cities, and Towns

Monte Cavo. 6 kilometers (3.7 miles) from Rocca di Papa to Monte Cavo's summit. If you're up for a nature excursion, head to Monte Cavo, an ancient volcanic peak. The hiking trails lead to incredible views over the Castelli Romani area and the Roman

Velletri. 15.6 kilometers (9.7 miles) via local roads. Although it borders the Castelli Romani, Velletri is considered a separate historic town. It's known for its impressive Cathedral of San Clemente and Palazzo Ginnetti, as well as its wine production. Velletri offers a combination of cultural and culinary experiences.

Velletri's Defensive Walls

Rocca di Papa Festivals Throughout the Year

La Mangialonga

Summer

La Mangialonga is a non-competitive 7-kilometer walk that takes participants through the scenic woods and archaeological sites of Rocca di Papa. Along the route, frequent stops offer tastings of traditional local foods, including pork meat, cold cuts, baked dishes, and wine from the Castelli Romani. The event combines outdoor recreation with the region's rich culinary heritage, creating a festive and communal atmosphere.

Octave of Our Lady of Mercy

Starts on the third Saturday of September and lasts for eight days

This religious festival is deeply rooted in Rocca di Papa's traditions and centers around the veneration of the Virgin Mary. The celebration begins with the public display of the sacred image of the Virgin, preserved in the Cathedral, during the traditional "Calata" ceremony. All week long, the city is treated to the image paraded on a Processional Machine. The event concludes on the following Sunday with the image's ascension back to its altar. This festival brings the parish community together in devotion and celebration.

Festa del Santo Patrono Carlo Borromeo (Patron Saint's Day)

Week of November 4th

Celebrating the Patron Saint of Rocca di Papa, Saint Carlo Borromeo, this week-long festival fills the town with concerts, traditional games, markets, and vibrant firework displays. The event honors the saint's legacy while fostering community spirit through a mix of religious and cultural activities.

CHAPTER THIRTY-FOUR

Latina Lights Up with the Magic of the Circus

A Premier Event on the International Circus Scene

Festa Internazionale del Circo

Where: Latina

When: Third Weekend in October

Average Festival Temperatures: High 21°C (70°F). Low 14°C (57°F).

Website: https://www.festivalcircoitalia.com/

Latina: A Modern City with Deep Roots

Latina, a relatively young city compared to many others in Italy, was founded on June 30, 1932, during the Fascist era. Initially named Littoria, the city was part of a large-scale project to reclaim the Pontine Marshes (Agro Pontino), a region plagued by malaria and underutilized for centuries. The successful land reclamation transformed the area into fertile farmland, and Latina became a model agricultural and industrial center. After World War II, the city was renamed Latina in 1946, reflecting a move away from its Fascist origins.

The town's unique history lies in its planned design and modernist architecture, showcasing the ideals of 20th-century urban planning. Today, Latina stands as a vibrant blend of history, agriculture, and culture, growing into a hub for festivals and international events.

Latina is located in the Lazio region, 60 kilometers (37 miles) south of Rome. It lies within the fertile plains of the Agro Pontino, bordered by the Tyrrhenian Sea to the west and the Lepini Mountains to the east. This strategic location provides a picturesque backdrop of rolling hills, farmlands, and sandy beaches along the coastline.

With a population of 130,000 residents, Latina is one of the largest cities in the Lazio region after Rome. It has a dynamic and diverse community, attracting people from rural areas, nearby towns, and even internationally because of its agricultural and industrial opportunities.

International Circus Festival of Italy

The International Circus Festival of Italy is a premier event in the global circus arts scene. Established in 1999 by the late Giulio Montico, a distinguished circus artist with a rich European career, the festival has grown significantly over the years. Montico's vision was to create a unique, non-itinerant event that would elevate the circus arts, providing a dignified platform for performers worldwide.

The festival is structured as a competition, attracting artists from all over the world who showcase a diverse range of acts, from classical circus traditions to innovative and experimental performances. Each year, approximately 100 artists from around 20 nations take part, performing in front of an international jury of experts.

Over the years, the festival has garnered significant recognition and support from various public institutions. Since 2002, the President of the Italian Republic has awarded medals to outstanding artists. The European Parliament, the Ministry of Cultural Heritage and Activities, and the Ministry of Foreign Affairs are among the institutions that have granted patronage to the event.

Besides the major performances, the festival includes various collateral events such as the "Circus Expo," showcasing circus-inspired art, and the "Caffè Letterario," a literary café discussing circus-themed literature. These activities contribute to the festival's mission of promoting circus culture to a broader audience.

Event Schedule

Thursday

Evening Performance: The festival typically opens with "Show A" at 9:00 PM, featuring a selection of competing acts.

Friday

Evening Performance: "Show B" begins at 9:00 PM, presenting a different lineup of performers.

Saturday / Sunday

Afternoon Performance: "Show B" is repeated at 4:30 PM.

Evening Performance: "Show A" is repeated at 9:00 PM.

Monday

Gala Show and Awards Ceremony: The festival culminates with a Gala Show and Awards Ceremony at 8:30 PM, where top performers are honored.

Tickets: Tickets can be purchased online through the festival's official website or at the box office near the Big Top from the start of October.

Walking Tour of Latina

#1. Piazza del Popolo
Piazza del Popolo is the central square of Latina and a vibrant gathering place for locals. The square is surrounded by significant Fascist-era architecture, including the Town Hall (Palazzo del Comune), which features a prominent clock tower. Built in the early 1930s, the square showcases the urban planning ideals of the time, with geometric designs and symmetrical layouts. Visitors can relax at outdoor cafes and appreciate the combination of old and new in the city's core.

#2. Palazzo M

Palazzo M, named for its M-shaped layout, was constructed as a Fascist headquarters in the 1930s. Today, it houses government offices and stands as a remarkable example of Rationalist architecture. The building's design is stark and functional, reflecting the architectural trends of the period. Visitors can explore its striking facade and the nearby gardens, which offer a peaceful respite.

#3. Museo Civico Duilio Cambellotti

Dedicated to the artist Duilio Cambellotti, this museum showcases a collection of works that highlight the Agro Pontino region's transformation during the Fascist era. Cambellotti's sculptures, paintings, and designs emphasize the connection between art and the reclamation of the marshlands. The museum is housed in a historic building and provides a deeper understanding of Latina's cultural and historical context.

#4. San Marco Cathedral

San Marco Cathedral is the main church in Latina, designed in a modern style with traditional elements. Built in the 1930s, it is dedicated to Saint Mark and reflects the city's relatively recent establishment. Inside, visitors can find beautiful mosaics and a peaceful atmosphere, making it an excellent spot for reflection and appreciation of the city's spiritual heritage.

#5. Torre Civica (Civic Tower)

Next to Piazza del Popolo, the Torre Civica is a symbolic structure of Latina. Built in the Fascist style, the tower was meant to represent the strength and vision of the new city. From the base, visitors can admire the tower's imposing design and its integration into the city's overall architectural theme.

Logistics

Train: Latina is accessible by train via the Latina Scalo station, located approximately 9 km (5.6 miles) outside the city center. From Latina Scalo, buses and taxis are available to take you into the city center.

Bus: Latina has an efficient local and regional bus network. Cotral operates buses that connect Latina to neighboring towns and Rome, with frequent service to and from the Anagnina Metro Station in Rome. Within Latina, the city's public transport system covers major areas, making it easy to navigate.

Car: Latina is well-connected by road. From Rome, take the SS148 Pontina, a direct highway that leads to Latina in about 1 hour. From Naples, follow the A1 Autostrada north, exiting at Frosinone, then take local roads to Latina. Driving is convenient for exploring nearby sites and towns.

Parking: Latina does not have a ZTL (Zona a Traffico Limitato) in its city center, making parking more straightforward than in older Italian cities. Free and paid parking options are available throughout the city, including near Piazza del Popolo and major landmarks like San Marco Cathedral. Public parking lots, such as those at Corso della Repubblica, offer convenient access to the chief attractions.

Restaurant Recommendations

Trattoria Sandalari. Address: Via Adua, 4
A charming Italian trattoria specializing in seafood and traditional dishes. The menu is simple, featuring high quality ingredients prepared with care. Guests appreciate the unbeatable quality and authentic flavors.

Testa O Croce Pizzeria. Address: Piazza Orazio, 10
A well-regarded pizzeria offering authentic Neapolitan-style pizzas. Customers love the Naples-style pizza and the welcoming environment, making it a favorite spot for both locals and visitors.

Accommodation

I would recommend two to three nights in town for the festival.

Hotel Europa. Address: Via Emanuele Filiberto, 14
A luxury hotel in the heart of Latina, opened in 2006. It offers a sophisticated atmosphere with a fully equipped meeting room, heated swimming pool, and wellness center. Guests appreciate its central location and friendly staff.

Day Trip Options: Nearby Sites, Cities and Towns

Sermoneta. 20 kilometers (12 miles) from Latina. A picturesque medieval hill town, Sermoneta is known for its well-preserved architecture and rich history.

The town's centerpiece is Castello Caetani, a fortress built in the 13th century that offers panoramic views of the surrounding countryside. Visitors can explore its ancient walls, grand halls, and a drawbridge that transports you back in time. Sermoneta is also a cultural hub, hosting concerts and events in its charming streets. Don't miss the town's vibrant local markets and artisan shops.

Ninfa Gardens (Giardini di Ninfa). 15 kilometers (9 miles). Often described as one of the most beautiful gardens in the world, Ninfa Gardens is a magical oasis built among the ruins of the medieval town of Ninfa. Created in the 1920s, the gardens feature exotic plants, romantic pathways, and streams fed by the Ninfa River. This UNESCO-listed site is a haven for nature lovers and photographers, with blooms changing with the seasons. Guided tours are available, offering insights into the site's history and botanical treasures.

Terracina. 50 kilometers (31 miles) from Latina. Terracina is a blend of history, culture, and coastal charm. The town's most iconic site is the Temple of Jupiter Anxur, perched atop Monte Sant'Angelo, offering breathtaking views of the Tyrrhenian Sea. Visitors can wander through the historic center, where Roman ruins blend seamlessly with medieval architecture. The lively promenade and sandy beaches make Terracina a perfect mix of culture and relaxation.

Latina Festivals and Sagre Throughout the Year

Sagra della Polenta

February

While not located directly in Latina, the nearby town of Sermoneta hosts the Sagra della Polenta in February, attracting many visitors from the region. This traditional food festival celebrates polenta, a staple of Italian cuisine. Attendees can enjoy various polenta dishes prepared according to local recipes, often accompanied by regional wines and live folk music.

The festival highlights the area's culinary heritage and offers a convivial atmosphere for both locals and tourists.

Festa di San Marco (St. Mark)

April 25

The Festa di San Marco honors Saint Mark, the patron saint of Latina. Celebrated annually on April 25, the festival features religious processions through the city streets, accompanied by music and communal prayers. The event fosters a sense of unity among residents and offers visitors insight into the city's spiritual traditions.

CHAPTER THIRTY-FIVE

Frascati's Toast to Tradition

Celebrating the Wine Harvest

F esta della Cortesia

Where: Frascati

When: Last week of October.

Average Festival Temperatures: High: 18°C (64°F). Low: 10°C (50°F).

Frascati Through Time: From Ancient Retreats to Timeless Charm

Frascati, in the Castelli Romani area, lies 20 kilometers (12 miles) southeast of Rome. Perched on the slopes of the Alban Hills, it offers panoramic views of Rome's skyline and is surrounded by fertile lands ideal for wine production. Its elevation (320 meters (1000 feet) above sea level) and mild climate have historically made it a desirable location for Roman elites seeking respite from the city's heat.

With ancient roots, Frascati was once part of the Latin League, a confederation of cities that played a significant role in ancient Roman history. During the Roman Empire, it became a retreat for the aristocracy, who built opulent villas amidst its rolling hills. One notable example is the Villa of Lucullus, a luxurious estate belonging to the famed Roman general and statesman. The town's strategic position near the Via Appia also contributed to its early prosperity.

Frascati flourished during the Renaissance and Baroque periods, when prominent families like the Aldobrandini commissioned lavish villas, many of which still stand as symbols of the town's aristocratic past. The Villa Aldobrandini, an architectural masterpiece, remains the most iconic and continues to attract visitors with its impressive gardens and frescoed interiors.

Renowned for its centuries-old wine production, Frascati is synonymous with its Frascati DOC[1], a light and refreshing white wine made from local grapes. This tradition dates back to ancient Roman times, earning the town a reputation as a significant center of viticulture in Italy.

Today, Frascati has a population of 20,000 residents and continues to thrive as a popular destination for both locals and tourists. Its proximity to Rome, cultural heritage, and charming piazzas make it an ideal day trip or retreat from the bustling capital. Whether exploring its historical villas, savoring its renowned wines, or enjoying its scenic landscapes, Frascati remains a timeless gem of the Castelli Romani.

Wine Harvest Festival

The Festa della Cortesia, a festival that honors the conclusion of the wine harvest, emerged as a way for the rich winemakers to express their gratitude to the workers who tirelessly toiled in the vineyards. Encapsulating the spirit of the festival, the

---

1. DOC (Denominazione di Origine Controllata) is an Italian wine classification that ensures the quality, authenticity, and geographic origin of a wine. Introduced in 1963, DOC wines must adhere to strict regulations regarding grape varieties, production methods, yield limits, and aging requirements, all tailored to reflect the unique characteristics of their specific region.

word "cortesia," meaning courtesy or kindness, highlights the values of generosity, community, and thanksgiving. This festival is one of Frascati's most important cultural events, celebrating not only the end of the harvest season but also the region's agricultural heritage and the bond between landowners and laborers.

History of the Festa della Cortesia

The Festa della Cortesia has its roots in the 17th century, a time when Frascati's vineyards were owned by wealthy aristocratic families who depended on seasonal laborers to tend to the vines and harvest the grapes. During the harvest season, vineyard workers, many of whom came from neighboring villages, would spend long days picking grapes and preparing them for the wine-making process. At the end of the harvest, it became customary for the landowners to host a feast to thank their workers, offering them food, wine, and entertainment.

Over time, this private celebration evolved into a larger public festival, as Frascati's winemaking industry expanded and became more central to the town's economy. By the 19th century, the festival had become an annual event, bringing together the entire community to celebrate the successful harvest and the region's wine culture. The festival was given its official name, Festa della Cortesia, in the early 20th century, and it has been held every year since, with some breaks during times of war or hardship.

The Festival

The Festa della Cortesia is held during the last week of October, marking the end of the grape harvest and the beginning of the wine-making process. It's a lively, multi-day event that includes concerts, fireworks displays, and exhibitions of traditional agricultural tools. The festival brings together locals, visitors, winemakers, and agricultural workers to celebrate the town's rich wine heritage and give thanks for the year's harvest.

Festival Events

Concerts and Live Music

The festival kicks off with a series of concerts held in Piazza San Pietro and other central squares in Frascati. Music options range from folk bands playing traditional Roman tunes to more contemporary performances by local artists.

The lively atmosphere is perfect for dancing. It is common to see people enjoying the music with a glass of Frascati wine in hand.

Exhibition of Agricultural Tools and Machinery

One of the unique aspects of the festival is the exhibition of traditional agricultural tools, which takes place in Piazza Marconi. Local farmers and artisans display vintage plows, wine presses, and other tools that were historically used in the vineyards and cellars of Frascati. This exhibition offers a fascinating glimpse into the town's agrarian past and highlights the craftsmanship involved in traditional wine production. In recent years, the exhibition has also featured modern agricultural machinery, showing how the industry has evolved while still honoring its roots.

Parades and Processions

The festival also includes a parade through the streets of Frascati, with participants dressed in historical costumes that reflect the town's agricultural past. Local families, farmers, and vineyard workers march together, carrying baskets of grapes, bottles of wine, and banners representing the town's wine guilds. The parade is accompanied by marching bands and flag bearers, adding to the festive atmosphere.

Fireworks Display

On the final evening of the festival, a spectacular fireworks display is held, lighting up the sky above Frascati's historic center. Fireworks launch from a famed villa, like Villa Aldobrandini, offering a breathtaking view. The fireworks symbolize the end of the harvest and the community's gratitude for a bountiful season.

Traditional Food and Wine

Throughout the festival, the streets of Frascati are lined with food stalls offering a variety of local specialties. Visitors can sample porchetta, a traditional Roman dish of slow-roasted pork, as well as fried polenta, pasta dishes, and cheeses from the surrounding countryside. Of course, the festival wouldn't be complete without Frascati wine, which is served in abundance. Many of the local wineries set up tasting booths, allowing visitors to try different varieties of wine, including Frascati Superiore and Cannellino di Frascati, both of which are renowned for their floral and fruity notes.

Agricultural Competitions

As part of the festival, local farmers and vineyard workers often compete in agricultural contests, such as grape-picking races or wine-pressing competitions. These events showcase the skills and techniques involved in traditional winemaking, and they offer a fun and engaging way for visitors to learn more about the grape harvest.

The festival offers a unique opportunity to experience traditional Roman hospitality, enjoy local food and wine, and learn about the history of wine-making in one of Italy's most famous wine regions. Whether you're a wine lover, a history enthusiast, or simply looking for a memorable experience in the heart of the Castelli Romani, the Festa della Cortesia is a must-see event.

Walking Tour of Frascati

#1. Piazza and Duomo di San Pietro

This central square is the heart of Frascati, and you'll find the town's Cathedral of St. Peter (Cattedrale di San Pietro Apostolo) here. The cathedral built in 1598 is known for its neoclassical façade and rich interior. It was heavily damaged during World War II but has since been restored.

Piazza Principale in Frascati

#2. Villa Aldobrandini

One of the grandest villas in the region, Villa Aldobrandini, was built in 1598 for Cardinal Pietro Aldobrandini, a nephew of Pope Clement VIII. The villa was designed by Giacomo della Porta, one of Michelangelo's pupils, and is a classic example of Renaissance architecture. The villa is renowned for its stunning gardens, fountains, and frescoed interiors. It sits atop a hill, offering panoramic views of Rome and the surrounding countryside. The villa is privately owned and is open only for events.

Villa Aldobrandini

#3. Scuderie Aldobrandini (Aldobrandini Stables)

Originally built in the 17th century to house the stables of Villa Aldobrandini, the Scuderie Aldobrandini has been restored and transformed into a modern exhibition space and museum.

The museum offers exhibits on the history of Frascati and the surrounding Castelli Romani area. It's a great way to delve into the town's culture.

#4. Villa Torlonia

Built in the 16th century, Villa Torlonia is another impressive historical villa in Frascati, though it has undergone various renovations over the centuries. It was once the residence of the Torlonia family, a prominent Roman noble family. The villa is surrounded by lush gardens, and although the interior is usually not open to the public, the gardens are a peaceful place for a stroll. Tickets can be purchased in advance. https://www.museivillatorlonia.it/en/infopage/biglietti

#5. Frascati Wine and Olive Oil Tasting

Frascati is famous for its white wine, and no trip to the town would be complete without a tasting experience. Head to a local enoteca (wine shop) or cantina to try Frascati Superiore, the local DOCG wine. Frascati wine has been produced in the region for over 2,000 years, dating back to ancient Roman times. Local wine shops are usually open daily. For additional information and scheduling wine tastings, refer to the following websites:

Antico Casale Mindari: https://minardifrascatiwinery.com/

Old Frascati Food and Wine: https://oldfrascati.com/

Azienda Bio De Sanctis: https://www.frascati-wine.it/

#6. Passeggiata (walk) Along Viale Vittorio Veneto

This picturesque boulevard is perfect for a late afternoon stroll. It leads up to the villa estates and offers beautiful views of the Roman countryside. The street is lined with local cafes and bakeries, where you can stop for a Frascati rosetta, a type of bread that's a specialty in the area.

#7. Palazzo Vescovile (Bishop's Palace)

From the 16th century, this was the seat of the bishops of Frascati. The building is a fine example of Renaissance architecture and offers insight into the religious and political history of the town. The palazzo houses some fascinating historical documents and artwork connected to the Roman Catholic Church.

Logistics

Train: Frascati has a direct train line to Rome's Termini Station, with frequent departures. The journey takes around 30 minutes, making it a quick and convenient option for travelers. The Frascati train station is centrally located, which is great for easy access to the town and nearby attractions.

Bus: Several bus lines also operate between Frascati and Rome, with routes connecting to various parts of the city, including metro stations. The bus ride can take longer than the train because of traffic, but it offers additional flexibility in terms of destinations within Rome.

Car: We arrived in Frascati by car and had no problems finding parking and getting around town, but the center is a ZTL (limited traffic zone).

Parking: For visitors not staying within the ZTL, it's advisable to park outside the restricted zone. Frascati offers several parking areas near the city center:

Parcheggio di Piazza Marconi, Parcheggio di Via Gregoriana or Parcheggio di Piazza San Pietro are all good options.

Recommended Restaurants

Gran Caffè Roma. Address: Piazza Roma 4

We arrived around nine in the morning and headed directly for the Gran Caffè Roma. It is on the main piazza when you arrive into town so parking is nearby. They have pastries and coffee, which you can enjoy outside in the warm morning sun.

Ristorante Belvedere dal 1933. Address: Piazza Giuseppe Garibaldi, 1

A historic restaurant with over 90 years of tradition, Belvedere dal 1933 offers both classic Roman dishes and stunning panoramic views of the surrounding countryside and Rome.

Accommodation

Usually I will say that for a sagra an overnight stay is unnecessary. But since this is a wine festival, you might consider a night or two in town.

Hotel Flora. Address: Viale Vittorio Veneto, 8

A refined 4-star hotel housed in a charming Liberty-style Roman villa from the late 19th century. The hotel features elegant rooms, a rooftop terrace with panoramic views, and a welcoming atmosphere perfect for a relaxing stay.

Villa Tuscolana. Address: Via del Tuscolo, km 1

A luxurious 4-star hotel in a stunning 16th-century villa on a hill overlooking Frascati. Guests can enjoy breathtaking views of the surrounding countryside, beautifully landscaped gardens, and access to spa facilities.

Day Trip Options: Nearby Sites, Cities, and Towns

Orvieto. 120 kilometers (74.6 miles) from Rome, Orvieto commands attention from its dramatic position atop a volcanic plateau. The city's crown jewel is its magnificent Gothic cathedral (Duomo di Orvieto), whose facade stands as one of Italy's most spectacular examples of religious architecture, adorned with intricate mosaics and sculptures. The city's fascinating underground network of caves and tunnels, carved into volcanic rock over millennia, tells the story of Etruscan and medieval life. The Pozzo di San Patrizio (St. Patrick's Well), a masterpiece of Renaissance engineering, descends 62 meters into the earth with its unique double-helix design. The city's museums, including the National Archaeological Museum and the Museum of the Cathedral (MODO), house significant collections spanning from Etruscan to medieval periods. Orvieto is also renowned for its white wine, Orvieto Classico DOC, produced in the surrounding vineyards since Etruscan times.

Velletri. 27 kilometers (16.8 miles) from Rome, Velletri stands as a historic city in the Castelli Romani region, boasting a rich cultural and architectural heritage. At its heart lies the Velletri Cathedral (Cattedrale di San Clemente), a magnificent structure dating back to the 4th century, showcasing an impressive blend of Renaissance and Baroque elements with masterful artworks by Gentile da Fabriano and Antoniazzo Romano. The city's architectural splendor continues with the 16th-century Palazzo Comunale, designed by celebrated architect Jacopo Barozzi da Vignola, while the Porta Napoletana (1511) offers glimpses into the city's medieval past. The Archaeological Museum houses an extensive collection spanning from proto-historic to medieval periods. Velletri's prestigious wine production reaches its cultural pinnacle during the annual Grape and Wine Festival each October.

Lanuvio. 20.8 kilometers (12.9 miles) from Rome, Lanuvio sits gracefully on the southern slopes of the Alban Hills, offering a compelling journey through ancient Roman history. The town's crowning glory is the Temple of Juno Sospita, whose ruins stand as testament to Lanuvio's significance in Roman religious life. The site includes well-preserved sections of the ancient sanctuary and architectural elements that highlight Roman engineering prowess. The town's medieval center features the baroque Collegiata di Santa Maria Maggiore, rebuilt in 1675, with its impressive artworks and architectural details. The picturesque Fountain of the Rocks (Fontana degli Scogli) adds to the town's charm, while the restored castle, Castello Colonna, offers panoramic views of the surrounding countryside. Lanuvio's archaeological museum houses important local finds, including votive offerings from the Temple of Juno and artifacts from nearby Roman villas.

Frascati Festivals Throughout the Year

Sant'Antonio Abate (Patron Saint of Animals)

January 17th

The festival of Sant'Antonio Abate has been celebrated in Frascati since medieval times, with records dating back to the 14th century. Saint Anthony the Abbot, also known as Anthony the Great, lived in Egypt from 251 to 356 AD and is revered as the patron saint of animals, farmers, and butchers. The tradition of blessing animals on his feast day spread throughout Italy during the Middle Ages, with Frascati adopting this custom because of its strong agricultural heritage.

The celebration begins at dawn with the ringing of church bells throughout Frascati. Local families bring their pets and farm animals to participate in the procession, which starts from the Church of Santa Maria in Vivario and winds through the historic center's narrow streets.

The procession includes traditional flag bearers, or sbandieratori, dressed in medieval costumes, accompanied by the local brass band playing traditional hymns. Farmers lead decorated farm animals through the streets, while residents proudly walk with their household pets. Members of local agricultural associations also take part, adding to the sense of community and celebration.

The procession culminates in Piazza San Pietro, where the town's senior priest conducts the blessing ceremony. Each animal receives an individual blessing, symbolizing protection for the coming year. The blessing is followed by the distribution of "panetti di Sant'Antonio" - small blessed bread rolls that are traditionally fed to animals for good health.

Festa dei Santi Patroni Filippo e Giacomo (Patron Saints' Day)

May 3rd

Saints Philip and James became the patron saints of Frascati in 1515 when Pope Leo X elevated the town's parish church to collegiate status. The church, now the Cathedral Basilica of St. Peter the Apostle, houses important relics of both saints. The festival's tradition began as a way to honor these patron saints and celebrate Frascati's elevated status within the Catholic Church. This festival includes a High Mass during which candles are offered to the saints. On select days, visitors can also enjoy free entry to the Aldobrandini stables.

San Giovanni Battista (St. John the Baptist)

June 23rd

The vibrant "Night of the Witches" festival transforms the town square into a feast for the senses, where locals honor St. John with traditional songs and spirited dances, while food vendors offer delicacies including the region's famous "lumacata," a celebrated ritual of snail tasting.

Festa del Borgo di San Rocco (Festival of the St. Rocco District)

Second week of September

Held in one of Frascati's oldest neighborhoods, this festival is a heartfelt tribute to San Rocco, protector against plagues and hardship. The celebration features processions, music, and family-friendly games, but its true charm lies in its local flavors and folk traditions. Visitors can sample fagioli e cotiche (slow-cooked beans with pork rind), a humble yet delicious Roman dish, while enjoying poetry recitals and storytelling in the local dialect, preserving the oral traditions of the Castelli Romani.

Mercatino d'Arte e d'Antiquariato (Art and Antique Market)

The first Sunday of each month

The streets come alive with vibrant stalls showcasing art, antiques, and occasionally modern art collections, alongside hobby materials and unique objects.

Winter Celebrations

November through January

CHAPTER THIRTY-SIX

Celebrating the Dedication of San Giovanni in Laterano

The Mother of All Churches

Festa della Dedicazione della Basilica di San Giovanni in Laterano

Where: Rome, Basilica di San Giovanni Laterano

When: November 9

Average Festival Temperatures: High 15°C (59°F). Low 10°C (50°F).

Saint John Lateran Basilica

Nestled in the heart of Rome, away from the bustling crowds of more famous landmarks, stands the Archbasilica of St. John Lateran. This is my favorite of the four papal basilicas, a place I love because it is full of treasures and feels somewhat off the beaten path despite its immense importance. My first visit here was a revelation, guided by an insightful audio tour that brought the basilica's rich history to life.

I am always struck by the sense of peace and historical depth this church offers. I find the cloister gorgeous and peaceful, its intricate mosaics on the columns inviting me to linger. Walking through the vast nave or simply watching bishops pass through the glass hallways of the Lateran Palace offers moments of quiet wonder. The Palace, which houses various administrative offices of the Diocese of Rome, gives rare glimpses into the everyday governance of the Church, making each visit feel like a peek behind the curtain of Catholic leadership.

What I love most about St. John Lateran is the contrast between its profound significance and its relative obscurity among tourists. As the Cathedral of Rome and the official ecclesiastical seat of the Pope, it is the most important church in Catholicism. Yet, compared to the crowds at St. Peter's Basilica or the Colosseum, St. John Lateran offers me a serene and intimate experience of Rome's religious heritage.

For individuals seeking to understand the depths of Rome's Christian history, St. John Lateran is an unmissable destination. Its walls echo with nearly two millennia of faith, politics, and art, telling a story that goes beyond mere tourism and touches the very foundations of Western civilization. On the following pages, we'll explore the rich tapestry of past events, architecture, and spiritual significance that makes St. John Lateran truly the "mother church" of Christian Rome.

St. John Lateran's story stretches back to the early days of Christianity in Rome. Originally built in the 4th century AD, it predates even the grand St. Peter's Basilica. Its full title, "Archbasilica of the Most Holy Savior and of Saint John the Baptist and John the Evangelist in the Lateran," reflects its rich historical and spiritual legacy. The basilica's foundations were laid in 324 AD by Emperor Constantine I, and it was subsequently dedicated by Pope Sylvester I.

For nearly a millennium, it served as the residence of the Popes before they relocated to the Vatican. Throughout its history, the basilica has demonstrated remarkable resilience, enduring multiple fires, earthquakes, and renovations while maintaining its sacred significance.

The basilica's current appearance showcases the magnificent Baroque renovations of the 17th and 18th centuries while preserving elements from its long history. The imposing façade, created by Alessandro Galilei in 1735, welcomes visitors with ancient bronze doors from the Roman Senate House, connecting modern pilgrims to the city's classical past.

Facade of the Archbasilica of St. John Lateran

The 13th-century Gothic baldachin (an ornate canopy structure supported by columns that stands over the papal altar, marking it as a place of special significance) rising majestically over the papal altar represents medieval craftsmanship at its finest, while the Cosmatesque floor below (a distinctive medieval Roman style of geometric stone inlay using colored marble and glass, created by the Cosmati family workshop) displays intricate geometric patterns that have captivated visitors for centuries. The nave ceiling, designed by the renowned architect Borromini, crowns this sacred space with its breathtaking artistry, completing a harmonious blend of architectural styles that span nearly two millennia.

Feast of the Dedication

One of the most significant events associated with St. John Lateran is the annual Feast of the Dedication, celebrated on November 9th. This feast is not just a local Roman observance but a universal celebration in the Catholic Church, underscoring the basilica's significance.

Origins and Significance

The feast commemorates the original dedication of the basilica in 324 AD. As the "mother church" of Christendom, St. John Lateran's dedication is a celebration of the unity and universality of the Catholic Church. It serves as a reminder of the Pope's role as the Bishop of Rome and the universal pastor of the Church.

Celebrations and Traditions

Solemn Mass and Procession. The celebration of St. John Lateran's dedication centers around a solemn morning Mass, typically held at 10:00 AM. This profound ceremony, often presided over by a high-ranking Church official or sometimes the Pope himself, incorporates special prayers of dedication and gratitude that honor the basilica's pivotal role in Church history. The Mass draws an impressive gathering of clergy, pilgrims, and faithful from across the globe, creating a truly international celebration of faith. The procession begins after mass.

Processions and Public Festivities. Throughout the day, religious processions wind their way around the basilica and neighboring areas, creating a tapestry of movement and devotion. These processions bring together local clergy, parishioners, and visiting pilgrims in a shared expression of faith. The surrounding Laterano neighborhood embraces the celebration, often organizing local events that complement the religious observances and create a festive atmosphere throughout the area.

Cultural and Educational Activities. The celebration extends beyond religious ceremonies to include enriching cultural and educational activities. Visitors can take part in specialized guided tours that illuminate the basilica's architectural magnificence and artistic treasures. Scholars and experts offer engaging lectures and seminars exploring St. John Lateran's heritage and significance, while special exhibitions showcase precious religious artifacts and historical documents that tell the story of this ancient church.

Musical Performances. Music fills the basilica throughout the celebration, with magnificent concerts featuring the church's grand organ. Choirs and orchestras perform both traditional and contemporary religious compositions, their music resonating through the vast space just as it has for centuries. These performances add a profound spiritual and artistic dimension to the festivities.

Charitable Initiatives. The feast day also serves as an important catalyst for charitable initiatives. Catholic organizations often choose this significant date to launch or promote their humanitarian projects. Special collections and fundraising events are organized, with proceeds supporting both the basilica's preservation and various charitable causes, embodying the Church's commitment to serving others.

Spiritual Significance

The Feast of the Dedication of St. John Lateran transcends mere historical commemoration, serving as a powerful symbol of the Church's unity, continuity, and universality. For Catholics worldwide, this feast offers a multifaceted opportunity for spiritual growth and reflection. It invites the faithful to deepen their sense of connection to the broader Church community, fostering a feeling of solidarity with Catholics across the globe.

The occasion also prompts individuals to renew their commitment to the faith, reaffirming their beliefs and dedication to living out Catholic teachings. Furthermore, the feast encourages contemplation of the rich background and traditions of Catholicism, allowing believers to appreciate the depth and breadth of their religious heritage. Lastly, it provides a focused moment for prayer, particularly for the Pope and the Church's ongoing mission in the modern world, uniting the faithful in their support for the Church's spiritual and social endeavors.

Attending the Feast at St. John Lateran

The Feast of the Dedication of St. John Lateran offers a unique opportunity to experience this historic basilica at its most crucial moment. While more solemn and focused on the Church's history than other major Roman religious festivals, it still draws a substantial crowd of locals, clergy, and pilgrims who come to celebrate the basilica's importance to the Catholic Church.

Things to Know:

Arrive Early: To secure a good seat for the Mass, it's advisable to arrive well in advance, as the basilica fills up quickly on this important day.

Public Transportation: St. John Lateran is easily accessible by public transport: Metro: Take Line A to the San Giovanni stop or Bus: Various routes serve the area.

Participation: While the main Mass is the centerpiece of the celebration, visitors can also take part in processions, attend educational events, or simply explore the basilica and its surroundings.

Dress Code: As with all major churches in Rome, modest dress is required. Shoulders and knees should be covered.

Walking Tour of St. John Lateran

#1. The Apostle Statues

A stunning highlight of St. John Lateran's interior is the magnificent series of apostle statues that line the basilica's nave. Created in the early 18th century, these larger-than-life Baroque masterpieces command attention and reverence from all who enter. Each statue occupies its own carefully designed niche, creating a powerful visual rhythm that draws visitors through the sacred space. The artists took great care to imbue each apostle with distinct characteristics and symbolic attributes, allowing the faithful to identify and connect with these pillars of the early Church.

The brilliant white marble of these sculptures creates a striking contrast against the basilica's rich interior, where colorful marbles and elaborate frescoes provide a magnificent backdrop. This artistic choice serves to emphasize the apostles' spiritual significance while contributing to the overall baroque splendor of the space. These impressive statues replaced an earlier set of medieval sculptures, marking a significant transformation in the basilica's artistic evolution and reflecting the Church's embrace of baroque aesthetics. Their installation represented not just an artistic update, but a renewal of the basilica's commitment to visual storytelling and spiritual inspiration.

#2. The Cloister

Next to the basilica lies one of Rome's most serene spaces - the magnificent 13th-century cloister. This architectural jewel serves as a peaceful counterpoint to the basilica's grandeur, offering visitors a tranquil retreat from the main sanctuary. The cloister's most striking feature is its collection of exquisitely crafted twisted columns, adorned with intricate Cosmatesque mosaic work that shows the pinnacle of medieval craftsmanship.

The delightful cloister of San Giovanni in Laterano

The heart of the cloister features a carefully tended garden surrounded by covered walkways, creating an atmosphere of contemplative peace that has served generations of clergy and visitors. These walkways also house an impressive collection of architectural fragments and artifacts that chronicle the basilica's long history, each piece telling its own story of the church's evolution through time. The intimate scale of the cloister creates an interesting architectural contrast with the soaring spaces of the main basilica, offering visitors a uniquely varied experience of medieval sacred architecture.

#3. The Baptistery

The historic Baptistery of San Giovanni in Fonte stands near the basilica as one of Christianity's most ancient baptisteries. Dating back to Constantine's reign in the 4th century, this remarkable structure serves as a pristine example of early Christian architecture and its evolving traditions. The baptistery's distinctive octagonal design carries deep symbolic meaning, representing the eighth day of creation and the promise of new life through Christ - a powerful architectural expression of Christian theology.

Inside, the baptistery's walls come alive with stunning mosaics and frescoes that tell the story of baptism through sacred imagery. These artistic treasures, accumulated over centuries, create an immersive spiritual environment that has witnessed countless baptismal ceremonies. The baptistery's historical significance is further heightened by its unique status as Rome's sole baptistery for many centuries, underscoring St. John Lateran's central role in the early Christian church and its continued importance as the Cathedral of Rome.

#4. The Lateran Obelisk

In the piazza outside the basilica stands the magnificent Lateran Obelisk, an awe-inspiring monument that commands attention and admiration. This remarkable structure holds the distinction of being the largest standing Egyptian obelisk in the world, reaching an impressive height of 32.18 meters (105.6 feet), or 45.70 meters (149.9 feet) when including its ornate base. The obelisk's journey from its original home in Karnak, Egypt, to Rome represents a fascinating chapter in history, having been transported to the eternal city by Emperor Constantius II in 357 AD.

Lateran Obelisk

The obelisk found its current home through the vision of Pope Sixtus V, who orchestrated its re-erection in 1588 as a powerful symbol of Christianity's triumph over paganism. Today, it creates a dramatic visual dialogue with the basilica's Baroque façade, serving as a compelling introduction to the sacred complex. This juxtaposition of ancient Egyptian artistry and Christian architectural grandeur perfectly encapsulates Rome's unique ability to weave together different historical epochs and cultural traditions into a harmonious whole.

Each of these elements contributes to the rich tapestry of history, art, and faith that makes St. John Lateran unique. From the soaring apostle statues to the tranquil courtyard, from the baptistery to the monumental obelisk, these aspects of the church offer visitors a comprehensive view of Rome's religious and cultural heritage.

#5. The Scala Santa: A Sacred Staircase

Directly across the street from St. John Lateran lies another site of profound religious significance: the Scala Santa, or Holy Stairs. This sacred staircase offers visitors an exceptional and deeply moving pilgrimage experience that complements a visit to the basilica.

The Scala Santa is believed to be the very staircase that Jesus Christ climbed on his way to trial before Pontius Pilate in Jerusalem. According to tradition, St. Helena, mother of Emperor Constantine, had the stairs brought to Rome from Jerusalem in 326 AD. The staircase comprises 28 white marble steps, now encased in protective wooden risers to preserve them from the wear of countless pilgrims.

For centuries, the Scala Santa has been a site of intense devotion and pilgrimage. The faithful ascend the stairs on their knees as an act of penance and reflection on Christ's Passion. As they climb, many pilgrims pray on each step, often reciting the rosary, creating a sense of profound reverence and contemplation. At the top of the stairs, pilgrims reach the Sancta Sanctorum, or Holy of Holies, a private papal chapel containing important relics. This final destination adds to the spiritual significance of the climb, offering a moment of closeness to sacred history.

The Scala Santa is housed in a building known as the Lateran Palace, which was once the main papal residence before the move to the Vatican. This complex is rich in history and art, featuring several chapels and walls adorned with frescoes depicting scenes from Christ's Passion. Flanking the Holy Stairs are two additional staircases, allowing pilgrims to descend after their ascent. The entire building underwent significant restoration in the 16th century under Pope Sixtus V, preserving its importance in Rome's religious landscape.

The Scala Santa serves as a powerful complement to a visit to St. John Lateran. While the basilica represents the institutional and historical aspects of the Church, the Holy Stairs offer a more personal and contemplative experience. Together, these sites provide a comprehensive view of Rome's religious heritage, from monumental architecture to deeply personal acts of devotion.

Walking Tour Esquilino Neighborhood: 7 Nearby Attractions

#1. Two Recommended Bookstores

Libereria San Paolo and Libreria Romani are both here near San Giovanni. These are great bookstores and I always make a stop when I am in the area.

#2. Santi Quattro Coronati

A short walk north of San Giovanni, this venerable church is known for its fortress-like appearance and peaceful cloister. Santi Quattro Coronati stands as one of Rome's most formidable religious structures, built like a medieval fortress with high defensive walls and sturdy towers that date back to the 9th century. This architectural choice wasn't merely aesthetic - it served to protect the papal treasures and the church itself during the tumultuous Middle Ages when Rome faced numerous invasions.

The church's crowning jewel is its tranquil 13th-century cloister, where delicate double columns frame a garden that seems frozen in time. The Chapel of St. Sylvester, tucked away within its walls, contains an extraordinary cycle of 13th-century frescoes depicting the legend of Constantine and Pope Sylvester, serving as powerful propaganda for papal authority during medieval times. These frescoes remain remarkably well-preserved, their colors still vibrant after centuries, offering visitors a glimpse into medieval artistic techniques and political messaging.

#3. Basilica di San Clemente (Highly Recommended)

A 10-minute walk from San Giovanni, this distinctive basilica is built over three layers of history. The Basilica di San Clemente is a remarkable testament to Rome's layered history, functioning as a vertical time machine that takes visitors through three distinct eras of Roman civilization. The current church, dating from the 12th century, features stunning medieval mosaics in the apse, depicting an elaborate Tree of Life with intricate spiral patterns.

Descending to the first underground level (ticket required), visitors encounter a well-preserved 4th-century church, complete with frescoes depicting early Christian scenes and rare examples of medieval religious art. The lowest level reveals the remains of a 1st-century Roman house and a dark, atmospheric Mithraeum - a temple dedicated to the mystery cult of Mithras. This space also contains evidence of an ancient spring and Roman apartments, with walls still bearing the scorch marks from the Great Fire of 64 AD during Nero's reign. The sound of running water from an ancient Roman spring can still be heard echoing through these underground chambers, creating an immersive connection to the city's past.

#4. Santo Stefano Rotondo

This unique circular church is a short walk southwest of the Basilica. Santo Stefano Rotondo stands as Europe's oldest circular church, its unique architecture inspired by the Church of the Holy Sepulchre in Jerusalem. Built in the 5th century under Emperor Constantine, its concentric design features a central ring supported by 22 ancient Roman columns, creating a mesmerizing spatial effect that draws the eye upward toward the wooden ceiling.

The church is notorious for its 16th-century fresco cycle commissioned by Pope Gregory XIII, which depicts 34 scenes of martyrdom in graphic detail. These frescoes, while disturbing to modern sensibilities, served an important didactic purpose - they were used to prepare missionaries for the possibility of martyrdom in dangerous foreign lands. Each scene is meticulously labeled in Latin, Italian, and German, creating a macabre but historically significant testament to the church's role in Counter-Reformation education. The church's peaceful location on the Caelian Hill, set among gardens and pine trees, creates a striking contrast with its intense interior decoration.

#5. Villa Celimontana

A 15-minute walk west of San Giovanni, this beautiful park is home to gardens, ancient ruins, and the Church of Santa Maria in Domnica. It's a peaceful stop for those looking to relax amid greenery and history.

#6. Santa Croce in Gerusalemme

A 15-minute walk east of San Giovanni, Santa Croce in Gerusalemme stands as one of Rome's seven major pilgrimage basilicas. Its origins traced to the 4th century when St. Helena, mother of Emperor Constantine, ordered its construction to house sacred relics from Jerusalem. According to tradition, St. Helena incorporated soil from Jerusalem into the church's foundation, hence its name "in Jerusalem." The church underwent significant baroque renovations in the 18th century, giving it its current appearance with an imposing facade and dramatic interior. The most remarkable feature is its Chapel of Relics, which houses some of Christianity's most venerated objects: fragments believed to be from the True Cross, a nail from the Crucifixion, thorns from Christ's crown, and a piece of the titulus (the inscription placed above Christ's cross). The chapel also contains the finger bone of St. Thomas, which, according to tradition, he placed in Christ's wounds to verify the Resurrection.

The basilica's interior showcases remarkable artistic treasures beyond its relics. The apse features vibrant 15th-century frescoes depicting the Legend of the True Cross, while the barrel-vaulted ceiling is adorned with elaborate 18th-century frescoes celebrating the power of the Cross. The monastery adjacent to the church houses a library of ancient manuscripts and a Cistercian herb garden, continuing a medieval tradition of botanical study and medicinal plant cultivation. During Holy Week, the basilica becomes a focal point for Roman Catholic devotions, with pilgrims coming from around the world to venerate the relics of the Passion, making it a living testament to Rome's enduring role as a center of Christian pilgrimage.

#7. Porta Maggiore

This monumental ancient gate is a 5-minute walk north of Santa Croce in Gerusalemme. It's a key part of Rome's Aurelian Walls and features impressive arches, making it a brilliant spot for history enthusiasts.

Restaurant Recommendations near St. John Lateran

Trattoria Re di Roma. Address: Via Tuscolana 40/A, Piazza dei Re di Roma

Just a short walk from San Giovanni, this traditional trattoria offers classic Roman dishes with a focus on fresh ingredients. Known for its friendly atmosphere and reasonably priced menu, favorites include cacio e pepe, carbonara, and a variety of meat and fish options. It's perfect for a casual yet authentic dining experience.

I Buoni Amici. Address: Via Aleardo Aleardi 4

Located close to the Basilica of San Giovanni in Laterano, I Buoni Amici is a cozy restaurant known for its homemade pasta and traditional Roman dishes. The restaurant offers a warm, family-friendly atmosphere, with standout dishes like saltimbocca alla romana and bucatini all'amatriciana. It's a magnificent spot for a meal after visiting the nearby historical sites.

Accommodation: See Accommodation Detail Chapter for Rome hotel information. I would recommend a minimum of four nights for any trip to Rome.

St. John Lateran Festivals Throughout the Year

As the Mother Church of all churches in Rome and the world, the Archbasilica of St. John Lateran is not only the cathedral of the Bishop of Rome (the Pope), but also a center of some of the most solemn and symbolically rich celebrations in the Catholic liturgical calendar. In addition to the Feast of the Dedication on November 9, which commemorates the original consecration of the basilica in the 4th century, several other key events take place here throughout the year.

Holy Thursday Papal Mass

Thursday before Easter

Traditionally, the Pope celebrates the Mass of the Lord's Supper at St. John Lateran, marking the beginning of the Easter Triduum. The liturgy recalls Christ's establishment of the Eucharist at the Last Supper and involves the feet-washing ritual, recreating Jesus' act of humility and service toward his disciples. The atmosphere is reverent and powerful, as pilgrims from around the world gather to witness this ancient rite performed in one of Christianity's holiest spaces. The ceremony concludes with the solemn procession of the Blessed Sacrament, setting the tone for Good Friday's somber reflection.

Feast of the Ascension

May

Celebrated with a Solemn Pontifical Mass, the Feast of the Ascension honors the moment Christ rose to heaven in the presence of his disciples, completing his earthly mission. The liturgy at St. John Lateran often features incense, chanted prayers, and sacred music that elevate the spiritual experience. The basilica is adorned with fresh flowers and gold vestments as the faithful reflect on themes of hope, transformation, and the promise of eternal life.

Feast of Corpus Christi

June (60 days after Easter)

The Solemnity of the Body and Blood of Christ is marked by a Pontifical Mass, followed by a procession with the Blessed Sacrament within the basilica. This celebration holds special significance at the Lateran as it's the Cathedral of Rome and the Pope's own church. The procession traditionally includes members of Rome's ancient confraternities in their historic dress, while the basilica's interior is adorned with special tapestries and floral arrangements.

Following ancient custom, the ceremony includes the exposition of the Blessed Sacrament in a precious monstrance dating from the 18th century. The celebration concludes with Benediction from the high altar, which contains the ancient wooden altar said to have been used by the early popes.

Solemnity of the Nativity of St. John the Baptist

June 24

As the basilica is co-dedicated to St. John the Baptist, his nativity on June 24 is celebrated with Solemn Vespers and a Pontifical Mass. The celebration includes the veneration of relics associated with St. John the Baptist preserved in the basilica's Treasury. The day begins with the traditional blessing of holy water in the ancient baptistery, which dates back to Constantine's time and is the oldest baptistery in Christian Rome.

A distinctive feature of this celebration is the use of the basilica's choir performing medieval chants specific to the Lateran's liturgical tradition. The high altar is decorated with red vestments and hangings, reflecting the martyrdom of St. John the Baptist, and the celebration often includes a procession around the basilica's extensive cloisters, where participants can view the medieval Cosmatesque decorations by moonlight, as some celebrations continue into the evening.

CHAPTER THIRTY-SEVEN

Rhythms of Rome

Rome Comes Alive with the Soulful Sounds and Rhythms of the Annual Jazz Festival

R oma Jazz Festival

Where: Rome, primarily at Auditorium Parco della Musica

When: November (first three weeks).

Average Festival Temperatures: High 15°C (59°F). Low 10°C (50°F).

Event Website: https://romajazzfestival.it/

Jazz Fest Rome

Every November, the Eternal City resonates with the soulful rhythms and innovative sounds of jazz during the Rome Jazz Festival. This prestigious event, founded in 1976, has grown into one of Italy's premier music festivals, attracting jazz aficionados from around the globe. Set against the backdrop of Rome's rich cultural heritage, the festival offers a unique blend of world-class performances, educational experiences, and artistic collaborations that celebrate the past, present, and future of jazz.

History and Significance

The Rome Jazz Festival is an essential platform for both established jazz legends and emerging artists. Over the decades, it has hosted iconic performers like Miles Davis, Herbie Hancock, and Wayne Shorter, solidifying its reputation as one of Europe's most prestigious jazz festivals.

While rooted in jazz tradition, the festival embraces musical evolution, inviting contemporary and experimental jazz artists. This approach ensures a dynamic and ever-evolving lineup that honors jazz's rich history while pushing the boundaries of the genre.

The festival's significance extends beyond music. It serves as a cultural bridge, blending jazz with visual arts, literature, and cinema, reflecting Rome's deep artistic heritage and the universal language of music.

Jazz Fest Events

The Rome Jazz Festival typically runs for several weeks, usually starting in late October and continuing through early November. Tickets can be purchased in advance on the website. While the exact schedule varies each year, here's a general timeline:

Opening Night Gala. Usually the first Friday of November. Features a headline act at the Auditorium Parco della Musica.

Daily Performances. Throughout the festival, typically starting at 8:00 p.m. or 9:00 p.m. Concerts at various venues, including Auditorium Parco della Musica and local jazz clubs.

Workshops and Masterclasses. Daytime hours, 10:00 a.m. - 4:00 p.m. Educational sessions led by renowned musicians.

Late-Night Jam Sessions. Starting around 11:00 p.m. Spontaneous performances at local jazz clubs.

Closing Night Concert. Usually the last Sunday of the festival. A grand finale featuring multiple artists.

Festival Venues

1. **Auditorium Parco della Musica**

   ○ Main venue for large-scale concerts

   ○ Santa Cecilia Hall: Largest hall for headliners

   ○ Petrassi Hall: Smaller space for intimate performances

2. **Alexanderplatz Jazz Club**

   ○ Historic jazz club hosting late-night sessions

3. **Casa del Jazz**

   ○ Dedicated jazz venue offering performances and workshops

4. Various pop-up locations throughout Rome.

What to Expect

The Rome Jazz Festival delivers world-class performances that bring together international jazz legends and emerging talents from across the globe. Audiences can experience everything from classic bebop to cutting-edge contemporary fusion, showcasing the full spectrum of jazz expression. The festival's innovative programming creates unique artistic intersections, featuring collaborations between musicians and visual artists, dancers, and filmmakers, along with specially curated themed nights that explore cross-cultural musical exchanges.

Educational opportunities form a vital part of the festival experience, with comprehensive workshops diving into jazz theory, improvisation, and composition. Industry experts and veteran musicians lead engaging panel discussions exploring jazz history and contemplating the genre's future directions. As evening turns to night, the festival comes alive with spontaneous late-night jam sessions, where artists collaborate in intimate club settings, offering audiences an up-close perspective on pure jazz improvisation.

The festival extends beyond music to create a complete cultural immersion, featuring thoughtfully curated art exhibitions and film screenings that illuminate jazz's influence on visual media. Literary events explore the profound connection between jazz and literature, creating a multifaceted celebration of jazz's impact on global culture.

Local Customs and Traditions

- Aperitivo: Many Romans enjoy pre-concert aperitivo, a light meal with drinks. Join locals at nearby bars for this tradition.

- Late-Night Culture: Embrace Rome's nocturnal lifestyle by attending late-night jam sessions.

- Cafe Culture: Visit historic cafes like Antico Caffè Greco, where artists and musicians have gathered for centuries.

Practical Tips for Visitors

When planning your visit to the Rome Jazz Festival, securing tickets early is essential, particularly for headline performances, and multi-show passes often provide the best value for experiencing multiple concerts. Since performances take place in various venues with different ambient temperatures, dressing in layers will help ensure your comfort throughout the evening. Given the festival's vibrant late-night culture, especially during the impromptu jam sessions, prepare yourself for extended evenings of musical exploration.

The Rome Jazz Festival offers a unique blend of musical excellence, cultural exploration, and Roman charm. Whether you're a lifelong jazz enthusiast or a curious newcomer, the festival provides an unparalleled opportunity to experience world-class jazz in one of the world's most historic cities. From grand performances in modern concert halls to intimate jam sessions in cozy clubs, the festival captures the spirit of jazz in all its forms. As you wander Rome's ancient streets by day and lose yourself in the rhythms of jazz by night, you'll experience a musical journey that resonates with the eternal spirit of the city itself.

Dining Recommendations Near the Event

Dao Restaurant (Chinese). Address: Viale Parioli, 201 High-end Chinese cuisine, perfect for a pre-concert dinner near Auditorium Parco della Musica.

Ristorante Mimi e Coco. Address: Via del Governo Vecchio, 72 Cozy trattoria offering Roman classics, ideal for late-night dining after performances.

Gelateria dei Gracchi. Address: Via di Ripetta, 261 Artisanal gelato shop, great for a sweet treat between shows.

Accommodation

Accommodation Detail Chapter for hotel recommendations by area. I recommend a minimum of four nights for any trip to Rome.

CHAPTER THIRTY-EIGHT

Immersion Experience: Learn to Cook Like a Roman

Mastering Culinary Classics in the Eternal City

I magine returning from your Roman vacation not just with photos and souvenirs, but with the ability to recreate the iconic dishes of the Eternal City in your own kitchen! A cooking class in Rome offers exactly this: an opportunity to dive into the rich culinary traditions of Roman cuisine while crafting unforgettable memories. From rolling out fresh pasta to mastering the secrets of a perfect Amatriciana, this hands-on experience brings Rome's flavors to life in a way that dining out simply can't match.

Rome's culinary tradition is as eternal as its monuments, embedded in straightforward yet bold flavors that reflect its history and people. While exploring the city's trattorias and markets provides a taste of this heritage, joining a cooking class transforms your vacation into a journey of flavors, skills and connection. It's not just about food it's about immersing yourself in the culture and carrying a piece of Rome back home with you.

A Personal Slice of Rome: Our Culinary Adventure

During a to Rome, we joined a small cooking class in a cozy kitchen near the bustling Campo de' Fiori market. Our host, Maria, a passionate Roman chef, guided us (along with some new friends) through a full Roman menu, starting with the preparation of Cacio e Pepe, Amatriciana, and the creamy yet bold Carbonara, three pillars of Roman pasta dishes.

Maria's approach was hands-on and engaging. We learned to make fresh pasta from scratch, roll it to the perfect thickness, and master the delicate balance of flavors in the sauces. We discovered that guanciale (cured pork cheek) is non-negotiable in authentic Roman pasta dishes and perfected the timing of emulsifying pasta water with pecorino to create a silky sauce.

After the hard work, we gathered around the table with our newfound friends and enjoyed the fruits of our labor. The food at the end of a cooking class always tastes so good! No idea why. More than just eating, it involved laughter, connection, and ancient Roman craft.

Why Take a Cooking Class in Rome?

Deeper Cultural Immersion: Rome's culinary traditions are deeply tied to its history and identity. Cooking iconic Roman dishes offers a window into the city's soul.

Unforgettable Memories: There's something uniquely satisfying about creating a Roman feast from scratch and enjoying it with fellow travelers or locals.

Skills for Life: The techniques you learn will stay with you, allowing you to bring the flavors of Rome to your own table long after your trip ends.

A Unique Story: Dining at a Roman restaurant is great, but telling your friends, "I made Carbonara in a kitchen overlooking the rooftops of Rome," is unforgettable.

What to Expect in a Roman Cooking Class

Hands-On Cooking: You'll actively participate in preparing Roman dishes, from making fresh pasta to crafting traditional sauces like Amatriciana, Cacio e Pepe, and Carbonara.

Traditional Techniques: Learn time-honored methods such as perfecting a creamy carbonara without cream or using authentic Roman ingredients like pecorino cheese and guanciale.

Shared Meal: After cooking, you'll sit down to enjoy your creations with wine and good company.

Take-Home Recipes: Leave with detailed and now treasured recipes and tips to recreate your Roman feast at home.

Logistics: Finding and Booking a Class

Want to master authentic Roman cuisine? Join local experts for hands-on cooking classes, available for both groups and private sessions at various price points.

Roscioli (our #1 recommendation)

The brilliant cooks of Roscioli share their secrets!

Website: https://rimessaroscioli.com/cooking-classes/

Cook With Us in Rome

Specializes in small group classes that cover Roman classics.

Website: www.cookwithusinrome.com

A cooking class in Rome is more than just learning to cook: it's experiencing the city's lifestyle. It's about kneading dough like a Roman, simmering sauces in the same way generations have, and sipping wine while sharing stories around a table. These moments bring you closer to the essence of Rome and give you a skill set that turns memories into meals long after your vacation ends.

CHAPTER THIRTY-NINE

Campoli's Black and White Gold

Where Truffles and Tradition Meet

S agra del Tartufo

Where: Campoli Appennino

When: Two Weekends in November.

Average Festival Temperatures: High 14°C (57°F). Low 6°C (42°F).

Campoli Appennino: A Hidden Gem in Lazio's Mountains

Discover Campoli Appennino, a captivating town tucked away in Lazio's Frosinone province. Perched 650 meters above sea level in the Apennine Mountains, it offers stunning views of valleys and forests. The town borders the Abruzzo, Lazio, and Molise National Park, making it perfect for outdoor enthusiasts. Its landscape features verdant hills and fascinating karstic formations, including the legendary "Bear's Sinkhole," named for the magnificent creatures that once roamed these lands.

Founded by the ancient Samnites in a strategic location, Campoli Appennino later flourished under Roman rule. The Middle Ages transformed it into a fortified settlement, with medieval walls and towers still standing as silent witnesses to its past. Today, its 1,500 residents preserve the town's authentic character through winding cobblestone streets and traditional stone houses.

The town's soul lies in its connection to the land. The surrounding forests yield precious black and white truffles, making it a paradise for food lovers. This intimate community celebrates its heritage through vibrant festivals and time honored traditions.

Campoli Appennino offers an unforgettable blend of natural splendor, rich history, and culinary treasures. Visitors can wander medieval alleyways, take in mountain vistas, and savor truffle dishes in local eateries. The nearby national park provides endless opportunities for hiking and wildlife watching, immersing guests in the region's diverse natural wonders.

The Truffle Festival

The Sagra del Tartufo di Campoli Appennino was established as a celebration of the town's natural riches, particularly its prized black and white truffles, which have been a significant part of its identity for centuries. Campoli's location in the Apennine Mountains, with its rich, loamy soil and dense forests, creates the perfect environment for truffle growth. Historically, truffles have been foraged in this region by local farmers and hunters with the help of specially trained dogs.

The festival originated as a way to honor this culinary heritage and to promote Campoli Appennino's truffles to a broader audience. Over the years, it has grown into one of the most anticipated events in the region, drawing truffle enthusiasts, gourmands, and visitors from across Italy and beyond. The festival highlights the importance of truffles as both a cultural symbol and a valuable economic resource for the town.

What Are Truffles and Why Are They Celebrated?
Truffles are a type of subterranean fungus that grows symbiotically with the roots of certain trees, such as oaks, hazelnuts, and pines. They are highly prized for their unique and intense aroma, which enhances a variety of dishes. Truffles are

often referred to as "the diamonds of the kitchen" because of their rarity and high market value.

A Black Truffle

Campoli Appennino is renowned for producing both black truffles (Tuber melanosporum) and white truffles (Tuber magnatum pico). Black truffles are typically harvested in winter, while white truffles, considered even more prestigious, are gathered in late autumn. These truffles are celebrated not only for their gastronomic value but also for their role in preserving traditional truffle hunting techniques and the town's connection to its natural environment.

What Happens During the Sagra del Tartufo?

The festival takes place over two weekends in November, transforming the town into a vibrant hub of activity centered on truffles. Here's what visitors can expect during the Sagra del Tartufo:

1. **Truffle Tastings**
   The main square is filled with stalls offering fresh black and white truffles, truffle-based products like oils and sauces, and other local delicacies such as cheeses, cured meats, and wines.

2. **Truffle Hunts**
   Guided truffle hunting and demonstrations with trained dogs are one highlight of the festival. Visitors can join experienced truffle hunters in the nearby forests to learn about the art and science of truffle foraging. To book a truffle hunt in town during the festival or anytime the Podere Poggio a Campoli has daily offerings. Website: https://www.poggioacampoli.it/en/experiences-eng.html

3. **Cooking Demonstrations**
   Local chefs and culinary experts host live cooking demonstrations, showcasing traditional recipes and innovative dishes that highlight the unique flavor of truffles.

4. **Tastings and Gastronomy**
   The festival features an array of food stalls and pop-up restaurants where visitors can enjoy truffle-infused dishes, such as pasta, risotto, eggs, and even desserts. Wine pairings with local varieties further enhance the gastronomic experience.

5. **Cultural Events and Entertainment**
   Live music, folk dances, and theatrical performances provide entertainment throughout the weekend, creating a lively and festive atmosphere.

6. **Workshops and Educational Talks**
   Experts give presentations on the history of truffle cultivation, its ecological significance, and tips for incorporating truffles into everyday cooking.

7. **Craft Markets:** Visit markets featuring local artisans and traditional products, perfect for finding unique souvenirs.

8. **Competitions and Awards**
   The festival often includes competitions for the largest or most aromatic truffle, with prizes awarded to local truffle hunters.

The Sagra is a celebration of the town's heritage, a showcase of its natural bounty, and a communal gathering that brings people together to share in the joy of food, culture, and tradition. For anyone who appreciates fine cuisine or wants to experience the authentic charm of an Italian mountain town, this festival offers an unforgettable experience.

Walking Tour of Campoli

#1. Piazza Umberto I
Start your tour in the heart of Campoli Appennino at Piazza Umberto I, the town's main square. This lively hub is surrounded by traditional stone buildings and serves as the focal point for community gatherings and festivals, including the Sagra del Tartufo. From here, you can admire the panoramic views of the surrounding Apennine Mountains and valleys.

#2. Chiesa di San Pancrazio
A short walk from the main square takes you to the Church of San Pancrazio, a beautiful 16th-century structure dedicated to the town's patron saint. Inside, you'll find intricate frescoes and religious artifacts that reflect the town's deep spiritual roots. The church is also a key site during the town's religious celebrations.

#3. Medieval Walls and Porta di Mezzo
Head toward the remnants of Campoli's medieval walls, which once served as a fortification for the town. The Porta di Mezzo, an ancient gateway, is a striking example of the town's medieval architecture and provides a glimpse into its historical significance as a defensive stronghold.

#4. Bear's Sinkhole (Dolina del'Orso)
Walk to the edge of town to visit the Bear's Sinkhole, a fascinating geological feature that is one of Campoli's most unique attractions. This large karstic sinkhole has earned its name from its historical connection to the local bear population. Karstic refers to a landscape formed by water dissolving limestone or other soluble rocks. This creates depressions, caves, and sinkholes in the ground.

Bears are occasionally housed in a dedicated enclosure for conservation work focused on protecting the endangered Marsican brown bear. Visitors can explore marked trails with signs explaining both the sinkhole's limestone formation and local wildlife history.

#5. Abruzzo, Lazio, and Molise National Park Entrance
Conclude your tour at the entrance to the Abruzzo, Lazio, and Molise National Park, located just outside Campoli Appennino. This protected area offers stunning hiking trails, diverse flora and fauna, and opportunities for wildlife

spotting, including wolves and deer. It's a perfect place to immerse yourself in nature after exploring the town.

Logistics

Train: Campoli Appennino does not have a train station, but the closest major station is in Sora, approximately 16 kilometers (10 miles) away. From Sora, regional trains connect to Rome and other towns in Lazio. To reach Campoli Appennino from the station, visitors can take a taxi or a local bus.

Bus: The town is well-connected by Cotral buses, which provide regular service to and from nearby towns such as Sora, Posta Fibreno, and Cassino. These buses also link Campoli Appennino to larger transport hubs, making it accessible for travelers without a car. The primary bus stop is in town.

Car: Driving is the most convenient way to reach Campoli Appennino. From Rome, take the A1 Autostrada del Sole southbound and exit at Ferentino. Follow the signs for Sora and then Campoli Appennino. The drive is approximately 120 kilometers (75 miles) and takes about 1 hour and 45 minutes, offering scenic views of the Apennine foothills.

Parking: Campoli Appennino offers ample parking options near the town center and its attractions. Public parking lots are available, including areas close to Piazza Umberto I. During festivals like the Sagra del Tartufo, parking may be limited, so arriving early is recommended. The historic center has narrow streets and some restricted zones (ZTL), so it's best to park outside the ZTL and explore the town on foot.

Restaurant Recommendations

Il Tartufo. Address: Via San Gaspare del Bufalo 65

Il Tartufo specializes in Italian and Mediterranean cuisine, with a focus on truffle-based dishes. The restaurant offers a cozy atmosphere and is known for its generous portions and traditional flavors.

Trattoria 'La Torre' Da Peppe Olè Se Magna. Address: Via Treo 29

This trattoria offers Italian and Mediterranean dishes in a rustic setting. It's praised for its authentic cuisine and friendly service, making it a popular spot for both locals and visitors.

Le Grotte della Locanda. Address: Via Roma 8

Le Grotte della Locanda serves Italian cuisine in a unique cave-like environment. Known for its excellent service and traditional dishes, it provides a memorable dining experience.

Accommodation

Staying overnight is unnecessary for sagre. There are no hotels in the town of Campoli. Here are some hotels in towns nearby.

Mingone Hotel Ristorante. Address: Via Pietro Nenni 96, 03033 Arpino, Italy

A 3-star hotel featuring a garden, terrace, restaurant, and bar. Guests have appreciated its good location, free parking, friendly staff, and great breakfast.

Relais Colle Buono. Address: Via Colle Buono Serre di Conca 2, 03041 Alvito, Italy

A 4-star hotel offering a seasonal outdoor swimming pool, fitness center, garden, and terrace. Guests have highlighted its wonderful stay, relaxing environment, and great restaurant.

Day Trip Options: Nearby Sites, Cities, and Towns

Posta Fibreno. 12 kilometers (7.5 miles). On the edge of the Fibreno River and its stunning natural reserve, Posta Fibreno is known for its crystal-clear waters and unique floating islands. Visitors can enjoy birdwatching, nature trails, and peaceful boat rides, making it an ideal destination for nature lovers and families.

Abruzzo, Lazio, and Molise National Park. 5 kilometers (3 miles). This vast and biodiverse park is a must-visit for outdoor enthusiasts. Spanning three regions, it offers hiking trails, wildlife observation opportunities (including wolves and bears), and breathtaking mountain landscapes. Campoli Appennino serves as a gateway to the park. One of Italy's oldest national parks, established in 1923, it protects some of the country's most precious wildlife, including the rare Marsican brown bear and the Italian wolf. The park boasts over 150 kilometers of marked hiking trails ranging from simple nature walks to challenging mountain treks.

Spring brings a spectacular display of wildflowers, including rare orchids, while autumn paints the ancient beech forests in brilliant reds and golds. Bird watchers can spot golden eagles soaring above the limestone peaks, while patient observers might glimpse chamois gracefully navigating the rocky slopes. The park's visitor center in Campoli Appennino offers maps, guided tour information, and fascinating exhibits about local flora and fauna. For the best wildlife viewing opportunities, early morning or dusk visits are recommended, and the park's trained guides can lead you to the most promising observation points while sharing insights about the delicate mountain ecosystem.

Vicalvi Castle. 15 kilometers (9 miles). This medieval fortress perched on a hill offers panoramic views of the Comino Valley. Though partially in ruins, the castle's walls and towers still exude a sense of history and charm, making it a favorite spot for history buffs and photographers. Dating back to the 10th century, the castle complex includes a fascinating mix of architectural elements, from its Norman-style watchtower to its later medieval additions.

Visitors can explore the remains of the ancient chapel, walk along the preserved ramparts, and discover the castle's role as a strategic defensive position for the valley below. The hike up to the castle follows an ancient stone path, offering glimpses of wild herbs and flowers along the way. Time your visit for sunset when the golden light bathes the stone walls and creates stunning photo opportunities of both the castle and the rolling countryside below. The small village of Vicalvi at the base of the hill also deserves a quick stroll, with its narrow medieval streets and traditional stone houses.

Campoli Festivals Throughout the Year

Festa di San Pancrazio

May 12

This festival honors Campoli Appennino's patron saint, San Pancrazio. The celebration includes a solemn religious procession through the town's streets, traditional music, and a communal feast. The event reflects the town's deep-rooted spiritual heritage and devotion to its patron saint, uniting the community in a meaningful cultural and religious tradition.

Campoli Appennino Estate (Summer Festival)

Late August

The Summer Festival is a vibrant series of events held during the warmer months, featuring music, sports, entertainment, and cultural activities. It aims to celebrate the lively spirit of Campoli Appennino and its people, drawing both locals and visitors for an engaging communal experience.

Festa del Broccoletto

December 8

This festival celebrates Campoli Appennino's unique variety of broccoli, known as 'broccoletto.' The event showcases the town's agricultural heritage with tastings of broccoletto-based dishes, local products, and traditional music. It highlights the importance of agriculture to the town's economy and culture, offering visitors a chance to savor its authentic flavors.

CHAPTER FORTY

Festa dell' Immacolata: Initiating the Season of Light

Mary's Day, Christmas Way

F esta dell'Immacolata

Where: Rome & Beyond

When: December 8

Average Festival Temperatures: High 13°C (55°F). Low: 4°C (39°F).

Papal Tribute at Piazza Mignanelli: History and Significance

The central event of the Festa dell'Immacolata in Rome takes place at Piazza Mignanelli, near the iconic Spanish Steps. The focal point is the Column of the Immaculate Conception, a towering monument dedicated to the Virgin Mary (see my instagram for videos of this event @katerinaferraraauthor).

The column was erected in 1857 to commemorate Pope Pius IX's proclamation of the dogma of the Immaculate Conception in 1854. This dogma affirmed the belief that Mary, the mother of Jesus, was conceived without original sin. It was a landmark moment in Catholic theology and devotion to Mary.

The column itself is a significant piece of art and architecture. Standing 12 meters (40 feet) high, it was designed by architect Luigi Poletti, and its installation was a major engineering feat for the time. The base is adorned with sculptures of biblical figures associated with Marian devotion: Moses, David, Isaiah, and Ezekiel. At the top is a bronze statue of the Virgin Mary, created by sculptor Giuseppe Obici.

Inauguration of the Papal Tribute:
The tradition of the Papal Tribute to the Immaculate Conception began with Pope Pius XII in 1953. The Pope's annual visit to Piazza Mignanelli to lay flowers at the base of the column underscores the importance of Marian devotion in the Catholic Church and serves as a highly anticipated public display of faith.

Significance of the Ritual:

Floral Wreath: The floral wreath laid by the Pope is a symbol of purity and reverence for the Virgin Mary. It reflects the Church's veneration of Mary as a central figure in Catholicism and as a protector of the faithful.

Firefighters' Role: An integral part of the ceremony is the participation of Rome's firefighters. Using a ladder, they place a garland at the very top of the column, honoring Mary from the highest point of the monument. This gesture is both a display of skill and devotion, making it a unique aspect of the celebration.

Processions and Ceremonies:

7:00 a.m.

The day's events begin with a firefighter ascending the Column of the Immaculate Conception to place a floral wreath on the statue of the Virgin Mary.

8:30 a.m.

A procession from the Church of Santa Caterina da Siena in Via Urbana arrives at the Marian Column.

9:00 a.m.

The parish of Sant'Andrea delle Fratte conducts a procession to the column.

10:30 a.m.

Various groups, including workers from prominent Roman companies, knights and ladies of the Order of the Holy Sepulcher, and representatives from different Italian regions, pay homage to the Virgin Mary.

12:00 p.m.

The Spanish Ambassador to the Holy See, along with Spanish dignitaries, presents their respects.

3:30 p.m.

The pilgrimage organization Unitalsi leads a procession to the column.

3:45 p.m.

City officials of Rome take part in the homage.

4:00 p.m. the Main Event

The Pope arrives at Piazza Mignanelli to honor the Virgin Mary, laying a floral wreath at the base of the column. These processions and ceremonies reflect the deep Marian devotion in Rome, with various religious groups, civic organizations, and dignitaries taking part throughout the day. The culmination of the day's events is the Pope's tribute, attracting because of the sizeable crowds of faithful and visitors. Over the years, this event has become not just a religious observance but also a cherished cultural tradition in Rome, marking the beginning of the Christmas season in the city.

*For those planning to attend, it's advisable to arrive early because of the significant number of participants and spectators. The area around Piazza Mignanelli becomes quite crowded, especially during the Pope's visit. Public transportation is recommended, as traffic restrictions are typically in place during these events.

Other Key December 8th Events in Rome

On December 8th, Rome is vibrant with events marking the beginning of the Christmas season, coinciding with the Feast of the Immaculate Conception. Here are some notable happenings:

Piazza del Popolo Christmas Tree Lighting

The tree, a 22-meter fir from Como, will be illuminated on December 8th at 18:30. This ceremony signifies the city's festive spirit and is accompanied by the lighting of decorations along Via del Corso.

Vatican Nativity Scene and Christmas Tree

In St. Peter's Square, the Vatican unveils its Nativity scene and illuminates its Christmas tree on December 7th at 17:00. This year's Nativity scene hails from Grado, and the tree is a spruce from Ledro. The ceremony is presided over by Vatican officials and attracts visitors worldwide.

Exhibition of 100 Nativity Scenes

The "100 Presepi in Vaticano" exhibition showcases Nativity scenes from around the globe. Located under Bernini's Colonnade in St. Peter's Square, the exhibition runs from December 8th to January 6th. It offers a diverse display of artistic interpretations of the Nativity.

Piazza Navona Christmas Market

The historic Piazza Navona transforms into a festive market during the Christmas season. From December 1st to January 6th, the square is filled with stalls selling holiday treats, gifts, and decorations, providing a lively atmosphere for both locals and tourists.

Beyond Rome – Festa dell'Immacolata

Sagra del Pangiallo e della Polenta in Riano

Where: Piazza Piombino, Riano (33 kilometers (20 miles) north of Rome)

When: December 8 (and surrounding days)

The Riano Christmas Festival offers a rich array of attractions that blend traditional cuisine with holiday entertainment. The Pro Loco Riano operates food stands featuring local specialties, with particular emphasis on polenta and the town's signature dessert, pangiallo. This traditional sweet is crafted through a meticulous process of combining dried fruits, cocoa, liqueurs, and candied fruits, which are left to macerate for days before baking. Its distinctive name, meaning "yellow bread," comes from the egg batter coating that takes on a golden hue during baking.

The festival's Christmas market provides themed stalls perfect for holiday shopping, while children can experience the magic of Christmas at Santa's House. Throughout the event, visitors are treated to live music and street performances, creating a festive atmosphere for all ages. A unique highlight of the festival is the national archery competition organized by the "Arcieri di San Giorgio da Riano," adding a sporting element to the celebration's diverse offerings.

"Christmas is Coming" in Canale Monterano

Where: Canale Monterano along Corso della Repubblica (51 kilometers (31 miles) northwest of Rome)

When: December 8

"Christmas is Coming" in Canale Monterano creates a magical holiday atmosphere along Corso della Repubblica on December 8, transforming this historic street into a festive wonderland. The event features a diverse array of attractions beginning with an extensive artisanal and Christmas market, where visitors can browse handcrafted items and holiday-themed products perfect for seasonal gift-giving. Children are delighted by visits to Santa's House, where they can meet Father Christmas and share their Christmas wishes in a charming, festive setting.

The celebration includes the special inauguration of nativity scenes crafted by local community members, showcasing the area's creative talent and dedication to tradition. Families can embark on a whimsical journey through the Elf Kingdom, an enchanted space that brings the magical world of Santa's helpers to life.

CHAPTER FORTY-ONE

Christmas Lights and Decorations in Rome & Beyond

Illuminating Lazio

Christmas Magic in Rome & Lazio: A Festival of Light and Tradition

December 8 to January 6

Picture Rome at Christmas: ancient cobblestones glisten under twinkling lights, the scent of roasted chestnuts fills crisp winter air, and centuries-old piazzas transform into enchanted gathering places. This is when Rome sheds its summer crowds and dons its most intimate, magical atmosphere. As the saying goes, "Natale con i tuoi, Pasqua con chi vuoi" (Christmas with family, Easter with whom you choose) and during these special weeks, Rome welcomes you like family.

Average Festival Temperatures: High 12°C (54°F). Low 4°C (39°F).

Christmas Lights in Rome's Piazzas

During the festive season, Rome's piazzas come alive with enchanting Christmas lights and decorations, creating a magical atmosphere that captivates visitors and locals alike. Here are some must-visit piazzas:

- **Piazza Venezia**: The central location of Piazza Venezia features a towering Christmas tree adorned with thousands of sparkling lights, making it a focal point of the city's holiday celebrations.

- **Piazza Navona**: Renowned for its Christmas market, this piazza also boasts beautifully lit fountains and festive stalls. Piazza Navona hosts a lively Christmas fair with rides, games, and entertainment for children and families.

- **Piazza del Popolo**: The elegant square transforms into a winter wonderland with a mix of modern and traditional lighting, perfect for an evening stroll.

- **Campo de' Fiori**: This historic market square is adorned with twinkling lights, adding a cozy charm to its bustling atmosphere.

Rome's Festive Shopping Streets

Rome's streets are an essential part of its holiday magic. Here are the most iconic streets to experience:

- **Via del Corso**: The long stretch of Via del Corso features dazzling light displays, often with themes that change annually, making it a favorite for holiday shopping and strolling.

- **Via Condotti**: Known for luxury shopping, this street's elegant light displays are designed to complement its high-end boutiques.

- **Via Veneto**: The iconic street, famous for its La Dolce Vita allure, glows with festive lighting, offering a sophisticated holiday ambiance.

- **Trastevere**: The charming cobblestone streets of Trastevere are adorned with understated but enchanting lights, adding to the district's bohemian vibe.

Christmas Markets in Rome

Rome's Christmas markets are a delightful part of the festive season, offering unique gifts, local crafts, and seasonal treats:

- **Piazza Navona**: The most famous Christmas market in Rome is held here, featuring artisanal crafts, holiday sweets, decorations, and traditional toys. It's a perfect spot to soak up the festive atmosphere.

- **Auditorium Parco della Musica**: This cultural hub hosts a holiday market known as "Christmas World," showcasing international stalls, food, and entertainment.

- **Campo de' Fiori**: While not exclusively a Christmas market, the square has seasonal offerings during the holidays, including decorations and festive food items.

- **Piazza Mazzini**: This smaller market is popular for handmade crafts and unique gifts, offering a more local experience.

Nativity Scenes (Presepi)

Rome's tradition of presepi (nativity scenes) is a highlight of its Christmas celebrations. These artistic displays can be found throughout the city:

- **St. Peter's Square**: The grand nativity scene at the Vatican is a centerpiece of the city's Christmas decorations. It features life-sized figures and intricate details.

- **Basilica of Santa Maria Maggiore**: This church houses one of the oldest nativity scenes in Rome, crafted in the 13th century.

- **Piazza del Popolo**: A charming presepe is often displayed in the square, drawing crowds for its traditional craftsmanship.

- **Presepe dei Netturbini**: Created by Rome's sanitation workers, this unique nativity scene located on Via dei Cavalleggeri is a hidden gem worth visiting.

Key Churches with Christmas Decorations

Rome's churches showcase stunning decorations and special events during the holiday season:

- **St. Peter's Basilica**: Beyond the nativity scene, the basilica's interior is beautifully illuminated, and midnight Mass on Christmas Eve is a spiritual highlight.

- **Sant'Andrea della Valle**: This Baroque church is adorned with festive lights and often features a special presepe.

- **Santa Maria in Trastevere**: The historic church is lit up with golden hues, and its nativity scene is a must-see.

- **San Luigi dei Francesi**: Known for its stunning Caravaggio paintings, this church also features tasteful holiday decorations.

Rome Visiting Tips

Visit major piazzas and streets in the evening when Christmas lights create a magical atmosphere. Churches offer special holiday concerts and Masses throughout December. Traditional nativity scenes are displayed from early December through January 6th (Epiphany), providing glimpses into Italian Christmas traditions.

Christmas in Lazio: Towns Known for Their Festive Lights and Decorations

Civita di Bagnoregio

Known as the "dying town," Civita di Bagnoregio transforms into a magical Christmas village during the holiday season. Perched atop a hill, this medieval village is adorned with twinkling lights that highlight its cobblestone streets and ancient architecture.

- Where to Go: Stroll through the main square, Piazza San Donato, where a charming nativity scene is often set up. The entire village is illuminated, offering breathtaking views of the surrounding valley.

- Christmas Markets: While small, local vendors often set up stalls selling handmade crafts, local delicacies, and festive decorations.

- Church to Visit: The Church of San Donato in the main square hosts special Christmas events, including Mass and concerts, adding to the town's serene holiday atmosphere.

Sermoneta

This historic hilltop town is renowned for its medieval charm, which is amplified during the festive season. The streets and piazzas are beautifully illuminated, creating a warm and inviting holiday ambiance.

- Where to Go: Piazza del Popolo is the heart of Sermoneta's Christmas celebrations, featuring lights, decorations, and occasional live music.

- Christmas Markets: Sermoneta's Christmas market includes stalls selling local crafts, traditional foods, and holiday gifts. Don't miss the locally produced olive oil and wine.

- Church to Visit: The Cathedral of Santa Maria Assunta, with its Romanesque architecture, is adorned with festive decorations and hosts special holiday services.

Greccio

Known as the birthplace of the first live nativity scene, Greccio holds a special place in the history of Christmas traditions. The town celebrates with reverence and charm during the holiday season.

- Where to Go: Visit the historic Sanctuary of Greccio, where St. Francis of Assisi created the first nativity scene. The town's main square is also beautifully decorated.

- Christmas Markets: Greccio hosts a unique Christmas market that focuses on nativity-themed crafts and gifts. Visitors can find handmade figurines and local artisan products.

- Church to Visit: The Sanctuary of Greccio is a must-see, offering both spiritual significance and stunning holiday decorations.

Vetralla

Vetralla becomes a Christmas wonderland during the holiday season, with its famous "Christmas Kingdom" attracting visitors from all over Lazio.

- Where to Go: Explore the Victorian Village within the Christmas Kingdom, where you'll find Santa's House, illuminated pathways, and themed displays.

- Christmas Markets: The Christmas Kingdom features a variety of stalls offering festive treats, ornaments, and handmade gifts. There are also activities for children, such as storytelling and workshops.

- Church to Visit: The Church of San Francesco is beautifully decorated and often hosts concerts and holiday Masses.

Gaeta

Gaeta's "Favole di Luce" (Fairy Tales of Light) festival is a highlight of the holiday season in Lazio. The artistic light installations transform the town into a luminous wonderland.

- Where to Go: Start at Piazza della Libertà, where the largest installations are displayed. Wander along Lungomare Giovanni Caboto to enjoy more lights and festive scenes.

- Christmas Markets: Gaeta's Christmas market is located near the waterfront, offering a range of local foods, crafts, and holiday gifts. Try the traditional "tiella," a savory pie filled with seafood or vegetables.

- Church to Visit: The Cathedral of Saints Erasmus and Marciano is beautifully lit and decorated, making it a serene spot for holiday reflection.

Planning Your Christmas Visit

During Christmas week, hotels increase prices by 40%, so advance booking is essential. Restaurant reservations are crucial from December 23-26, when many venues are fully booked.

Transportation runs on reduced schedules December 25-26. Shops extend their hours until 8:00 PM from December 8-24 for holiday shopping.

Church service schedules are available at Tourist Information Points and posted on church doors. At markets, bring cash since many vendors don't accept cards.

CHAPTER FORTY-TWO

Tivoli's Annual Journey of Faith, Fire, and Culture

The Splendor of the Festa di Sant'Antonio Abate

F esta di Sant'Antonio Abate

Where: Tivoli

When: January 17

Average Festival Temperatures: High: 10°C (50°F). Low: 2°C (36°F).

Tivoli: A Historic Gem of Lazio

Tivoli, a charming town in the Lazio region of Italy, is renowned for its ancient history, stunning architecture, and breathtaking natural beauty. Nestled in the hills east of Rome, Tivoli has long been a favored destination for those seeking both artistic enrichment and serene landscapes. Its proximity to Rome makes it an ideal day trip or a quiet retreat from the bustling city.

Tivoli is located 30 kilometers (19 miles) east of Rome, easily accessible by train, car, or bus. On the western slopes of the Monti Tiburtini, part of the Apennine mountain range, the town enjoys a picturesque setting overlooking the Roman Campagna, the fertile plains surrounding Rome. The Aniene River, a tributary of the Tiber, flows through Tivoli, contributing to the town's iconic waterfalls and lush surroundings. This natural beauty has inspired poets, artists, and architects for centuries.

The town sits at an elevation of 235 meters (771 feet) above sea level, providing cooler temperatures than Rome during the summer months, which has historically made it a popular retreat for the Roman elite. Tivoli boasts a rich history that predates the founding of Rome. Originally known as Tibur, the town was established by the Sabines, one of Italy's ancient peoples, around the 13th century BC. By the 5th century BC, Tibur had become an important ally of Rome, though it kept a degree of autonomy.

In the Roman era, Tivoli became a favored location for wealthy Romans, who constructed luxurious villas to escape the heat and chaos of the capital. The most famous of these is Villa Adriana (Hadrian's Villa), a sprawling complex built by Emperor Hadrian in the 2nd century AD. The villa, now a UNESCO World Heritage Site, reflects the opulence and architectural innovation of the Roman Empire.

During the Middle Ages, Tivoli gained prominence as a fortified town and a religious center. Its strategic location made it a contested site among various factions, including the Papacy and the Holy Roman Empire. Many of the town's medieval structures, including churches and defensive walls, date back to this period.

In the Renaissance, Tivoli flourished once again, attracting artists, architects, and noble families. The construction of Villa d'Este, another UNESCO World Heritage Site, showcases the grandeur of this era with its elaborate fountains, gardens, and waterworks.

Festival of Saint Anthony the Abbot

Who is Saint Anthony Abbot?

Saint Anthony the Abbot, also known as Anthony of Egypt or Anthony the Great, was a Christian monk and one of the most prominent figures of early Christian monasticism. Born in 251 AD in Egypt, he devoted his life to asceticism, retreating to the desert to live in solitude and prayer. He is often called the "Father of Monks."

Anthony is celebrated for his profound spiritual insights and miraculous acts, including healing the sick and casting out demons. Over the centuries, he became a patron saint of animals and those who work with the land. His association with animals likely stems from medieval depictions of his life, where he is often shown accompanied by a pig, symbolizing his role as a protector of livestock.

The feast day, January 17, is also linked to ancient rural traditions marking the end of winter and the beginning of the agricultural year, blending Christian and pagan customs.

The Festival Traditions

The festival in Tivoli has been celebrated for centuries, rooted in the town's agricultural past. Tivoli's farmers and herders have long turned to Sant'Antonio for protection over their animals and livelihoods. This connection between the saint and the town's rural identity is reflected in the festival's traditions. In the Middle Ages, the festival grew in importance as it provided an opportunity for communal blessings and thanksgiving. Farmers would bring their animals to the local church to receive blessings, ensuring their health and productivity for the year ahead. Over time, the festival strengthened into a larger event, incorporating processions, bonfires, and cultural celebrations, while maintaining its spiritual essence.

Religious Ceremonies

Blessing of Animals: Following the morning mass, a priest performs the customary blessing of animals. Residents bring their pets, livestock, and even symbolic representations of animals to the church or designated square for this touching ceremony. It is believed this blessing protects animals from illness and ensures a prosperous year.

Procession of Saint Anthony

A solemn procession through the streets of Tivoli showcases an icon or statue of Sant'Antonio, carried by devotees. The route winds through the town's historic center, accompanied by prayers, music, and the participation of local clergy and community groups. Participants dress in traditional costumes, adding a historical and cultural dimension to the event.

Bonfires (Falò di Sant'Antonio)

One of the festival's most iconic elements is the lighting of bonfires in the evening. These fires symbolize purification, protection, and the banishment of evil spirits, echoing ancient pagan traditions. Residents gather around the bonfires to enjoy music, storytelling, and customary foods, fostering a sense of community.

Culinary Delights

The festival is also a time to savor local specialties, such as polenta, grilled meats, and sweet treats. Vendors set up stalls offering hot mulled wine and other winter comforts. Some dishes, like roasted chestnuts or pork-based delicacies, pay homage to Sant'Antonio's association with rural life and animals.

Entertainment and Cultural Events

The streets of Tivoli come alive with folk music, dancing, and performances by local bands or theatrical groups. Artisans and farmers often showcase their crafts and produce in a small market, celebrating the town's agricultural traditions.

Festival Events

The Festa di Sant'Antonio Abate in Tivoli is a cherished annual event that combines religious devotion with vibrant community activities. While specific schedules can vary each year, the festival typically includes the following events:

January 17: Feast Day of Sant'Antonio Abate

8:00, 9:00, 10:00, and 11:00 a.m.

Morning Masses are held at the Church of Sant'Antonio Abate on Via Maggiore.

Tamburellare Performances: Traditional drummers perform after the morning Masses, adding a festive rhythm to the celebrations.

Following the 11:00 a.m. Mass

Animal Blessings, the blessing of animals takes place after mass, honoring Sant'Antonio as the patron saint of animals.

Afternoon Rosary and Mass: In the afternoon, the Rosary is recited, followed by a Solemn Mass presided over by the Bishop of Tivoli and Palestrina.

Evening

The day concludes with a concert by the Associazione Culturale "Città di Tivoli," featuring traditional and contemporary music.

Walking Tour of Tivoli

#1. Piazza Garibaldi

Begin the tour at this picturesque square, which offers sweeping views of the countryside and the historic Porta del Colle. Enjoy a coffee at one of the nearby cafes.

#2. Villa d'Este

A UNESCO World Heritage Site, Villa d'Este is a Renaissance masterpiece renowned for its spectacular gardens, intricate fountains, and richly decorated interiors. Built in the 16th century for Cardinal Ippolito II d'Este, the villa exemplifies the grandeur of its time and reflects the cardinal's ambition to rival the glories of ancient Rome. Designed by Pirro Ligorio, the gardens and waterworks use innovative engineering to create gravity-fed fountains without pumps, showcasing the ingenuity of Renaissance landscape architecture.

Fountains of Villa d'Este

The gardens feature a network of terraces, pathways, and lush greenery, interspersed with over 500 fountains, pools, and waterfalls. Highlights include the Fountain of Neptune, which dominates the lower garden with its powerful cascade, and the Organ Fountain, which produces musical sounds through a water-powered mechanism, a technological marvel of its era.

Inside the villa, the frescoed interiors are equally captivating, with vibrant depictions of mythology, nature, and celestial themes adorning the walls and ceilings. Rooms such as the Hall of the Fountain provide a glimpse into the opulent lifestyle of the cardinal and his guests. Allow 1–2 hours to explore the villa and its gardens. Be sure to pause at the many viewpoints offering sweeping vistas of the Roman Campagna, adding to the villa's allure as a serene retreat and a cultural treasure.

Booking ahead is recommended: https://www.villadeste.com/

#3. Chiesa di San Francesco (St. Francis)

The Chiesa di San Francesco stands as one of Tivoli's most significant medieval religious monuments, dating back to the 13th century. Its austere Romanesque facade belies an interior rich with historical treasures, including fragments of 14th-century frescoes that hint at the church's original decorative splendor. The adjacent cloister, built in the 14th century, features delicate double columns supporting graceful arches, creating a contemplative space where monks once walked.

The church has witnessed numerous historical events, including a visit by St. Francis himself in 1223. A particular highlight is the Gothic portal with its intricate stone carvings, while the bell tower, though partially rebuilt over the centuries, remains an excellent example of medieval architectural practices. The church's interior chapels contain several notable artworks, including a 15th-century wooden crucifix and baroque altarpieces.

#4. Anfiteatro di Bleso

The Anfiteatro di Bleso constructed in the 1st century AD during the reign of Emperor Trajan, represents a fascinating example of Roman provincial architecture. Though smaller than Rome's Colosseum, it could still accommodate approximately 3,500 spectators, a significant portion of Tivoli's ancient population. The remaining structure reveals sophisticated engineering techniques, including a complex system of underground passages and chambers that were used to house animals and gladiators before performances.

The amphitheater's elliptical design, measuring roughly 80 meters (260 feet) by 60 meters (190 feet), follows classical Roman architectural principles. Today, visitors can still observe the original seating arrangements, parts of the arena floor, and some of the service corridors, providing insight into how these spectacular entertainment venues functioned.

#5. Temple of Vesta and Temple of Sibyl

The Temple of Vesta and Temple of Sibyl, perched dramatically on Tivoli's acropolis, represent some of the best-preserved examples of Republican Roman temple architecture outside Rome. The Temple of Vesta, built in the 1st century BC, is particularly remarkable for its circular design and Corinthian columns, of which ten of the original eighteen remain standing. This temple's position on the edge of a deep gorge created by the Aniene River made it a symbol of Tivoli visible from miles away.

The nearby Temple of Sibyl, actually dedicated to Tiburnus (the mythical founder of Tivoli), features a rectangular plan and was built around the 2nd century BC. From their vantage point, visitors can enjoy breathtaking views of the surrounding valley and the Rocca Pia, a formidable 15th-century fortress commissioned by Pope Pius II. The fortress's four cylindrical towers dominate the skyline, while its strategic position protected both Tivoli and the road to Rome. The temple's location offers spectacular views at sunset, when the golden light illuminates the ancient stone and creates dramatic shadows across the valley.

#6. Ponte Gregoriano and Parco Villa Gregoriana

The Ponte Gregoriano and Parco Villa Gregoriana represent one of Italy's most remarkable fusions of natural beauty and human engineering. A masterpiece of 19th-century landscape design, the park was commissioned by Pope Gregory XVI in the 1830s following a devastating flood. The pope's engineers, led by Clemente Folchi, redirected the Aniene River through a double tunnel carved into Monte Catillo, creating the spectacular Great Cascade - a 120-meter waterfall that thunders through the gorge.

Visitors can explore the park's multiple levels of paths and stairways, glimpsing ancient Roman ruins including the remains of the Republican-era Villa of Manlius Vopiscus and the foundation of an ancient necropolis. The Neptune Grotto, formed by centuries of water erosion, creates an otherworldly atmosphere with its massive chambers and natural arches. With a diverse ecosystem of ferns, moss, and local flora thriving in the perpetually moist microclimate of its waterfalls, the park's botanical richness is equally impressive.

The original Roman acqueduct remains visible, demonstrating the site's historical importance in Rome's water management system. From the walking trails, the cascades are visible from many viewpoints, each highlighting the unique interplay between the natural gorge and human structures.

#7. Piazza Rivarola

Piazza Rivarola is the lively heart of Tivoli, blending medieval charm with everyday local life. Surrounded by historic buildings, the square is home to artisan shops where ceramists and craftspeople create ceramics, metalwork, and carvings, often inspired by the gardens of Villa d'Este.

In the evening, locals gather for the passeggiata, enjoying regional dishes like porchetta at nearby cafes. The piazza also hosts seasonal markets and festivals, including a popular autumn olive oil celebration. Winding medieval alleys nearby reveal hidden workshops and unique handmade treasures.

#8. Villa Adriana (Hadrian's Villa)

A short ride or bus trip from the town center, this Roman archaeological site is a must-see if time allows. Explore its vast complex of baths, temples, and the iconic Maritime Theatre.

What to See at Hadrian's Villa

This sprawling complex covers over 120 hectares, with only a portion accessible to visitors. The villa features an eclectic mix of Roman, Greek, and Egyptian influences, reflecting Hadrian's travels and vision.

Maritime Theater

A circular pool surrounding an artificial island. This unique structure was likely Hadrian's private retreat within the villa. The island contained a small Roman domus (house) with sleeping quarters, baths, and even a library.

Maritime Theater in Tivoli

Canopus and Serapeum

Inspired by the Egyptian city of Canopus, this elongated pool is framed by statues of gods and mythological creatures, creating a dramatic and serene setting. At one end is the Serapeum, a semi-circular pavilion thought to have been a dining area for Hadrian and his guests. Its arched structure and decorative features exemplify Roman engineering at its peak.

Piazza d'Oro (Golden Square)

This was one of the villa's most opulent spaces, featuring a grand courtyard surrounded by columns and elaborate mosaics. The purpose of this area is debated, but it may have been a reception hall or leisure area.

Large Baths and Small Baths

These two complexes show the importance of bathing in Roman culture. The Large Baths were for public use, while the Small Baths were likely reserved for Hadrian and his inner circle.

Pecile

A vast rectangular portico that originally surrounded a pool, the Pecile was designed for walking and relaxing. Its design was inspired by the Stoà Poikílē in Athens, reflecting Hadrian's admiration for Greek culture.

Heliocaminus Bath

Named after the sun (Helios), this bathhouse was ingeniously designed to use solar heating. It is one of the oldest examples of this technology in Roman architecture.

Greek and Latin Libraries

These spaces housed Hadrian's vast collection of texts in Greek and Latin, reflecting his intellectual pursuits and appreciation for literature.

Tickets: Tickets can be purchased on-site or online. I always advise to book at least one week ahead so you are not disappointed on a sold-out day.

https://villae.cultura.gov.it/en/the-locations/villa-adriana/

Logistics

Train: Tivoli boasts a train station served by the FL2 regional line, which connects Rome's Tiburtina station to Tivoli. Trains run approximately every 30 minutes during peak times, with a journey duration of about 50 minutes. This option is convenient for travelers preferring public transport.

Bus: Several bus services operate between Rome and Tivoli, offering an alternative to train travel. Buses typically depart from Rome's Ponte Mammolo station and arrive at Tivoli's main square, Piazza Garibaldi. The journey takes around 1 hour, depending on the traffic conditions. This option is suitable for those looking for direct routes to the town's center.

Car: Driving to Tivoli from Rome is straightforward, with a distance of about 30 kilometers (19 miles). The fastest route is via the A24 highway, taking approximately 35 minutes under optimal traffic conditions.

Parking: Parking in Tivoli, especially near major attractions like Villa d'Este, can be challenging because of limited spaces and ZTL zones. There are multi-level public parking garages within a couple of blocks of the entrance to Villa d'Este, but they fill fast in busy seasons, and on-street parking is hard to find. It's advisable to arrive early to secure a spot. Always check for signage indicating ZTL areas to avoid fines.

Dining Recommendations

Sibilla. Address: Via della Sibilla, 50

A historic restaurant established in 1720, offering traditional Italian cuisine in a picturesque setting. Near ancient Roman temples, it features a garden with views of the Aniene River. Signature dishes include fettuccine with truffle and a variety of fresh seafood. Reservations are recommended.

Trattoria da Gabriella. Address: Vicolo Santa Croce, 22

A cozy and authentic Italian trattoria known for its generous portions and warm atmosphere. Popular dishes include Cacio e Pepe and other traditional Roman pastas. A favorite among both locals and tourists.

Avec 55. Address: Via Domenico Giuliani, 55

A modern restaurant offering a fresh take on traditional Italian cuisine. The menu features seasonal, innovative dishes and an extensive wine list. Its contemporary decor and attentive service make it ideal for a refined dining experience.

Ristorante Antiche Terme di Diana. Address: Via dei Sosii, 6

Nestled within ancient caves, this restaurant provides a unique historical ambiance. The menu highlights regional specialties, including homemade pastas and locally sourced meats, offering a blend of history and culinary excellence.

Accommodation

For the festival I recommend two to three nights in town.

*Hotel Torre Sant'Antonio. Address: Vicolo Sant'Antonio, 35

Housed in a 14th-century tower, this boutique hotel offers two private rooms, each occupying an entire floor. The interiors blend antique furnishings with modern amenities, curated by architect owners. Guests can enjoy panoramic views of the historic center on the upper floors.

Affittacamere Al Seminario. Address: Vicolo del Duomo, 1

This guesthouse offers simple yet comfortable rooms with free Wi-Fi and TVs. Its central location makes it convenient to explore Tivoli's attractions, and the terrace provides a pleasant spot to relax.

Hotel Cristallo Relais. Address: Via Maremmana Inferiore Km 0,500

This 3-star hotel features modern rooms with free Wi-Fi, an on-site restaurant, and an outdoor pool. It offers free parking and is a short distance from Tivoli's principal attractions.

Hotel Le Rose. Address: Via Tiburtina Valeria, 330

This 2-star hotel offers basic accommodations with free Wi-Fi and an on-site restaurant. It provides free parking and is a budget-friendly option for visitors.

*Directly on the procession route for the Festa di Sant'Antonio.

Day Trips: Nearby Sites, Cities and Towns

Palestrina: This charming town lies 25 kilometers (16 miles) southeast of Tivoli and is famous for the National Archaeological Museum of Palestrina, housed in the ancient Sanctuary of Fortuna Primigenia. The museum showcases fascinating artifacts from ancient Rome and the pre-Roman period. Palestrina also offers lovely streets to wander and splendid views of the surrounding countryside.

Castel Madama: 12 kilometers (7.5 miles) northeast of Tivoli, this quaint medieval village is known for its well-preserved castle, Castello Orsini, and its charming cobbled streets. It's a peaceful escape with stunning views of the Roman countryside and a slower pace compared to Tivoli or Rome.

Tivoli Festivals Throughout the Year

Tiburtino Carnival

Typically held in February or early March, aligning with the traditional carnival season.

The Tiburtino Carnival traces its origins to the late 16th century, coinciding with Cardinal Ippolito d'Este's residence in Tivoli. Today, the Carnival includes float parades, markets, concerts, theater performances, exhibitions, masked balls, and children's parties, infusing the town's old quarters with vibrant celebrations.

Sagra delli Ghiozzi (Pasta)

Traditionally held in May; specific dates may vary annually.

This sagra celebrates "Ghiozzi," a traditional pasta dish unique to Tivoli's culinary heritage. The festival offers attendees the opportunity to savor this local specialty, prepared according to time-honored recipes, highlighting the town's pasta traditions.

Festa di San Lorenzo (Festival of Saint Lawrence)

August 10th

Saint Lawrence, martyred on August 10, 258 AD, is venerated as Tivoli's patron saint. The festival begins with a solemn Mass at the Cathedral of San Lorenzo, where relics of the saint are displayed. A procession follows, winding through Tivoli's historic streets, accompanied by clergy, local officials, and residents.

Pizzutello Grape Festival (Sagra dell'Uva Pizzutello)

First weekend in September

One of Italy's oldest grape festivals, the Pizzutello Grape Festival, dates back to 1845. It honors the "Pizzutello" grape, also known as "uva corna," a variety native to Tivoli and recognized as a Slow Food presidium. The festival features tastings, cultural events, and exhibitions that celebrate the town's viticultural heritage.

Spring Celebrations

February through April

CHAPTER FORTY-THREE

The Vibrant Masks of Ronciglione

A Carnival Legacy, Celebration Through the Ages

Carnivale Roncligione

Where: Ronciglione

When: February / March (Dependent on date of Easter)

Average Festival Temperatures: High 15°C (59°F). Low 5°C (41°F).

Event Website: https://www.carnevaledironciglione.org/it/

Ronciglione: Where Tradition and Festivity Thrive

Nestled in the verdant hills of Lazio, Ronciglione is a picturesque town known for its rich history, cultural heritage, and vibrant festivals. In the Province of Viterbo, 60 kilometers (37 miles) northwest of Rome, this charming town offers a blend of medieval architecture, natural beauty, and timeless traditions.

Ronciglione is situated on the slopes of the Cimini Mountains, overlooking the Vico Lake, a volcanic lake that enhances the town's scenic allure. The surrounding landscape is characterized by lush forests, rolling hills, and fertile lands, making it a haven for nature lovers and outdoor enthusiasts. Its strategic location historically made Ronciglione a key stop along ancient trade routes, contributing to its cultural and economic significance.

The origins of Ronciglione date back to the Etruscan era, with evidence of settlements in the region. During the Middle Ages, the town flourished under the control of prominent noble families, such as the Prefetti di Vico and later the Farnese. Its well-preserved medieval quarter reflects the architectural styles of these periods, with narrow cobblestone streets, historic churches, and imposing towers.

In the Renaissance, Ronciglione became an important center of production, particularly for armaments and copper objects, which were traded widely. The town's prosperity continued into the Baroque era, as seen in its artistic and cultural developments. Today, Ronciglione retains its historical charm while embracing modernity.

With a population of 8,000 residents, Ronciglione is a close-knit community that values its traditions and cultural heritage. The residents, known as *ronciglionesi*, take pride in their town's festivals and culinary delights, which draw visitors from across Italy and beyond.

Ronciglione offers a captivating mix of history, natural beauty, and vibrant traditions. Visitors can explore its medieval quarter, enjoy panoramic views of Lake Vico, and immerse themselves in the town's festive spirit during its renowned Carnevale di Ronciglione. Whether wandering through its historic streets or savoring local delicacies, Ronciglione provides an authentic taste of Lazio's cultural heart.

Carnevale di Ronciglione

Picture yourself in 1538: Pope Paul III Farnese has just declared three days of revelry to celebrate his son's new role as Duke. The streets of Ronciglione erupt in celebration - a moment that would spark one of central Italy's most beloved carnival traditions.

Today's Carnevale di Ronciglione still pulses with that Renaissance spirit, most dramatically in the "Corse dei Barberi" - thundering riderless horse races that have thrilled spectators since the 1600s. Originally part of August's feast of San Bartolomeo, these heart-stopping races found their true home in the carnival celebrations, where they continue to showcase the town's deep equestrian heritage.

The carnival transforms Ronciglione's medieval streets into a living theater. Masked revelers in elaborate period costumes sweep past centuries-old stone walls, while allegorical floats tell stories both ancient and modern. Each element of the celebration from the traditional processions to the local foods and music weaves together the town's past and present.

At its heart, Carnevale represents humanity's age-old desire to turn the world upside down, if only for a few weeks. The name itself comes from "carnem levare" (to remove meat), marking this period of indulgence before Lent's fasting begins. While every Italian town celebrates differently, each tradition - whether Venice's masked balls or Ronciglione's racing horses - shares this spirit of joyful rebellion against the ordinary.

Events at Carnevale di Ronciglione

The Carnevale di Ronciglione spans several days, with events concentrated during the so-called "fat week" and the Sundays leading up to Lent. While the exact schedule can vary each year, a typical lineup includes:

Opening Ceremony: The carnival officially begins with the arrival of the "King of Carnival," welcomed by the townspeople with great fanfare. This symbolic figure presides over the festivities, embodying the spirit of celebration. The carnival season officially opens when citizens roll out the red carpet for the King of Carnival, but the real spectacle unfolds during "fat week." For over 300 editions, the Corso di Gala has brought thousands to the streets, where locals showcase their creativity through stunning handmade costumes and masks. Allegorical floats wind through the medieval streets while bands and folk dancers fill the air with music and movement.

Corso di Gala (Gala Parade): Held on multiple Sundays, this grand parade features thousands of participants in colorful masks and costumes, showcasing the creativity and craftsmanship of local artisans. The procession includes allegorical floats, marching bands, and folk dance troupes, creating a lively and joyous atmosphere.

Ride of the Hussars: On Shrove Thursday (Thursday before Ash Wednesday), horsemen in 19th-century uniforms gallop through town, recreating a Napoleonic tradition. The spectacle commemorates a French hussar captain who paraded his dragoons to impress a local lady during the French occupation.

Corse dei Barberi (Riderless Horse Races): The Corse dei Barberi represents one of Italy's most dramatic and historically significant carnival traditions, with roots stretching back to medieval times when similar races were held in Rome along Via del Corso. In Ronciglione, these races take place along the town's principal thoroughfare, with riderless horses thundering through the narrow cobblestone streets at breathtaking speeds.

Each horse, known as a "barbero," is carefully selected and trained for months before the event, typically chosen from breeds known for their speed and agility. The horses are adorned with elaborate decorative harnesses and plumes, continuing a tradition that dates back to when noble families would sponsor horses to represent their interests.

The race itself follows strict traditional protocols. Before the start, each horse is brought to the starting line in a ceremony that includes the blessing of the animals. The horses run approximately one kilometer through the historic center, guided only by the cheering crowds and their own instincts. Traditional wooden barriers, known as "steccati," line the course to protect spectators while maintaining the authentic atmosphere of the historical event. The winning horse brings great prestige to its owner and stable, with the victory celebrated in a ceremony that includes the presentation of a palio (ceremonial banner) painted by local artists.

Masquerade Balls and Street Performances: Throughout the carnival period, various masquerade balls are organized, along with street performances by artists and musicians, enhancing the festive ambiance.

Culinary Events: Food stalls and local eateries offer traditional dishes and sweets associated with Carnevale, allowing visitors to indulge in the culinary delights of the region.

Closing Ceremony: The grand finale of Ronciglione's Carnival unfolds on Shrove Tuesday with the dramatic "Death of King Carnival." As night falls, a torchlit procession winds through the streets, led by black-hooded members of the Company of Penitence and the Company of Good Death.

The King's widows wail in mock grief, following their doomed sovereign while Death stalks behind, scythe in hand. Ancient characters known as cerusici (medieval surgeons) join the procession, adding to its theatrical flair. The climax arrives when King Carnival - represented by an elaborate papier-mâché puppet - makes his final ascent into the night sky aboard a colorful hot-airpapier mâché balloon. Below, the town erupts in a raucous wake of music, wine, and masked revelry, one last burst of joy before the solemnity of Lent begins.

Special Festival Foods of Carnivale in Ronciglione

Polenta: Known as polentari, the makers of this traditional dish serve up creamy polenta topped with various savory accompaniments. It's a warm and hearty dish perfect for the winter festivities.

Beans: Fagiolari prepare bean dishes, often stewed with herbs and sometimes sausage, reflecting the rustic flavors of the region.

Tripe: Tripparoli offer tripe dishes, a classic Roman delicacy often cooked with tomato sauce, herbs, and cheese. It's a must-try for those looking to experience authentic local flavors.

Fritters: Frittellari specialize in making a variety of fritters. These delicious, fried treats can be sweet or savory, providing a perfect snack as you stroll through the festivities.

Fregnacce: Fregnacciari prepare fregnacce, typical pancakes rolled up and seasoned with sugar, pecorino cheese, and cinnamon. This unique combination of flavors is sure to tantalize your taste buds.

Macaroni in Chamber Pots: On Monday, known as the day of the Pitalata, the Red Noses distribute macaroni kept warm in chamber pots, washed down with excellent red wine. It's a quirky and fun tradition that adds to the carnival's charm.

These dishes are integral to the Carnival's celebration and provide a taste of the local culinary traditions. Enjoy the festivities and the delicious food!

Walking Tour of Ronciglione

#1. Duomo dei Santi Pietro e Caterina (St. Peter and Saint Catherine)

The Duomo dei Santi Pietro e Caterina stands as one of the finest examples of Baroque ecclesiastical architecture in the Lazio region, its imposing presence dominating Ronciglione's skyline. Commissioned in 1671 by Cardinal Altieri and designed by the renowned architect Pietro da Cortona, the cathedral represents the height of Roman Baroque style, with its magnificent dome serving as a visual anchor for the entire town. The facade features elegant proportions with classical elements, including paired Corinthian columns and elaborate stone carvings that frame the main portal.

The interior showcases the full splendor of 17th-century religious art and architecture. Leading to a dramatic crossing under the dome, the central nave, flanked by side chapels, features intricate frescoes depicting scenes from the lives of Saints Peter and Catherine. The dome itself, rising 40 meters (130 feet) above the floor, is adorned with trompe l'oeil paintings that create an illusion of ascending into heaven, executed by Giuseppe Passeri in 1688. Of particular note are the side chapels, each rich with marble decoration, gilded stucco work, and important paintings by artists of the Roman school.

The cathedral also houses several important relics, including fragments believed to be from St. Catherine's vestments, displayed in ornate reliquaries. The sacristy contains a collection of precious liturgical objects and vestments dating from the church's founding, providing insight into the evolution of religious ceremonies over three centuries.

#2. Medieval Quarter

Wander through the narrow cobblestone streets of Ronciglione's medieval district, where ancient stone houses, arches, and charming alleyways evoke the town's historical past. This area offers a glimpse into the architectural styles and urban planning of the Middle Ages.

#3. Fontana degli Unicorni (Fountain of the Unicorns)

Built in the 16th century, this unique fountain features sculptures of unicorns, symbolizing purity and fantasy. It serves as a central gathering spot and reflects the town's artistic traditions.

#4. Castello di Ronciglione (Ronciglione Castle)

The Castello di Ronciglione, originally constructed in the 11th century under the Prefetti di Vico family, stands as a commanding testament to the town's medieval military importance. The castle's strategic position atop a volcanic outcrop provided crucial control over the Via Cassia and surrounding valleys, making it a vital stronghold throughout the Middle Ages. Its most significant transformation came in the 15th century when the Farnese family converted it from a purely military fortress into a more refined, noble residence, while maintaining its defensive capabilities. The castle's architectural evolution blends medieval military features, including its massive circular tower, battlements and arrow slits with Renaissance elements such as the covered open balcony (loggia) and expanded residential quarters.

The fortress complex includes multiple towers, each offering spectacular views across the Cimini Mountains and Lake Vico. Standing 30 meters tall, the main tower, featuring walls over three meters thick, was once home to the castle's garrison. The interior, though partially modified over centuries, still retains several original features, including vaulted chambers, a medieval chapel, and sections of 15th-century frescoes commissioned by the Farnese family. The castle's courtyard, with its well-preserved Renaissance well and decorative stonework, provides insight into how the structure developed from a military installation to a symbol of noble power and refinement.

#5. Chiesa di Santa Maria della Provvidenza

The Chiesa di Santa Maria della Provvidenza represents a fascinating architectural journey through Italian religious history, with its structure evolving from an 11th-century Romanesque foundation to include later Baroque modifications. A harmonious blend of Romanesque and 17th-century Baroque styles, unique to the area, is achieved by the church's facade, which retains its original Romanesque features including a rose window and stone arcades. The bell tower, with its distinctive medieval stonework and rounded arches, remains one of the best-preserved examples of Romanesque architecture in the area.

The interior houses an exceptional collection of 15th-century frescoes, predominantly created by artists of the Viterbo school. These works include a remarkable cycle depicting scenes from the life of the Virgin Mary, notable for their use of rich ultramarine blues and gold leaf typical of the period. The main altar features an especially venerated 13th-century wooden Madonna, known as the "Madonna della Provvidenza," which has been the focus of local devotion for centuries. The church's side chapels contain additional artistic treasures, including a series of 16th-century paintings and intricate marble inlays that showcase the evolution of religious art from the medieval to the baroque period. Recent restoration work has uncovered previously hidden frescoes beneath layers of plaster, providing new insights into the church's artistic heritage and its importance as a center of religious life in medieval Ronciglione.

#6. Piazza Principe di Napoli
This central square serves as the heart of Ronciglione's social life. Surrounded by historic buildings, cafes, and shops, it's an ideal place to relax and observe daily life in the town.

#7. Porta Romana
As one of the ancient gateways to the town, Porta Romana stands as a reminder of Ronciglione's medieval defenses. The gate leads visitors into the historic center, marking the transition from the modern to the ancient parts of the town.

#8. Lake Vico
A short distance from the town center, this volcanic lake is surrounded by natural beauty and offers recreational activities such as boating, fishing, and hiking. The lake's serene environment provides a peaceful retreat from the bustling town.

Logistics

Train: The nearest train station to Ronciglione is in Capranica-Sutri, located approximately 10 kilometers (6 miles) away. Regional trains connect Capranica-Sutri to major cities, including Rome and Viterbo. From the station, local buses or taxis can bring visitors directly to Ronciglione.

Bus: Ronciglione is well-connected by regional buses that link it to nearby towns such as Viterbo, Sutri, and Rome. Cotral buses provide regular service, with the main stop conveniently located in the town center, making it an accessible option for those traveling without a car.

Car: To arrive by car from Rome, take the A1 Autostrada del Sole northbound and exit at Magliano Sabina. From there, follow regional roads toward

Ronciglione via the SP1 Cimina road. The drive is approximately 60 kilometers (37 miles) and takes about an hour, offering scenic views of the Lazio countryside.

Parking: Ronciglione has several parking areas outside the ZTL (Limited Traffic Zone) to accommodate visitors. Parking options include designated lots near the historic center, such as those on Via della Valle or Piazza Principe di Napoli. These parking areas allow easy access to the town while respecting the restrictions of the ZTL. It's advisable to arrive early during festivals or peak tourist seasons to secure a spot.

Restaurant Recommendations

Il Divino. Address: Via San Giovanni, 4
In the historic center, Il Divino offers a diverse menu featuring Italian, pizza, seafood, and Mediterranean dishes. Patrons appreciate its cozy atmosphere, friendly service, and high-quality ingredients.

La Corte dei Prefetti di Vico. Address: Vicolo del Montone, 1
This elegant restaurant specializes in Italian cuisine, with standout dishes like pappardelle with ragout. Its charming ambiance and proximity to the Duomo make it a must-visit for those seeking a fine dining experience.

Antica Osteria Donna Gloria. Address: Viale Giuseppe Garibaldi, 90
A traditional trattoria located within the historic village, this restaurant serves authentic Italian dishes in a rustic setting. Known for its warm hospitality, it's a favorite among locals and visitors alike.

Accommodation

Relais Sans Soucis & Spa. Address: Via dei Noccioleti, 18.
Near Lake Vico, this hotel provides comfortable accommodations with modern amenities. Its location offers easy access to both the historic center and natural attractions.

The Carnivale website also has a page of hotels and accommodations: https://www.carnevaledironciglione.org/it/turismo_6/dove-dormire_16/

Day Trips: Nearby Sites, Cities and Towns

Bolsena: The journey from Ronciglione to Bolsena covers approximately 52 kilometers (32 miles). By car, this trip typically takes around 1 to 1.5 hours, depending on traffic. In 1263, Bolsena became the site of one of the most famous Eucharistic miracles in Catholic history, strengthening faith worldwide. According to tradition, a German priest named Peter of Prague, struggling with doubts about the doctrine of transubstantiation, was celebrating Mass at the Basilica of Santa Cristina. During the consecration, the host began to bleed, with the blood staining the altar cloth (corporal). This miraculous event affirmed the belief in the real presence of Christ in the Eucharist and inspired Pope Urban IV to establish the Feast of Corpus Christi in 1264. Today, visitors can explore the Basilica of Santa Cristina, where the miracle occurred, including the Chapel of the Miracle, adorned with frescoes depicting the event, and the ancient catacombs beneath the church.

Sutri. Distance from Ronciglione: 12 kilometers (7.5 miles). Sutri is home to an ancient Roman amphitheater carved directly into the tuff rock, an Etruscan necropolis, and the Madonna del Parto church, built within a rock-cut chamber. Its archaeological park provides insights into the town's rich past, spanning Etruscan, Roman, and medieval periods. The blend of historical sites within a compact area makes Sutri a fascinating destination for a day trip.

Ronciglione Festivals and Sagre Throughout the Year

Festa di San Bartolomeo

August 24

The Festa di San Bartolomeo represents one of Ronciglione's most significant religious and cultural celebrations, transforming the town's medieval streets each August 24th. Beginning at dawn, the festival starts with church bells ringing, followed by a solemn High Mass in the Duomo dei Santi Pietro e Caterina. The highlight is an elaborate procession where a centuries-old statue of San Bartolomeo is carried through the historic center on a richly decorated platform (carro), accompanied by religious confraternities in traditional dress, local clergy, and town officials. Enjoy a spectacular fireworks display from

Castello di Ronciglione and lively traditional folk music and dancing in the streets this evening. Local families prepare special dishes associated with the feast day, including a traditional pasta dish called "maccheroni di San Bartolomeo" served with a rich meat sauce that's been simmered for hours according to ancient family recipes.

Sagra della Nocciola (Hazelnut Festival)

Late August

The Sagra della Nocciola celebrates the region's renowned hazelnut harvest, a crop that has been central to the area's economy since medieval times. The festival showcases the versatility of the local "Tonda Gentile Romana" hazelnut variety, prized by chocolatiers worldwide. Local producers offer tastings of traditional products including torrone (nougat), nocciole tostate (roasted hazelnuts), and various pastries and liqueurs made from the nuts.

Palio di San Bartolomeo

Late August

The Palio di San Bartolomeo brings history to life through a series of competitive events between Ronciglione's historic contrade (districts). Each contrada, distinguished by unique colors and emblems, fields teams in traditional competitions including archery, flag throwing (sbandieratori), and the "Corsa dei Sacchi" (sack race) along the medieval streets. The archery competition holds particular significance, recalling the town's military history and its strategic importance in defending the papal territories.

Participants wear meticulously researched historical costumes from the Renaissance period, and the events are preceded by a magnificent historical parade featuring hundreds of costumed participants, musicians playing period instruments, and displays of ancient crafts. The winning contrada receives a hand-painted silk banner (palio) created by local artists, which is proudly displayed in their district church until the following year's competition. The festival concludes with a grand medieval feast where traditional dishes are served at long tables in the town's main square, fostering community bonds and celebrating Ronciglione's rich cultural heritage.

CHAPTER FORTY-FOUR

The Historic Fair of Grottaferrata

Centuries of Celebration

Fiera Nazionale di Grottaferrata

Where: Grottaferrata

When: Last Week in March.

Average Festival Temperatures: High: 16°C (61°F). Low: 8°C (46°F).

Event Website: https://www.fieradigrottaferrata.it/la-fiera.html

Grottaferrata

For a comprehensive history of Grottaferrata along with detailed information on logistics, day trips, restaurants, and accommodations, please refer to the Celebrating San Nilo in Grottaferrata Chapter earlier in this text.

Annual Fair of Grottaferrata

Calling this festival a fair doesn't quite do it justice. The Fiera Nazionale di Grottaferrata dates back to <u>at least</u> 1462, as documented by Pope Pius II in his Commentarii. The Pope observed that the fair was often lively, stating that it "rarely ends without a murder, as the people sweat wine." To curb this violence, papal authorities imposed strict regulations, threatening severe punishments for those caught with weapons. [1]

The fair's roots stretch even deeper into history, back to 1004 and the founding of the Abbey of Santa Maria di Grottaferrata. What began as religious pilgrimages for the Feast of the Annunciation developed naturally into a bustling marketplace, as savvy merchants realized that crowds of worshippers made excellent customers.

Today's fair maintains that vibrant energy, minus the medieval mayhem. Each March, the ancient abbey grounds and surrounding streets transform into a wonderland of sights, sounds, and flavors. Local nonnas share centuries-old recipes alongside trendy food trucks. Master artisans demonstrate traditional crafts while tech startups showcase sustainable innovations. You might find yourself sampling a glass of locally-produced Frascati wine while watching demonstrations, or learning ancient basket-weaving techniques before joining a workshop on urban farming.

Food remains at the heart of the fair. Follow your nose to stalls piled high with wheels of pecorino romano cheese, glistening porchetta fresh from the spit, and still-warm loaves of crusty bread. Local vintners offer tastings of wines grown in the volcanic soils of the Castelli Romani, each glass carrying hints of the region's rich terroir. The evening air fills with the aroma of roasting chestnuts and the sound of traditional folk music.

The entertainment spans from traditional to contemporary. One moment you're watching medieval flag throwers perform gravity-defying tosses, the next you're joining an impromptu dance party as local bands take the stage. Children dash between puppet shows and modern rides while their parents browse everything from handcrafted jewelry to cutting-edge home technologies.

Pack a light jacket for the cool March evenings and comfortable walking shoes - you'll want to explore every corner of this sprawling celebration. From its wine-soaked origins to its current blend of tradition and innovation, the Fiera

---

1. National Fair of Grottaferrata – History, on fieradigrottaferrata.it. URL consulted on 02-10-2024 (archived from the original URL on 2 May 2009).

Nazionale di Grottaferrata continues to capture the spirit of this remarkable town, offering visitors a taste of both its storied past and dynamic present.

Free admission and open to the public every day from 10:00 a.m. to 9:00 p.m.

For Accommodation, Restaurant Recommendations, Logistics, Day Trips **see Chapter 28 Celebrating San Nilo in Grottaferrata.**

CHAPTER FORTY-FIVE

Festa di San Benedetto in Montecassino

Celebrations at the Legendary Abbey

F esta di San Benedetto

Where: Monte Cassino

When: March 21

Average Festival Temperatures: High: 11°C (53°F). Low 2°C (36°F).

Abbey Website: https://abbaziamontecassino.it/

The History of Montecassino and Its Legendary Abbey

Perched high on a rocky hill overlooking the town of Cassino in southern Italy, the Abbey of Montecassino stands as a testament to faith, resilience, and spiritual renewal. Founded in the early 6th century by St. Benedict of Nursia, the abbey is the cradle of Western monasticism and one of the most historically significant monasteries in the Christian world.

Montecassino Abbey

Who Is San Benedetto / St. Benedict?

San Benedetto, or St. Benedict of Nursia (480–547 AD), is widely regarded as the father of Western monasticism. Born into a noble Roman family, he left the chaos of the city to live as a hermit near Subiaco, seeking a life of solitude and devotion. His wisdom and holiness drew followers, and he soon became a spiritual leader. Benedict's most enduring legacy is the *Rule of St. Benedict*, a practical guide for monastic life that balances prayer, work, and study. This *Rule* became the foundation of Benedictine monasticism, influencing Christian spirituality and European culture for centuries.

St. Benedict is also remembered for his miracles and deep humility, with stories of healing, exorcisms, and surviving an assassination attempt attributed to him. He died on March 21, 547 AD, and was proclaimed the Patron Saint of Europe in 1964 by Pope Paul VI. His teachings continue to inspire both monastic and secular communities, offering timeless wisdom on discipline, community, and faith.

The Foundation by St. Benedict (529 AD)

The story of Montecassino begins in 529 AD, when St. Benedict, seeking solitude and spiritual inspiration, arrived at this strategic hilltop. Here, on the ruins of an ancient Roman temple dedicated to Apollo, he established a monastery that would become the birthplace of the Benedictine Rule—a detailed guide for monastic life focused on prayer, work (ora et labora), and communal living. The Rule of St. Benedict would go on to influence countless monastic communities across Europe, shaping Christian spirituality for centuries.

Benedict's vision turned Montecassino into a center of religious devotion, education, and hospitality. The monastery not only housed monks who lived according to his Rule but also welcomed pilgrims and offered aid to the surrounding communities.

Medieval Glory and Cultural Significance

In the centuries following its foundation, Montecassino became a beacon of learning, faith, and culture. Its monks preserved and copied ancient manuscripts, helping to safeguard classical knowledge during the so-called "Dark Ages." The abbey's scriptorium gained renown as a center of intellectual activity, producing illuminated texts that combined artistic beauty with theological depth.

By the 8th and 9th centuries, Montecassino had grown in prominence, supported by kings and popes alike. Charlemagne, the great ruler of the Holy Roman Empire, is said to have visited the abbey and granted it protection and privileges. This royal patronage further cemented its role as a spiritual and cultural hub.

Cloister at Montecassino

Destruction and Rebirth

The history of Montecassino is also marked by cycles of destruction and reconstruction, mirroring the resilience of its community.

First Destruction (581 AD): Montecassino faced its first major trial when it was sacked by the Lombards, forcing the monks to flee to Rome.

Reconstruction (718 AD): With the support of Pope Gregory II, the abbey was rebuilt and resumed its central role in monastic and spiritual life.

The pattern of destruction and renewal continued over the centuries:

Second Destruction (883 AD): Saracen raiders plundered the abbey, leaving it in ruins.

Third Destruction (1349 AD): A devastating earthquake leveled much of the structure, prompting yet another reconstruction effort.

Despite these trials, Montecassino endured, each rebirth serving as a testament to its enduring spiritual significance.

World War II and the Fourth Destruction (1944)

The most dramatic chapter in Montecassino's history came during World War II. In 1944, the abbey, mistakenly believed to be a German stronghold, was heavily bombed by Allied forces during the Battle of Montecassino. The destruction was near total, reducing the historic monastery to rubble and claiming the lives of many civilians who had sought refuge there.

Following the war, a massive reconstruction effort was undertaken, meticulously rebuilding the abbey to its former glory. Completed in 1964, the new structure faithfully restored the original design while incorporating modern elements. Pope Paul VI consecrated the new abbey and declared St. Benedict the Patron Saint of Europe, further solidifying its importance as a symbol of resilience and faith.

Today, the Abbey of Montecassino is not only a functioning monastery but also a pilgrimage site, museum, and cultural landmark. Visitors come from around the world to experience its breathtaking architecture, learn about its storied past, and pay homage to St. Benedict. The abbey's history reflects the timeless power of faith and human determination to rebuild and renew in the face of adversity.

With its majestic hilltop location, centuries of cultural contributions, and a profound spiritual legacy, Montecassino remains a cornerstone of Western Christianity and a living monument to the Rule of St. Benedict.

The Festival of St. Benedict

The Abbey of Montecassino in Italy hosts several festivals and events throughout the year. One of the most notable is the Festival of San Benedetto, which lasts an entire week and culminates in the Terra Sancti Benedicti procession on March 21st. This event features a large procession in costume through the central streets of Cassino.

Additionally, the abbey offers themed spiritual workshops and retreats focusing on monastic spirituality, the Rule of St. Benedict, and contemplation. These retreats provide a unique opportunity to experience the spiritual atmosphere of the abbey.

The festival has deep historical roots, dating back to the establishment of the abbey in 529 AD by Saint Benedict himself. Over the centuries, this festival has evolved into a week-long event filled with various activities and ceremonies.

Key Events During the Festival:

Religious Ceremonies: The festival includes several religious services and masses held at the abbey, celebrating the life and contributions of Saint Benedict.

Historical Reenactments: Participants often engage in reenactments of significant events from Saint Benedict's life, bringing history to life for visitors.

Cultural Events: The festival features a range of cultural events, including traditional music, dance performances, and art exhibitions showcasing the rich heritage of the region.

Procession of Terra Sancti Benedicti: The highlight of the festival is the Terra Sancti Benedicti procession on March 21st. This grand procession involves participants dressed in historical costumes parading through the streets of Cassino. The procession symbolizes the historical and spiritual significance of the abbey and its founder. The procession is a vibrant and colorful celebration that brings the history and spirituality of the abbey to life, allowing participants and spectators to experience the legacy of Saint Benedict in a unique and engaging way.

The festival not only celebrates the legacy of Saint Benedict but also brings together the local community and visitors from around the world to experience the rich cultural and spiritual heritage of Montecassino

Walking Tour / Key Sites

The Abbey of Montecassino is one of the most renowned monasteries in the world, rich in history, art, and spirituality. Visitors can explore its magnificent architecture, sacred relics, and cultural treasures, all while enjoying breathtaking views of the Italian countryside. Here's a comprehensive guide to the highlights of the abbey:

#1. The Basilica

At the heart of the abbey stands the Basilica, a stunning reconstruction after the devastation of World War II. This sacred space features intricate baroque design, marble inlays, and gold-leaf decorations, faithfully rebuilt to its original splendor.

Highlights include the tomb of St. Benedict and St. Scholastica, located under the main altar, is a must-see for pilgrims including beautiful frescoes depicting scenes from the lives of the saints. The ceiling frescoes and intricately detailed chapels showcasing the artistry of the Benedictine tradition.

#2. The Cloisters

The abbey has several cloisters, offering peaceful spaces for reflection and a chance to admire the architecture. The most notable include: Cloister of Bramante: named after the famous Renaissance architect, this area features elegant arcades and statues of St. Benedict and St. Scholastica. And the Cloister of Paradise: A serene space filled with flowers, a fountain, and a view of the surrounding hills.

#3. The Crypt

Beneath the basilica lies the Crypt, an intimate space adorned with mosaics and dedicated to St. Benedict and St. Scholastica. This sacred area contains relics and offers a quieter, more spiritual experience.

#4. The Museum

The Montecassino Museum is a treasure trove of artifacts showcasing the abbey's historical and cultural significance.

Highlights include ancient manuscripts and illuminated texts created by the monks, religious art, including paintings, statues, and sacred relics. There are often exhibits on the Battle of Montecassino, including photographs and items related to the abbey's reconstruction.

#5. The Library

The abbey's library is world-renowned for its collection of rare books and manuscripts. Although not all parts of the library are open to the public, visitors can admire its legacy and importance through guided tours or museum exhibits.

#6. The War Memorial and Cemetery

The Polish War Cemetery, near the abbey, commemorates the soldiers who died during the Battle of Montecassino in 1944. This site provides a poignant reminder of the abbey's role in World War II and is worth visiting for its historical significance.

#7. The Panoramic Views

From the abbey, visitors can enjoy spectacular views of the Liri Valley and surrounding mountains. The abbey's hilltop location makes it an ideal spot for photography and quiet contemplation of the Italian countryside.

#8. The Abbey Gift Shop

Before leaving, stop by the gift shop, where you can purchase souvenirs, books, and products made by the monks, including herbal remedies, honey, and liqueurs.

Logistics

Train: 1.5 hours from Rome Termini to Cassino station. Taxi or shuttle to the abbey (~10-15 minutes).

Bus: Buses run from Rome to Cassino and take around 2-3 hours. Local bus or taxi to the abbey.

Car: Take the A1 Autostrada del Sole, exit at Cassino, and follow signs to Montecassino. Drive takes ~1.5 hours.

Parking: Free parking available near the abbey; arrive early on busy days.

Restaurant Recommendations

Ristorantino da Nonna Giuseppina. Address: Via Manlio Zincone, 49

An unforgettable dining experience where time has stood still. Known for its authentic Central-Italian cuisine and the best pasta dishes.

Masseria Montecassino. Address: Via Montecassino, Località Albaneta

A charming restaurant offering Mediterranean and Italian dishes with a focus on fresh, local ingredients. Its rustic elegance and peaceful setting near the countryside create a perfect escape from the busy town center.

Accommodation

For the festival I recommend two to three nights in town.

Hotel Forum Palace S.R.L. Address: Via Montecassino

A comfortable 3-star hotel offering modern amenities and a convenient location near the abbey. Ideal for travelers seeking both value and proximity to the main historic sites.

Forum Palace Hotel & Experience Spa. Address: Via Montecassino

A 4-star hotel with a spa, restaurant, and beautiful views of the abbey. Perfect for a relaxing stay.

Day Trips: Nearby Sites, Cities, and Towns

Abbey of Fossanova. The Abbey of Fossanova, located 58 kilometers from Rome, stands as one of Italy's most perfectly preserved Cistercian monasteries, its 12th-century architecture rising majestically from the tranquil countryside. This masterpiece of medieval engineering and spiritual design represents the first example of Gothic architecture in Italy, showcasing the transition from Romanesque to Gothic styles that would later influence religious buildings throughout the peninsula.

The complex is particularly notable as the place where the great theologian St. Thomas Aquinas spent his final days in 1274, adding a profound historical significance to its already considerable architectural importance. Visitors can explore the harmonious complex, including the magnificent church with its soaring pointed arches and refined simplicity - hallmarks of Cistercian design philosophy.

The serene cloister features elegant double columns and finely carved capitals, while the monastic refectory, one of the finest examples of its kind, demonstrates the perfect balance between functionality and aesthetic beauty characteristic of Cistercian architecture. The abbey's austere yet elegant design reflects the Cistercian order's commitment to simplicity and spiritual focus, with carefully planned architectural elements that direct light and create spaces conducive to contemplation and prayer.

Pompeii. Located 140 kilometers (87 miles) from Montecassino, Pompeii stands as one of the world's most remarkable archaeological treasures, its streets and buildings preserved in haunting detail by the catastrophic eruption of Mount Vesuvius in 79 BC. This ancient Roman city offers visitors an unparalleled glimpse into daily life during the height of the Roman Empire, with its sophisticated urban planning and architectural achievements frozen in time by the volcanic disaster.

The site's highlights include the grand Forum, which once served as the city's political and commercial heart, and the mysterious Villa of the Mysteries, renowned for its enigmatic frescoes depicting what many scholars believe to be initiation rites into a Dionysian cult. Archaeologists' poignant plaster casts of eruption victims, created by filling voids left by decomposed bodies in the ash, offer a deeply moving testament to the human tragedy, while the well-preserved amphitheater provides insight into Roman entertainment and social life. The site's remarkably preserved streets, complete with wheel ruts, stepping stones, and electoral graffiti, allow visitors to walk in the footsteps of ancient Romans, making Pompeii an essential destination for anyone interested in experiencing the tangible remains of Roman civilization.

Reggio di Caserta: Just 55 kilometers (35 miles) from Montecassino, the city of Caserta is crowned by the magnificent Royal Palace of Caserta (Reggia di Caserta), an 18th-century architectural masterpiece that ranks among Europe's largest and most impressive royal residences. This UNESCO World Heritage Site, commissioned by the Bourbon King Charles III of Naples and designed by architect Luigi Vanvitelli, rivals Versailles in its grandeur and scale. The palace complex showcases the height of Baroque and Neoclassical design, with its 1,200 rooms featuring richly decorated state apartments, a magnificent grand staircase, and the stunning Court Theater.

The palace grounds extend over 235 acres of formal gardens, creating one of the most spectacular examples of Italian garden design. Visitors can explore the vast landscaped park with its long cascade of fountains and water features, including the dramatic Great Cascade with its mythological sculptures. The English Garden, added later under Ferdinand IV, offers a more naturalistic landscape with exotic plants, artificial ruins, and hidden grottos, providing a striking contrast to the formal Italian gardens. The palace complex stands as a testament to the power and artistic patronage of the Bourbon dynasty, making it an essential destination for anyone interested in European royal history, architecture, or garden design.

Montecassino Festivals Throughout the Year

Carnival Celebrations

February (exact dates vary based on Lent)

Cassino's Carnival festivities are a vibrant pre-Lenten celebration featuring colorful parades, costumes, and community events. This lively festival is perfect for visitors seeking to experience traditional Italian Carnival customs, music, and joyful atmosphere.

Easter Processions

Holy Week (March or April, depending on the liturgical calendar)

During Holy Week, Cassino hosts solemn processions and religious ceremonies that honor the Passion of Christ. These events reflect the town's deep Christian roots and offer visitors a chance to witness heartfelt devotion and historical traditions.

Summer Music Festivals

June to August

Throughout the summer, Cassino comes alive with music festivals spanning classical, contemporary, and popular genres. Performances are held in scenic venues, providing visitors with a mix of cultural and entertainment experiences in the warm Italian summer evenings.

Autumn Food Festivals

September to November

These festivals celebrate Cassino's rich culinary heritage, featuring local produce, traditional dishes, and regional wines. A must-visit for food lovers, these events showcase the area's gastronomic excellence and community spirit.

Christmas Markets and Events

December 8- January 6

During the festive season, Cassino transforms with twinkling lights, artisan markets, and holiday-themed events. Visitors can enjoy shopping for handmade goods, savoring seasonal treats, and soaking in the charming holiday ambiance.

CHAPTER FORTY-SIX

Ladispoli's Artichoke Extravaganza

Hearts of Gold

Sagra del Carciofo

Where: Ladispoli

When: 2nd weekend in April, typically a three-day weekend.

Average Festival Temperatures: High: 17°C (63°F). Low: 11°C (53°F).

Ladispoli: Where History and Tradition Savor the Artichoke

The town of Ladispoli is a destination where history intertwines seamlessly with gastronomy, offering an enriching experience for visitors. Founded in 1888 by Prince Ladislao Odescalchi, Ladispoli's story stretches back far beyond its modern establishment. Its origins lie in the ancient world, where it was home to the Etruscans, who established a bustling port city known as Alsium. This strategic coastal location flourished under Etruscan culture, leaving behind traces of their civilization that still pique the curiosity of history enthusiasts today.

Under Roman rule, Alsium transformed into a luxurious resort town for the empire's elite. It became a retreat for some of the most notable figures in Roman history, including Pompey and Julius Caesar. The allure of its pristine shores and proximity to Rome made it an enviable haven for those seeking leisure and escape. However, the town's fortunes shifted during the turbulent Gothic Wars, when it was destroyed and left in ruins.

In the 12th century, a fortified settlement known as Castrum Pali rose from the ashes, marking the medieval period of the area's history. This small but resilient community laid the foundation for what would later become modern Ladispoli. It wasn't until the late 19th century that Prince Odescalchi envisioned a new future for the area, developing it into a refined seaside resort. This transformation attracted wealthy Romans, drawn by the town's fresh sea breezes and idyllic surroundings, seeking a respite from the sweltering heat of the city.

Today, Ladispoli stands as a vibrant seaside town that effortlessly blends its historical legacy with its modern appeal. Its streets, rich with the echoes of its storied past, provide the perfect setting for events like the annual Artichoke Festival. With its unique combination of cultural depth and coastal charm, Ladispoli offers visitors a chance to indulge their taste buds while stepping back in time.

The Birth of a Tradition: The Roman Artichoke Festival

In the charming coastal town of Ladispoli, spring heralds more than just blooming flowers, it marks the return of the beloved "Sagra del Carciofo Romanesco," or Roman Artichoke Festival. This celebration of the humble yet revered artichoke has become a cornerstone of local culture and a major draw for food enthusiasts from across Europe.

The festival's roots trace back to 1950 when the founders of the newly formed Pro Loco, while brainstorming at the restaurant "La Tripolina," struck upon a brilliant idea. In an effort to revitalize Ladispoli, they spotlighted the town's local specialty: the artichoke. This highly valued vegetable, widely grown in the area, would make Ladispoli known worldwide.

The inaugural Roman Artichoke Festival took place on April 2, 1951, and its success surpassed all expectations. The event garnered significant media attention, boosted tourism, and invigorated the local economy. Word of Ladispoli's exceptional artichokes spread to northern markets like Florence, Padua, Bologna, and Verona, which began requesting large quantities of the prized vegetable.

Artichoke's Ready for the Festival

A Festival of Flavors and Art

Today, the Artichoke Festival has evolved into a multifaceted celebration that engages all the senses. During the three-day extravaganza, visitors can expect the following.

Culinary Showcases: Local chefs and home cooks demonstrate their artichoke expertise, offering both traditional and innovative preparations. The classic "Carciofi alla romana," baked upside down in a flavorful bath of olive oil, garlic, mint, and parsley, is a perennial favorite. But adventurous eaters will also find artichoke-based desserts and other creative concoctions.

Artichoke Sculptures: One of the festival's unique and visually striking features is the artichoke sculpture competition. The town square transforms into an open-air gallery, showcasing impressive artworks crafted entirely from artichokes. From towering horses to gentle turtles, these artistic masterpieces celebrate the artichoke in all its glory. Visitors marvel at the creativity and skill on display, with special recognition awarded to the most innovative and visually stunning sculpture.

Food Fair: Food stalls line the streets, offering a myriad of artichoke dishes for tasting and purchase. Visitors can sample everything from simple grilled artichokes to complex artichoke-based pastas and risottos. Many stalls offer free artichoke samples, allowing event-goers to discover the many versatile ways this culinary gem can be prepared.

Cultural Performances: The celebration is not just about food. Music, dance, and parades add to the festive atmosphere, showcasing local traditions and talent. The streets come alive with the sounds of traditional music and the sight of colorful costumes.

Agricultural Tours: For those interested in the cultivation process, guided tours of local artichoke fields are available. Visitors can learn about the agricultural practices that make Ladispoli's artichokes so special, from planting to harvest.

Cooking Competitions: Local chefs and home cooks compete to create the most innovative or delicious artichoke dish, judged by a panel of experts and lucky festival attendees.

Artisanal Products: Beyond fresh artichokes and prepared dishes, visitors can purchase artichoke-based products like spreads, oils, and even liqueurs to take home as souvenirs.

The Star of the Show: Carciofo Romanesco

The Roman artichoke, or "carciofo romano," isn't just any vegetable. It boasts the prestigious IGP (Protected Geographical Indication) label. This certification, similar to the DOC status of wines, ensures that these artichokes are grown in specific regions, guaranteeing their authenticity and quality. Only one other artichoke in Italy, the Carciofo di Paestum from Campania, shares this honor.

The history of the artichoke in this region stretches back to ancient times. Cultivated in the Mediterranean since 400 BC, it has been a Lazio staple since the Etruscan era. The vegetable's journey is fascinating, even making its way to France with Catherine de' Medici and later to Thomas Jefferson's beloved Monticello gardens. Jefferson held the artichoke in such high esteem that he used it as a codeword in his secret correspondence.

Ladispoli's artichokes are renowned for their sweet and robust flavor. They're often enjoyed simply, with minimal seasoning, allowing their inherent flavor to stand out. The lack of thorns and chokes in these varieties makes them particularly prized for cooking.

A Taste of Tradition

Festival-goers can indulge in a variety of artichoke dishes that showcase the vegetable's versatility:

- **Stuffed Artichokes**: A classic preparation where artichokes are filled with a savory mixture of breadcrumbs, Parmesan cheese, garlic, and herbs, then baked to perfection.

Carciofo alla Romana

- **Fried Artichokes**: Crispy, golden-brown artichoke hearts or slices that offer a satisfying crunch.

- **Artichoke Pasta**: From simple aglio e olio preparations with tender artichoke pieces to more complex filled pastas, artichokes shine in these dishes.

- **Artichoke Risotto**: Creamy Arborio rice slowly cooked with artichoke hearts, resulting in a dish that epitomizes spring.

- **Artichoke Pizza**: Traditional pizza gets a gourmet twist with the addition of marinated artichoke hearts.

- **Grilled Artichokes**: Simply prepared with olive oil, garlic, and lemon, these showcase the natural flavor of the vegetable.

- **Artichoke Salad**: Fresh, often raw, artichoke slices are combined with other spring vegetables in light, refreshing salads.

Beyond Ladispoli: Artichoke Festivals Across Italy

While Ladispoli's festival may be the most renowned, artichoke celebrations span the Italian peninsula, each highlighting local varieties and traditions:

Sezze, Lazio: Held in mid-April, this event showcases the enormous round artichokes called cimaroli and the cone-shaped violet-leaved violetta variety. These exceptionally tender artichokes are prepared in six different ways and served alongside the famous breads of Sezze.

Chiusure, Tuscany: Dedicated to the local "Carciofo di Chiusure" variety, this April festival combines culinary delights with music and cultural activities.

Paestum, Campania: Celebrating the Paestum artichoke variety, this event features tastings, cooking demonstrations, and entertainment, held in April.

Cerda, Sicily: On April 25th each year, this village near Palermo honors its agricultural heritage with a festival centered on its prized artichokes, which are distributed throughout Italy and exported abroad.

Sant'Angelo, Sicily: Held in Sant'Angelo Muxaro, about an hour's drive from Ragusa, this April festival offers various artichoke dishes through numerous food stalls.

Jesi, Marche and **Uri, Sardinia**: These festivals in March and April respectively celebrate their local artichoke varieties with culinary events, tastings, and cooking competitions.

These festivals not only celebrate the artichoke but also offer a window into the diverse regional cultures and culinary traditions of Italy.

The Festival's Evolution and Impact

Throughout the years, the Artichoke Festival has significantly increased in size and importance.

In 2001, it gained status as a national fair due to increased participation from exhibitors across Italy. The same year, the Romanesco artichoke was awarded PGI (Protected Geographical Indication) status, further cementing its importance.

The celebration is now recognized as the oldest event dedicated to artichokes, despite numerous attempts to replicate its success elsewhere. It has consistently aimed to promote the artichoke and its benefits, while also showcasing Ladispoli to a broader audience.

A unique feature of the festival is the "Bi-Settimana Gastronomica," a two-week event that precedes the major celebration. During this time, the city's top chefs present a variety of fixed-price artichoke-based menus, from appetizers to desserts, further extending the celebration.

The weeks leading up to the festival see local restaurants competing to create innovative artichoke dishes, turning the entire town into a gastronomic playground. This culinary celebration marks the beginning of the region's tourist season, drawing visitors eager to explore the versatile world of artichokes and the charming town of Ladispoli.

From its humble beginnings as a local gathering to its current status as a food phenomenon, Ladispoli's Artichoke Festival offers a unique blend of culinary delights, cultural experiences, and historical charm. Whether you're a food enthusiast, history buff, or simply looking for a taste of authentic Italian culture, this springtime celebration promises an unforgettable experience in the heart of Lazio.

Walking Tour of Ladispoli

#1. Piazza Rossellini

Piazza Rossellini is named after the famous Italian film director Roberto Rossellini, who frequently visited Ladispoli. This central square is a great starting point, often hosting local events and markets.

#2. Torre Flavia

Torre Flavia stands as a haunting reminder of the region's maritime history. Constructed in 1568 under Pope Pius V as part of a defensive network of coastal watchtowers, it was designed by architect Flavio Orsini, from whom it takes its name. Originally standing 20 meters high, the tower included three floors with defensive positions, a cistern for water collection, and a sophisticated system of smoke signals to communicate with nearby towers.

The gradual erosion of the coastline over centuries has created its current partially submerged state, with about half the tower now standing in the Mediterranean waters. The site is surrounded by a protected wetland area of 45 hectares that serves as a crucial habitat for various bird species, including kentish plovers and little terns. Recent conservation efforts have focused on stabilizing the remaining structure while maintaining its romantic, semi-ruined appearance.

#3. Castello Odescalchi

Castello Odescalchi represents one of the most significant examples of medieval military architecture in the Lazio region. Originally constructed in the 9th century as a Carolingian fortress, it was extensively renovated by the powerful Orsini family in the 16th century, who transformed it into a more comfortable noble residence while maintaining its defensive capabilities.

Redesigned in the 17th century, the castle gardens boast geometric Italian parterres, rare plants, and secret grottoes. The interior houses an impressive collection of art and artifacts spanning several centuries, including Renaissance paintings, medieval armor, and a library containing rare manuscripts.

The castle's great hall, with its 16th-century frescoes depicting scenes from Roman history, is particularly noteworthy. The structure still belongs to the Odescalchi family, who have opened portions of it to the public. Abstract stained glass windows and a contemporary marine-material crucifix are among the modern interpretations of traditional religious art inside.

#4. Chiesa di Santa Maria del Rosario

Chiesa di Santa Maria del Rosario stands as a bold example of mid-20th century religious architecture. Completed in 1957, the church was designed by architect Ennio Canino who took inspiration from naval architecture to create a structure that symbolically connects the town's maritime heritage with its spiritual life. The building's most striking feature is its curved roof that resembles an upturned ship's hull, supported by dramatic concrete ribs that create a sense of movement and flow. Modern interpretations of traditional religious art are featured inside, including abstract stained glass windows that bathe the space in colored light and a contemporary crucifix crafted from marine materials.

The church's bell tower, standing separate from the main building, echoes the design of a lighthouse, further reinforcing the maritime theme. The plaza in front of the church, paved in a pattern suggesting waves, serves as a gathering space for the community and hosts religious processions during major festivals.

#5. Stabilimento Balneare (Beach club) Columbia

Stabilimento Balneare Columbia is one of the oldest beach establishments in Ladispoli.

#6. Necropoli di Monteroni (30-minute walk or short bus ride)

The Necropoli di Monteroni stands as a remarkable testament to Etruscan civilization (an advanced pre-Roman culture that flourished in central Italy from 800 to 300 BC), with its complex of tombs dating back to the 7th-6th centuries BC offering invaluable insights into ancient burial practices and religious beliefs. Many tomb types, from simple pit graves to elaborate chamber tombs carved into the volcanic tuff, are found in the necropolis spanning several hectares.

The most impressive structures are the multi-chambered family tombs, which feature vestibules, main chambers, and side rooms that once contained elaborate funeral goods and painted decorations. Some tombs still retain traces of their original architectural elements, including carved columns, benches, and niches that would have held funeral urns and offerings.

The site's layout reflects the Etruscan belief in the afterlife, with tombs arranged to mimic the houses of the living. The necropolis includes several architectural styles, from modest single-chamber tombs to more elaborate multi-room complexes that belonged to wealthy families. Archaeological excavations have revealed a wealth of artifacts, including ceramic vessels, bronze objects, and jewelry, many of which are now housed in regional museums. The surrounding area also features ancient quarries where the Etruscans extracted the tuff stone used in tomb construction, providing additional insight into their engineering and construction techniques.

Particularly noteworthy are the drainage systems carved into the rock to prevent water damage to the tombs, demonstrating the advanced engineering capabilities of the Etruscan civilization. While many of the portable artifacts have been removed for preservation, the site's architectural features and rock-cut facades continue to provide valuable information about Etruscan funeral customs and social hierarchy.

The necropolis's location, set against the backdrop of the Mediterranean landscape, creates an atmospheric connection to this ancient civilization that once dominated central Italy.

#7. La Posta Vecchia Hotel

La Posta Vecchia Hotel was once a Roman villa, later owned by J. Paul Getty, and converted into a luxury hotel. While the hotel is private, you can admire its beautiful exterior and imagine its glamorous past or stay during your visit!

Logistics

Train: The most convenient way to reach Ladispoli from Rome. The train station is centrally located, making it easy to access the events.

Bus: Less frequent than trains, but connections are available from Rome and other nearby towns.

Car: To drive from Rome to Ladispoli, take the Strada Statale 1 (SS1), commonly known as the Via Aurelia. This route begins in Rome and heads northwest towards Ladispoli. The journey covers approximately 25 miles (40 kilometers) and typically takes around 40 minutes, depending on traffic conditions.

Parking: Regarding parking in Ladispoli, it's important to be aware of any Zona a Traffico Limitato (ZTL) areas, which are restricted traffic zones commonly found in Italian towns to reduce congestion and protect historic centers. Parcheggio Piazza Rossellini: A public parking area near the town center, offering convenient access to local shops and the beach. Or Parcheggio Via Firenze: A parking lot situated close to the principal shopping streets, providing easy access to the commercial area.

Restaurant Recommendations

Ristorante La Tripolina. Address: Piazza della Vittoria, 14

In the heart of Ladispoli, La Tripolina offers authentic Italian cuisine with a focus on fresh seafood. Known for its charming atmosphere and excellent service, it's a perfect spot to end your tour.

Dalla Sora Franca. Address: Via Duca degli Abruzzi, 133

This traditional trattoria is a local favorite, known for its home-style Italian cooking. With a warm, family-friendly atmosphere, it's a great place to experience authentic local flavors.

La Locanda del Pescatore. Address: Via Orazio Marini, 10

La Locanda del Pescatore is renowned for its fresh seafood dishes and traditional Roman cuisine. With its cozy ambiance and focus on local ingredients, it offers a true taste of the region.

Accommodation

Overnight stays are unnecessary for sagre, however if you plan to stay I recommend two to three nights in town.

La Posta Vecchia. Address: Palo Laziale, Via Palo Laziale

A luxurious 5-star hotel nestled on the coast of Ladispoli, La Posta Vecchia is a meticulously restored Roman villa once owned by John Paul Getty. This property offers an unparalleled blend of historic charm and modern comfort, with opulent interiors featuring antique furnishings, Renaissance art, and archaeological relics unearthed on the grounds.

Guests can enjoy panoramic sea views, a Michelin-starred restaurant, an elegant spa, and beautifully landscaped gardens. The hotel also provides direct access to the beach, making it a perfect retreat for those seeking exclusivity and relaxation.

Miramare. Address: Via Trieste, 3

Miramare is a charming 3-star hotel conveniently near Ladispoli's historic center, offering stunning sea views. The hotel features comfortable rooms, many with private balconies overlooking the Tyrrhenian Sea. Its prime location allows guests easy access to local attractions, restaurants, and the beach, all within walking distance.

Miramare is known for its welcoming atmosphere and excellent value, making it a superb choice for travelers seeking a pleasant seaside stay. Guests can enjoy a continental breakfast in the morning and a friendly, attentive staff ready to assist with local recommendations.

Day Trip Options: Nearby Sites, Cities, and Towns

Cerveteri. 13 kilometers, 8 miles from Ladispoli. This nearby town is home to the UNESCO World Heritage Site of the Necropolis of Banditaccia, one of the most impressive Etruscan archaeological sites in Italy. The necropolis features thousands of tombs, some dating back to the 9th century BC, arranged in a city-like plan. The on-site museum offers further insights into Etruscan civilization. After exploring the ancient tombs, take a stroll through Cerveteri's medieval center, dominated by the impressive Ruspoli Castle.

Civitavecchia. 35 kilometers (22 miles) from Ladispoli. Known as the principal port of Rome, Civitavecchia offers more than just cruise ships and ferry terminals. Its roots trace back to Roman times, when Emperor Trajan developed the harbor, parts of which can still be seen today. A stroll along the historic port reveals remnants of the Roman docks, medieval fortifications, and the striking Forte Michelangelo, a Renaissance-era fortress attributed in part to Michelangelo, who designed its central tower.

Ferries depart for Sardinia, Sicily, the Tuscan Islands, Spain, Tunisia and Corsica (France).

Visit the National Archaeological Museum of Civitavecchia, located in a former papal customs house, to explore Roman and Etruscan artifacts uncovered in the region. Just steps away is the Cattedrale di San Francesco d'Assisi, the town's main church, set on a lively square ideal for people-watching. For a relaxing break, walk the lungomare (seafront promenade) lined with cafes and gelaterie, or enjoy fresh seafood at one of the waterfront restaurants.

Ladispoli Festivals Throughout the Year

Festa di San Giuseppe (St. Joseph).

March 19

Ladispoli celebrates its patron saint, Saint Joseph (San Giuseppe), with a vibrant festival each year. The Festa di San Giuseppe is held on March 19, coinciding with the traditional feast day of Saint Joseph. This celebration is a significant event in Ladispoli's cultural calendar, featuring a variety of activities that reflect the town's rich heritage. Festivities include religious processions through the streets, traditional music and dance performances, and communal feasts where locals and visitors can enjoy regional delicacies. One of the culinary highlights of the festival is the opportunity to taste the first artichokes of the season, a local specialty, along with zeppole di San Giuseppe, cream-filled pastries traditionally associated with Saint Joseph's Day.

The Festa di San Giuseppe offers a unique opportunity for visitors to immerse themselves in the local traditions of Ladispoli, experience the town's communal spirit, and enjoy its culinary delights. Taking part in this festival provides insight into the deep-rooted customs that continue to shape the cultural identity of this picturesque Italian town.

Summer Cultural Events

During the summer months, Ladispoli comes alive with a series of cultural events, including art exhibitions, music performances, and local festivals that showcase the town's traditions and folklore. These events provide both locals and visitors with opportunities to engage in the vibrant cultural scene of Ladispoli.

CHAPTER FORTY-SEVEN

Celebrating Rome's Timeless Birthday

From Ancient Times to Today

N atale di Roma

Where: Rome Centro Storico

When: April 21

Average Festival Temperatures: High: 19°C (66°F), Low: 9°C (48°F).

Event Website: https://www.natalidiroma.it/*The website has great photos of the event.

Rome's Birthday Celebration

#FestaFusion 2025. In 2025 (and again in 2038) Easter Sunday will fall very near the Natale di Roma celebration, allowing you to attend both festivals.

Natale di Roma (Rome's Birthday) is a major annual celebration marking the founding of Rome. According to Roman tradition, the city was founded by Romulus on April 21st, 753 BC, making April 21st the official birthday of Rome. This ancient festival has transformed into a lively modern celebration that honors the city's long and storied history with historical reenactments, parades, and cultural events.

It's a citywide event filled with cultural activities that pay tribute to Rome's ancient history, and it's a perfect blend of historical reenactments, processions, and modern entertainment. The day honors the city's past while offering Romans and visitors alike a festive, engaging atmosphere.

Where Does Natale di Roma Take Place?

The principal celebrations occur in several key historical locations throughout Rome, with the most significant events taking place at:

- **Circus Maximus:** This ancient stadium is one of the primary locations for reenactments, including gladiator battles, Roman army drills, and parades featuring actors dressed as ancient Romans.

- **Roman Forum:** This iconic area hosts many of the historical processions and offers a dramatic backdrop for speeches, reenactments, and commemorations.

- **Via dei Fori Imperiali:** This road connecting the Colosseum to the Roman Forum is often closed off for parades, historical demonstrations, and celebrations.

- **Piazza del Campidoglio:** This square is home to official speeches and special events related to Rome's history.

I've been to a lot of festivals, but nothing quite compares to the unique mix of history, pageantry, and pure fun that is Natale di Roma. This is Rome's birthday celebration, and it's truly one of the most captivating festivals I've ever experienced.

What makes Natale di Roma truly special is how it transforms the entire city into an immersive historical experience. As you wander through Rome's ancient heart during the festival, you're not just a spectator, — you become a part of history itself. The cobblestone streets that have witnessed millennia of triumphs and tribulations now pulse with the energy of reenactors, paraders, and enthusiastic visitors from around the world.

We enjoy all of Italy's festivals, but there's something magical about Natale di Roma that sets it apart. Perhaps it's the sight of fully armored legionaries marching past the Colosseum, or the sound of ancient Roman music echoing through the Forum. Maybe it's the way the setting sun paints the sky in hues of orange and pink, casting a warm glow over the citywide celebration. Whatever it is, this festival captures the essence of Rome in a way that's both educational and fun.

In this chapter, we'll explore the various aspects of Natale di Roma, from the grand historical reenactments to the cultural events that bring ancient Rome to life. We'll delve into the spectacle of the Corteo Storico parade, the excitement of gladiatorial displays, and the quieter moments of enlightenment in museums and lectures. Whether you're a history buff, a culture enthusiast, or simply someone who loves a wonderful celebration, Natale di Roma offers something for everyone.

So, join me as we step back in time and forward in celebration, experiencing the birthday party of one of the world's most iconic cities. Welcome to Natale di Roma — where every year, for a few magical days, we all become citizens of ancient Rome.

Key Events During Natale di Roma

1. Historical Reenactments: Rome's Living History

These captivating reenactments are the crown jewel, transforming the Eternal City into a vibrant, living museum. As you wander through Rome's ancient heart, you'll find yourself transported back in time, surrounded by the sights, sounds, and even smells of antiquity.

These vibrant reenactments transform Rome's ancient stones into a living breathing city during Natale di Roma. Hundreds of historically accurate participants fill the streets from stern legionaries in gleaming armor to dignified senators in flowing togas. Vestal Virgins tend their sacred duties while gladiators prepare for combat and merchants hawk their wares just as they did two millennia ago. Even emperors make appearances accompanied by their elaborate entourages.

The spectacle unfolds through carefully choreographed gladiatorial matches precise military drills and grand parades that capture the pomp of Imperial Rome. Many of the reenactors are historians or archaeologists ensuring exceptional accuracy in everything from weapon details to behavioral portrayals. They demonstrate ancient crafts and daily life activitiesoffering visitors glimpses into the practical aspects of Roman civilization.What makes these reenactments truly special is their interactive nature.

The participants stay firmly in character allowing visitors to "converse" with ancient Romans and learn about their lives firsthand. This creates perfect photography opportunities with costumed figures posed against Rome's authentic ancient backdrops. Through these immersive experiences the city's silent ruins transform into a bustling metropolis helping modern visitors grasp the grandeur and vitality of ancient Rome in a way that mere imagination cannot match.

2. The Grand Parade: A March Through Time

The grand parade, known as the "Corteo Storico," stands as the pinnacle of Rome's historical reenactments, transforming the city's streets into a living tableau of ancient glory. Over 1,500 meticulously costumed participants bring history to life, from stern legionaries in gleaming armor and red cloaks to dignified senators in white togas with purple trim. Vestal Virgins glide past in their distinctive veiled attire, while gladiators stride through the crowds, their presence evoking the ancient games. Musicians playing authentic replica instruments accompany graceful dancers performing traditional Roman choreographies, while magnificent horse-drawn chariots thunder through the streets.

The procession follows a route rich in historical significance, beginning at the Circus Maximus before winding along the Via dei Fori Imperiali, where ancient ruins stretch out on either side. The parade creates an unforgettable spectacle as it passes the Colosseum and threads through the Roman Forum, finally ascending to its conclusion atop the Capitoline Hill, Rome's sacred religious and political center.

The parade unfolds as a feast for the senses, with sunlight dancing off polished armor and banners fluttering in the spring breeze. The air fills with the authentic soundscape of marching caligae, powerful buccinae blasts, and the thunder of approaching chariots, while fragrant incense wafts through the air. Key moments punctuate the celebration, including the Vestal Virgins tending a portable flame and legionaries demonstrating precise military formations. Ornate litters carry costumed "emperors" through the streets, while musicians and dancers perform at strategic locations.

Drawing inspiration from the Roman Triumph, this meticulous recreation serves as a living bridge between past and present, offering modern visitors a powerful reminder of Rome's enduring influence on Western civilization.

3. Fireworks Display

In the evening, a spectacular fireworks display lights up the sky over the Tiber River, offering a festive and celebratory conclusion to the day's events. This display is set against the backdrop of Rome's ancient monuments, providing a truly breathtaking experience.

4. Cultural and Educational Events: Bringing Ancient Rome to Life

The festival goes beyond spectacle, offering a rich array of cultural and educational events that delve deep into Roman history, art, and civilization. These events cater to history enthusiasts, families, and curious visitors alike, providing engaging ways to learn about ancient Rome.

Lectures and Conferences: Distinguished historians and archaeologists gather to share their expertise through engaging lectures and conferences, presenting topics that range from daily life in ancient Rome to military tactics and the role of women in Roman society. These talks are thoughtfully presented in multiple languages, ensuring international visitors can fully participate in these enlightening discussions.

Museum Exhibits: Museums across the city complement these scholarly offerings with special exhibitions, extended hours, and guided tours, while interactive displays allow visitors to handle carefully crafted replicas of ancient artifacts.

Guided Tours: Expert guides lead specialized tours through archaeological sites, often including areas typically closed to the public. These tours weave engaging narratives, following themes like "In the Footsteps of Julius Caesar" or exploring the architectural marvels of Imperial Rome. Particularly memorable are the evening tours of monuments like the Colosseum, where the play of light and shadow creates an entirely different perspective on these ancient structures.

Workshops and Demonstrations: Hands-on learning takes center stage through various workshops and demonstrations. Participants can try their hand at Roman coin minting, create intricate mosaics, or explore the fascinating world of ancient Roman cuisine. These practical sessions are complemented by demonstrations of ancient crafts and technologies, bringing the skills of the past vividly to life. The festival's film program features carefully selected historical documentaries and movies set in ancient Rome, often followed by enlightening discussions with historians or filmmakers who provide deeper context.

Film Screenings: Showings of historical documentaries and films set in ancient Rome, often followed by discussions with historians or filmmakers.

Children's Activities: Young visitors are especially well-served by the festival's children's programming. Interactive storytelling sessions bring Roman myths and legends to life, while "Junior Archaeologist" programs let children experience the excitement of archaeological discovery through mock digs. Creative workshops allow young participants to design and create their own Roman-inspired costumes, helping them connect personally with the historical period through hands-on creativity.

5. Official Ceremonies

Rome's mayor and other dignitaries often take part in official ceremonies, giving speeches that reflect on Rome's history and its future. These events are typically held at the Piazza del Campidoglio.

Natale di Roma is a vibrant and thrilling way to experience the history and culture of the Eternal City. Whether you're drawn by the historical reenactments, the parades, or the cultural events, the festival offers a unique and immersive celebration of Rome's legendary past. Visitors and locals alike can enjoy the festive atmosphere, connect with the city's ancient roots, and take part in this enduring celebration of Rome's 2,700+ years of history.

Restaurant Recommendations for the Areas of the Festival

1. Near Circus Maximus:

   - Osteria Circo: Traditional Roman cuisine with a view of Circus Maximus.

   - Il Bocconcino: Cozy trattoria offering authentic Roman dishes.

2. Along Via dei Fori Imperiali:

   - Aroma: Michelin-starred restaurant with a breathtaking view of the Colosseum.

   - Venus: Rooftop restaurant with panoramic views of the ancient ruins.

3. Near the Colosseum:

   - Li Rioni: Popular pizzeria with a local atmosphere.

   - Hostaria da Nerone: Traditional Roman cuisine in a charming setting.

   - Oppio Caffè: Casual dining with a terrace overlooking the Colosseum.

4. Near the Roman Forum:

   - Antica Taverna: Classic Roman dishes in a rustic setting.

   - Sacello: Upscale dining with a view of the Forum.

Accommodation: See Accommodation Detail Chapter for information about hotels in Rome. I recommend a minimum of four nights in Rome.

CHAPTER FORTY-EIGHT

Civitavecchia, A Harbor of History and Tradition

Hundreds of Years of Celebrations

F esta di Santa Fermina

Where: Civitavecchia

When: April 28

Average Festival Temperatures: High 16°C (62°F). Low 12°C (53°F).

Civitavecchia: Chronicles of a Timeless Port

Civitavecchia, which translates to "Ancient Town," is a historic port city in the Lazio region. It has served as a critical maritime hub since its foundation by the Etruscans. Later, during the Roman Empire, Emperor Trajan established the Portus Traiani (Trajan's Port) around 106 AD, further solidifying the city's role as a key gateway for trade and travel in the Mediterranean. Over the centuries, Civitavecchia has witnessed the rise and fall of empires, with its strategic location making it a coveted site for military and economic purposes.

During the Middle Ages, the city came under Papal control, contributing to its religious and cultural heritage. Civitavecchia's resilience through wars and natural disasters has left a rich tapestry of historical landmarks, including its medieval walls, forts, and its historic cathedral.

Civitavecchia is situated along the Tyrrhenian Sea, approximately 70 kilometers (43 miles) northwest of Rome. Its coastal location has defined its identity as a port city. The city's natural harbor is one of its most distinctive features, protected by a crescent-shaped coastline and overlooked by the iconic Forte Michelangelo, a fortress commissioned by Pope Julius II and completed by Michelangelo Buonarroti.

The surrounding area includes rolling hills and fertile plains, which historically supported agriculture and trade. Its proximity to Rome and its connection via the Aurelia road and railway have made it a vital transportation link.

As of the most recent census, Civitavecchia has a population of 52,000 residents. The city is a dynamic blend of locals who have long relied on maritime industries, and a growing community of visitors and expatriates attracted by its historical charm, convenient location, and vibrant cultural scene. Thie port serves as the "port of Rome" for cruise ships as well as ferries traveling to Sicily, Sardinia, Corsica, and Spain.

The Festival of Santa Fermina

The festival is a vibrant blend of religious ceremonies, historical reenactments, and communal activities. It includes a solemn procession, traditional music, and the blessing of the sea, symbolizing Santa Fermina's protection over sailors and the maritime community.

Santa Fermina: Her Life and Connection to Civitavecchia

Santa Fermina, also known as Saint Firmina, is believed to have lived in the 3rd century. According to tradition, she was the daughter of Calpurnius, the prefect of Rome. Fermina devoted herself to Christianity and chose a life of prayer and seclusion near Amelia in Umbria. During the persecution of Christians under Emperor Diocletian, she suffered martyrdom.

Her connection to Civitavecchia is rooted in legend. It is said that during a sea voyage to Centumcellae (modern-day Civitavecchia), a violent storm threatened her ship. Through her prayers, the storm calmed, and she safely reached the port. She is believed to have lived for a time in a grotto near the port, over which Fort Michelangelo was later built. This association has made her the patron saint of Civitavecchia and sailors.

History of the Festival

Although a start date for this festival is not documented, it is safe to say that Santa Fermina has been celebrated for centuries. Her veneration in Civitavecchia dates back to at least the medieval period, when her role as protector of sailors and the city became firmly established. Given her connection to the region through both legend and the construction of Fort Michelangelo over her grotto, it's likely that devotion to her began shortly after these events, potentially as far back as the Renaissance.

The festival has strengthened over the years, incorporating various cultural and historical elements, but its core purpose remains the celebration of Santa Fermina's enduring legacy and her significance to the people of Civitavecchia.

Festival Events

April 25 to April 27

5:45 p.m.

The Triduum of preparation takes place in the Cathedral, with the prayer of the Rosary at 5:45 pm, followed by the Eucharistic celebration at 6:30 pm.

April 28

8:30 a.m.

Holy Mass: The day begins with a Holy Mass in the Chapel of Santa Fermina at Fort Michelangelo, celebrated by the local bishop.

5:00 p.m.

Historic Parade: Following the Mass, a historic parade featuring costumed figures from the 17th century and flag bearers from Amelia, the city associated with Santa Fermina's martyrdom, proceeds through the principal streets of the historic center.

Blessing of the Sea: At the harbor, a devotional candle is lit, and the sea is blessed. Fallen sailors are honored with a laurel wreath, while ships in the harbor sound their horns in tribute.

The Patron Saint Festival of Santa Fermina continues to be a significant event in Civitavecchia, fostering a sense of community and preserving the rich cultural heritage of the city. Patron Saint Festival of Santa Fermina in Civitavecchia encompasses a variety of celebrations beyond the religious ceremonies. The festivities include:

Cultural Events: The festival features cultural activities such as concerts, art exhibitions, and theatrical performances. For instance, in previous years, the opera "The Martyrdom of Santa Ferma" has been performed to inaugurate the celebrations.

Historical Reenactments: Participants dressed in period costumes reenact historical events related to Santa Fermina, adding a vibrant and educational aspect to the festivities.

Sporting Events: Traditional sporting competitions, such as the Palio Marinaro, a historic rowing race among the city's districts, are organized to honor the maritime heritage of Civitavecchia.

Communal Feasts: Local communities come together to enjoy traditional dishes and local wines, fostering a sense of unity and shared cultural identity.

These activities contribute to a festive atmosphere throughout the city, allowing both residents and visitors to engage with Civitavecchia's rich cultural and historical heritage during the celebration of Santa Fermina.

Walking Tour of Civitavecchia

#1: Fort Michelangelo

This imposing fortress, constructed in the 16th century, was designed to protect Civitavecchia's port. Commissioned by Pope Julius II and completed under Michelangelo's supervision, it is a masterpiece of Renaissance military architecture with sturdy walls and cylindrical towers that create an iconic impression of the city. Fort Michelangelo is closely tied to the story of Santa Fermina, as the chapel within the fort was built in her honor, marking the grotto where she is said to have lived. A visit here offers historical significance, architectural grandeur, and stunning views of the harbor.

Castello Santa Severa

#2: Port of Civitavecchia (Porto di Traiano)

Known as Porto di Traiano, the port has served as a vital maritime hub since its construction during Emperor Trajan's reign in the 2nd century AD. It has played a key role in trade and transportation for millennia and continues to be a bustling harbor welcoming cruise ships and ferries. Visitors can stroll along the harbor to see remnants of ancient Roman engineering while enjoying the lively atmosphere.

#3: Cathedral of San Francesco d'Assisi

Dedicated to St. Francis of Assisi, this cathedral was built in the 17th century and showcases elegant Baroque architectural details. Having been restored after damage during World War II, it stands as a symbol of resilience. Inside, the serene space is adorned with frescoes and sculptures, offering a peaceful retreat for visitors.

#4: Piazza Leandra

The oldest square in Civitavecchia, Piazza Leandra is a charming and historically significant spot surrounded by colorful buildings. Named after Leandro, a local figure who contributed to the city's early development, it exudes a quaint and lively ambiance. Visitors can relax at a café, enjoy the picturesque surroundings, and immerse themselves in local culture.

Bastion of the Medieval Fortress

#5: Rocca Medievale (Medieval Fortress)

This historic fortress, overlooking the city, dates back to the 9th century. It has undergone many modifications over the centuries, reflecting Civitavecchia's strategic importance. Exploring the preserved sections of the fortress provides an opportunity to appreciate its historical legacy and take in panoramic views of the city and the Tyrrhenian Sea.

#6: Porta Livorno

Porta Livorno, a monumental gateway built in the 18th century, serves as an elegant entrance to the historic city center. Near the port, it symbolizes Civitavecchia's importance as a maritime city. Its grand archway is a magnificent spot for photos and an iconic part of the city's landscape. Visitors can walk through Porta Livorno to explore the charming streets and discover more about Civitavecchia's vibrant past.

#7: Thermal Baths of Trajan (Terme Taurine)

Located outside the city center, these ancient Roman baths are an archaeological treasure. Built in the 1st century AD, the baths were frequented by Roman elites and include well-preserved structures such as pools, mosaics, and a calidarium. A visit to this site offers a fascinating glimpse into ancient Roman leisure culture and engineering.

Logistics

Train: Civitavecchia is well-connected to Rome by train, with the closest station being Civitavecchia Train Station, in the heart of the town and just a short walk from the port and city center. The distance to Rome is approximately 70 kilometers (43 miles), and the journey takes about 1 hour via the regional Trenitalia trains. Trains run frequently throughout the day, making it a convenient option for travelers.

Bus: Several bus lines connect Civitavecchia to Rome, including Cotral buses that operate between the town and key destinations like Cornelia or Saxa Rubra metro stations in Rome. The distance is also 70 kilometers (43 miles), and the travel time ranges from 1.5 to 2 hours, depending on traffic.

Car: Driving from Rome to Civitavecchia is straightforward. Take the A12/E80 Autostrada, heading northwest towards Civitavecchia. The distance is approximately 70 kilometers (43 miles), and the drive takes about 1 hour. The route is well-maintained, with clear signage directing you to the town and port areas.

Parking: Parking in Civitavecchia is relatively easy, especially for visitors who want to avoid the ZTL (Zona a Traffico Limitato) areas in the historic center. Safe and convenient parking options include the Port Mobility parking lots, near the cruise terminal and well-marked on approach roads. Additional parking areas are available outside the town center, such as along Via XVI Settembre or near the Civitavecchia Train Station, offering easy access to the primary sites while staying outside restricted zones.

Port of Civitavecchia: Civitavecchia serves as one of Italy's most important maritime gateways, with its bustling port handling a comprehensive network of ferry connections throughout the Mediterranean. From its well-organized terminals within the easily accessible port area, travelers can embark on journeys to numerous destinations across the region. Regular services connect to multiple ports in Sardinia, including Olbia and Porto Torres, while routes to Sicily serve both Palermo and Termini Imerese.

The port also maintains vital links to Corsica, offering tourists and locals alike access to this French Mediterranean island. For those seeking to venture further, international routes include regular services to Barcelona, Spain, and connections to Tunisia in North Africa. Additional Mediterranean destinations are served seasonally or on specific schedules, making Civitavecchia a crucial intersection point for maritime travel in the region. The port's modern facilities and central location within the harbor area ensure convenient access for passengers, whether they're beginning their journey or incorporating ferry travel into a broader Mediterranean itinerary.

Restaurant Recommendations

Ristorante Ideale. Address: Via Aurelia Sud, 27

A cozy, family-run restaurant known for its authentic Roman and Mediterranean cuisine. Specialties include fresh seafood dishes like spaghetti alle vongole and grilled catch-of-the-day, as well as classic Italian pasta and desserts. The welcoming atmosphere and attentive service make it a local favorite.

Pizzeria Del Ghetto. Address: Via Luigi Cadorna, 17

A casual spot offering some of the best wood-fired pizzas in town. Known for its thin crust and creative toppings, the menu also includes calzones and traditional Italian antipasti. Perfect for a relaxed meal with friends or family.

Accommodation

For the festival, I recommend two to three nights in town.

Hotel San Giorgio. Address: Viale Giuseppe Garibaldi, 34

A 4-star hotel housed in a prestigious historic building dating back to the late 1800s, in the heart of the historic center near the train station and port. It offers elegant rooms, a rooftop terrace with sea views, and an on-site restaurant specializing in Italian cuisine.

Hotel de La Ville. Address: Viale della Repubblica, 4

This 4-star hotel is in a charming 19th-century building on the main road, offering elegant rooms with classic décor. Amenities include a restaurant serving Italian dishes, a bar, and proximity to the train station and seafront.

Day Trips: Nearby Sites, Cities, and Towns

Tuscania. 40 kilometers (25 miles) from Civitavecchia. Tuscania is a picturesque hilltop town with ancient roots, tracing its origins back to the Etruscan civilization. In medieval times, it flourished as a significant trading and cultural hub. Its Romanesque churches, such as San Pietro and Santa Maria Maggiore, are architectural masterpieces, showcasing intricate frescoes and carvings.

The surrounding countryside offers panoramic views, making it a favorite for artists and photographers. Wander through its historic center to discover narrow cobblestone streets and charming squares.

Cerveteri. 35 kilometers (22 miles) from Civitavecchia. Cerveteri is renowned for its Etruscan heritage and the Necropoli della Banditaccia, a UNESCO World Heritage Site. The necropolis features tombs dating back to the 9th century BCE, providing a glimpse into Etruscan funeral rites and daily life. The Cerite National Museum houses artifacts excavated from the area, including jewelry, pottery, and sculptures. Cerveteri's quaint town center, with its medieval architecture and vibrant markets, adds to its charm.

Monte Argentario. 95 kilometers (59 miles) from Civitavecchia. Monte Argentario is a scenic peninsula in southern Tuscany, originally an island connected to the mainland by two sandy isthmuses. It has a rich history as a strategic port during the Roman and Spanish eras. The charming ports of Porto Santo Stefano and Porto Ercole are highlights, offering colorful harbors, seafood restaurants, and historic fortifications. Nature enthusiasts can explore the coastal trails, secluded beaches, and crystal-clear waters perfect for snorkeling and diving.

Civitavecchia Festivals and Sagre Throughout the Year

Ferragosto

August 15

A national holiday celebrated with particular enthusiasm in Civitavecchia, Ferragosto marks the Assumption of the Virgin Mary. The day is filled with beach outings, communal meals, and fireworks, embodying the Italian love for festivity and togetherness.

Sagra dell'Uva (Grape Festival)

September

The Sagra dell'Uva transforms Civitavecchia each September into a celebration of the region's rich viticultural heritage, with activities centered on the historic port area and winding through the medieval streets. The festival showcases local wines, particularly those produced from the indigenous grape varieties that thrive in the volcanic soils of northern Lazio. Local wineries set up elaborate stands where visitors can sample both young and aged wines, including the area's renowned white wines made from Trebbiano and Malvasia grapes.

Traditional grape-pressing demonstrations use historic equipment to show visitors the ancient methods of wine production, while local experts offer guided tastings that explore the unique characteristics of wines from different microclimates within the region. The celebration features parades of decorated farm wagons laden with grapes, competitions for the best home-produced wine, and evening concerts where traditional folk groups perform songs related to the harvest.

Local restaurants create special menus pairing regional wines with traditional harvest-time dishes, such as pasta alla vendemmia (harvest pasta) and wild boar stews.

Festa di Santa Cecilia

November 22

The Festa di Santa Cecilia on November 22nd honors the patron saint of music with a rich program of events that highlight Civitavecchia's musical traditions. The festival begins with a solemn Mass at the Cathedral, featuring performances by the cathedral choir singing sacred music spanning several centuries. Throughout the day, the town's historic squares and churches host concerts ranging from classical chamber music to traditional folk ensembles.

A highlight is the evening procession where the statue of Santa Cecilia is carried through the streets, accompanied by the town's historic band playing traditional marches. Local music schools take part by organizing student performances, while professional musicians from the region offer masterclasses and workshops.

The festival culminates in a grand concert at the Teatro Traiano, the town's historic theater, where local and visiting orchestras perform works dedicated to Santa Cecilia. The event also includes a special recognition of the town's music teachers and longtime members of local musical organizations, celebrating their contribution to maintaining Civitavecchia's rich musical heritage.

CHAPTER FORTY-NINE

Experiencing Holy Week and Easter in the Eternal City

Rome's Sacred Traditions

La Settimana Santa & La Pasqua

Where: Rome & Beyond

When: April (varies)

Average Festival Temperatures: High 18°C (65°F). Low 8°C (47°F).

Holy Week and Easter

Pilgrims visiting Rome during Holy Week will have the rare opportunity to be in the city for Easter. Throughout Holy Week, major events take place like the Papal Mass on Easter Sunday and the Way of the Cross on Good Friday.

In April 2022, I embarked on what would become one of the most beautiful journeys of my life, spending Holy Week and Easter in Rome with my family. Words cannot capture the magic of those days. Rome seemed to glow with an otherworldly light as spring breathed new life into the city. The mornings greeted us with a crisp coolness that gradually yielded to the warm embrace of the

Mediterranean sun. With each passing day, I felt more deeply connected to the rhythm of this ancient city, its cobblestone streets and timeless piazzas resonating with centuries of faith and tradition.

The experience of Holy Week and Easter in Rome transcends mere tourism; it's an immersion into living history, a chance to be part of something greater than oneself. From the solemn processions to the jubilant Easter Mass, every moment felt significant, every sight etched permanently in my memory.

I cannot recommend this experience highly enough. If you're considering when to visit Rome, let me assure you: Holy Week and Easter are, without a doubt, the most special times to be in this extraordinary city. It may well be the crowning jewel of all the celebrations Rome offers!

Join me as I guide you through the vibrant traditions and awe-inspiring events that make Easter in Rome an unparalleled experience.

Palm Sunday (Domenica delle Palme): Where History Meets Faith

As I stood in St. Peter's Square on Palm Sunday, the air thick with anticipation and the scent of olive branches, I felt the weight of centuries of tradition. This day, marking the beginning of Holy Week and commemorating Jesus Christ's triumphant entry into Jerusalem, was more powerful than I could have imagined.

Events in Rome

Mass at St. Peter's Square: Witnessing the Pope lead the special Mass was truly awe-inspiring. As Pope Francis processed through the square, carrying palms and re-enacting Jesus' entry into Jerusalem, I felt transported through time. The celebration of the Eucharist that followed was deeply moving. (Note: Tickets are required, and I recommend securing them well in advance.)

Traditional Processions: While the Vatican events were grand, I found equal beauty in the smaller processions throughout Rome. Walking through the ancient streets, joining locals carrying olive branches, I was struck by the intimacy of these neighborhood celebrations. Using olive branches instead of palm fronds was a delightful surprise, and I love the practical wisdom behind it. As a local explained to me, Italy's abundance of olive trees that need regular pruning makes this an ingenious, eco-friendly tradition. It felt like a beautiful blend of faith, sustainability, and Italian practicality.

A Tale of Palms, Popes, and Perseverance

During my visit, I was captivated by a story I'd read in R.A. Scotti's book "Basilica" (which I heartily recommend to anyone interested in the history of St. Peter's). It's a tale that exemplifies the spirit of innovation and determination that built the Vatican we see today.

In 1586, Pope Sixtus V faced a monumental challenge: moving a 320-ton Egyptian granite obelisk to the center of St. Peter's Square. This wasn't just any obelisk–it had stood witness to St. Peter's martyrdom and had resisted relocation for centuries. Even Michelangelo had deemed the task impossible.

The winning solution came from Domenico Fontana, whose ingenious plan involved an intricate system of ropes, pulleys, and manpower. On the day of the move, with 907 men and 145 horses assembled, Rome held its breath. The Pope had decreed silence on pain of death, adding to the tension.

As the operation began, disaster loomed–the ropes started to smoke. In that critical moment, a sailor from Bordighera broke the silence, shouting, "Acqua alle funi!" (Water the ropes!). This simple suggestion saved the day; the ropes did not break.

In a beautiful twist of fate, the Pope granted Bordighera and his family the perpetual honor of providing Easter palms to St. Peter's–a tradition that continues to this day. Fontana, for his part, was knighted and richly rewarded.

Standing in St. Peter's Square on Palm Sunday, holding my olive branch, I couldn't help but feel connected to this rich tapestry of history.

Holy Monday to Holy Wednesday

A Time for Reflection and Exploration

As I discovered during my visit, the early days of Holy Week offer a unique blend of spiritual reflection and opportunities for exploration. While the grand events were yet to come, these days held their own quiet power. At this point, there were no crowds in town.

Holy Monday: Traditionally marking Jesus' cleansing of the temple, I found this day set a tone of purification and renewal. The city seemed to hold its breath, preparing for the days ahead.

Holy Tuesday: As we reflected on Jesus' predictions of betrayal, I was struck by the human drama at the heart of the Easter story. The weight of these ancient events felt palpable in Rome's historic streets.

Holy Wednesday: This day commemorates Judas' conspiracy with the Sanhedrin. The air of anticipation in Rome was almost tangible.

Personal Experiences and Tips:

During these quieter days, we took time to explore Rome more extensively. The walking tours included in this guide are based on my planning for this week. They will allow you to discover hidden gems and iconic sites alike. I'd recommend using these days to immerse yourself in Rome's rich history and culture - it adds depth to the Easter experience.

My cousin Susie and I took a *treno veloce* (fast train, 90 minutes) to Florence on Tuesday. While it meant missing some events in Rome, it offered a beautiful contrast and a chance to see how other parts of Italy prepare for Easter. If you can, I highly recommend a side trip. Just make sure you plan your return to Rome in time for the Holy Week events.

For those staying in Rome, consider visiting some of the less-known churches. I found that smaller, neighborhood churches often offered more intimate and deeply moving services during these days.

Remember to pace yourself; the most intense and crowded days are yet to come. Use this time to reflect, explore, and prepare yourself spiritually and physically for the profound experiences ahead.

As Holy Wednesday drew to a close, I felt a sense of anticipation building. The quiet reflection set the stage for upcoming events. I felt grateful for this preparation time.

Holy Thursday (Giovedì Santo)

The Last Supper Remembered

Holy Thursday marks a pivotal moment in the Easter story, commemorating the Last Supper when Jesus instituted the Eucharist and washed his disciples' feet. This day in Rome marked a palpable turning point, deepening the solemnity of the season.

From my experience, Rome remained relatively quiet from Palm Sunday through Holy Wednesday. However, on Holy Thursday, I noticed a significant increase in visitors. By Good Friday evening, during the Via Crucis, the city was bustling with pilgrims and tourists. If you're looking for a quieter Rome experience, I'd recommend arriving on the Saturday before Palm Sunday or on Palm Sunday itself. This timing allows you to settle in and explore the city more peacefully before the crowds arrive.

Key Events in Rome on Giovedi Santo:

- Chrism Mass

- Mass of the Lord's Supper

- Washing of the Feet (Lavanda dei Piedi)

- Adoration and Altars of Repose

Personal Reflection: Holy Thursday in Rome was a day of contrasts for me. The grandeur of the papal ceremonies juxtaposed with the intimate moments of prayer and reflection in smaller churches created a rich tapestry of experiences. I found the Giro delle Sette Chiese particularly meaningful. Walking through Rome's nighttime streets, moving from one sacred space to another, felt like a physical embodiment of a spiritual journey.

As the day ended, I sensed the city's atmosphere shifting. The growing crowds buzzed with anticipation. Holy Thursday set the stage for the profound events of Good Friday. I was privileged to be part of this ancient tradition in Rome.

Good Friday (Venerdì Santo): A Night of Solemn Reflection

Good Friday, the day Christians commemorate the Passion and Crucifixion of Jesus Christ, is marked by profound and moving events in Rome. The city takes on a somber yet deeply spiritual atmosphere as pilgrims and visitors gather to participate in centuries-old traditions.

Celebration of the Passion of the Lord: In the afternoon, the Pope presides over this solemn liturgy at St. Peter's Basilica. The service includes reading from the Gospel of John, venerating the Cross, and Holy Communion, creating a reverent atmosphere for the day.

Via Crucis (The Way of the Cross) at the Colosseum (highly recommended): The highlight of Good Friday in Rome is undoubtedly the Stations of the Cross, or Via Crucis, held at the Colosseum. This tradition, dating back to the 18th century, creates an unforgettable experience for all who attend.

As night falls, thousands of pilgrims, visitors, and religious figures gather around the illuminated Colosseum. The Pope leads the procession, guiding the faithful through the Stations of the Cross. Each station represents a moment in Christ's journey to Calvary, accompanied by prayers and hymns in multiple languages.

Personal Experience: The Via Crucis is truly a remarkable event. Under the moon and stars, beside the Colosseum, amidst fellow pilgrims, an indescribable unity and spiritual reflection emerge. The multilingual nature, with prayers and readings in various languages, emphasizes the universal nature of the observance. It was quite crowded outside the Colosseum where we attended, but my understanding is Rome will start holding the event inside the Colosseum again this year.

Practical Information:

Tickets are not required, but attendees must pass through security checkpoints.

- Large bags are not permitted, so travel light. All bags are searched.

- Be prepared for a crowd–thousands attend this event each year.

Broadcast: For those unable to attend in person, the Via Crucis is broadcast worldwide, making it one of the most widely watched Good Friday observances globally.

The Colosseum at moonrise when we entered for the Via Crucis, Way of the Cross with Pope Francis.

The combination of the ancient Colosseum–once a site of martyrdom–with the timeless story of Christ's sacrifice creates a deeply moving experience. With flickering torches, prayers in multiple languages, and faithful from all corners of the world, this Good Friday in Rome is a unique and memorable event. It's not just a religious ceremony, but a profound cultural experience that resonates with many, regardless of their faith background.

Rome & Beyond Good Friday

Frascati: The streets of Frascati host a traditional Via Crucis (Way of the Cross) with reenactments of the Passion of Christ. The procession begins at sunset, with local residents portraying biblical figures and carrying illuminated torches through the medieval streets. The event concludes at the Cathedral of San Pietro with special prayers and hymns.

Grottaferrata: A solemn procession led by monks of the Abbey through the streets, accompanied by prayers and Byzantine chants. The unique blend of Eastern and Western Christian traditions makes this celebration particularly special, featuring ancient Greek hymns and traditional Orthodox elements.

Marino: The historic center becomes the setting for a dramatic reenactment of the Passion of Christ. Local actors portray key biblical figures while moving through elaborately decorated stations of the cross. The evening procession is illuminated by hundreds of candles, creating a deeply moving atmosphere.

Genzano di Roma: A solemn procession through the town's streets, with artistic displays reflecting the Passion of Christ. The event features traditional sculptures and paintings carried by confraternities in historical dress, while local choirs perform traditional lamentation hymns.

Ariccia: A dramatic and emotional procession through the town's baroque streets, featuring a 17th-century statue of the Dead Christ and Mary in mourning. The route passes under the iconic Bernini bridge, while participants carry traditional symbols of the Passion.

Orte: The ancient Dead Christ Procession illuminates the medieval city center with torchlight as seven historic brotherhoods converge at the Mother Church of St. Croce. The procession features the Dead Christ's coffin carried by 14 men, followed by the Float of the Lady of Sorrows. Participants include Cyreneans bearing chains and crosses, and figures representing Veronica and the Three Crying Marys. At Libertà Square, the brotherhoods form a heart shape while singing the "Miserere," before returning to share traditional bread among the participants.

Holy Saturday (Sabato Santo)

A Day of Quiet Anticipation

Holy Saturday, also known as the Easter Vigil, is a day of quiet reflection and anticipation in the Christian calendar. It commemorates the day Jesus lay in the tomb before his resurrection. While less outwardly eventful than Good Friday or Easter Sunday, Holy Saturday holds deep spiritual significance and culminates in one of the most beautiful and symbolic services of the liturgical year.

Daytime in Rome and Beyond

While Rome becomes more filled with Easter visitors on Holy Saturday, my cousin Susie and I explored beyond the city limits. We ventured into the Castelli Romani, a cluster of picturesque towns in the Alban Hills southeast of Rome.

We visited Frascati, Ariccia, Castel Gandolfo, Nemi, Genzano di Roma, Rocca di Papa and Grottaferrata. Luckily for us I had a friend from the area who knew their way around, had a car, and could transport us all over these beautiful villages.

Our day trip offered a unique glimpse into Italian Easter traditions outside the bustling capital. In these small towns, we witnessed a flurry of preparatory activity that contrasted with Rome's solemnity. Families lined up at local butcher shops, patiently waiting to collect their lamb for the traditional Easter Sunday feast. The streets were alive with residents running last-minute errands, their arms full of flowers, foods, and other holiday essentials.

In the smaller churches of the Castelli Romani, we observed the symbols and statues used for the Holy Week processions, including various statues of *Cristo Morto* (Christ after His removal from the Cross) in front of the altars. Each statue, a poignant representation of Jesus in repose, reflects the community's deep reverence and devotion, setting the stage for the solemn rituals of Holy Week.

For visitors to Rome during Holy Week, a day trip to the surrounding towns can offer a peaceful retreat and a chance to experience local culture away from the city's grand religious ceremonies. It provides a different perspective on how Italians observe this important religious holiday, blending spiritual tradition with family customs and culinary preparations.

The Easter Vigil (Vigilia Pasquale): The focal point of Holy Saturday is the Easter Vigil, which begins after sundown at St. Peter's Basilica, led by the Pope. This ancient service is rich in symbolism and tradition:

- Service of Light: The vigil begins in darkness, symbolizing the darkness of the tomb. The Paschal candle, representing the light of Christ, is lit from a new fire and carried into the darkened basilica. The light spreads as candles held by the faithful are lit from this single flame, gradually illuminating the entire church.

- Liturgy of the Word: This extended part of the service includes several readings from the Old and New Testaments, tracing salvation history from Creation to Resurrection. The Gloria is sung for the first time since Lent, often with bells ringing.

- Baptismal Liturgy: The Pope blesses the baptismal water, and the faithful renew their baptismal vows. New members are received into the Church through baptism during this service.

- Liturgy of the Eucharist: The vigil concludes with the celebration of the Eucharist, marking the joyous transition to Easter.

The Easter Vigil is considered the "mother of all vigils" in the Catholic tradition. It's a time of waiting and preparation, symbolizing the faithful's vigilant anticipation of Christ's return. The vigil's progression from darkness to light powerfully represents the movement from death to life central to the Easter story.

Practical Information for Visitors:

- While the main vigil is held at St. Peter's, many churches throughout Rome hold their own Easter Vigil services.

- The Vatican service is ticketed and extremely popular. Those wishing to attend should request tickets well in advance.

- The vigil typically lasts 3-4 hours, concluding around midnight with the ringing of bells and the illumination of church lights to celebrate the resurrection.

Easter Sunday (Pasqua)

Easter Sunday, celebrating the Resurrection of Jesus Christ, is the pinnacle of the Christian calendar. In Rome, this day is marked by grand celebrations and deeply moving spiritual experiences.

Easter Mass at St. Peter's Square: The Pope celebrates a solemn Mass in St. Peter's Square, attended by thousands of pilgrims and broadcast globally.

Personal Experience: Attending Easter Mass in St. Peter's Square is an unforgettable experience. As we took our seats near the obelisk, the atmosphere was electric with anticipation. The square was a sea of people, pilgrims, tourists, and locals alike, all gathered for this momentous occasion.

As the Mass began, a hush fell over the crowd. The spring sun shone brightly, casting a warm glow over the assembled faithful. What struck me most was the truly universal nature of the celebration. The Mass proceeded in multiple languages, Latin, English, Spanish, and others, each section seamlessly transitioning to the next. The multilingual approach beautifully represented the Church's global reach and believers' unity across the globe.

Despite the thousands in attendance, there was an incredible sense of intimacy. The Pope's words, amplified across the square, seemed to reach everyone individually. The shared responses of the crowd, the collective moments of silence and reflection, all contributed to a profound sense of community and shared faith.

Mass in St. Peter's Square and façade of St. Peter's Basilica

Urbi et Orbi Blessing: Following the Mass, the Pope delivers the "Urbi et Orbi" ("To the City and the World") blessing from the central loggia of St. Peter's Basilica. This special blessing, given on Easter and Christmas, often includes the Pope's reflections on global issues and prayers for peace and unity.

Pope in the Popemobile: In 2022, we were fortunate to get a closer view of Pope Francis thanks to his tour in the Popemobile after Mass and the Blessing. This added a personal touch to an already memorable day.

Practical Information for Attending Easter Mass:

Getting tickets for Easter Mass in St. Peter's Square can be challenging, but it is worthwhile. Here's what we learned:

- Tickets are distributed through the Prefecture of the Papal Household. Requests should be made well in advance (we started about 4 months ahead) on the Vatican website. Tickets are then collected in the morning prior to Mass.

- Arrive early to clear security (no large bags permitted) and secure good seats.

- Be prepared for crowds - even with assigned seating, standing crowds may fill the aisles.

The atmosphere of joy, hope, and unity that permeates St. Peter's Square on Easter Sunday is truly one-of-a-kind, making it a profound highlight of any visit to Rome during Holy Week. The morning was cool, but by the end of mass, our jackets were no longer needed.

Chairs setup in Piazza San Pietro for Easter Mass

Easter Monday (La Pasquetta)

In Italy, Easter Monday, known as "Pasquetta" (Little Easter), is a public holiday that serves as a joyful continuation of the Easter celebrations. This day is traditionally dedicated to relaxation, outdoor activities, and social gatherings, offering a perfect balance to the solemnity of Holy Week.

Traditions and Activities in Rome:

Outdoor Gatherings: Romans typically spend this day with family and friends, enjoying picnics or day trips to the countryside. The city's parks and gardens, such as Villa Borghese or the Pincio Gardens, become lively hubs of activity.

Day Trips: Many locals take quick trips to nearby towns in the Castelli Romani or to the coast, embracing the spring weather and the opportunity to explore beyond the city.

Special Masses: While less common than on Easter Sunday, some churches may hold special Masses or services for those seeking a spiritual component to their day.

For Visitors:

- Be aware that many shops and restaurants may be closed, so it's wise to plan.

- Public transportation usually runs on a holiday schedule.

This relaxed and festive day serves as a fitting conclusion to Holy Week in Rome, a period that showcases the city's deep spiritual roots and rich cultural heritage. From the solemnity of Good Friday to the joy of Easter Sunday and the relaxation of Pasquetta, Holy Week in Rome offers a profound and multifaceted experience for both locals and visitors, leaving lasting memories of this special time.

Important Churches in Rome that have Mass on Palm Sunday and Easter

In Rome, several important churches, besides St. Peter's Basilica, hold significant Palm Sunday and Easter Masses. These churches are often historic and are deeply connected to the religious and cultural heritage of the city. If you are unable to secure tickets for mass at St. Peter's Square here is a list of some of other options:

Other Papal Basilicas: Basilica of St. John Lateran (San Giovanni in Laterano). Basilica of St. Mary Major (Santa Maria Maggiore). Basilica of St. Paul Outside the Walls (San Paolo Fuori le Mura).

Basilica of Santa Maria in Trastevere (St. Mary in Trastevere). In the Trastevere district, this basilica is one of the oldest churches in Rome dedicated to the Virgin Mary. It is celebrated for its beautiful mosaics and historical significance.

Basilica of Santa Maria sopra Minerva (St. Mary over Minerva's Roman Temple). Near the Pantheon, this is one of the few Gothic churches in Rome. It houses the tombs of St. Catherine of Siena and Fra Angelico.

Chiesa del Gesù (Church of the Gesù / Jesuit Order). The mother church of the Jesuit order, near Piazza Venezia. It is renowned for its Baroque architecture and its significance to the Society of Jesus.

Basilica of San Clemente (St. Clement). Famous for its layered history, this basilica is built over a fourth-century church, which itself is above a first-century Roman house.

Basilica of San Lorenzo fuori le Mura (St. Laurence outside the walls). One of the seven pilgrimage churches of Rome, it is dedicated to St. Lawrence and is one of the oldest basilicas in the city.

Basilica of Sant'Andrea della Valle (St. Andrew of the Valley). Near the Campo de' Fiori, this basilica is known for its gigantic dome and Baroque art.

Church of Sant'Ignazio di Loyola (St. Ignatius of Loyola). Another Jesuit church in Rome, renowned for its breathtaking ceiling frescoes and its connection to St. Ignatius of Loyola.

Easter Treats

Easter in Italy is celebrated with a variety of traditional foods that vary by region, but several dishes are commonly enjoyed across the country. These foods often reflect the season and have deep cultural and religious significance. Traditional Easter foods in Italy - an overview.

1. **Colomba Pasquale.** The "Colomba Pasquale," or Easter Dove, is a sweet, yeast bread similar to Panettone (which is popular at Christmas), but it is shaped like a dove or a cross. It's made with flour, eggs, sugar, and butter, and is typically studded with candied peel and topped with pearl sugar and almonds.

2. **Torta Pasqualina.** This savory pie originates from Liguria and is made with layers of thin pastry filled with a mixture of ricotta, spinach (or chard), Parmesan cheese, and often whole boiled eggs. The pie is said to symbolize the resurrection because of the eggs hidden inside.

3. **Agnello (Lamb).** Lamb is a traditional Easter dish in many parts of Italy, symbolizing purity and sacrifice. It is often roasted and served with potatoes and herbs like rosemary and garlic.

4. **Casatiello.** It is a savory, traditional bread from Naples, typically prepared during the Easter season. It's made from a rich dough that incorporates lard or butter, filled with a combination of cured meats like salami and ham, along with cheeses, such as pecorino or provolone.

5. **Pastiera Napoletana.** This is a traditional Neapolitan dessert made with a crust of short crust pastry filled with a mixture of ricotta, cooked wheat grains, eggs, sugar, and orange flower water. It's often flavored with cinnamon and candied citrus peel.

6. **Uova di Pasqua** (Chocolate Easter Eggs). In modern times, chocolate Easter eggs have become a widespread tradition across Italy. Eggs in Italy are unlike those in America. The chocolate eggs can be as big as your purse or even your suitcase. They are hollow and they have toys inside, stuffed animals, almost like an Easter basket inside of an egg. They can cost 60, 100, even 500 euros. It is a unique tradition.

7. **Salami and eggs.** Especially common in Southern Italy, this dish is a simple yet hearty meal that involves cooking slices of salami and eggs together. It is often served at Easter Sunday breakfast.

Casatiello

Navigating Lazio

Your Ultimate Rome Planning Guide

CHAPTER FIFTY

Savoring the Flavors of Rome

A Culinary Journey Through Eternal City Delights

R ome's culinary heritage is as rich and layered as its ancient history. While visitors often come for the monuments and art, they soon discover that the city's cuisine tells an equally compelling story of tradition, innovation, and the art of transforming simple ingredients into extraordinary flavors. In Rome, every meal is an opportunity to experience centuries of culinary wisdom passed down through generations.

The Soul of Roman Cooking

Roman cuisine is built on a foundation of simplicity and respect for ingredients. Unlike the elaborate preparations found in other Italian regions, Roman dishes often feature just a handful of carefully chosen components. This minimalist approach demands perfection in both ingredients and technique, as there's nowhere to hide imperfections in a dish of just cheese, pepper, and pasta.

The city's cooking traditions also reflect its history of resourcefulness. Many beloved Roman dishes originated in the cucina povera (poor kitchen) tradition, where humble ingredients were transformed into satisfying meals. Today, these same dishes are celebrated in high-end restaurants and neighborhood trattorias alike.

Essential Roman Dishes

1. **Cacio e Pepe**

   A simple yet delicious pasta dish made with just three ingredients: pecorino romano cheese, freshly cracked black pepper, and pasta (usually tonnarelli or spaghetti). The heat from the pasta melts the cheese, creating a creamy, peppery sauce that clings to the noodles.

   Why try it? It's a perfect example of Roman cuisine's ability to create extraordinary flavor from humble ingredients.

2. **Carbonara**

   Another iconic Roman pasta, carbonara is made with guanciale (cured pork cheek), pecorino romano, eggs, and black pepper. The eggs create a rich, creamy sauce (without any cream) that coats the pasta, usually spaghetti or rigatoni.

   Why try it? A must-try for any pasta lover, carbonara is Roman comfort food at its finest, with guanciale adding a savory, crispy contrast to the creamy sauce.

3. **Amatriciana**

   A classic pasta sauce made with guanciale, tomatoes, and pecorino romano cheese. Bucatini, a thick, hollow pasta, is traditionally used to absorb the robust flavors of the sauce.

   Why try it? Amatriciana is a rich and tangy dish that balances the salty pork with the sweetness of tomatoes, showcasing the depth of Roman pasta traditions.

4. **Saltimbocca alla Romana**

   Thin slices of veal topped with prosciutto and sage, then sautéed in white wine and butter. The name "saltimbocca" means "jump in the mouth," reflecting the dish's burst of flavor.

   Why try it? A classic Roman main course that is simple, yet the combination of flavors from the veal, prosciutto, and sage is unforgettable.

5. **Carciofi alla Romana**

Roman-style artichokes, these are cooked in olive oil with garlic, mint, and parsley. The artichokes are typically stuffed and slowly braised until tender.

Why try it? Artichokes are a staple of Roman cuisine, and this dish highlights their delicate flavor with a simple preparation that lets the vegetable shine.

6. **Carciofi alla Giudia**

This is a deep-fried version of artichokes, a famous dish from the Roman Jewish tradition. The artichokes are fried twice, resulting in a crispy, golden exterior with a tender inside.

Why try it? A standout dish from Rome's Jewish ghetto, it's both a flavorful and historical experience for food lovers.

7. **Trippa alla Romana**

Roman-style tripe (the stomach lining of a cow) is slow-cooked in a tomato sauce with pecorino romano, garlic, and mint. It's a rich, hearty dish traditionally enjoyed by locals.

Why try it? For adventurous eaters, this dish represents the Roman tradition of using every part of the animal, creating a rich and flavorful meal from humble ingredients.

8. **Abbacchio alla Romana**

This dish comprises roast lamb, often marinated with garlic, rosemary, and olive oil, then slow-cooked until tender and juicy. It's typically served with potatoes.

Why try it? It's a favorite dish around Easter but is enjoyed year-round in Rome. The lamb is succulent and full of earthy flavors from the herbs.

9. **Supplì**

A popular Roman street food, supplì are deep-fried rice balls typically stuffed with mozzarella and seasoned with tomato sauce. The crispy exterior gives way to a gooey, cheesy center.

Why try it? Supplì are an indulgent snack or starter and are the Roman version of the more widely known Sicilian arancini.

10. **Coda alla Vaccinara**

A slow-cooked oxtail stew, simmered with tomatoes, celery, and wine. The oxtail is cooked until it's incredibly tender and flavorful.

Why try it? It's a hearty, traditional dish that reflects Rome's working-class roots, perfect for wintry days or for those wanting to experience authentic Roman comfort food.

11. **Gnocchi alla Romana**

Unlike the more common potato-based gnocchi, Roman gnocchi are made from semolina flour. The dough is shaped into discs, baked with butter and parmesan cheese, resulting in a golden, crispy top and a creamy center.

Why try it? This dish offers a different take on gnocchi, unique to Rome and rich with buttery, cheesy flavors.

12. **Maritozzo**

A traditional Roman pastry, maritozzo is a soft, sweet bun filled with whipped cream. Historically, it was often given to brides-to-be by their grooms.

Why try it? Maritozzo is a beloved Roman dessert, perfect for breakfast or as a sweet treat during a day of sightseeing.

13. **Puntarelle**

A type of chicory, puntarelle is a popular Roman salad ingredient, typically served with an anchovy, garlic, and vinegar dressing.

Why try it? Puntarelle has a distinctive crunch and a slightly bitter taste, perfectly balanced by the salty, tangy anchovy dressing, making it a must-try Roman side dish.

14. **Porchetta**

Although originally from the countryside outside of Rome, porchetta (roasted pork) is incredibly popular in Roman cuisine. It is seasoned with garlic, rosemary, and other herbs, then roasted until the skin is crispy and the meat is tender.

Why try it? Porchetta sandwiches are a common sight at Roman markets and food stalls, and they are delicious, savory, and satisfying.

15. **Tiramisu**

Although it originated in northern Italy, tiramisu is a favorite dessert in

Rome. It's made from layers of coffee-soaked ladyfingers, mascarpone cheese, and cocoa powder.

Why try it? Tiramisu is an iconic Italian dessert, and in Rome, you'll find excellent versions of this creamy, coffee-flavored delight.

16. **Bonus: Pizza al Taglio**

Pizza al taglio (pizza by the slice) is a Roman invention, where pizza is baked in large rectangular trays and sold by weight. Toppings can range from classic margherita to more elaborate combinations.

Why try it? It's a convenient and delicious way to enjoy pizza while exploring the city, with endless topping possibilities and a crispy yet chewy crust typical of Roman pizza.

Understanding Roman Meal Structure

To truly appreciate Roman cuisine, it helps to understand how locals approach their meals. A typical Roman meal might begin with antipasti (appetizers) like supplì or local cured meats, followed by a primo (first course) of pasta such as carbonara or amatriciana. The secondo (main course) often features meat or fish dishes like saltimbocca alla romana, accompanied by contorni (side dishes) such as puntarelle or carciofi alla romana.

Seasonal Considerations

Roman cuisine follows the rhythms of the seasons closely. Spring brings tender artichokes, perfect for carciofi alla romana and alla giudia. Summer sees light, fresh preparations, while autumn and winter welcome heartier dishes like coda alla vaccinara. Understanding these seasonal specialties helps visitors align their culinary explorations with Rome's natural bounty.

Street Food Culture

While Rome excels at formal dining, some of its most beloved foods are enjoyed on the go. Pizza al taglio, served in rectangular slices and sold by weight, represents Rome's practical approach to quick meals. Supplì, those perfectly crispy rice balls with molten cheese centers, offer a satisfying snack between sightseeing stops.

CHAPTER FIFTY-ONE

Best Coffee and Pastries in Rome: A Neighborhood Guide

A Taste of Tradition

The sweet side of Rome deserves special attention. From historic coffee houses to family-run bakeries, these establishments are essential to experiencing Roman daily life.

Trust me! Order a Cornetto con Crema,
the perfect Italian treat to start your day!

Pasticcerie and Coffee Near Campo de' Fiori

Roscioli Caffè Pasticceria (My favorite Pasticceria!). Address: Piazza Benedetto Cairoli, 16

A local favorite, Roscioli offers both a bakery and coffee shop experience. Known for its artisanal breads, pastries, and top-quality espressos, Roscioli is a must-stop for anyone visiting the Campo de' Fiori area. Don't miss their famous maritozzi (Roman cream buns) or their selection of cornetti, perfect with a cappuccino. Signature Item: Make sure and try their Maritozzo!!

Roscioli Mornings

Forno Campo de' Fiori. Address: Piazza Campo de' Fiori, 22

A historic bakery just off the famous Campo de' Fiori market, this spot is known for its pizza bianca but also serves excellent pastries and coffee.

Sant'Eustachio Il Caffè. Address: Piazza di Sant'Eustachio, 82

Famous for its signature creamy espresso, Sant'Eustachio has been serving coffee in Rome since 1938. It's a brilliant spot to enjoy a traditional Italian coffee alongside a pastry like a cornetto or a ciambella. I always buy coffee at Sant'Eustachio to bring home. When they ask if you want the coffee sweet just say "Yes!"

Pasticcerie and Coffee Near the Spanish Steps

Antico Caffè Greco. Address: Via dei Condotti, 86

Established in 1760, Antico Caffè Greco is one of Rome's oldest coffeehouses. It's famous for its classic espresso served in a charming historic setting.

Ciampini Roma. Address: Piazza di San Lorenzo in Lucina, 29

Known for its gelato and pastries, Ciampini offers a sophisticated atmosphere near the Spanish Steps. Whether it's a croissant in the morning or a sweet tart in the afternoon, their selection of treats and expertly made coffee will enhance any visit to the area.

Pasticceria D'Angelo. Address: Via della Croce, 10

A family-run pasticceria near the Spanish Steps, D'Angelo is known for its delicious variety of sweets, including tiramisu, cornetti, and cannoli.

Pasticcerie and Coffee Near the Vatican

Sciascia Caffè 1919. Address: Via Fabio Massimo, 80/A

Known for its exquisite espresso and vintage atmosphere, Sciascia Caffè is a hidden gem near the Vatican. It's a glorious spot for a quiet break with a traditional Italian pastry and a cup of their famous rich coffee.

Pasticceria Bonci. Address: Via della Meloria, 83

Famous for its artisan bread and pastries, Bonci is a favorite stop for those seeking high-quality baked goods near the Vatican. Their cakes and biscuits are top-notch, and their cornetti are perfect with an espresso for breakfast.

Pasticcerie and Coffee in Trastevere

Pasticceria Valzani. Address: Via del Moro, 37a

Valzani is a family-run pasticceria that has been serving up sweets since 1925. Famous for its traditional Roman pastries.

Bar San Calisto. Address: Piazza di San Calisto, 3

A classic Roman bar where you can enjoy coffee, pastries, and gelato.

CHAPTER FIFTY-TWO

Best Dining & Gelato in Rome: A Neighborhood Guide

Where to Eat in Rome

Rome's dining scene is as diverse as its neighborhoods, with each area offering its own interpretation of the city's beloved cuisine. From historic trattorias to modern bistros, here's your guide to finding exceptional meals throughout the Eternal City.

Near Piazza Navona

This historic piazza offers a perfect blend of tourist-friendly and authentically Roman dining options.

Da Francesco. Address: Piazza del Fico, 29

Known for its traditional Roman cuisine, Da Francesco is famous for its pizza and pasta dishes. It's a cozy, local favorite that draws both tourists and Romans for its authentic flavors and welcoming atmosphere.

Cul de Sac. Address: Piazza di Pasquino, 73

One of Rome's oldest wine bars, Cul de Sac offers a vast selection of Italian wines paired with regional dishes. Its cozy, informal setting makes it ideal for sampling local specialties like Roman-style tripe and pasta dishes.

Pizzeria Da Baffetto. Address: Via del Governo Vecchio, 114

A Roman institution, Da Baffetto is famous for its thin-crust pizzas. Be prepared for a lively, bustling atmosphere, as the restaurant is popular with both locals and visitors seeking classic Roman pizza.

Near the Spanish Steps

The elegant shopping district surrounding the Spanish Steps houses some of Rome's most refined dining establishments.
Il Gabriello. Address: Via Vittoria, 51

Il Gabriello is a hidden gem offering a refined take on traditional Roman cuisine. Known for its cozy, elegant ambiance, the restaurant serves dishes like tonnarelli cacio e pepe and fresh seafood.

Ristorante Nino. Address: Via Borgognona, 11

A Roman classic, Nino is a traditional trattoria offering Tuscan-influenced Roman dishes. Famous for its bistecca alla fiorentina and handmade pastas, it's a long-standing favorite near the Spanish Steps.

Hostaria Romana. Address: Via del Boccaccio, 1

This restaurant offers classic Roman dishes like cacio e pepe and saltimbocca. Known for its friendly service and lively atmosphere, Hostaria Romana provides a true Roman dining experience.

Near the Vatican

After visiting St. Peter's Basilica and the Vatican Museums, these nearby restaurants offer welcome respite and excellent cuisine.

Ristorante Arlu (this is my favorite in the area. I visit EVERY trip!). Address: Borgo Pio, 135

Located just a short walk from St. Peter's Basilica, Arlu is a family-run restaurant serving Roman classics with a modern twist. Known for its friendly service and cozy atmosphere, it offers fresh pasta, meat dishes, and excellent desserts.

La Zanzara. Address: Via Crescenzio, 84

A trendy bistro near the Vatican, La Zanzara offers a mix of traditional Italian dishes and creative cuisine. Popular with both locals and tourists, it's known for its lively ambiance, pizza, and regional Roman dishes.

Hostaria Dino e Toni. Address: Via Leone IV, 60

A classic Roman trattoria known for its generous portions and lively atmosphere. Dino e Toni serves traditional Roman dishes, such as carbonara, amatriciana, and hearty meat dishes, in a family-style setting.

Taverna Angelica. Address: Piazza Americo Capponi, 6

This elegant restaurant near the Vatican is known for its sophisticated Roman and Mediterranean cuisine. Taverna Angelica offers a seasonal menu that emphasizes fresh ingredients, including homemade pasta and seafood.

In Trastevere

This charming neighborhood across the Tiber River maintains its reputation for authentic Roman cuisine and lively atmosphere.

Da Enzo al 29 (My favorite in the area. Consistently delicious!). Address: Via dei Vascellari, 29

A small, family-run trattoria in Trastevere known for its authentic Roman cuisine. Da Enzo serves traditional dishes like carbonara, amatriciana, and oxtail, made with fresh, local ingredients. The cozy setting and friendly service make it a must-visit.

Osteria der Belli. Address: Piazza di Sant'Apollonia, 11A

A local favorite offering traditional Roman and Sardinian cuisine. Known for its fresh seafood and homemade pasta, Osteria der Belli is a charming spot to enjoy authentic Italian flavors in a relaxed setting.

Trattoria da Teo. Address: Piazza dei Ponziani, 7A

Famous for its seasonal dishes and traditional Roman fare, Trattoria da Teo is in a quieter part of Trastevere. Its menu includes fresh artichokes, homemade pasta, and daily specials, all served in a warm, rustic atmosphere.

Antica Trattoria Da Carlone. Address: Via della Luce, 5

A traditional Roman trattoria known for its rich and flavorful pasta dishes, especially the carbonara and cacio e pepe. The generous portions and friendly service make it a popular spot for both locals and visitors.

Tonnarello. Address: Via della Paglia, 1

One of the busiest and most beloved spots in Trastevere, Tonnarello serves classic Roman cuisine, with standout dishes like cacio e pepe and gnocchi. Its lively atmosphere and generous portions keep both tourists and locals coming back.

Near the Pantheon

The area surrounding Rome's most perfectly preserved ancient monument offers dining options as impressive as the architecture.

Armando al Pantheon. Address: Salita dei Crescenzi, 31

A historic restaurant just steps from the Pantheon, Armando al Pantheon offers traditional Roman dishes with a focus on quality ingredients. The menu includes classic Roman pastas and hearty meat dishes, all served in an intimate setting.

Da Fortunato al Pantheon. Address: Via del Pantheon, 55

Known for its elegant ambiance and excellent Roman cuisine, Da Fortunato al Pantheon has been serving guests for decades. The restaurant specializes in Roman classics like saltimbocca and amatriciana, and also offers a fine selection of wines.

Ristorante Alfredo alla Scrofa. Address: Via della Scrofa, 104

Famous for creating the original "Fettuccine Alfredo," this historic restaurant near the Pantheon is a must-visit for fans of classic Italian dishes. The elegant interior and timeless menu make it a popular choice for a special night out.

Il Bacaro. Address: Via degli Spagnoli, 27

A small, intimate restaurant offering a blend of Roman and Tuscan cuisine. Il Bacaro is known for its fresh, seasonal ingredients and cozy, romantic atmosphere. It's the go-to spot for a romantic dinner near the Pantheon.

Ristorante La Tavernetta 48. Address: Via degli Spagnoli, 48

A cozy and traditional Roman trattoria offering hearty Roman dishes like rigatoni alla carbonara, cacio e pepe, and saltimbocca. Known for its welcoming service and homey atmosphere, it's a superb choice for a classic Roman meal in the center of the city.

Top-Rated Gelato in Rome

Gelateria del Teatro. Address: Via dei Coronari, 65/66

Tucked along a charming cobblestone street near Piazza Navona, Gelateria del Teatro is a favorite for inventive, natural flavors like sage and raspberry, lavender and white peach, and rich dark chocolate. The gelato is made in-house behind a glass wall, so you can watch the artistry unfold as you order. The location and quality make this a standout stop.

Come il Latte. Address: Via Silvio Spaventa, 24/26

Located near Via XX Settembre, this creamy and elegant gelateria offers rich textures and premium ingredients. Known for its signature white and dark chocolate fountains, Come il Latte drizzles every cone or cup with melted chocolate. Flavors range from classics like pistachio and hazelnut to more indulgent varieties like ricotta with caramelized figs.

Otaleg. Address: Via di San Cosimato, 14A (Trastevere)

"Gelato" spelled backward, Otaleg lives up to its name with a creative approach to traditional recipes. The master gelataio here is renowned for precision and quality, creating flavors like pear and gorgonzola, zabaione, or licorice, alongside perfect versions of chocolate and fruit sorbets. Located in lively Trastevere, it's worth the walk for something truly unique.

CHAPTER FIFTY-THREE

Itineraries for Rome and Must-See Sights

Explore Rome at Your Own Pace

Rome is a city best discovered on foot, where every cobblestone street holds surprises. These itineraries are designed to maximize your time by grouping nearby sites together, minimizing travel time, and including strategic breaks. Whether you're here for 3, 5, or 8 nights, you'll experience Rome's spiritual and cultural treasures while walking efficiently between locations.

Three Perfect Days in Rome: An Insider's Guide

Day 1: Vatican Treasures & Prati Elegance

Start your Roman adventure early at St. Peter's Basilica, when morning light streams through Michelangelo's dome and the crowds are still sleeping. Enter through the lesser-known Vatican post office security line to skip the usual queues. Inside, make your Holy Door pilgrimage before admiring the Pietà's delicate beauty and Bernini's soaring Baldacchino.

Climb the dome early while temperatures are cool - the 551 steps reward you with breathtaking views over the Vatican gardens and Rome's sea of terracotta roofs. By afternoon, you're ready for the Vatican Museums (pre-book 2 p.m. tickets to dodge peak crowds). Take your time in the Raphael Rooms before the grand finale of the Sistine Chapel.

Exit through Porta Sant'Anna into Prati, where elegant art nouveau buildings house some of Rome's finest boutiques. As sunset approaches, wander the cobblestone lanes of Borgo Pio before dinner at intimate Ristorante Arlu. End your night capturing the magic of St. Peter's Square illuminated against the dark sky.

Day 2: Ancient Rome's Stones & Jewish Heritage

Greet Rome's grande dame, the Colosseum, right as she wakes (8:30 a.m. entry recommended). Let the morning light play on ancient stones as you explore the arena where gladiators once fought. The Roman Forum naturally beckons next - follow in Caesar's footsteps before ascending Capitoline Hill for panoramic views.

By lunchtime, the Jewish Ghetto calls with its tempting restaurants and fascinating history. Pause at the whimsical Turtle Fountain before discovering Rome's layers at the Basilica of San Clemente, where each underground level reveals another century. If your feet protest, bus 87 connects these sites seamlessly.

Cross the scenic Ponte Sisto at sunset for dinner in lively Trastevere, but first, join the locals for aperitivo around Campo de' Fiori's vibrant market square.

Day 3: Sacred Heart of Rome

Begin at the Basilica of St. Mary Major when its golden mosaics catch the morning light. A short walk brings you to St. John Lateran, the Pope's official cathedral, and the adjacent Holy Stairs - climbed by pilgrims on their knees for centuries.

After lunch near the perfectly preserved Pantheon, embark on a walking loop connecting Rome's most beautiful piazzas and churches. Admire Bernini's fountains in Piazza Navona, peek into Sant'Agnese's baroque splendor, and marvel at Sant'Andrea della Valle's frescoed dome. Time your arrival at the Aventine Hill's famous keyhole for sunset views of St. Peter's perfectly framed.

End your Roman holiday with a memorable dinner near Piazza Navona before a final passeggiata through the illuminated historic center, where every corner tells a 2,000-year-old story.

Pro Tips:

- Book "skip-the-line" tickets for major sites

- Carry water and wear comfortable shoes

- Many churches require covered shoulders and knees

- Early morning and evening hours offer the best light for photos and fewer crowds

Five Days in Rome: A Spiritual & Cultural Journey

Day 1: Sacred Heart of the Vatican

Begin your journey at St. Peter's Basilica when the morning light first touches its dome. At 7 AM, you'll have this sacred space almost to yourself. Make your Holy Door pilgrimage before descending into the crypt to visit the papal tombs. The dome climb offers spectacular morning views, but the genuine treasure comes with a pre-booked Scavi tour taking you deep beneath the basilica to the ancient necropolis.

After lunch, enter the Vatican Museums at 2 p.m. when tour groups thin out. Save time by exiting through the Sistine Chapel directly to St. Peter's (a route usually reserved for tour groups). Pro tip: art at the Cipro metro station entrance and end near St. Peter's, avoiding backtracking.

As evening falls, explore the atmospheric Borgo streets before dining near Castel Sant'Angelo, where the fortress lights create a magical backdrop.

Day 2: Eastern Basilicas' Sacred Path

Start at St. John Lateran, Rome's cathedral and the Pope's official seat. Visit the ancient baptistry and climb the Holy Stairs on your knees as pilgrims have done for centuries. Follow the tree-shaded Via Carlo Felice to the Basilica of the Holy Cross in Jerusalem, home to precious relics.

Continue to St. Mary Major's glittering mosaics before discovering Santa Prassede, a hidden jewel housing stunning Byzantine art. Bus 40 Express offers an easy return to the center. Spend your evening in charming Monti, where local life unfolds beneath Trajan's illuminated column.

Day 3: Rome's Layers Revealed

Journey along the ancient Appian Way to the Catacombs of San Callisto when they first open, exploring Rome's early Christian history in the quiet morning hours. Bus 118 from Circo Massimo makes the journey simple.

At San Clemente Basilica, descend through three levels of Roman history, from medieval church to early Christian basilica to ancient Roman temple. Continue to the Colosseum and Forum, following the paths of emperors to Capitol Hill.

Watch the sunset paint the sky from Michelangelo's perfect Campidoglio plaza before dining in the atmospheric Jewish Ghetto.

Day 4 (Rome Option): Sacred Heart of Historic Rome

Begin at the Pantheon when early light streams through its oculus, then discover Santa Maria Sopra Minerva's hidden Michelangelo and Sant'Ignazio's trompe l'oeil ceiling. Thread through narrow, shaded alleys connecting Piazza Navona's baroque churches to the Chiesa Nuova.

Cross the Tiber for an evening in Trastevere, culminating at the golden mosaics of Santa Maria in Trastevere. Dine on the quiet back streets where locals still gather.

Day 4 (Day Trip Option): Orvieto's Hilltop Majesty

Venture north by train to Orvieto, a stunning Umbrian town perched on volcanic rock and rich in medieval charm. Take the funicular up from the train station to reach the town center. Begin with the awe-inspiring Duomo di Orvieto, adorned with golden mosaics and frescoes by Luca Signorelli that predate Michelangelo's Sistine Chapel.

Wander cobblestone alleys, explore Etruscan caves beneath the city, and enjoy a relaxed lunch with sweeping views of the Umbrian countryside. Don't miss the Pozzo di San Patrizio, a double-helix well that spirals 175 feet deep.

Orvieto is ideal for travelers who want a taste of small-town Italy without an overnight stay. Direct trains from Roma Termini make this an easy, enriching day trip.

Day 5: Art, Beauty & Reflection

Reserve early entry to the Borghese Gallery to admire Bernini's masterpieces in peace. Stroll the Villa Borghese gardens to Santa Maria della Vittoria for Bernini's transcendent St. Teresa.

Climb the Spanish Steps to Trinità dei Monti before indulging in Via Condotti's elegant shops. End your pilgrimage with dinner near the Trevi Fountain, followed by a night walk through Rome's illuminated heart.

If you have the energy left head to Piazza del Popolo and the Basilica di Santa Maria del Popolo.

Essential Tips:

- Book Scavi tour and Borghese Gallery months ahead

- Dress modestly for churches (covered shoulders/knees)

- Carry water and wear comfortable walking shoes

- Many sites close during lunch (12:30-3:30)

- Early morning and evening offer best light for photos

- Consider purchasing the Roma Pass which offers transport and some museum entries.

Eight Days in Rome: A Deep Exploration

[Days 1-5 as previously detailed, then continue with:]

Day 6 (Rome Option): Art Treasures & Hidden Churches

Start at the Capitoline Museums when they open, exploring the world's oldest public museums. Descend to the atmospheric Mamertine Prison where Saints Peter and Paul were held, then climb the steep steps to Santa Maria in Aracoeli's gilded interior.

The afternoon unfolds in the opulent Palazzo Doria Pamphilj, where aristocratic rooms house masterpieces still in their original setting. Follow Via dei Coronari's antique shops to three remarkable churches: San Luigi dei Francesi's dramatic Caravaggios, Sant'Agostino's hidden Raphael, and the riverside elegance of San Giovanni dei Fiorentini.

End your day with dinner amid Campo de' Fiori's evening bustle, followed by a moonlit stroll through the Jewish Ghetto's quiet lanes.

Day 6 (Day Trip Option): Tivoli's Villas and Waterfalls

Escape the city for the day with a quick trip east to Tivoli, a hilltop town famous for its spectacular villas and cascading gardens. Start with Villa d'Este, where Renaissance fountains dance among manicured hedges and shaded terraces. The sound of rushing water and cool mist offer a refreshing contrast to Rome's heat.

Continue to Villa Adriana, Emperor Hadrian's vast countryside retreat, a masterpiece of Roman engineering and imagination. Wander among ancient pools, libraries, and mosaics in a tranquil setting of olive groves and ruins. If time allows, visit Villa Gregoriana, where forest trails lead to gorges and waterfalls.

Return to Rome in time for a quiet dinner in Monti or Trastevere. Tivoli is reachable by regional train from Roma Tiburtina or via a guided tour.

Day 7: Papal Retreat & Wine Country

Escape to Castel Gandolfo, the Pope's summer residence, on an early train. Tour the Apostolic Palace's state rooms and meander through manicured papal gardens with stunning lake views. Pro tip: Book the Vatican Museums' combined ticket that includes train travel.

Venture to nearby Albano Laziale for lunch in a family trattoria before wine tasting in Frascati's historic cellars. Consider a detour to Ariccia, where the scent of roasting porchetta fills medieval streets. Return to Rome for dinner along the Tiber, where twinkling lights reflect on the river.

Day 8: Secret Rome

Begin on the Aventine Hill, visiting its trio of peaceful churches before discovering Rome's best views through the famous keyhole. Stroll through the Orange Garden and Rose Garden (blooming May-June), then descend the picturesque Clivo di Rocca Savella toward the river.

Explore Testaccio's vibrant food scene. This authentic neighborhood was built atop Monte Testaccio, an artificial hill composed of millions of discarded ancient Roman amphora shards from the city's bustling trade. It now offers Rome's best market lunch.

In the afternoon and evening, lose yourself in Trastevere's cobblestone labyrinth, where golden lanterns cast their glow on centuries-old trattorias and the air fills with laughter and aromas of Roman cuisine. Cap your Roman adventure with a moonlit stroll across ancient bridges spanning the Tiber, watching the city's eternal lights dance on its dark waters, a farewell worthy of Rome's timeless magic.

Trevi Fountain

Essential Planning Tips:

- See Securing Tickets for Rome's Sights (Chapter 54).

- Make lunch and dinner reservations along your route so you don't get desperate and eat at a tourist trap.

- Use metro, bus, or taxi (FreeNow app allows you to order a taxi to your location) for longer distances.

- Schedule indoor activities 12:00 to 3:00 p.m. during the summer. Start early morning/evening for outdoor sites in summer.

- Carry water bottle - Rome has free fountains everywhere, and the water is drinkable.

CHAPTER FIFTY-FOUR

Securing Tickets for Rome's Busiest Sites

A Strategic Guide

R ome's most iconic sites draw millions of visitors each year. The key to a successful visit lies in strategic planning and advance booking. There's nothing more frustrating than spending precious vacation hours standing in preventable queues, so let's explore how to navigate Rome's busiest attractions efficiently.

The Vatican Complex

The Vatican Museums and Sistine Chapel represent one of Rome's most visited attractions, requiring careful planning to avoid lengthy wait times. While St. Peter's Basilica offers free entry, the museums require tickets that should be purchased well in advance through the official Vatican Museum's website (www.museivaticani.va).

Visiting the Vatican Scavi, the Necropolis beneath St. Peter's Basilica, is one of the most extraordinary and exclusive experiences in Rome. This sacred underground site is believed to contain the tomb of Saint Peter, making it a place of profound spiritual and historical significance. The tour takes you beneath the basilica, through ancient Roman burial chambers and mausoleums, culminating at the humble grave marked as Peter's resting place.

Access is highly restricted: only about 250 people per day are allowed, and advance reservations are mandatory through the Vatican Excavations Office. Visitors must be at least 15 years old, and appropriate modest dress is required (covered shoulders and knees). The tour is led by an official Vatican guide, lasts approximately 90 minutes, and offers a deeply moving insight into early Christian history and the foundations of the Catholic Church. It is not included with standard basilica entry and must be booked separately, often several months in advance.

https://www.basilicasanpietro.va/en/products/the-necropolis

The Colosseum Complex

As of October 2023, visiting the Colosseum requires more planning than ever before. All tickets must now be nominative, meaning they're tied to a specific visitor's identity. This measure prevents unauthorized reselling but requires careful attention during booking.

The basic ticket (approximately €16) includes access to the Colosseum, Roman Forum, and Palatine Hill, valid for 24 hours from first use. Purchase tickets through the official Parco Colosseo website or trusted vendors, and remember that identity checks are mandatory at entry. Name changes are permitted once, up to seven days before your visit.

The Borghese Gallery

This treasure trove of Renaissance and Baroque art requires a different approach. With strictly limited two-hour visiting slots, tickets often sell out weeks in advance. Book directly through the gallery's official website (www.galleriaborghese.beniculturali.it) and consider joining a guided tour to make the most of your limited time. The museum's masterpieces by Caravaggio, Bernini, and Raphael deserve careful planning to ensure you don't miss this spectacular collection.

Historic Sites and Landmarks

Both the Pantheon and Trevi Fountain now require tickets during peak seasons. Book Pantheon tickets in advance on the official website to skip long lines. For the Spanish Steps, entry is free, but visiting early in the morning or late at night offers the best experience with fewer crowds.

Tour Guides versus Self Guided Tours

While self-guided walking tours offer flexibility, a local guide can add rich insight, historical context, and access to hidden gems. Many visitors find that hiring a guide, especially for places like the Roman Forum or Vatican City, enhances the experience. Booking in advance is recommended during busy seasons. Audio tours and maps are useful, but a guide can bring Rome's layered history to life. Below are some Rome-based tour operators offering historical, cultural, food, and art tours:

1. **Walks of Italy:** Specializes in small group tours with expert guides, covering key sites like the Vatican, Colosseum, and more. Website: www.walksofitaly.com

2. **Rome Private Guides**: Offers private and small group tours with licensed guides, focusing on personalized experiences in Rome's major landmarks. www.romeprivateguides.com

3. **The Roman Guy:** A popular operator providing guided tours of iconic sites such as the Vatican Museums and the Colosseum. Website: www.theromanguy.com

4. **LivItaly Tours:** Known for intimate, small-group and private tours, LivItaly covers everything from the Vatican to immersive food experiences. Website: www.livitaly.com

5. **Angel Tours:** Provides small group tours with a personal touch and even special art tours. www.angeltours.eu

Each of these tour operators offers unique experiences that cater to different interests, from food and art to history and religion.

Documentation Requirements:

Carry valid ID matching ticket names (especially for the Colosseum)

By planning and booking strategically, you can transform what could be hours of waiting into enriching experiences at Rome's magnificent sites. Remember that during the Jubilee Year, religious sites will see increased pilgrim traffic, making planning even more crucial for a smooth and meaningful visit.

CHAPTER FIFTY-FIVE

Accommodation Detail

Stay in Style: A Complete Guide to Finding the Perfect Area and Hotel for Your Unforgettable Roman Adventure

Rome's magic begins with choosing the right location. The perfect neighborhood can transform your experience from a typical tourist visit into an authentic Roman adventure. Each area has its own character, and I'll guide you through the best spots to base yourself during your stay.

Understanding Rome's Hotel Options

When searching for the perfect stay in Rome, location and comfort level are key considerations. While maps can be overwhelming due to Rome's sprawling neighborhoods, platforms like Booking.com for hotels and Airbnb for apartments offer user-friendly tools to narrow your search by area and budget.

Hotel Star Classifications

To help you choose the right accommodation, here's what each hotel rating typically offers:

One-Star Hotels provide basic, clean accommodations with essential amenities and daily housekeeping. These budget-friendly options are ideal for travelers who primarily need a comfortable place to sleep.

Two-Star Hotels step up the comfort level with more spacious rooms, en-suite bathrooms, and basic technology like TVs and phones. Many offer Wi-Fi and simple breakfast service, perfect for budget-conscious travelers seeking added convenience.

Three-Star Hotels strike an excellent balance between comfort and value. Expect comfortable rooms with work spaces, on-site dining options, 24-hour reception, and amenities like room service and parking. Some properties may feature fitness centers or pools, making them ideal for travelers wanting reliable comfort without luxury pricing.

Four-Star Hotels deliver upscale experiences with spacious, well-appointed rooms and premium amenities. These properties typically feature multiple dining venues, extensive facilities including spas and fitness centers, and enhanced services like concierge and valet parking. They're perfect for travelers seeking luxury touches without five-star prices.

Five-Star Hotels represent the pinnacle of hospitality, offering impeccable service and world-class amenities. Guests enjoy luxurious rooms with high-end furnishings, gourmet restaurants, extensive facilities, and personalized services like butler assistance. These properties cater to those seeking an exceptional experience where every detail is carefully curated.

Beyond the traditional star system, you'll also find ultra-luxury and boutique properties that offer unique experiences, often in exclusive settings or historic buildings.

Recommended Hotels by Area

Piazza Navona Area (Personal Favorite)

This historic center location offers easy access to Rome's main attractions. The five-star Hotel Raphael impresses with its eco-friendly approach and stunning rooftop views, while the four-star Hotel Genio provides classic Roman elegance.

For a more intimate experience, the Navona Theater Hotel offers contemporary comfort at three-star pricing – I can personally vouch for its charm from my recent stay.

Hotel Raphael – Relais & Châteaux (5 stars). Address: Largo Febo, 2

A luxury eco-friendly hotel offering an impressive rooftop terrace with panoramic views of the city. The hotel features elegant rooms suites with designer furnishings.

Hotel Genio (4 stars). Address: Via Giuseppe Zanardelli 28

Located right in the center of Rome Hotel Genio offers classical Roman architecture and a rooftop terrace with stunning views of Piazza Navona and St. Peter's Basilica. This elegant hotel is a fantastic option for travelers wanting proximity to Rome's most famous piazzas and landmarks.

Navona Theater Hotel (3 stars). Address: Vicolo dei Granari 3

**This is where I stayed my last visit. It is very nice. This boutique 3-star hotel is a cozy and modern accommodation option in the centro storico. Its contemporary design and convenient location just 1 minute from Piazza Navona make it ideal for visitors looking for style and comfort without breaking the bank.

Spanish Steps Area

The area around the Spanish Steps combines historic elegance with premier shopping opportunities. The five-star Hotel d'Inghilterra Roma embodies refined luxury, housed in a historic building just steps from Via Condotti's designer boutiques. For a more intimate experience, Hotel Condotti offers four-star boutique charm with personalized service. Budget-conscious travelers will appreciate Hotel Scalinata di Spagna, a charming three-star property offering spectacular city views from its position atop the Spanish Steps.

Hotel d'Inghilterra Roma–Starhotels Collezione (5 stars). Address: Via Bocca di Leone, 14

Steeped in history and sophistication, this elegant retreat sits at the heart of Rome's most coveted address, where the Spanish Steps meet the fashion-filled

Via Condotti. Behind its storied walls, timeless Roman grandeur mingles with contemporary luxury, creating an oasis for discerning travelers who dream of stepping out their door into the city's most glamorous shopping district and iconic landmarks.

Hotel Condotti (4 stars). Address: Via Mario de' Fiori, 37

This charming boutique hotel is located right by the Spanish Steps and Via Condotti, one of the best shopping streets in Rome. It offers an intimate atmosphere with modern comforts and personalized service, ideal for visitors wanting both comfort and proximity to major sites.

Hotel Scalinata di Spagna (3 stars). Address: Piazza della Trinità dei Monti, 17

This quaint 3-star hotel offers stunning views over Rome and is located just steps from the top of the Spanish Steps. Known for its cozy atmosphere, Scalinata di Spagna offers a warm and comfortable stay with all the major landmarks within walking distance.

Vatican Area

Staying near the Vatican provides easy access to St. Peter's Basilica and the Vatican Museums while offering a more residential atmosphere. The Starhotels Michelangelo Rome stands out as a sophisticated four-star option, artfully blending modern comfort with traditional Roman style just minutes from St. Peter's Square. For travelers seeking value, Hotel Paolo II provides a peaceful three-star retreat in a historic building, offering tranquility while remaining close to major attractions.

Starhotels Michelangelo Rome (4 stars). Address: Via della Stazione di S. Pietro, 14

Just a few minutes' walk from St. Peter's Basilica, Starhotels Michelangelo combines modern comfort with traditional Roman style.

Hotel Paolo II (3 stars). Address: Via Paolo II, 3

A charming, budget-friendly option, Hotel Paolo II offers modern rooms in a peaceful area near the Vatican. In a historic building, it provides a quiet retreat from the hustle and bustle while being just minutes from St. Peter's Square.

Trastevere District

Trastevere captures Rome's bohemian spirit with its cobblestone streets and lively atmosphere. The four-star Donna Camilla Savelli Hotel, housed in a converted 17th-century convent, offers an oasis of calm with its serene garden and elegant rooms. Hotel Santa Maria provides a quintessential Trastevere experience at the three-star level, featuring a charming courtyard garden perfect for morning coffee or evening aperitivos (happy hours). For contemporary style, Hotel Ripa Roma offers modern design and spacious accommodations, ideal for those who appreciate updated comforts in this historic neighborhood.

Donna Camilla Savelli Hotel (4 stars). Address: Via Garibaldi 7

Housed in a 17th-century former convent this beautiful 4-star hotel offers a serene garden.

Hotel Santa Maria (3 stars). Address: Vicolo del Piede 2

A cozy and charming 3-star hotel Hotel Santa Maria offers a peaceful escape with a beautiful courtyard garden in the heart of Trastevere. Its warm atmosphere and personalized service make it an ideal retreat for couples or families.

Hotel Ripa Roma (4 stars). Address: Via degli Orti di Trastevere 3

A modern hotel in the lively Trastevere district Hotel Ripa Roma offers contemporary design with spacious rooms. It's well-suited for travelers looking for a stylish and comfortable stay with easy access to Trastevere's vibrant dining and nightlife.

Pantheon Area

Staying near the Pantheon puts you in the heart of ancient Rome with easy access to major landmarks. The Grand Hotel De La Minerve delivers five-star luxury and spectacular rooftop views in a historic setting. The three-star Albergo del Senato has earned a reputation for exceptional service and unbeatable views directly facing the Pantheon. Similarly positioned, Hotel Abruzzi offers comfortable three-star accommodations with the bonus of waking up to one of Rome's most iconic monuments.

Albergo del Senato (3 stars). Address: Piazza della Rotonda, 73

A classic Roman hotel with an unbeatable location directly in front of the Pantheon. Albergo del Senato offers elegant rooms, a rooftop terrace, and traditional charm, perfect for those looking to stay in the heart of historic Rome.

Grand Hotel De La Minerve (5 stars). Address: Piazza della Minerva, 69

A luxury 5-star hotel offering a perfect blend of classic elegance and modern amenities. Located just steps from the Pantheon, this historic hotel boasts a rooftop terrace with panoramic views, ideal for travelers seeking a lavish experience.

Hotel Abruzzi (3 stars). Address: Piazza della Rotonda, 69

Offering stunning views of the Pantheon from many rooms, this charming 3-star hotel is perfect for those wanting a central location. Perfect for travelers who desire to wake up to Rome's iconic sites.

Accommodation Options in Italy

#1. Hotels

Best for:

- Travelers seeking traditional hospitality services

- Those preferring reliable amenities and 24/7 reception

- Short-term stays and city breaks

- Business travelers

Key booking platforms:

- Booking.com: Largest selection of Italian hotels

- Hotels.com: Offers loyalty rewards and frequent deals

- Expedia.com: Good for package deals with flights

#2. Private Rooms, Apartments, B&Bs

Types available:

- Family-run B&Bs: Common in residential neighborhoods

- Converted historic properties

- Modern guesthouses

- Boutique B&Bs in city centers

- Rooms in traditional Italian homes

Popular platforms:

- Booking.com: Verified reviews and secure booking

- BedandBreakfast.com: Specialized B&B listings

- Airbnb: Largest variety of apartments

- VRBO: Focus on entire properties

#3. Rural Accommodations

Agriturismo

For Agriturismo experiences, guests can immerse themselves in authentic Italian farming traditions through olive oil production, wine making, and hands-on pasta making classes. Many properties offer guided farm tours where visitors can interact with animals and participate in seasonal activities like grape or olive harvests. Traditional cheese making demonstrations provide insight into artisanal production methods passed down through generations.

Winery Stays

At Italian winery accommodations, visitors can enjoy intimate wine tasting sessions featuring estate-produced wines, often paired with local specialties. Guided vineyard tours explain the terroir and viticulture practices unique to each region. Many estates offer behind-the-scenes demonstrations of the wine-making process from harvest to bottling. Evening experiences typically include gourmet dining featuring regional cuisine paired with estate wines. Educational programs range from informal tastings to structured courses on wine appreciation, viticulture, and the history of Italian wine making.

Booking platforms:

- Agriturismo.it: Specialized in farm stays

- ItalyFarmStay: Curated rural experiences

- Direct booking through individual properties

#4. Hostels

Hostels offer budget-friendly accommodations, often with shared rooms and communal facilities. They're great for solo travelers looking to meet others.

Hostelworld: Largest hostel database

Hostelling International: Focus on quality standards

#5. Campsites

Italy has many campsites for outdoor enthusiasts, ranging from basic to well-equipped sites with amenities like pools and restaurants.

Eurocampings: Comprehensive campsite database

ACSI: Camping card discounts

Booking Accommodations for Festivals

Book Early: If you're planning to attend a festival, aim to book your accommodation at least 6 months in advance when possible. This is crucial for securing the best locations and rates.

Central Locations: Getting a spot in the center of town is key for fully immersing yourself in the festival atmosphere. These prime locations fill up quickly, so early booking is essential.

Festival Periods: Plan to stay more than one night. Be especially proactive about booking for summer festivals and other popular events. These periods see a significant influx of visitors.

Local Insights: Some accommodations may offer special packages or insights for festival attendees. Don't hesitate to reach out directly and ask about any festival-related perks or information they might offer.

By planning and securing your accommodation early, you'll be well-positioned to fully enjoy Italy's vibrant festival culture without the stress of last-minute booking scrambles.

References & Resources

CHAPTER FIFTY-SIX

Festival Calendar

Dates, Cities, and Celebrations Across Rome and Lazio

January

January 17: Festa di Sant'Antonio Abate in Tivoli

February

February/March: Carnivale in Ronciglione

March

Last week in March: Fiera Nazionale in Grottaferrata

March 21: Festa di San Benedetto in Montecassino

Varies March/April: Holy Week and Easter

April

April, 2nd weekend: Sagra del Carciofo in Ladispoli

April 21: Natale di Roma in Rome

April 28: Festa di Santa Fermina in Civitavecchia

May

May: Cicero Festival in Arpino

May 1: Festa di Sant'Ambrogio Martire in Ferentino

May, first two weeks: Festa della Madonna delle Grazie in Nettuno

May 26-27: Festa di San Filippo Neri in Rome

June

June: Infiorata in Genzano di Roma

June, first Sunday: Sagra delle Fragole (Strawberry) in Nemi

June: Festa del Corpus Domini in Rome

June 29: Festa di San Pietro e San Paolo in Rome

End of June: Frascati International Festival of the Villas of Tusculum

July

July, first two weeks: Liri Blues Festival in Isola del Liri

July, Saturday after July 16: Festa dei Noantri in Trastavere

July, last Sunday: Sagra delle Pesche (Peach) in Castel Gandolfo

August

August 5: Festa della Madonna della Neve in Rome

August 15: FestaFusion Roma in Rome

August 16: FestaFusion Rocca Priora in Rocca Priora

September

September 3: Macchina di Santa Rosa in Viterbo

September, first weekend: Sagra della Porchetta in Ariccia

September, third weekend: Sagra del Pane Casareccio IGP and Del Santo Padrono in Genzano di Roma

September 26: Festa di San Nilo in Grottaferrata

September, last week: Sagra del Fungo in Bracciano

October

October, first Sunday: Sagra dell'Uva in Marino

October, 10 days mid-October: Festa di Cinema in Rome

October, third weekend: Festa Internazionale del Circo in Latina

October, third weekend: Sagra della Castagna in Rocca di Papa

October, last week: Festa della Cortesia in Frascati

November

November two weekends: Sagra del Tartufo in Campoli Appennino

November 9: Festa della Dedicazione della Basilica di San Giovanni in Laterano in Rome

November, first three weeks: Roma Jazz Festival in Rome

December

December 8: Festa dell'Immacolata in Rome

December 8 to January 6: Christmas Decorations and Markets in Rome & Lazio

CHAPTER FIFTY-SEVEN

Alphabetical Index of Locations with Events

Ariccia, Sagra della Porchetta, September

Arpino, Cicero Festival, May

Bracciano, Sagra del Fungo, September

Campoli Appennino, Sagra del Tartufo, November

Castel Gandolfo, Sagra delle Pesche (Peach), July

Civitavecchia, Festa di Santa Fermina, April

Ferentino, Festa di Sant'Ambrogio Martire, May

Frascati, International Festival of the Villas of Tusculum, June

Frascati, Festa della Cortesia, October

Genzano di Roma Infiorata, June

Genzano di Roma, Sagra del Pane, September

Grottaferrata, Festa di San Nilo, September

Grottaferrata, Fiera Nazionale, March

Isola del Liri, Liri Blues Festival, July

Ladispoli, Sagra del Carciofo (Artichoke), April

Latina, Festa Internazionale del Circo, October

Rome, Christmas, December

Marino, Sagra dell'Uva (Grape), October

Montecassino, Festa di San Benedetto, March

Nemi, Sagra delle Fagole (Strawberry), June

Nettuno, Festa della Madonna delle Grazie, May

Rocca di Papa, Sagra della Castagna, October

Rocca Priora, FestaFusion Rocca Priora, August

Rome, Festa di San Filippo Neri, May

Rome, Festa del Corpus Domini, June

Rome, Festa della Madonna della Neve, August

Rome, FestaFusion Roma, August

Rome, Festa di Cinema, October

Rome, Festa della Dedicazione della Basilica di San Giovanni in Laterano, November

Rome, Roma Jazz Festival, November

Rome, Festa dell'Immacolata, December

Rome, Natale di Roma, April

Rome, Holy Week and Easter, April

CHAPTER FIFTY-EIGHT

Glossary of Key Terms

A Bit of Italian & Key Words to Enhance Your Journey

Basilica: A term derived from the official building of a Greek magistrate, Basileus. In antiquity, it was a roofed building with a double colonnade used for law courts, assemblies, or markets. In the Christian era, it meant a characteristic type of church building with a high nave and two or four aisles. Usually oriented to the west. basilicas usually have windows on the elevated part of the walls (clerestory) where the roof meets the wall. A basilica is the shape of Catholic churches since the 4th century. The Pope has given a basilica special privileges as a major church.

Benedictines: St. Benedict of Nursia (c. 480-547) founded the oldest order of Western monks. 529AD. The Benedictine rules formed the basis of western monasticism. The primary task was to cultivate liturgy and prayer. Physical labor, scholarly and artistic work supplemented this.

Blue Flag Beaches: The Blue Flag is an international certification awarded to beaches, marinas, and sustainable boating tourism operators that meet high environmental and safety standards. It is granted by the Foundation for Environmental Education (FEE), a non-profit organization, and is recognized worldwide as a symbol of clean and well-managed beaches.

Brotherhoods: The brotherhoods, or "confraternite" in Italian, are religious lay organizations that play a crucial role in preserving and celebrating local traditions of the region. These brotherhoods have deep historical roots, often dating back centuries, and are named after various saints or religious concepts.

Byzantine architecture: This style relates to the architecture developed in the Byzantine or Eastern Roman Empire. Characterized by enormous domes, mosaics, rounded arches, and spires.

Campanile: A bell tower of an Italian church. Sometimes a watchtower for the town, the bell tower, grew in importance during the Renaissance.

Centro Storico: The historic center of town.

Chiesa di: Church of followed usually by a saint's name.

Chiesa Madre: Mother church or the most important church in town. This is not a duomo or cathedral.

Cinquecento: A term shortened in Italian from mille-cinquecento. It means the 1500s or the 16th century.

Cistercians: The Cistercians are a monastic Catholic order that has its origins in the reformed Benedictine monastery of Citaeux founded in 1098. The new order set out to achieve fully the ideal from the Rule of St. Benedict.

Confraternite: Religious brotherhoods composed of laypeople dedicated to prayer, charity, and community service, especially within Catholic traditions. Confraternities in Italy, including those in Sicily, are often responsible for organizing and participating in religious processions during major festivals. During events such as the Festa di Santa Rosalia in Palermo, the confraternities don traditional garments, typically long tunics and capes, carrying banners and religious symbols. They play a key role in maintaining the solemnity and spiritual focus of the event, embodying centuries-old traditions of faith and devotion.

Consul: A Roman consul was one of the highest-ranking elected officials in the Roman Republic. After the overthrow of the Roman monarchy, the Romans introduced the office of consul around 509 BC. The Roman Republic elected two consuls each year to serve jointly for a one-year term. They held significant power and responsibility.

Corpus Domini: Corpus Domini is the Latin term for the Solemnity of the Most Holy Body and Blood of Christ, a major feast in the Catholic Church. Commonly referred to as Corpus Christi in English, this celebration honors the real presence of Jesus Christ in the Eucharist. It is traditionally celebrated on the Thursday after Trinity Sunday or, in many places, moved to the following Sunday to encourage broader participation.

Corso & Via: Street.

DOC: DOC stands for Denominazione di Origine Controllata (Designation of Controlled Origin) in Italian. It is a quality assurance label for Italian wines, cheeses, and other agricultural products. This classification guarantees that the product meets strict production standards and comes from a specific geographic area.

Duomo or Cattedrale: These are all referred to as the town's Cathedral but they have different significance. Cathedral means the main church of the diocese where the bishop's seat is located. Duomo is the Italian word for cathedral, but both Duomo and Cattedrale are used when seeking the bishop's seat in Italy.

Municipio: Town hall or city hall.

Piazza: Square, as an element of urban layout.

Reformation: A major religious movement from within the Catholic Church that began in Germany in 1517 at the instigation of Martin Luther. His challenge of the practices and doctrines of the Roman Catholic Church ultimately led to the establishment of the Protestant churches.

Romanesque: A term used to describe forms of Roman architecture such as rounded arches, columns, capitals, and vaults that were used in buildings in the early Middle Ages. The term Romanesque covers the period from about 1000 to the point when Gothic began.

CHAPTER FIFTY-NINE

Patron Saints of Lazio in Alphabetical Order

The Saint Protectors of the Cities in this Guide

S ant'Ambrogio Martire (Saint Ambrose)

Saint Ambrose is the patron saint of Ferentino, Italy. He was a soldier in the Roman army who was martyred for his Christian faith in the 4th century during the persecutions under Emperor Diocletian. According to tradition, he endured several tortures while steadfastly refusing to renounce Christianity, and was ultimately beheaded in Ferentino around 304 AD. His relics are preserved and venerated in the Cathedral of Ferentino (Duomo di Ferentino), and his feast day is celebrated on August 1st with great solemnity in the city, including religious processions and civic celebrations.

This Sant'Ambrogio should not be confused with the more widely known Saint Ambrose of Milan (Sant'Ambrogio di Milano) who was a bishop and doctor of the Church. The saints' following has been important to the local identity and religious traditions of Ferentino since medieval times.

Sant'Antonio Abate (Saint Anthony the Abbot)

Also known as Anthony the Great, he was one of the first Christian monks and is considered the founder and patriarch of desert monasticism. Born in Egypt around 251 AD, he gave away his inheritance to live an ascetic life in the desert. He is often portrayed with a pig and a bell, and is the patron saint of animals, skin diseases, and firefighters, with his feast day on January 17.

San Benedetto (St. Benedict)

San Benedetto of Montecassino (c. 480–547) was an Italian monk, theologian, and founder of Western monasticism. Born in Norcia, he withdrew from the chaos of Roman society to live as a hermit in Subiaco, where his piety attracted disciples. Around 529, he established the Abbey of Montecassino, a center of religious life and learning. There, he wrote the Rule of Saint Benedict, a guide for monastic life emphasizing prayer, work (ora et labora), and community living, which became the foundation of Benedictine spirituality and influenced monastic practices worldwide.

San Filippo Neri (Saint Philip Neri)

Known as the "Apostle of Rome" and the "Humorous Saint," Philip Neri lived in the 16th century during the Counter-Reformation. He founded the Congregation of the Oratory and was known for his joyful spirituality and practical jokes that taught spiritual lessons. His heart was physically enlarged by divine love, verified upon his death, and he is the patron saint of joy and humor.

San Giovanni (Saint John)

One of Jesus' closest disciples and the author of the Gospel of John, three epistles, and the Book of Revelation. He was the only apostle who didn't forsake Jesus during his crucifixion and was entrusted with the care of Mary. Known as the "Beloved Disciple," he is often represented by an eagle and is the patron saint of love, loyalty, and friendship.

San Nilo (Saint Nilus)

A Greek monk of the 10th century who founded the monastery of Grottaferrata near Rome. He was known for his ascetic life, prophecies, and miracles, particularly in southern Italy. His monastery became an important center of Byzantine culture in Italy, and he worked to bridge the Eastern and Western churches during his lifetime.

San Paolo (Saint Paul)

Originally a persecutor of Christians, Paul's dramatic conversion on the road to Damascus transformed him into one of Christianity's most influential apostles. He wrote many epistles in the New Testament and spread Christianity throughout the Roman Empire. Known for his missionary journeys and theological writings, he is the patron saint of missionaries, evangelists, and writers.

San Pietro (Saint Peter)

The chief of the apostles, Peter, was a fisherman whom Jesus called to be the rock upon which he would build his Church. Given the keys to the kingdom of heaven, he became the first Pope and leader of the early Christian church. He was martyred by crucifixion upside down in Rome, and his tomb lies beneath St. Peter's Basilica.

Santa Firmina (Saint Firmina)

A 3rd-century virgin martyr from Amelia, Italy, who was persecuted during the reign of Diocletian. She refused to renounce her Christian faith despite torture and threats. She is particularly venerated in central Italy, especially in Umbria, and is often depicted holding a palm branch symbolizing martyrdom.

San Rocco (Saint Roch)

A 14th-century French nobleman who gave away his wealth to care for plague victims throughout Italy. He miraculously cured many by making the sign of the cross over them. After contracting the plague himself, he retreated to a forest where a dog brought him bread daily. He is the patron saint against plagues and epidemics.

Santa Rosa (Saint Rose)

St. Rose was a 13th-century Italian saint known for her mystical experiences and public preaching from age 10. She defended the papacy against Emperor Frederick II and was exiled for her bold proclamations. She is the patron saint of Viterbo and is often depicted holding roses or scattered with rose petals.

CHAPTER SIXTY

Editing and Photo Credits

Acknowledging the Editor and Those Who Made This Journey Brighter

A very special thank you to my editor, Pamela Zale

Pam, thank you for your sharp eye, steady guidance, and heartfelt enthusiasm throughout this journey. Your insight helped shape every page, and your belief in this Puglia project never wavered. I'm deeply grateful for your care, precision, and the joy you brought to the process. This book is all the better because of you.

Photo Credits

Arpino gate. Vagabanda, Public domain, via Wikimedia Commons.

Arpino Locals in Period Dress. gerry.scappaticci, CC BY 2.0 <https://creativecommons.org/licenses/by/2.0>, via Wikimedia Commons.

Facade St. John Lateran. Berthold Werner, Public domain, via Wikimedia Commons.

Papal Palace Viterbo. Jean-Pierre Dalbéra from Paris, France, CC BY 2.0 <https://creativecommons.org/licenses/by/2.0>, via Wikimedia Commons.

All Other Photos are my Own.

CHAPTER SIXTY-ONE

Select Bibliography

Great Reads for those who Love Italy

Broers, Michael. Napoleon: The Spirit of the Age, 1805-1810. Faber & Faber, 2018.

Furet, François. Napoleon and the Transformation of Europe. Harvard University Press, 1990.

Hibbard, Howard. Michelangelo: Painter, Sculptor, Architect. Harper & Row, 1974.

Langdon, Helen. Caravaggio: A Life. Farrar, Straus and Giroux, 1998.

Lowe, Norman. Italy in the Era of the World Wars 1915-1945. Routledge, 2002.

McBrien, Richard P. Lives of the Popes. HarperCollins, 2000.

Scotti, R.A. Basilica: The Splendor and the Scandal: Building St. Peter's. New York: Viking, 2006. - Recommended Reading.

Wittkower, Rudolf. Bernini: The Sculptor of the Roman Baroque. Phaidon Press, 1955.

Thank You & Please Leave a Review

Reviews Enhance a Book's Discoverability

T hank you for reading the *Ultimate Festival and Travel Guide Rome & Beyond*. It is the third in the Travel Italy Series.

If the guide enhanced your travel planning, I'd greatly appreciate it if you could leave a review on Amazon. Your feedback not only helps other travelers, but also supports this book's success.

I sincerely hope you have enjoyed this tour through Lazio via its festivals. I would love to hear about your own festival adventures! Connect with me on Instagram, where I share hundreds of videos from the festivals of Rome and Italy, perfect for a sneak peek before your trip.

For even more travel inspiration, visit my blog for deeper dives into Lazio's stunning beaches and off-the-beaten-path gems, which are not covered extensively in this guide. https://katerinaferrara.com/blog/

Thank you for being part of this journey, and I look forward to hearing about yours!

Wishing you the safest and happiest travels!

Katerina Ferrara

Scan here to link to
the book and leave
a review!

Connect with Me

Free Italy Travel Resources and More

Newsletter / Travel News

Sign up for my newsletter and stay updated with insider secrets about Italy's charming towns, vibrant festivals, and mouthwatering food, things you won't find in any travel guide. Stay updated with the latest on festivals, tours, podcasts, and special insights that go beyond the book! https://katerinaferrara.com/

*KaterinaFerrar
a.com*

Immersion Travel by Katerina Ferrara Blog

Looking for even more hidden gems in Italy? My blog is packed with insider tips, from secret beaches tucked away on Italy's lesser-known coastlines to self-guided walking tours that take you off the typical tourist path. Whether you're planning a relaxing escape or an adventurous exploration, you'll find everything you need to create unforgettable Italian journeys. Subscribe at for exclusive travel insights and start uncovering Italy's best-kept secrets! www.katerinaferrara.com

Immersion Travel Podcast and YouTube

Looking for the real Italy? Step beyond the tourist trail with the Immersion Travel Podcast and YouTube series, where I take you deep into Italy's most captivating regions. From hidden festivals and authentic food spots to spiritual walks and backstreet wonders, each episode brings you insider stories, expert tips, and cultural treasures you won't find in typical travel guides.

Podcast

https://podcasts.apple.com/us/podcast/immersion-travel-italy/id1795327762

YouTube

https://www.youtube.com/@ImmersionTravelItaly

Katerina on Instagram

@KaterinaFerraraAuthor

Corrections / Updates / Suggestions Oops!

Even the best of us can make mistakes. I would appreciate your help in making my content better. Please visit the book page here:

https://katerinaferrara.com/ultimate-festival-and-travel-guide-rome-and-beyond/and scroll down to the book feedback button.

About the Author: Katerina Ferrara

Festival Follower and Founder of Immersion Travel Italy

Katerina Ferrara is a published author and the founder of Immersion Travel Italy, a company dedicated to creating unforgettable travel experiences in Italy. With over 25 years of exploring Europe, Katerina has developed a deep love for immersing herself in the diverse cultures, traditions, and culinary delights of the places she visits. Fluent in Italian, she effortlessly connects with locals and travelers alike, bringing an insider's perspective to her travel writing.

Katerina jokes that she lives her life on a perpetual diet, not for vanity, but to prepare for the next irresistible festival in Italy. Her ultimate dream is to inspire **Festival Followers,** travelers who prioritize experiencing incredible festivals first and then explore the surrounding sites while immersing themselves in local traditions. She believes festivals offer a unique lens into a region's heart and culture, making them the perfect starting point for any adventure.

An avid hiker and fitness enthusiast, Katerina incorporates her passion for staying active into her travels, often seeking out scenic trails, walking tours, and outdoor adventures that connect her to the natural beauty of a destination (while making room for just a little more gelato).

When she's not exploring new destinations or writing, Katerina enjoys sharing her travel insights and tips with fellow adventurers, inspiring them to delve deeper into the cultural richness of the places they visit—and maybe even discover their own favorite festival.

Website: https://katerinaferrara.com/

Follow the Immersion Travel Podcast on Spotify

Also Available on Apple Itunes:

https://podcasts.apple.com/us/podcast/immersion-travel-italy/id1795327762

Katerina's YouTube Channel:

https://www.youtube.com/@ImmersionTravelItaly